Classical Mythology

Classical Mythology

Mark P. O. Morford

and

Robert J. Lenardon

DAVID McKAY COMPANY, INC.
New York

CLASSICAL MYTHOLOGY

Sixth Printing, March 1975

ISBN: 0-679-30028-7

LIBRARY OF CONGRESS CATALOG CARD NUMBER: 78-124550

MANUFACTURED IN THE UNITED STATES OF AMERICA

*Dedicated to the
memory of
William Robert Jones,
teacher, scholar, and
friend.*

Preface

Our experience in teaching courses in classical mythology to large undergraduate classes has convinced us of the need for a new and comprehensive survey that will be useful to readers who have little or no background of classical knowledge. We must acknowledge our debt to predecessors in the field, most especially the works of Röscher, Preller, Robert, and Rose. Our method, however, has taken us beyond these convenient but secondary sources to the classical authors themselves. The compendium of the second century A.D. attributed to Apollodorus has been drawn upon where legends could not be conveniently found in earlier authors, but we have preferred where possible to make extensive use of Homer, Hesiod, the *Homeric Hymns,* Pindar and the Lyric Poets, and the tragedians, among Greek authors; among Latin authors, of Vergil and Ovid. We have provided our own translations of many of the original passages, so that the reader may have knowledge of the classical sources upon which modern discussion of the legends is based. It has proved more practical to give extensive translations in Part I, most especially of passages from the *Homeric Hymns* to the various gods; in dealing with saga and local legends (Part II) we have resorted more to paraphrase in the interests of conciseness and clarity, although even here we have included a generous amount of the classical sources in translation. In writing the book we have each taken the major responsibility for certain sections— Professor Lenardon for the Introduction, Part I and Chapter 24, and Professor Morford for Parts II and III (other than Chapter 24) and the illustrations; we have each read and criticized the other's contributions and take joint responsibility for the whole.

Consistency in spelling has proved impossible to attain. In general we have adopted Latinized forms (*Cronus* for *Kronos*) or spellings generally accepted in English-speaking countries (*Heracles,* not *Herakles*); the Greek final *-ōs* has been kept, as in *Minos.* In doubtful cases we have accepted the spelling given by Gordon Kirkwood in his *Short Guide to Classical Mythology* (New York, 1959). We have generally used the Greek forms of names where there is a separate Latin equivalent (Aphrodite, not Venus); this rule obviously does not apply in the chapter on Roman Legends. The Index provides cross-references to both the Greek and Roman names.

We have received help and encouragement from many colleagues, students, and friends. Our colleague, the late Professor W. Robert Jones, until his death in 1968, gave generously to us of his time and wisdom. Mr. Gordon Hill and the late Mr. Charles Hillard, of David McKay's, were more patient and encouraging than we deserved; Miss Ellen B. Karge and Mr. Charles A. McCloud were helpful in providing material for the writing of Chapter 24. Dr. Arta Johnson has provided patient and detailed criticism of the manuscript and has undertaken the labor of compiling the index. Mrs. Mark Morford has helped us in selecting the illustrations and in typing much of the manuscript, while Mrs. Colette Armstrong, Mrs. Nicholas Genovese and Miss Joann Phillips typed the remaining parts of the manuscript. To all these persons we extend our thanks.

Mark P. O. Morford   Robert J. Lenardon
November, 1970

Contents

Part III—The Survival of Classical Mythology

Illustrations follow pages 116, 212, 308

Classical Mythology

Introduction

Webster's Third New International Dictionary gives the following definition of myth: "a story that is usually of unknown origin and at least partially traditional, that ostensibly relates historical events usually of such character as to serve to explain some practice, belief, institution, or natural phenomenon, and that is especially associated with religious rites and beliefs." This indeed is as good a definition as any, clear and all-inclusive, highlighting the essential meanings of the word in its most general sense. Many specialists in the field of mythology, however, are not satisfied with such a broad interpretation of the term "myth." They attempt to distinguish "true myth" or "myth proper" from other varieties, and seek to draw distinctions in terminology between it and other words often used synonymously, such as legend, saga, and folk tale.[1] Thus, for some, myth must be ancient and of anonymous origin (according to Gayley "myths are born, not made." [2]); others demand that they invariably be concerned with nature and provide explanations for its phenomena (i.e., real myths are nature stories and etiological); still others would expand their definition to include tales dealing with all circumstances of human life, although they might also insist upon the presence of the divine or supernatural for authenticity. There are those who argue that myths must have once been believed, although subsequently they come to be regarded as incredible. Thus Christian dogma for them may be excluded from mythological study (although to non-Christians it may be viewed as incredible),[3] and so on. Robert Graves, for example, distinguishes true myth, which for him is "the reduction

[1] Sometimes fable is also applied as a general term, but it is better to restrict its meaning to designate a story in which the characters are animals endowed with human traits, the primary purpose being moral and didactic.

[2] Charles Mills Gayley, *The Classic Myths in English Literature and in Art* [Boston: Ginn and Co. (new edition, 1939)], p. 2.

[3] This emphasis upon the unbelievable in myths is reflected in the common association of the words myth and mythical with what is incredible, fantastic, or untrue.

1

to narrative shorthand of ritual mime performed on public festivals, and in many cases recorded pictorially on temple walls, vases, seals, bowls, mirrors, chests, shields, tapestries, and the like," from twelve other categories, such as: philosophical allegory, satire or parody, minstrel romance, political propaganda, theatrical melodrama, realistic fiction.[4]

The definitions set forth by Rose in his invaluable handbook have deservedly won wide acceptance. His distinctions are clear, serviceable, and enlightening; although inevitably artificial per se, they are by no means intended to be adopted as rigid. In reality the criteria merge and the lines of demarcation blur. For him, true myth or myth proper is ultimately "the result of the working of naive imagination upon the facts of experience."[5] It is to be distinguished from folk tale, whose major function is to present a story primarily for the sake of entertainment, and from saga, which, however fanciful and imaginative, is rooted in historical fact.[6] Rarely, if ever, do we find a pristine, uncontaminated example of any one of these forms.

Theories on the meaning and interpretation of myth (which also usually provide bases for a hypothesis about origins) have been legion. Only a few of the more important and persistent attitudes will be mentioned here; indeed some have already been touched upon.[7]

The two major approaches in the analysis of myth have been

[4] Robert Graves, *The Greek Myths*, vol. 1 (Baltimore: Penguin Books, 1955), p. 10. His interpretation of Greek mythology is based on the assumption that there once existed an early matriarchal and totemistic system in Europe with the worship of a Great Mother Deity, the White Goddess, and the subsequent invasion of a patriarchal society from the North and East.

[5] H. J. Rose, *A Handbook of Classical Mythology* 6th ed. (London: Methuen, 1958), pp. 12–14.

[6] "Legend" may be used as a general term like "myth" in its broadest sense. Often, however, it is defined as equivalent to saga and made to refer to stories inspired by actual persons and events. Rose prefers the German word *Märchen* for the designation of folk tales (fairy tales, of course, belong in this category).

[7] Philip Freund, *Myths of Creation* (New York: Washington Square Press, 1964) provides a stimulating view of mythical analysis and theory. Both Gayley (pp. 1–2, 431–449) and Rose (pp. 1–15) offer more conventional and concise surveys.

what may be termed the rational and the metaphorical. Rationalistic interpreters insist upon explaining all that is incredible or fantastic in mythology in terms of what is naturally possible. Such a realistic viewpoint is labeled Euhemerism, as a result of the theories of an ancient Greek, Euhemerus (ca. 300 B.C.), who claimed that the gods of legend were merely deified men–Zeus, for example, was a king of old in Crete, who deposed his father Cronus. Metaphorical interpretations, on the other hand, stem from the belief that ancient tales hide profound meanings deep within them; commentators on the Bible who find the most sublime insights in the most obscure texts belong to this school. Thus it is assumed that all myths are allegories (and allegory, after all, is a sustained metaphor) setting forth their secret mysteries in obscure symbols that have to be deciphered. Some adherents to this approach go as far as to argue that these symbols reveal fundamental "truths" that are the same for all people (although arrived at independently) and essentially religious in nature, for example, the concept of monotheism.

The dissection of ancient tales has often been inspired by a quest for the "Ur-myth." This pursuit can take more than one guise. Attempts may be made to determine the original version of each and every myth, with philology, history, archaeology, and other related disciplines employed as aids; sometimes it turns out that a later rather than an earlier extant rendition may reveal most primitive aspects of a tale most clearly. On the other hand, this pursuit of origins has led to the thesis of a single Ur-myth, whose theme and content provide the essential core and meaning of all true myths. Thus, myths are not only defined as fundamentally of a ritual nature but further they are all ultimately derived from a single Ur-ritual, for example, one in which a king was killed and replaced each year. Or, to provide another example, myths are not only primarily concerned with natural phenomena but, more particularly, may be reduced to a few (if not only one) elementary cosmological conceptions dealing with the sky, the sun, the moon, or the stars.

Finally the significant and all-pervasive theories of Freud and Jung must be mentioned. Freud saw the resemblances between myths and dreams and defined myths as primitive man's attempts to release the repressed desires of his dream fantasies. Myths, then, reflect waking man's efforts to systematize the incoherent visions and impulses of his sleep world. The patterns in the imaginative world of children, savages, and neurotics are similar, and these patterns are revealed in the motifs of myth. One of the most early and basic patterns is that of the Oedipus story, in which the son kills the father in order to possess the mother. From the ensuing sense of guilt and sin emerges the conception of God as Father who must be appeased and to whom atonement must be made. In fact, according to Freud, the Oedipus complex has inspired the beginning not only of religion but all ethics, art, and society. Jung probes even more deeply into the archetypal patterns of dreams and myth. The persistent reveries of a race, its collective unconscious, are the impersonal projection of the myth-forming elements in the unconscious psyche—the stuff of both dreams and myths is similar, but dreams are individual and personal, while myths are collective and impersonal.

It is obvious that the comparative analysis of myths among various societies has played an important role in the evolution of many of these theories. Frazer's monumental *The Golden Bough* bears testimony to the fecundity and imagination of the anthropologist in his study of primitive peoples, ancient and modern; Frazer's work, in particular, had a marked influence upon Freud. The mores, the rites, and the stories of present-day savage tribes in the Congo or along the Nile will (hopefully) reveal the true essence of myth and elucidate the character and development of other mythologies, including those of Greece and Rome. Parallels unquestionably do exist, but analogies are fraught with innumerable deceptions for every single truth that they may divulge. It is a fact that prominent themes recur (often apparently quite independently) in the mythical thinking of widely divergent peoples and societies; [8] the character and attributes of sky deities are (of course?) strikingly similar; creation stories often contain identical episodes, such as a flood (was this a phenomenon experienced commonly in early times?); certainly the one-eyed giant emerges again and again as a universal figure of folk tales (reasons can be found to explain this recurrence, too). Yet, despite everything,

---

[8] A recurrent or basic theme in mythology is sometimes referred to as a mythologem.

a vast gulf separates the musings of the Zulus or Fiji Islanders and the sophisticated and sublime mythological thinking evolved by the Greeks and the Romans. The realization of this difference is fundamental.[9] Our earliest literary sources (Homer and Hesiod) provide artistic presentations of intellectual and spiritual concepts of the highest order. This is not to deny their primitive origins but to stress the fact of a lengthy period of evolution, about which we have to surmise so much on the tenuous basis of so little in terms of archaeological and anthropological evidence.

Early myth (and now we must apply to the word all its broadest connotations) was primitive art, primitive philosophy, primitive science, and primitive history. The first mythmakers (surely it is right to speak in terms of individuals) were the poets, the artists, the philosophers, the religious teachers, the scientists, and the historians of their tribes who sought to explain, to inform, and to delight. It is often emphasized that the explanations (however aesthetic) are inevitably wrong, but how can one presume to evaluate the imaginative solely in terms of the demonstrable and concrete? Zeus may not pour rain from the heavens or hurl thunder and lightning (our mythmaker is a bad scientist), but the literal image is not the only "truth" his pictures may contain; the conception of deity is beyond science, that is, metaphysical (the mythmaker is not always a bad theologian, and in fact is often a very good one). These early anonymous visionaries, then, sought to give meaningful answers in terms of intelligence, sensitivity, imagination, and beauty. But they were limited. How far removed from them are the artists of Greece and Rome (even "Homer" and "Hesiod" have a real existence by comparison)? Whatever the original version of the Oedipus story (i.e., its Ur-myth, or should we say Ur-saga?), it is the dramatic treatment by Sophocles that has established and imposed the mythical pattern for all time—it is he, the poet, who forces us to see and to feel the universal im-

---

[9] One should use terms like "pagan" and "heathen" with caution, when referring to practices, stories, and beliefs of the ancient world. These words can be innocuous, meaning simply non-Jewish, non-Christian, or non-Mohammedan, or they may be made deliberately derogatory, suggesting the primitive and inferior. Too often they are thoughtlessly and carelessly applied, and (intentionally or not) leave the vague and disturbing impression of something like savage jungle rites, hardly applicable to Periclean Athens or Augustan Rome.

plications. His art is self-conscious and literary, aesthetically of the highest order, the end product, as it were, of the working of naive imagination upon the facts of experience and history. Savage myth and literary myth are an inextricable unity and yet worlds apart. Those who define primitive myth in terms of timeless universals imposed upon the real world and somehow profoundly different from it do little more than attempt to put into words the nature and essence of all artistic expression and experience.[10]

Literary myth is the primary concern of this book. Many of the important myths exist in multiple versions of varying quality, but usually one ancient treatment has been most influential in establishing the prototype for all subsequent art and thought. Insofar as possible the original text of this dominant version is provided in this book; hopefully even a literal translation is better than a bald and eclectic paraphrase in which the essential spirit of literary myth is stifled for the sake of scientific analysis. It is a commonplace to say that myths are by nature good stories, but some are more childish, confused, and repetitious than others. The good ones are usually good because they have survived in a form molded by a great artist. For this and other reasons conjectures and arguments about the origin, nature, and evolution of various deities and stories have been kept to a minimum. These questions are, of course, important (however rash and absurd some of the answers that have been postulated), but we have kept in mind our major purpose—the transmission of the myths themselves as recounted in the Greek and Roman period. The theories we have included are in one way or another basic, important, and interesting. The wildest hypotheses have deliberately been ignored; it is well-known that the most prolific and imaginative mythmakers are the very ones who write about myth. In the last analysis, choice has been personal and eclectic, if not completely erratic.

In connection with myth based ultimately upon history (more specifically, if you like, saga or legend), a knowledge of some of the essential background is necessary for fuller appreciation and

[10] See Mircea Eliade, *Myth and Reality,* translated from the French by Willard R. Trask (New York: Harper & Row, 1963) for a deeply philosophical analysis, interpretation, and definition of myth.

understanding. Only the briefest of sketches can be provided here.[11] The study of prehistoric Greece and the Aegean is particularly fascinating because of the contributions that are continually being provided by archaeology and philology. Our knowledge literally advances day by day as scholars shed new light (and raise fresh problems as well) on many areas, not least of all those involving religion and mythology.

This progress has been made possible primarily through the efforts of one brilliant pioneer, Heinrich Schliemann, who, because of his love of Greek antiquity in general and Homer in particular, was inspired by a faith in the ultimate historical authenticity of Greek legend.[12] Certainly archaeology had existed in earlier periods, but it usually meant little more than treasure hunting and tomb robbing; Schliemann has rightly earned the title Father of Modern Archaeological Excavation and Study. In the 1870s he went to Troy, Mycenae, and Tiryns and confirmed the reality of the wealth, grandeur, and power of the cities, kings, and heroes of Minoan-Mycenaean saga. Sir Arthur Evans followed at the turn of the century, unearthing the splendid and grand complex of the Palace of Minos at Cnossus in Crete. A whole new world had been opened up.

For a long time it was believed that Greece had not been inhabited before the Neolithic period. But we know today that the country was settled in Paleolithic times (before 70,000 B.C.). With the present state of excavation and study, the culture of this early period appears tentative and no direct links can be established with the later Greeks. Evidence for the Neolithic period (ca. 6000–3000 B.C.) is more abundant. Archaeology has revealed settled agricultural communities (i.e., outlines of houses, pottery, tools, and graves). It is conjectured that the Neolithic

[11] Emily Vermeule, *Greece in the Bronze Age* (Chicago: University of Chicago Press, 1964) offers an excellent survey and contains an important bibliography.

[12] Schliemann's life and career are the material for a bizarre and exciting success story. He amassed a fortune so that he could prove the validity of his convictions, which he pursued with passion. Several biographies are available: the one by Emil Ludwig, *Schliemann, the Story of a Gold-Seeker,* translated from the German by D. F. Tait (Boston: Little, Brown, 1931) is particularly attractive.

inhabitants came from the East and the North.[13] For our purposes it is noteworthy that evidence of religion seems apparent; particularly significant are little female idols, their sexuality exaggerated by the depiction of swollen belly, buttocks, and full breasts. Male figures also are found (some ithyphallic), although in far fewer numbers. Was a fertility mother-goddess worshipped in this early period, and perhaps already associated with a male consort?

The Stone Age gave way to the Bronze Age in Greece, Crete, and the Islands with an invasion from the East (the movement was from Asia Minor across the Aegean to the southern Peloponnesus up into Greece). This people was responsible for the building of the great Minoan civilization of Crete. The Bronze Age is divided into three major periods: Early, Middle, and Late; these periods are also labeled according to geographical areas. Thus the Bronze Age in Crete is designated as Minoan (from the tradition of king Minos); for the Islands the term is Cycladic (the Cyclades are the islands that encircle Delos); in Greece it is called Helladic (Hellas is the Greek name for the country). The Late Bronze Age on the mainland (i.e., the late Helladic period) is also identified as the Mycenaean Age, from the citadel of power (Mycenae) dominant in Greece during this period. The chronology with the terminology is as follows: [14]

3000–2000 B.C.	Early Bronze Age	Early Minoan, Cycladic, Helladic
2000–1600 B.C.	Middle Bronze Age	Middle Minoan, Cycladic, Helladic
1600–1100 B.C.	Late Bronze Age	Late Minoan, Cycladic, Helladic; also the Mycenaean Age

[13] Some scholars prefer to speak of a progressive movement of cultural ideas rather than an actual migration and invasion of peoples for this and subsequent periods.

[14] More precise chronology and further subdivisions within the periods established by the specialists are not reproduced here.

The Minoan civilization grew to maturity in the Middle Bronze Age and reached its pinnacle of greatness in the following period (1600–1400). The palace at Cnossus was particularly splendid (although another at Phaestus is impressive, too). The excavations confirm the tradition (as interpreted later, for example, by Thucydides) that Cnossus was the capital of a great thalassocracy and that Minoan power extended over the islands of the Aegean and even the mainland of Greece. Tribute was in all probability exacted from her allies or her subjects; the complex plan of the palace at Cnossus suggests the historical basis for the legend of the Minotaur. The fact that Cnossus had no walls (unlike the fortress citadels of Hellas) suggests that her security depended upon ships and the sea. The sophistication of Minoan art and architecture implies much about the civilization, but more particularly the painting and the artifacts reflect a highly developed sense of religion, for example, the importance of the bull in ritual, the dominant role of a snake-goddess, the sacred significance of the double ax.[15] It seems fairly clear that the worship of a fertility mother-goddess was basic in Minoan religion.

About 1400, Cretan power is eclipsed (archaeology reveals signs of fire and destruction) and the focus of civilization shifts to the mainland of Greece. Did the Greeks overthrow Cnossus and usurp the Minoan thalassocracy? Was an earthquake solely responsible for the eclipse of this island power? Theories abound but there is no general agreement except insofar as scholars may be divided into two groups: those who stress the dominant influence of the Minoans on the mainland civilization and refuse to attribute the downfall of Crete to a Mycenaean invasion as against those who argue for Mycenaean (Greek) encroachment and eventual control of the island.[16]

On the mainland of Greece, the Middle Bronze Age (or Middle

[15] For a more detailed interpretation of the evidence in terms of Minoan-Mycenaean religion, see W. K. C. Guthrie, "The Religion and Mythology of the Greeks," rev. ed. of *The Cambridge Ancient History*, vol. 2, ch. 40 (New York: Cambridge University Press, 1961, preliminary fascicle edition); he provides the essential bibliography.

[16] Joseph Alsop, *From the Silent Earth, A Report on the Greek Bronze Age* (New York: Harper & Row, 1964) presents a fascinating account of the relationships between the Minoans and Mycenaeans. Although popular in tone, his research is accurate and his arguments convincing.

Helladic period) was ushered in by an invasion from the North and possibly the East. These Nordic Indo-Europeans are the first Greeks (i.e., they spoke the Greek language) to enter the peninsula; gradually they created a civilization (usually called Mycenaean) that reached its culmination in the Late Helladic period (1600–1100).[17] They learned much from the Minoans; their painting, palaces, and pottery are strikingly similar, but there are some significant differences. Schliemann was the first to excavate at Mycenae, the kingdom of the family of Atreus, corroborating the appropriateness of the Homeric epithet, "rich in gold." Cyclopean walls typically surround the complex palace of the king and the homes of the aristocracy; the entrance to Mycenae was particularly splendid, graced as it was with a relief on which two lions or lionesses flanking a column were sculptured—presumably the relief was of political and religious significance, perhaps the emblem of the royal family. A circle of shaft graves within the citadel, set off in ritual splendor, has revealed a hoard of treasures —masks of beaten gold placed on the faces of the corpses, exquisite jewelry, and beautifully decorated weapons. Larger (and later) tholos tombs (also typical of Mycenaean civilization elsewhere and confirming a belief in the afterlife) built like huge beehives into the sides of hills below the palace complex were dramatically and erroneously identified by Schliemann as both the treasury of Atreus and the tomb of Clytemnestra. But the fact remains that Mycenae was the kingdom of Agamemnon, just as other Mycenaean sites unearthed by Schliemann and subsequent archaeologists have definite links with saga, for example, Tiryns (the home of Heracles) and Thebes (the domain of Oedipus). Carl W. Blegen has discovered the palace of Nestor at Pylos in western Greece, settling once and for all the controversy waged over the identification of the site. The plan of the palace can be clearly distinguished; in particular the megaron (central room with an open hearth) is beautifully preserved.

The religion of the Mycenaeans was in many respects like that of

[17] Some believe that a later wave of invaders (ca. 1600) are to be specifically identified as the Achaeans in Homer; for all intents and purposes it is better to consider Achaeans virtually an equivalent term for the Mycenaean Greeks.

the Minoans, but again some important differences may be detected. The northern invaders of 2000 worshiped in particular a sky-god, Zeus, and in general their religious attitudes were not unlike those mirrored in the world of Homer's celestial Olympians. How different from the spiritual atmosphere of the Minoans dominated by the conception of a fertility mother-goddess, with or without a male counterpart! At any rate, Greek mythology seems to accommodate and reflect the union of these two cultures, as we shall see in Chapter 1.

Clay tablets inscribed with writing have been found on the mainland (an especially rich hoard was found at Pylos). These tablets were baked hard in the conflagrations that destroyed these Mycenaean fortresses when they fell before the onslaught of the invading Dorians.[18] The key to the decipherment of the Linear B tablets was discovered in 1952 by Michael Ventris who was killed in 1956 in an automobile accident. His friend and collaborator, John Chadwick, has written for the layman a fascinating account of their painstaking and exciting work on the tablets, one of the most significant scholastic and linguistic detective stories of this or any other age.[19] Important for our study is the finding of the names of familiar deities of classical Greece, Zeus and Hera (listed as a pair), Poseidon, Hermes, Athena, Artemis, Eileithyia (Eleuthia in the tablets), and the name Dionysus (a startling discovery, since it has usually been assumed that the worship of Dionysus did not come to Greece until later); also identified is an early form of the word Paean, which was later applied as a title or epithet for Apollo. Similarly, Enualios appears, a name identified in classical times with Ares. The word Potnia (mistress or lady) is frequent, and thus support is added to the theory that the Mycenaeans

[18] Linear A tablets (Linear B is derived from the Linear A script) have been found on Crete but have not yet been deciphered; apparently Minoan Linear A is not Greek. Linear B tablets (which we now know are written in an early form of Greek) have also been found at Cnossus with provocative implications for historical reconstruction. A recent assessment of the controversial evidence and a hostile criticism of Evans's methods and attitudes is offered by Leonard R. Palmer, *Mycenaeans and Minoans*, 2d ed. (New York: Alfred A. Knopf, 1965).

[19] John Chadwick, *The Decipherment of Linear B*, 2d ed. (New York: Cambridge University Press, 1958).

as well as the Minoans worshiped a goddess of the mother-fertility type, and the concept of chthonian deities that this implies was merged with that of the Olympians. The gods are listed in the tablets as the recipients of offerings which suggests ritual sacrifice and ceremonial banquets, for example, of animals, olive oil, wheat, wine, honey, and so forth.

Schliemann and Wilhelm Dörpfeld were pioneers at Troy. Blegen has continued work at the site and the results have been published by the Princeton University Press for the University of Cincinnati in a series of learned volumes.[20] Troy was settled in the Early Bronze Age and survived until the time of Constantine the Great (fourth century A.D.). Nine major settlements can be distinguished, of which Troy 1–5 are of the Early Bronze Age and 6–7 of the Middle and Late Bronze Ages. Troy 2 is especially interesting because of a series of caches or "treasures" that Schliemann discovered. The remains suggest that this settlement was significantly wealthy—a fact possibly accounted for by trade in pottery, timber, and woolen textiles (8000 to 10,000 terra-cotta whorls or buttons have been unearthed); perhaps tolls also were levied on those who traversed the territory of the Trojans by water or by land. The various settlements in the early period, despite numerous earthquakes and fires, bear witness to the tenacious survival of the inhabitants of the site.

Troy 6 marks the beginning of the Middle Bronze Age; the technique of pottery and the use of the horse indicate that the founders of this settlement were Greeks, the earliest to set foot in Asia Minor, a branch of those invaders who were the first Hellenes to enter the peninsula of Hellas and introduce the culture of the Middle Helladic period. The monumental fortification walls of Troy 6 are particularly impressive, and Dörpfeld identified this settlement as the great city of king Priam. According to Blegen, however, Troy 6 was destroyed by an earthquake and it

---

[20] Like the reports of Blegen's excavations at Pylos, they are a monumental testimony to the scientific precision of modern archaeological procedures. Blegen has provided a readily accessible and highly readable account of the excavations at Troy for the general reader: Carl W. Blegen, *Troy and the Trojans, Ancient Peoples and Places*, vol. 33 (New York: Praeger, 1963).

is Troy 7 (Troy 7a, to be exact) that is Priam's city, since (among other things) signs of a siege and fire can be detected, indicative of the Trojan War. The historical date of the fall of Troy is placed around 1250, some years earlier than that of the most commonly accepted tradition, that is, 1184.[21] The destruction of Troy 7b (ca. 1100) marks the troublesome period of transition from the Late Bronze Age to the age of Iron throughout the eastern Mediterranean.

The Trojan War, then, is a historical fact. The great leaders of the major Aegean kingdoms banded together to sail against Troy. We must, of course, look for concrete and prosaic causes, but about these we can only conjecture. Did Troy because of her strategic position hold a monopoly upon colonization and trade in the region of the Hellespont, the entrance to the rich area of the Black Sea? Were the Mycenaeans making a grand bid for power with the conquest of Cnossus, a raid upon Egypt, and the destruction of Troy? Yet the romance of poetic saga has a reality, too. We have a right to believe that there was once an Agamemnon and a Nestor, an Achilles and a Hector, who lived and died, no matter how fictitious the details of the legend that they inspired. Is it incurably romantic to cling to the belief that handsome Paris and beautiful Helen ran away together in the grip of Aphrodite, providing the inciting cause for a great war that has become immortal?

The Greeks returned from Troy in triumph, but it was not long afterwards that their splendid kingdoms were eclipsed. The invasion of the Dorians from the North and East (racial and linguistic "relatives" of the earlier invaders of 2000) brought an end to the great Minoan–Mycenaean Age. The traditional date, around 1100, is challenged by some archaeologists who would place the Dorian invasion of Hellas about one hundred years earlier, around 1200 B.C. With the Dorians came an age of Iron. For a time, darkness descends upon the history of Greece, a darkness that is only gradually dispelled with the emergence of the two great Homeric

[21] Not everyone is convinced by Blegen's chronology and historical reconstruction; some view the remains of Troy 7a as too insignificant for the glorious tradition of Priam's city and would look back to the earlier identification of Troy 6 as more likely and by no means impossible.

epics, the *Iliad* and the *Odyssey,* in the ninth and eighth centuries
B.C. The stories of the earlier period were kept alive by oral recita-
tion, transmitted by bards like those described in the epics themselves. "Homer" almost certainly belongs to Asia Minor or one
of the islands (e.g., Chios) off the coast. In the cities of this area
in this period, we find that monarchy is the prevailing institution;
significantly enough the social and political environment for the
bard of this later age is not unlike that of his predecessors in the
great days of Mycenae.

Most important of all for an appreciation of the cumulative
nature of the growth of the legends is the realization that there
were two major periods of creative impetus (i.e., pre-Dorian and
post-Dorian), however continuous the line of oral transmission.
Thus Homeric epic maintains remarkably well the fiction of the
earlier Bronze Age, but nevertheless on occasion betrays its own
era of iron; to mention but one example, archaeology shows us
that burial was prevalent in the Mycenaean age, but in Homer
cremation is common. The saga of the Argonauts reflects an interest in the Black Sea that is historical—but was this interest
Mycenaean or do the details belong to the later age of Greek
colonization (ca. 800–600)? The legend as we have it must be a
composite product of both eras. The Theseus story blends in
splendid confusion Minoan-Mycenaean elements with facts of the
later historical period of monarchy in Athens.

The Homeric poems were eventually set down in writing; this
was made possible by the invention of an alphabet. The Greeks
borrowed the symbols of the Phoenician script and used them to
create a true alphabet, distinguishing by each sign individual vowels
and consonants, unlike earlier scripts (such as Linear B) in which
syllables are the only linguistic units. This stroke of genius, by the
way, is typically Greek in its brilliant and inventive simplicity;
surely no one of our countless debts to Greek civilization is more
fundamental. Is the invention of the Greek alphabet and the setting down of the Homeric epics coincidental? Presumably the
dactylic hexameter of epic cannot be reproduced in the clumsy
symbols of Linear B. At any rate, when tradition tells us that
Cadmus taught the natives to write, we may wonder whether he
is supposed to have instructed them in Mycenaean Linear B or
the later Greek alphabet.

Part I

The Myths of Creation; The Gods

CHAPTER 1

Myths of Creation

There were many myths about the creation among the Greeks and Romans, and many parallels to them may be found in other mythologies, such as Egyptian, Sumerian, Babylonian, and Hebraic. Homer (ca. 800 B.C.)[1] has Oceanus and Tethys responsible for the origin of the gods (*Iliad*, 14.201) and reflects a primitive belief in the geographical nature of the universe as a flat disc with hills, touched at its rim by the vast dome of the heavens. The deity Oceanus is the stream of ocean that encircles the earth. But Homer does not by any means provide a complete account of genesis. Hesiod (ca. 700), as far as we can tell, was the first to give literary expression to a systematic explanation of how the gods, the universe, and mankind came into being. At any rate his is the earliest account that has survived, and it may be considered the classic Greek version in many respects; the genealogical scheme is presented in his *Theogony,* while his *Works and Days* adds significant details.

Hesiod invokes the Muse in the manner of epic (*Theogony,* 108 ff.): "Tell me how first gods, earth, rivers, the boundless sea . . . the shining stars, and the wide heavens above came into being." His answer is that first of all Chaos came into being. The Greek word *Chaos* means a "yawning." For Hesiod, then, Chaos is a void. How close we are in spirit to the investigations of the early pre-Socratic philosophers who sought a primal world substance is a difficult question. Thales (ca. 540) seems to provide a startling break with mythological and theological concepts when he claims water to be the source of everything, with shattering implications for both science and philosophy. Hesiod is not so

[1] All dates given henceforth will be B.C. unless otherwise indicated.

17

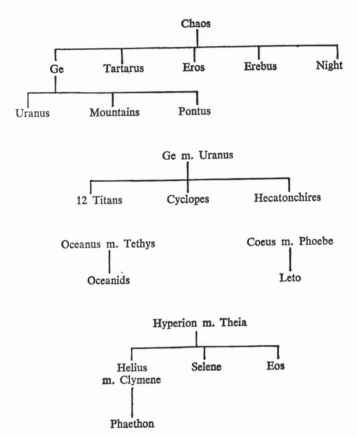

Fig. 1. Descendants of Chaos

revolutionary. From Chaos, Hesiod continues, came Gaea or Ge (Earth), Tartarus (a dim place in the depths of the ground), Eros (Love), Erebus (the gloom of Tartarus), and dark Night.

Love naturally appears early, and quite typically is a potent force in tales of creation and more especially procreation. Hesiod characterizes Eros by one of his many descriptive touches, which strive to lift his didacticism to the realm of poetry (*Theogony*, 120–123): "most fair among the immortal gods, who loosens the limbs and overcomes judgment and sagacious counsel in the breast of gods and men."

Another myth of creation is found in *The Birds,* a comedy by the fifth-century playwright Aristophanes. For all its mock heroism and burlesque of religious philosophical speculation and vocabulary, this account reflects earlier theory and illustrates both the multiplicity of versions and the primacy of Eros. A chorus of birds proves that the birds are much the oldest of all the gods by the following tale (683 ff.):

Chaos, Night, black Erebus, and broad Tartarus were first. But Ge, Aer [the lower atmosphere], and Uranus [Sky] did not exist. In the vast hollows of Erebus first of all black-winged Night, alone, brought forth an egg, from which Eros, the desirable, burst forth like a swift whirlwind, his back glistening with golden wings. He mingled in broad Tartarus with Chaos, winged and dark as night, and hatched our race of birds and first led it to light. There was no race of immortals before Eros caused all things to mingle. From the mingling of couples, Uranus, Oceanus, Ge, and the immortal race of all the blessed gods came into being.

The Eros responsible for this fury of procreation may very well be the same Eros who is in the later tradition appropriately called Phanes (the one who first shone forth or gave light to creation) and Protogonus (first-born). If so, we have in Aristophanes a parody of a myth that was the basis of a religion ascribed to Orpheus in which the world-egg was a dominant symbol. Orphism has as its fundamental features a dogma, ritual, and a belief in purification with an afterlife of reward and punishment. Orpheus and Orphism will be discussed in their proper place and with them other religions similar in nature, designated generically as mystery religions.[2] The link between myth and profound religious thought and experience in the ancient world is a continuing and fascinating theme.

Ovid, a Roman poet of the Augustan Age, and thus writing some seven hundred years after Hesiod, provides another classic account of genesis, different in important respects from that of Hesiod. Ovid is eclectic in his sources. Not only Hesiod but also the speculations of later Greek and Roman thought are definite influences,

[2] For the Orphic myth of creation in particular, see pp. 258–259.

in particular those of Empedocles (a fifth-century philosopher) with his theory of four basic elements (earth, air, fire, and water) as the primary materials of the universe. Ovid's Chaos (*Metamorphoses*, 1.1–75) is not a gaping void but rather a crude and unformed mass of elements in strife from which a god (not named) or some higher nature formed the order of the universe.[3] Ovid's poem *Metamorphoses*, which concentrates upon stories that involve transformations of various sorts, could very well provide a basic text for a survey of mythology. We shall on occasion reproduce Ovid's versions, since it is often his poetic, sensitive, and sophisticated treatment that has dominated subsequent tradition. But we must remember that Ovid is Roman and late, and that his mythology is far removed in spirit and belief from that of earlier conceptions. Mythology for him is little more than poetic fodder, however attractive the end product may be. The poetic and the real world of Hesiod and Ovid are poles apart.

But let us return to Hesiod (*Theogony*, 123–138). Night and Erebus (both sprung from Chaos) united and produced Aether (the bright upper atmosphere) and Day. Ge (also sprung from Chaos) first of all brought forth Uranus (Heaven or Sky) "equal to herself so that he might surround and cover her completely and be a secure home for the blessed gods forever." Ge thus produced Uranus alone, without Love the desirable, and also brought forth Mountains and Pontus (the sea). But then she lay with Uranus and bore the Titans.

The personification and deification of sky and earth as Uranus and Ge and their physical union represent basic recurring themes in mythology. Uranus is the male principle, a god of the sky; Ge, the female goddess of fertility and the earth. Worship of them may be traced back to very early times; sky and rain, earth and fertility are fundamental concerns and sources of wonder to primitive agricultural peoples. The rain of Uranus might, for example, be imagined as his seed that fertilizes the hungry earth and makes her conceive. Thus develops the concept of a sacred marriage (the Greek phrase *hieros gamos* is the technical term), and the sky-god

---

[3] The concept of god creating something out of nothing is not found in the Greek and Roman tradition.

and the earth-goddess (for example, Uranus and Ge, Cronus and Rhea, and Zeus and Hera) appear again and again under various names and guises to enact this holy rite.

The worship of the female earth divinity has many important facets, and she may assume the dominant role in the partnership with her male consort. But whatever her name and however varied her worship, she is significant in all periods, either maintaining her own identity or lurking behind, influencing, and coloring more complex and sophisticated concepts of female deity. Ge, Themis, Cybele, Rhea, Hera, Demeter, and Aphrodite are all, either wholly or in part, divinities of fertility. Indeed some scholars are ready to find Ge's presence in every goddess and are deeply suspicious of even the most circumspect virgin deities. Certainly the emotional, philosophical, religious, and intellectual range of the worship of the mother-goddess is vast. It may run the gamut from frenzied orgiastic celebrations with the castration of her devoted priests to a sublime belief in spiritual communion and personal redemption; from a blatant emphasis upon the sexual attributes and potency of the female to an idealized vision of love, motherhood, and virgin birth.

The Titans, offspring of Uranus and Ge, are twelve in number: Oceanus, Coeus, Crius, Hyperion, Iapetus, Theia, Rhea, Themis, Mnemosyne, Phoebe, Tethys, and the last-born, Cronus, "wily and most terrible, who hated his lusty father" (*Theogony,* 137–138). They are for the most part deifications of various aspects of nature, important for their progeny, although a few assume some significance in themselves. In the genealogical labyrinth of mythology, all lineage may be traced back to the Titans and to the other powers originating from Chaos. From these beginnings Hesiod proceeds to create a universe both real and imagined, physical and spiritual, peopled with gods, demigods, deified or personified abstractions, animals, monsters, and men; we cannot list them all here, but it is from his system that we shall select the most important figures. At the moment it is expedient only to define the nature of some of the early deities and to describe their more influential offspring. Several of the Titans are best considered in pairs, since the six brothers must mate with their six sisters, at least in the beginning.

Oceanus and his mate Tethys produce numerous children, the Oceanids, three thousand daughters and the same number of sons, spirits of rivers, waters, and springs, many with names and some with mythological personalities. Hesiod provides an impressive list, but he admits (*Theogony,* 369–370) that it is difficult for a mortal to name them all, although people know those belonging to their own area.[4]

The Titan Hyperion is a god of the sun, more important than his sister and mate Theia. They are the parents of Helius, Selene, and Eos. Helius, like his father, is a sun-god. Duplication of divinities is common in the early scheme of things; they may exist side by side or their names and personalities may be confused. Very often the younger generation will dominate the older and usurp its power.

The conventional picture of the sun-god is in harmony with the Homeric conception of geography described before. The sun-god dwells in the East, crosses the dome of the sky with his team of horses, descends into the stream of Oceanus in the West and sails back to the East, chariot and all. Mimnermus, a Greek poet of the seventh century, provides a description (fr. 10):

Helius has as his lot toil day after day and there is never any rest either for him or his horses, when rosy-fingered dawn (Eos) leaving the stream of Ocean makes her way up into the sky. But a beautiful hollow cup, winged and of precious gold, fashioned by the hands of Hephaestus, bears him, sleeping deeply, from the land of the Hesperides to the country of the Ethiopians, where he makes his swift chariot and horses stand, until rising dawn comes. Then the son of Hyperion mounts his chariot.

A well-known story concerns Phaethon, the son of Helius by one of his mistresses, Clymene. According to Ovid's account (*Metamorphoses,* 1.747–779; 2.1–366), Phaethon was challenged by the accusation that the sun was not his real father at all. His mother, Clymene, however, swore to him that he was truly the child of Helius and told him that he should, if he so desired, ask his father, the god himself. Ovid describes in glowing terms the

---

[4] Included are many important rivers such as the Nile, Alpheus, and Scamander, to mention only three in this world, and the Styx, an imaginary one in the realm of Hades.

magnificent palace of the sun, with its towering columns, gleaming with gold and polished ivory, splendid in both material and workmanship. Phaethon, awed by the grandeur of his surroundings, is prevented from coming too close to the god because of his radiance; Helius, however, confirms Clymene's account of Phaethon's parentage, lays aside the rays that shine around his head and orders his son to approach. He embraces him and promises on an oath sworn by the river Styx that the boy may have any gift that he likes so that he may dispel his doubts once and for all. Phaethon quickly and decisively asks that he be allowed to drive his father's chariot for one day. The sun tries in vain to dissuade him, but Phaethon in his eagerness pays no attention. Helius must abide by his dread oath and reluctantly leads the youth to his chariot, fashioned exquisitely by Vulcan,[5] of gold, silver, and jewels that reflect the brilliant light of the god. The chariot is yoked; Helius anoints his son's face as protection against the flames, places the rays on his head, and with heavy heart advises him on his course and the management of the horses and tries for the last time to dissuade him.

Phaethon, young and inexperienced, is unable to control the four winged horses who speed from their usual path. The chariot races to the heights of heaven, creating havoc by the intensity of the heat, then hurtles down to earth. Ovid delights in his description of the destruction and transformations that result. (Two examples from many must suffice. On earth, because of the heat at this time, the Ethiopians acquired their dark skins and Libya became a desert). Earth herself was ablaze and unable to endure her fiery anguish any longer. Jupiter in answer to her prayer hurls his thunder and lightning and shatters the car, dashing Phaethon to his death. The river Eridanus received and bathed him, and nymphs buried him with the following inscription upon his tomb: "Here is buried Phaethon, charioteer of his father's car; he could not control it, yet he died after daring great deeds." His sisters (daughters of the sun) in their mourning for Phaethon were turned into trees, from whose bark tears flowed, which were hardened into amber by the sun and dropped into the river. Away in Liguria

[5] When a Roman version of a myth is recounted, the Roman names of the original text will be used. Vulcan is Hephaestus, Jupiter is Zeus, etc.

his cousin, Cycnus, mourned for him, and he, too, changed and became a swan.

Selene, daughter of Hyperion and Theia, is a goddess of the moon. Like her brother Helius, she drives a chariot, although hers usually has only two horses. Only one famous myth is linked with Selene, and that concerns her love for the handsome youth, Endymion, who is usually depicted as a shepherd. On a still night Selene saw Endymion asleep in a cave on Mount Latmus (in Caria). Night after night, she lay down beside him as he slept. There are many variants to this story, but in all the outcome is that Zeus granted Endymion perpetual sleep with perpetual youth. This may be represented as a punishment (although Endymion is given some choice) because of Selene's continual absence from her duties in the heavens, or it may be the fulfillment of Selene's own wishes for her beloved.

Many stories about the god of the sun, whether he be called Hyperion, Helius, or merely the Titan, were transferred to the great god Apollo, who, although in all probability not originally a sun-god, was considered as such in the classical period. Thus Phaethon may be the son of Apollo. The confusion is caused for several reasons. The sun-god and Apollo share the same epithet, Phoebus, which means "bright." Apollo's twin sister, Artemis, became associated with the moon, although originally she probably was not a moon-goddess. Thus Selene and Artemis merge in identity, just as do Hyperion, Helius, and Apollo. Artemis, like Selene, as a moon-goddess is associated with magic, since the link between magic and the worship of the moon is close.[6] Apollo and Artemis themselves have a close link with the Titans. The Titan Coeus mates with his sister Phoebe, and their daughter Leto bore Artemis and Apollo to Zeus. Coeus and Phoebe are little more than names to us, but Phoebe is the feminine form of Phoebus, and she herself may very well be another moon-goddess. Phoebe became an epithet of Artemis, just as Phoebus is applied to Apollo. Again the identification of Apollo and Artemis with the sun and the moon is evident and confirmed by genealogy.

Eos, the third child of Hyperion and Theia, is goddess of the

[6] Hecate, goddess of the moon, ghosts, and black magic, is but another aspect of both Selene and Artemis.

dawn, and like her sister Selene drives a two-horsed chariot. Her epithets in poetry are appropriate, for instance, rosy-fingered and saffron-robed. She is an amorous deity. Aphrodite, the goddess of love, caused her to long for young mortals perpetually because she caught her mate Ares in Eos's bed. Orion, Cleitus, and Cephalus were all beloved by Eos, but her most important mate is Tithonus, a handsome youth of the Trojan royal house. Eos carried off Tithonus; their story is simply and effectively told in the *Homeric Hymn to Aphrodite* (5.218–238):

> Eos went to Zeus, the dark-clouded son of Cronus, to ask that Titho-nus be immortal and live forever. Zeus nodded his assent and accom-plished her wish. Poor goddess, she did not think to ask that her be-loved avoid ruinous old age and retain perpetual youth. Indeed as long as he kept his desirable youthful bloom, Tithonus took his pleasure with early-born Eos of the golden throne by the stream of Oceanus at the ends of the earth. But when the first gray hairs sprouted from his beau-tiful head and noble chin, Eos avoided his bed. But she kept him in her house and tended him, giving him food, ambrosia, and lovely garments. When hateful old age oppressed him completely and he could not move or raise his limbs, the following plan seemed best to her. She laid him in a room and closed the shining doors. From within his voice flows faintly and he no longer has the strength that he formerly had in his supple limbs.

Later writers add that eventually Tithonus was turned into a grasshopper.

By far the most important Titans are Cronus and Rhea, but be-fore we consider them we must again take up Hesiod's account (*Theogony,* 139–210). In addition to the Titans, Uranus and Ge bore Brontes (Thunder), Steropes (Lightning), and Arges (Bright), who were called Cyclopes (Orb-Eyed) because they each had only one eye in the middle of their forehead. They in their might and skill forged the thunder and lightning.[7] Uranus and Ge also bore Cottus, Briareus, and Gyes, who were even more overbearing and monstrous than the Cyclopes; they each had a hundred arms and hands and fifty heads and were named

[7] These Cyclopes are distinct from the Cyclops Polyphemus and his fel-lows.

the Hecatonchires (hundred-handed or -armed). Hesiod says that
these were the most terrible children of Uranus and Ge, and from
the beginning their own father hated them. His account is worth
reproducing in full:

As each of his children was born, Uranus hid them all in the depths
of Ge and did not allow them to emerge into the light. And he delighted
in his wickedness. But huge Earth in her distress groaned within and
devised a crafty and evil scheme. At once she created gray adamant and
fashioned a great sickle and confided in her dear children. Sorrowing in
her heart she urged them as follows: "My children born of a presumptuous father, if you are willing to obey, we shall punish his evil insolence. For he was the first to devise shameful actions." Thus she spoke.
Fear seized them all and not one answered. But great and wily Cronus
took courage and spoke to his dear mother: "I shall undertake and accomplish the deed, since I do not care about our abominable father.
For he was the first to devise shameful actions." Thus he spoke. And
huge Earth rejoiced greatly in her heart. She hid him in an ambush and
placed in his hands the sickle with jagged teeth and revealed the whole
plot to him. Great Uranus came leading on night and desirous of love
lay on Ge, spreading himself over her completely. And his son from his
ambush reached out with his left hand and in his right he seized hold
of the huge sickle with jagged teeth and swiftly cut off the genitals of
his own dear father and threw them so that they fell behind him. And
they did not fall from his hand in vain. Earth received all the bloody
drops that fell and in the course of the seasons bore the strong Erinyes
and the mighty giants (shining in their armor and carrying long spears
in their hands) and nymphs of ash trees (called Meliae on the wide
earth). And when first he had cut off the genitals with the adamant and
cast them from the land on the swelling sea, they were carried for a
long time on the deep. And white foam arose about from the immortal
flesh and in it a maiden grew. First she was brought to holy Cythera,
and then from there she came to sea-girt Cyprus. And she emerged
a dread and beautiful goddess and grass rose under her slender feet.
Gods and men call her Aphrodite, and the foam-born goddess because
she grew amid the foam, and Cytherea of the beautiful crown because
she came to Cythera, and Cyprogenes because she arose in Cyprus
washed by the waves. She is called too Philommedes (genital-loving)
because she arose from the genitals.[8] Eros attended her and beautiful

___

[8] Perhaps an intentional play upon the word *philommeides*, laughter-
loving, a standard epithet of Aphrodite.

desire followed her when she was born and when she first went into the company of the gods. From the beginning she has this honor, and among men and the immortal gods she wins as her due the whispers of girls, smiles, deceits, sweet pleasure, and the gentle delicacy of love.

The stark power of this passage is felt even in translation. Its brutal and transparent illustration of basic motives and forces in man's nature provides fertile material for modern psychology: the youngest son whose devotion to his mother is used by her against the father, the essentially sexual nature of love, the terror of castration. The castration complex of the Freudians is the male's unconscious fear of being deprived of his sexual potency, which springs from his feeling of guilt because of his unrecognized hatred of his father and desire for his mother. Hesiod provides literary documentation for the elemental psychic conscience of mankind.

In this view is it Hesiod's art that gets to the essence of things? Or is it that he is close to the primitive expression of the elemental in man's nature? It is a commonplace to say that although elements of the more grotesque myths may be detected in Greek literature, they were humanized and refined by the Greeks and transformed by their genius. Yet it is also true that these primitive elements were retained deliberately and consciously because of the horror, shock, and revelation that they contain. The Greeks did not suppress the horrible and horrifying; they selected from it and used it boldly with profound insight and sensitivity. Thus Hesiod's account may reflect a primitive myth, the ultimate origins of which we can never really know, but his version gives it meaning with an artistry that is far from primitive.[9]

Aphrodite and Eros will be considered more fully in a later chapter, and the Erinyes (spirits of vengeance for blood-guilt) will subsequently play an important role. Now we must return to Hesiod's account of how Cronus and his sister Rhea usurped the powers and the functions of their parents Uranus and Ge.

Hesiod tells of the union of Cronus and Rhea and the birth of their important offspring: Hestia, Demeter, Hera, Hades, Posei-

---

[9] Hesiod's myths of divine succession have many parallels in Phoenician, Babylonian, Hurrian, and Hittite texts.

don, and Zeus, and how Cronus devoured all these children, except
Zeus. Hesiod relates (*Theogony,* 453–506):

> Great Cronus swallowed his children as each one came from the womb
> to the knees of their holy mother, with the intent that no other of the
> illustrious descendants of Uranus should hold kingly power among the
> immortals. For he learned from Ge and starry Uranus that it was fated
> that he be overcome by his own child. And so he kept vigilant watch
> and lying in wait he swallowed his children. A deep and lasting grief
> took hold of Rhea and when she was about to bring forth Zeus, father
> of gods and men, then she entreated her own parents, Ge and starry
> Uranus, to plan with her how she might bring forth her child in secret
> and how the avenging fury of her father, Uranus, and of her children
> whom great Cronus of the crooked counsel swallowed, might exact
> vengeance. And they readily heard their dear daughter and were per-
> suaded, and they counseled her about all that was destined to happen
> concerning Cronus and his stout-hearted son. And they sent her to the
> town of Lyctus in the rich land of Crete when she was about to bring
> forth the youngest of her children, great Zeus. And vast Ge received
> him from her in wide Crete to nourish and foster. Carrying him from
> there Ge came first through the swift black night to Dicte. And taking
> him in her hands she hid him in the deep cave in the depths of the holy
> earth on thickly wooded Mt. Aegeum.[10] And she wrapped up a great
> stone in infant's coverings and gave it to the son of Uranus, who at
> that time was the great ruler and king of the gods. Then he took it in
> his hands, poor wretch, and rammed it down his belly. He did not
> know in his heart that there was left behind, in the stone's place, his
> son unconquered and secure, who was soon to overcome him and drive
> him from his power and rule among the immortals.

Cronus and Rhea are once again deities of sky and earth,
doublets of Uranus and Ge, and like them their union represents
the enactment of the universal holy marriage. But in the tradition
Cronus and Rhea have a more specific reality than their parents.
Cronus appears in art as a majestic and sad deity, sickle in hand.
He rules, as we shall see, in a golden age among men, and after
he is deposed by Zeus, he retires to some distant realm, sometimes
designated as the Islands of the Blessed, one of the Greek conceptions of paradise.

[10] There is trouble in the text concerning Hesiod's identification of the
mountain as Dicte or Aegeum.

Rhea, too, has a definite mythological personality, although basically she represents another one of the many names and guises of the all-pervading and important mother-goddesses of earth and fertility. She sometimes is equated with Cybele, an Oriental goddess who intrudes upon the classical world; worship of her involved frenzied devotion and elements of mysticism; her attendants played music on drums and cymbals and her myth involves a handsome young lover subordinate to her, named Attis.

It is of great significance that Hesiod places the birth of Zeus on the island of Crete and we can detect in his version some of the basic motives in the creation of myth.[11] Variations and additions occur in later writers who state that after Rhea brought forth Zeus in a cave on Mt. Dicte, he was fed by bees and nursed by nymphs on the milk of a goat named Amalthea. Curetes (the word means young men) guarded the infant and clashed their spears on their shields so that his cries would not be heard by his father Cronus. These attendants and the noise they make suggest the frantic devotees of a mother-goddess: Ge, Rhea, or Cybele. The myth is etiological in its explanation of the origin of rites connected with her worship.

This story may also reflect history: the amalgamation of at least two different peoples or cultures in the early period. When the inhabitants of Crete (ca. 3000) began to build their great civilization and empire, the religion that they developed (insofar as we can ascertain) was Mediterranean in character, looking back to earlier eastern concepts of a mother-goddess. The northern invaders who entered the peninsula of Greece (ca. 2000) bringing with them an early form of Greek and their own gods (chief of whom was Zeus) built a significant Mycenaean civilization on the mainland, but it was strongly influenced by the older, more sophisticated power of Crete. The myth of the birth of Zeus reads very much like an attempt to link by geography and genealogy the religion and deities of both cultures. Zeus, the Nordic male god of the Indo-Europeans, is born of Rhea, the Oriental goddess of motherhood and fertility.

Two dominant strains in the character of subsequent Greek

[11] Another version places the birth on the mainland of Greece in Arcadia

thought can be understood at least partly in terms of this thesis. W. K. C. Guthrie identifies this dual aspect of the religion of classical Greece in the contrast between the Olympian gods of Homer and the cult of the mother-goddess Demeter at Eleusis. His clear and forceful explanation is worth quoting.

The Mother-goddess is the embodiment of the fruitful earth, giver of life and fertility to plants, animals and men. Her cult takes certain forms, involving at least the more elementary kinds of mysticism, that is, the belief in the possibility of a union between the worshipper and the object of his worship. Thus the rites, may take the form of adoption as her son or of sexual communion. Orgiastic elements appear, as in the passionate, clashing music and frenzied dancing employed by the followers of Rhea or Cybele. . . . What an essentially different atmosphere we are in from that of the religion of the Achaean heroes described by Homer. There we are in clear daylight, in a world where the gods are simply more powerful persons who might fight for or against one, with whom one made bargains or contracts. The Achaean warrior did not seek to be born again from the bosom of Hera. He was indeed the reverse of a mystic by temperament.[12]

We can detect the ramifications of this paradox again and again in many places, but perhaps we feel it most clearly in the mysticism and mathematics that permeate Greek philosophical attitudes: the numbers of Pythagoras and the immortality of the soul in Orphic doctrine; the dichotomy of Platonic thought and Socratic character in the search for clarity and definition through rational argument coupled with the sound of an inner voice, the depths of a trance, and divine revelation in terms of the obscure and profound symbols of religious myth. God is a geometer and a mystic.

[12] W. K. C. Guthrie, *The Greeks and Their Gods* (Boston: Beacon Press, 1955), p. 31.

CHAPTER 2

Zeus's Rise to Power; The Creation of Man

When Zeus had grown to maturity, Cronus was beguiled into bringing up all that he had swallowed, first the stone and then the children. This very stone was exhibited at Delphi in ancient times; it was not large and oil was poured over it every day, and on festival days, unspun wool was placed upon it. Zeus then waged war against his father with his disgorged brothers and sisters as allies: Hestia, Demeter, Hera, Hades, and Poseidon. Allied with him as well were the Hecatonchires and the Cyclopes, for he had released them from the depths of the earth where their father Uranus had imprisoned them because of his hatred. The Hecatonchires were invaluable in hurling stones with their hundred-handed dexterity, and the Cyclopes forged for him his mighty thunder and lightning. On the other side with Cronus were the Titans with the important exception of Themis and her son Prometheus, both of whom allied with Zeus. But Atlas, the brother of Prometheus, was an important leader on the side of Cronus.

The battle was of epic proportions, Zeus fighting from Mt. Olympus, Cronus from Mt. Othrys. The struggle was said to have lasted ten years, the traditional length for a serious war, be it this one or the famous conflict of the Greeks against the Trojans. An excerpt from Hesiod will convey the magnitude and ferocity of the conflict (*Theogony,* 678–721).

The boundless sea echoed terribly, earth resounded with the great roar, wide heaven trembled and groaned, and high Olympus was shaken from its base by the onslaught of the immortals; the quakes came thick and fast and, with the dread din of the endless chase and mighty weapons, reached down to gloomy Tartarus. Thus they hurled their deadly weapons against one another. The cries of both sides as

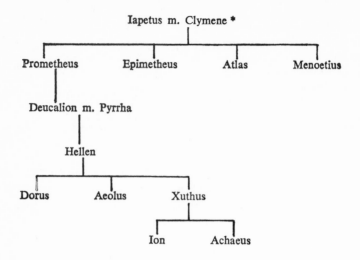

Fig. 2. The family of Prometheus

* The mother of Prometheus is Ge-Themis according to Aeschylus.

they shouted reached up to starry heaven, for they came together with a great clamor.

Then Zeus did not hold back his might any longer, but now immediately his heart was filled with strength and he showed clearly all his force. He came direct from heaven and Olympus hurling perpetual lightning, and the bolts with flashes and thunder flew in succession from his stout hand with a dense whirling of holy flame. Earth, the giver of life, roared, everywhere aflame, and on all sides the vast woods crackled loudly with the fire. The whole of the land boiled, and as well the streams of Ocean, and the barren sea. The hot blast engulfed the earth-born Titans and the endless blaze reached the divine aether; the flashing gleam of the thunder and lightning blinded the eyes even of the mighty. Unspeakable heat possessed Chaos. The sight seen by the eyes and the sound heard by the ears were as if Earth and wide Heaven above collided; for the din as the gods met one another in strife was as great as the crash that would have arisen if Earth were dashed down by Heaven falling on her from above. The winds mingled the confusion of tremor, dust, thunder, and the flashing bolts of lightning (the shafts of great Zeus) and carried the noise and the shouts into the midst of both sides. The terrifying clamor of fearful strife arose and the might of their deeds was shown forth. They attacked one another and fought relentlessly in mighty encounters until the battle was decided. Cottus, Briareus, and Gyes, insatiate of battle, were among the foremost to rouse the bitter strife; they hurled three hundred rocks, one right after another, from their staunch hands and covered the Titans with a cloud of missiles and sent them down far beneath the broad ways of the earth to Tartarus and bound them in harsh bonds, having conquered them with their hands even though they were great of spirit. The distance from Earth to gloomy Tartarus is as great as that of Heaven from Earth.

The Hecatonchires guarded the Titans imprisoned in Tartarus. Atlas was punished with the task of holding up the sky. Some say that after Zeus became secure in power he eventually relented and gave the Titans their freedom.

Another threat that Zeus had to face was from giants that Earth produced to challenge the new order of the gods, or that had been born when the blood from the mutilation of Uranus fell upon the ground; these monstrous creatures are called Gegeneis, which means earth-born. Details of the battle are many and varied, but it is generally agreed that the struggle was fierce, ending with the imprisonment of the giants under the earth, usually in volcanic regions where they betray their presence by the violence of their natures. Thus, for example, the giant Enceladus writhes under Mt. Aetna in Sicily. One of the most vicious of the giants was Typhoeus or Typhon. He sometimes joins the other giants in their conflict with the gods or he may do battle alone, as in Hesiod's account (*Theogony,* 820–880).

When Zeus had driven the Titans from heaven, vast Gaea brought forth the youngest of her children through the love of Tartarus and the agency of golden Aphrodite. The hands of the mighty god were strong in any undertaking and his feet were weariless. From the shoulders of this frightening dragon a hundred snake heads grew, flickering their dark tongues; fire blazed from the eyes under the brows of all the dreadful heads, and the flames burned as he glared. In all the terrible heads voices emitted all kinds of amazing sounds; for at one time he spoke so that the gods understood, at another his cries were those of a proud bull bellowing in his invincible might; sometimes he produced the pitiless roars of a courageous lion, or again his yelps were like those of puppies, wondrous to hear, or at another time he would hiss; and the great mountains resounded in echo.

Now on that day of his birth an irremediable deed would have been accomplished and he would have become the ruler of mortals and immortals, if the father of gods and men had not taken swift notice and thundered loudly and fiercely; the earth resounded terribly on all sides and as well the wide heaven above, the sea, the streams of Ocean, and the depths of Tartarus. Great Olympus shook under the immortal feet of the lord as he rose up and Earth gave a groan. The burning heat from them both, with the thunder and lightning, scorching winds, and flaming bolts reached down to seize the dark-colored sea. The whole land was aboil and heaven and the deep; and the huge waves surged around and about the shores at the onslaught of the immortals, and a quake began its tremors without ceasing. Hades who rules over the dead below shook, as did the Titans, the allies of Cronus, in the bottom of Tartarus, from the endless din and terrifying struggle. When Zeus had lifted up the weapons of his might, thunder and lightning and the blazing bolts, he leaped down from Olympus and struck, and blasted on all sides the marvelous heads of the terrible monster. When he had flogged him with blows, he hurled him down, maimed, and vast Earth gave a groan. A flame flared up from the god as he was hit by the bolts in the glens of the dark craggy mountain where he was struck down. A great part of vast earth was burned by the immense conflagration and melted like tin heated by the craft of artisans in open crucibles or like iron which although the hardest of all is softened by blazing fire and melts in the divine earth through the craft of Hephaestus. Thus the earth melted in the flame of the blazing fire. And Zeus in the rage of his anger hurled him into broad Tartarus.

From Typhoeus arise the winds that blow the mighty rains; but not Notus, Boreas, and Zephyr [1] that brings good weather, for they are sprung from the gods and a great benefit for mortals. But the others from Typhoeus blow over the sea at random; some fall upon the shadowy deep and do great harm to mortals, raging with their evil blasts. They blow this way and that and scatter ships and destroy sailors. Men who encounter them on the sea have no defense against their evil. Others destroy the lovely works of men born on the earth over the vast blossoming land, filling them with dust and harsh confusion.[2]

[1] Notus is the South Wind; Boreas, the North Wind; and Zephyr, the West Wind.

[2] Later versions have it that Heracles was an ally of Zeus in the battle; the giants could only be defeated if the gods had a mortal as their ally. In addition Earth produced a magic plant that would make the giants invincible; Zeus by a clever stratagem plucked it for himself.

The attempt of the giants Otus and Ephialtes to storm heaven by piling the mountains Olympus, Ossa, and Pelion upon one another is sometimes linked to the battle of the giants or treated as a separate attack upon the power of Zeus. In fact there is considerable confusion in the tradition concerning details and characters in the battle of the giants (Gigantomachy) and the battle of the Titans (Titanomachy). Both conflicts may be similarly interpreted as reflecting the triumph of the more benign powers of nature over the more wild powers or the victory of civilization over savagery. At any rate they very likely represent the historical fact of conquest and amalgamation when, in about 2000, the Greek-speaking invaders brought with them their own gods, with Zeus as their chief, and triumphed over the deities of the existing peoples in the peninsula of Greece.

Thus far in the creation and ordering of the universe no mention has been made of man. Several versions of his birth existed in the ancient world side by side. Very often he is the creation of Zeus alone, or Zeus and the other gods, or both immortals and mortals spring from one and the same source. An important tradition depicts Prometheus as the creator of man and sometimes woman is fashioned later and separately through the designs of Zeus.

After he has described the creation of the universe and animal life out of the elements of Chaos, Ovid goes on to tell about the birth of man, depicting the superiority and lofty ambition of this highest creature in the order of things (*Metamorphoses,* 1.76–88).

Until now there was no animal more godlike than these and more capable of high intelligence and able to dominate all the rest. Then man was born; either the creator of the universe, originator of a better world, fashioned him from divine seed or earth, recently formed and separated from the lofty aether, retained seeds from its kindred sky and was mixed with rain water by Prometheus, the son of Iapetus, and fashioned by him into the likeness of the gods who control all.[3] While other animals look down to the ground, man was given a lofty visage and ordered to

---

[3] A fragment attributed to Hesiod (number 268) adds that Athena breathed life into the clay. At Panopea in Boeotia stones were identified in historical times as solidified remains of the clay used by Prometheus.

look up to the sky and fully erect lift his face to the stars. Thus earth that had been crude and without shape was transformed and took on the figure of man unknown before.

Ovid goes on to describe the four ages of man: gold, silver, bronze, and iron. But we shall excerpt rather Hesiod's earlier account of these ages, which for him are five in number, since he feels compelled to include an age of heroes. After he has recounted the story of Pandora and her jar, his introduction to the description of the five ages suggests the multiplicity of versions of the creation of man and man's early career, and the futility of even attempting a reconciliation of the diverse accounts (*Works and Days*, 106–201).

If you like, I shall offer a fine and skillful summary of another tale and you ponder it in your heart: how gods and mortal men came into being from the same origin. At the very first the immortals who have their homes on Olympus made a golden race of mortal men. They existed at the time when Cronus was king in heaven, and they lived as gods with carefree hearts completely without toil or trouble. Terrible old age did not come upon them at all, but always with vigor in their hands and their feet they took joy in their banquets removed from all evils. They died as though overcome by sleep. And all good things were theirs; the fertile land of its own accord bore fruit ungrudgingly in abundance. They in harmony and in peace managed their affairs with many good things, rich in flocks and beloved of the blessed gods.

But then the earth covered over this race. Yet they inhabit the earth and are called holy spirits, who are good and ward off evils, as the protectors of mortal men, and are providers of wealth, since they keep watch over judgments and cruel deeds, wandering over the whole earth wrapped in air. For they have these royal prerogatives. Then those who have their home on Olympus next made a second race of silver, far worse than the one of gold and unlike it both physically and mentally. A child was brought up by the side of his dear mother for a hundred years, playing in his house as a mere baby. But when they grew up and reached the measure of their prime they lived for only a short time and in distress because of their senselessness. For they could not restrain their wanton arrogance against one another and they did not wish to worship the blessed immortals or sacrifice at their holy altars, as is customary and right for men. Then in his anger Zeus the son of Cronus hid them away because they did not give the blessed gods who inhabit Olympus their due. Then the earth covered over this race, too. And they dwell under the earth and are called blessed by mortals, and although second, nevertheless honor attends them also.

Father Zeus made another race of mortal men, the third, of bronze and not at all like the one of silver; terrible and mighty because of their spears of ash, they pursued the painful and violent deeds of Ares. They did not eat bread at all but were terrifying and had dauntless hearts of adamant. Great was their might, and unconquerable hands grew upon their strong limbs out of their shoulders. Of bronze were their arms, of bronze were their homes, and they worked with bronze implements. Black iron there was not. When they had been destroyed by their own hands, they went down into the dark house of chill Hades without leaving a name. Black death seized them, although they were terrifying, and they left the bright light of the sun.

But when the earth covered over this race, too, again Zeus the son of Cronus made still another, the fourth on the nourishing earth, valiant in war and more just, a godlike race of heroic men, who are called demigods, and who preceded our own race on the vast earth. Some evil war and dread battle destroyed under seven-gated Thebes in the land of Cadmus as they battled for the flocks of Oedipus; the end of death closed about others after they had been led in ships over the great depths of the sea to Troy for the sake of Helen of the beautiful hair. Some father Zeus, the son of Cronus, sent to dwell at the ends of the earth where he has them live their lives; these happy heroes inhabit the Islands of the Blessed with carefree hearts by the deep swirling stream of Ocean. For them the fruitful earth bears honey-sweet fruit that ripens three times a year. Far from the immortals Cronus rules as king over them; for the father of gods and men released him from his bonds. Honor and glory attend these last in equal measure.

Far-seeing Zeus again made still another race of men who live on the nourishing earth. Oh, would that I were not a part of the fifth generation of men, but either had died before or had been born later. Now indeed the race is of iron. For they never cease from toil and woe by day, nor from being destroyed in the night. The gods will give them difficult troubles, but good will be mingled with their evils. Zeus will destroy this race of mortal men, too, whenever it comes to pass that they are born with gray hair on their temples. And a father will not be in harmony with his children nor his children with him, nor guest with host, nor friend with friend, and a brother will not be loved as formerly. As they grow old quickly they will dishonor their parents, and they will find fault, blaming them with harsh words and not know-ing respect for the gods, since their right is might. They will not sus-tain their aged parents in repayment for their upbringing. One will destroy the city of another. No esteem will exist for the one who is true to an oath or just or good; rather men will praise the arrogance and evil of the wicked. Justice will be might and shame will not exist. The evil man will harm the better man, speaking against him unjustly and he will swear an oath besides. Envy, shrill and ugly and with evil delight, will attend all men in their woe. Then Aidos and Nemesis both [4] will forsake mankind and go, their beautiful forms shrouded in white, from the wide earth to Olympus among the company of the gods. For mortal men sorry griefs will be left and there will be no defense against evil.

The bitterness and pessimism of this picture of his own age of iron are typical of Hesiod's general crabbed, severe, and moral out-look. But his designation of the five ages reflects a curious blend of fact and fiction. Historically his *was* the age of iron, introduced into Greece at the time of the Dorian invasion (ca. 1100), bring-ing the age of bronze to a close. Hesiod's insertion of an age of heroes reflects the fact of the Trojan War which he cannot ignore.

This conception of the deterioration of the human race has been potent in subsequent literature, both ancient and modern. The vision of a paradise in a golden age when all was well inevitably holds fascination for some, whether imagined as long ago or merely in the good old days of their youth. Vergil in his fourth eclogue celebrates gloriously the return of a new golden age ushered in by the birth of a child. The identity of this child has long been in dis-pute, but the poem itself was labeled Messianic because of the sublime and solemn nature of its tone, reminiscent of the prophet Isaiah.

It would be wrong to imply that the theory of man's degenera-tion was the only one current among the Greeks and Romans. Prometheus's eloquent testimony in Aeschylus's play, translated on pp. 45–46, of his gifts to men rests upon the belief in progressive stages from savagery to civilization. A similar but more sober and scientific statement of human development, made by some of the

---

[4] Aidos is a sense of modesty and shame; Nemesis, righteous indignation against evil.

Greek philosophers and Lucretius, the Roman poet of Epicure-
anism, provides a penetrating account of man's evolution that in
many of its details is astoundingly modern.[5]

In the *Theogony* (506–616) Hesiod tells the story of Prometheus and his conflict with Zeus, with man as the pawn in this
gigantic clash of divine wills, and of the creation of woman.

Iapetus led away the girl Clymene, an Oceanid, and they went together in the same bed; and she bore to him a child, stout-hearted
Atlas; she also brought forth Menoetius, of very great renown, and
devious and clever Prometheus, and Epimetheus [6] who was faulty
in judgment and from the beginning was an evil for men who work
for their bread. For he was the first to accept from Zeus the virgin
woman he had formed. Far-seeing Zeus struck arrogant Menoetius
with his smoldering bolts and hurled him down into Erebus because
of his presumption and excessive pride. Atlas stands and holds the
wide heaven with his head and tireless hands through the force of
necessity at the edge of the earth, in the sight of the clear-voiced Hesperides; this fate Zeus in his wisdom allotted him. And he bound
devious and wily Prometheus with hard and inescapable bonds, after
driving a shaft through his middle; and roused up a long-winged eagle
against him that used to eat his immortal liver. But all the long-winged
bird would eat during the whole day would be completely restored in
equal measure during the night. Heracles the mighty son of Alcmene
of the lovely ankles killed it and rid the son of Iapetus from this evil
plague and released him from his suffering, not against the will of
Olympian Zeus who rules from on high, so that the renown of Theban-
born Heracles might be still greater than before on the bountiful earth.
Thus he respected his famous son with this token of honor. Although
he had been enraged, the mighty son of Cronus gave up the anger that
he had held previously because Prometheus had matched his wits
against him.

For when the gods and mortal men quarreled at Mecone,[7] then

[5] *De Rerum Natura*, 5.783–1457.

[6] Aeschylus has Themis as the mother of Prometheus, sometimes identified
as Ge-Themis, to show that she is a goddess of earth, who possesses oracular
power and is associated with justice. The name Prometheus means "fore-
thinker" or "the one who plans ahead"; Epimetheus means "afterthinker"
or "the one who plans too late." Prometheus is often called merely "the
Titan," since he is the son of Iapetus.

[7] An early name of Sicyon.

Prometheus with quick intelligence divided up a great ox and set the pieces out in an attempt to deceive the mind of Zeus. For the one group in the dispute he placed flesh and the rich and fatty innards on the hide and wrapped them all up in the ox's paunch; for the other group he arranged and set forth with devious art the white bones of the ox, wrapping them up in white fat. Then the father of gods and men spoke to him: "Son of Iapetus, most renowned of all lords, my fine friend, how partisan has been your division of the portions!" Thus Zeus whose wisdom is immortal spoke in derision. And wily Prometheus answered with a gentle smile, as he did not forget his crafty trick. "Most glorious Zeus, greatest of the gods who exist forever, choose whichever of the two your heart in your breast urges." He spoke with crafty intent. But Zeus whose wisdom is immortal knew and was not unaware of the trick. And he foresaw in his heart evils for mortal men, which would be accomplished. He took up in both his hands the white fat, and his mind was enraged, and anger took hold of his heart as he saw the white bones of the ox arranged with crafty art. For this reason the races of men on earth burn the white bones for the immortals on the sacrificial altars. Zeus the cloud-gatherer was greatly angered and spoke to him: "Son of Iapetus, my fine friend, who know thoughts that surpass those of everyone, so you have then not yet forgotten your crafty arts." Thus Zeus whose wisdom is immortal spoke in anger. From this time on he always remembered the deceit and did not give the power of weariless fire out of ash trees to mortal men who dwell on the earth.

But the noble son of Iapetus tricked him by stealing in a hollow fennel stalk the gleam of weariless fire that is seen from afar. High-thundering Zeus was stung to the depths of his being and angered in his heart as he saw among men the gleam of fire seen from afar. Immediately he contrived an evil thing for men in recompense for the fire. The renowned lame god, Hephaestus, fashioned out of earth the likeness of a modest maiden according to the will of the son of Cronus. Bright-eyed Athena clothed and arrayed her in silvery garments and with her hands arranged on her head an embroidered veil, wondrous to behold. And Pallas Athena put around her head lovely garlands of budding flowers and greenery. And she placed on her head a golden crown that the renowned lame god himself made, fashioning it with his hands as a favor to his father Zeus. On it he wrought much intricate detail, wondrous to behold, of the countless animals which the land and the sea nourish; many he fixed on it, amazing creations, like living creatures with voices; and its radiant loveliness shone forth in profusion. When he had fashioned the beautiful evil in recompense for the blessing of fire, he led her out where the other gods and men were, exulting in the raiment provided by the gleaming-eyed daughter of a mighty father. Amazement took hold of the immortal gods and mortal men as they saw the sheer trick, from which men could not escape.

For from her is the race of the female sex, the ruinous tribes of women, a great affliction, who live with mortal men, helpmates not in ruinous poverty but in excessive wealth, just as when in overhanging hives bees feed the drones, conspirators in evil works; the bees each day the whole time to the setting of the sun are busy and deposit the white honeycombs, but the drones remain within the covered hives and scrape together the toil of others into their own belly. Thus in the same way high-thundering Zeus made women, conspirators in painful works, for mortal men; and he contrived a second evil as recompense for the blessing of fire; whoever flees marriage and the troublesome deeds of women and does not wish to marry comes to ruinous old age destitute of anyone to care for him. He does not lack a livelihood while he is living but when he has died, distant relatives divide up the inheritance. And again even for the one to whom the fate of acquiring a good and compatible wife in marriage falls as his lot, evil continually contends with good throughout his life. Whoever begets mischievous children lives with a continuous sorrow in his breast; in heart and soul the evil is incurable. Thus it is not possible to go beyond the will of Zeus nor to deceive him. For not even the goodly Prometheus, son of Iapetus, got out from under his heavy wrath and a great bondage held him fast, even though he was very clever.

Once again Hesiod's dominant note is despair. He provides another equally dismal account of Prometheus in the *Works and Days* (47–105); despite some minor repetitions it is worth quoting for its elaboration of the theft of fire and its variations on the creation of woman. The evil is now specifically named; she is Pandora, which means "all gifts," and she has a jar.[8]

Zeus angered in his heart hid the means of human livelihood because wily Prometheus deceived him. And so he devised for men sorrowful troubles. He hid fire. Then the good son of Iapetus, Prometheus, stole it for men from wise Zeus in a hollow reed, without

---

[8] The name suggests a link with the typical conception of the fertility mother-goddess.

Zeus who delights in thunder seeing it. But then Zeus the cloud-gatherer was roused to anger and spoke to him: "Son of Iapetus, who know how to scheme better than all others, you are pleased that you stole fire and outwitted me—a great misery for you and men who are about to be. As recompense for the fire I shall give them an evil in which all may take delight in their hearts as they embrace it."

Thus he spoke and the father of gods and men burst out laughing. He ordered renowned Hephaestus as quickly as possible to mix earth with water and to implant in it a human voice and strength and to fashion the beautiful and desirable form of a maiden, with a face like that of an immortal goddess. But he ordered Athena to teach her the skills of weaving at the artful loom, and golden Aphrodite to shed grace about her head and painful longing and sorrows that permeate the body. And he commanded the guide Hermes, slayer of Argus, to put in her the mind of a bitch and the character of a thief.

Thus he spoke and they obeyed their lord Zeus, son of Cronus. At once the famous lame god molded out of earth the likeness of a modest maiden according to the will of Zeus. Bright-eyed Athena clothed and arrayed her, and the Graces and mistress Persuasion adorned her with golden necklaces. The beautiful-haired Seasons crowned her with spring flowers and Pallas Athena fitted out her body with every adornment. Then the guide and slayer of Argus contrived in her breast lies and wheedling words and a thievish nature, as loud-thundering Zeus directed. And the herald of the gods put in her a voice, and named this woman, Pandora, because all who have their homes on Olympus gave her a gift, a bane to men who work for their bread.

But when the Father had completed this sheer impossible trick he sent the swift messenger of the gods, the renowned slayer of Argus, to bring it as a gift for Epimetheus. And Epimetheus did not think about how Prometheus had told him never to accept a gift from Olympian Zeus but to send it back in case that in some way it turned out to be evil for mortals. But he received the gift and when indeed he had the evil he realized.

Previously the races of men used to live completely free from evils and hard work and painful diseases, which hand over men to the Fates. For mortals soon grow old amidst evil. But the woman removed the great cover of the jar with her hands and scattered the evils within and for men devised sorrowful troubles. And Hope alone remained within there in the unbreakable home under the edge of the jar and did not fly out of doors. For the lid of the jar stopped her before she could, through the will of the cloud-gatherer Zeus who bears the aegis. But the other thousands of sorrows wander among men, for the earth and the sea are full of evils. Of their own accord diseases roam among men some by day, others by night bringing evils to mortals in silence, since Zeus in his wisdom took away their voice. Thus it is not at all possible to escape the will of Zeus.

The etiology of the myth of Prometheus is perhaps the most obvious of its many fascinating elements. It explains procedure in the ritual of sacrifice and the origin of fire; in the person of Pandora the existence of evil and pain in the world is accounted for. Prometheus himself is the prototype of the culture god or hero ultimately responsible for all the arts and sciences.[9] The theme of the theft of fire springs from a widespread notion that fire originally belonged in heaven not on earth.

The elements in the myth of the creation of woman also reveal attitudes common among early societies. Hesiod's version is in keeping with his insular and suspicious nature. But the implications of his story have wider ramifications. Pandora, like Eve, for example, is created after man and she is responsible for his troubles. Why should this be so? The answer is complex, but inevitably it must lay bare the prejudices and mores inherent in the social structure. But some (like Hesiod?) detect as well the fundamental truths of allegory and see the woman and her jar as symbols of the drive and lure of procreation, the womb and birth and life, the source of all our woes.

Details in the story of Pandora are disturbing in their tantalizing ambiguity. What is Hope doing in the jar along with countless evils? If it is a good, it is a curious inclusion. If it too is an evil, why is it stopped at the rim? What then is its precise nature, whether a blessing or a curse? Is Hope in the last analysis the one thing that enables man to survive the terrors of this life and inspires him with lofty ambition? Yet is it also by its very character delusive and blind, luring him on to prolong his misery? It is tempting to see in Aeschylus's play *Prometheus Bound* an interpretation and elaboration; man was without hope until Prometheus gave it to him along with fire. But the hope bestowed is called blind; is the epithet merely ornamental or deliberately descriptive? The pertinent dia-

[9] He was worshiped by the potters in Athens alongside Hephaestus with whom he has several things in common.

logue between Prometheus and the chorus of Oceanids runs as follows (248–252):

Prometheus: I stopped mortals from foreseeing their fate.
Chorus: What sort of remedy did you find for this plague?
Prometheus: I planted in them blind hopes.
Chorus: This was a great advantage that you gave mortals.
Prometheus: And besides I gave them fire.

Fundamental to the depictions of both Hesiod and Aeschylus is the conception of Zeus as the oppressor of mankind and Prometheus as mankind's benefactor. In Aeschylus the clash of divine wills echoes triumphantly through the ages. His portrait, more than any other, offers the towering image of the Titan, the bringer of fire, the vehement and weariless champion against oppression, the mighty symbol for art, literature, and music of all time.

Aeschylus's play *Prometheus Bound* begins with Kratos (Strength) and Bia (Force), brutish servants of an autocratic Zeus, having brought Prometheus to the remote and uninhabited land of Scythia. Hephaestus accompanies them. Kratos urges Hephaestus to obey the commands of Father Zeus and bind Prometheus in bonds of steel and pin him with a stake through his chest to the desolate crags. It was Hephaestus's own brilliant "flower" of fire, deviser of all the arts that Prometheus stole, and for this error ("sin" is not an inappropriate translation) he must pay to all the gods "so that he might learn to bear the sovereignty of Zeus and abandon his love and championship of man."

Aeschylus, with great skill and economy, provides us with the essentials for the conflict and the mood of the play. The struggle between a harsh, young, and angry Zeus is pitted violently against the defiant determination of a glorious and philanthropic Prometheus. Aeschylus even manages to characterize the brutish Kratos, the unreasonable and monstrous henchman of a tyrannical Zeus. Kratos is the willing and anxious supporter of a new regime rooted in might, the one thing that he can understand; to him forceful power is the key to all: "Everything is hard except to rule the gods. For no one except Zeus is free." Hephaestus by contrast is a foil. He is sensitive, humane, curses his craft, hates the job he has to do, and pities the sleepless torment of Prometheus.

An important theme is echoed by Hephaestus in his realization that Zeus has seized supreme rule of gods and men only recently: "The mind of Zeus is inexorable; and everyone is harsh when he first comes to power." The contrast is presumably with the later Zeus who will have learned benevolence through experience, wisdom, and maturity. Certainly Zeus, fresh from his triumphant defeat of his father and the Titans, might indeed be uneasy and afraid. He may very well suffer the same fate as Cronus or Uranus before him. And Prometheus, his adversary, knows the terrifying secret: Zeus must avoid the sea-nymph Thetis in his amorous pursuits, as she is destined to bear a son mightier than his father. In this knowledge lies Prometheus's defiant power and the threat of Zeus's ultimate downfall.

The first utterance of Prometheus after Kratos, Bia, and Hephaestus have done their work is glorious, capturing the universality of his great and indomitable spirit:

O divine air and sky and swift-winged breezes, springs of rivers and countless laughter of sea waves, earth, mother of everything, and all-seeing circle of the sun, I call on you. See what I, a god, suffer at the hands of the gods.

In the course of the play Prometheus expresses his bitterness because, although he with his mother fought on the side of Zeus against the Titans, this is his reward. It is typical of the tyrant to forget and turn against his former allies. Prometheus lists the many gifts that he has given to mankind for whom he suffers now (442–506):

Prometheus: Listen to the troubles that there were among mortals and how I gave them sense and mind, which they did not have before. I shall tell you this not out of any censure of mankind but to explain the good intention of my gifts. In the beginning they had eyes to look, but looked in vain, and ears to hear, but did not hear, but like the shapes of dreams they wandered in confusion the whole of their long life. They did not know of brick-built houses that face the sun or carpentry, but dwelt beneath the ground like tiny ants in the depths of sunless caves. They did not have any secure way of distinguishing winter or blossoming spring or fruitful summer, but they did everything without judgment, until I showed them the rising and the setting of the stars, difficult to discern.

And indeed I discovered for them numbers, a lofty kind of wisdom, and letters and their combination, an art that fosters memory of all things, the mother of the Muses' arts. I first harnessed animals enslaving them to the yoke to become reliefs for mortals in their greatest toils, and I led horses docile under the reins and chariot, the delight of the highest wealth and luxury. No one before me discovered the seamen's vessels which with wings of sail are beaten by the waves. Such are the contrivances I, poor wretch, have found for mortals, but I myself have no device by which I may escape my present pain.

Chorus: You suffer an ill-deserved torment, and confused in mind and heart are all astray; like some bad doctor who has fallen ill, you yourself cannot devise a remedy to effect a cure.

Prometheus: Listen to the rest, and you will be even more amazed at the kinds of skills and means that I devised; the greatest this: if anyone fell sick, there existed no defence, neither food nor drink nor salve, but through lack of medicines they wasted away until I showed them the mixing of soothing remedies by which they free themselves from all diseases. I set forth the many ways of the prophetic art. I was the first to determine which dreams would of necessity turn out to be true and I established for them the difficult interpretation of sounds and omens of the road and distinguished the precise meaning of the flight of birds with crooked talons, which ones are by nature lucky and propitious, and what mode of life each had, their mutual likes, dislikes, and association; the smoothness of the innards and the color of the bile that would meet the pleasure of the gods, and the dappled beauty of the liver's lobe. I burned the limbs enwrapped in fat and the long shank and set mortals on the path to this difficult art of sacrifice, and made clear the fiery signs, obscure before. Such were these gifts of mine. And the benefits hidden deep within the earth, copper, iron, silver, and gold—who could claim that he had found them before me? No one, I know full well, unless he wished to babble on in vain. In a brief utterance learn the whole story: all arts come to mortals from Prometheus.

When Hermes, Zeus's messenger, appears in the last episode, Prometheus is arrogant and insulting in his refusal to bow to the threats of more terrible suffering and reveal his secret. The play ends with the fulfillment of the promised torment; the earth shakes and cracks, thunder and lightning accompany wind and storm as

Prometheus, still pinned to the rock, is plunged by the cataclysm beneath the earth; there he will be plagued by the eagle daily tearing his flesh and gnawing his liver. Prometheus's final utterance echoes and affirms the fiery heat and mighty spirit of his first invocation: "O majesty of earth, my mother, O air and sky whose circling brings light for all to share. You see me, how I suffer unjust torments."

Any dogmatic interpretation of Aeschylus's tragedy is impossible. We know that it was part of a trilogy, the other plays of which have survived only in name and fragments. We have the titles of three additional plays on the Prometheus legend attributed to Aeschylus: *Prometheus the Fire-Bearer, Prometheus Unbound,* and *Prometheus the Fire-Kindler.* This last may be merely another title for *Prometheus the Fire-Bearer,* or possibly it was a satyr play belonging either to the Prometheus trilogy itself or another on a different theme. We cannot even be sure of the position of the extant *Prometheus Bound* in the sequence. Thus details in the final outcome as conceived by Aeschylus are unknown. It seems certain that Heracles, probably through the agency of Zeus (as in Hesiod), was responsible for the release of Prometheus who yielded his fatal secret to Zeus. Conflicting and obscure testimony has Chiron, the centaur, involved in some way, as Aeschylus seems to predict; Chiron wounded by Heracles gives up his life and immortality in the bargain for the release of Prometheus.[10]

As we have seen, the growing maturity of Zeus and eventual wisdom of Prometheus was very likely a dominant theme in the Prometheus trilogy. In this way the character of Zeus can most easily be reconciled with the power and justice of his deity that we knew from other plays of Aeschylus. In the series of exchanges between Prometheus and the various characters who come to witness his misery, the scene with Io is particularly significant in terms of eventual reconciliation and knowledge. She herself tells of her suffering and wanderings for which Zeus is ultimately responsible. But Prometheus, with the oracular power of his mother, foretells the final peace that Io will find in Egypt with the birth of her son

[10] Chiron possibly dies for Prometheus and bestows his immortality upon Heracles.

Epaphus.[11] Secure in power, Zeus has now become the supreme and benevolent father of both gods and men.

Prometheus had a son, Deucalion, and Epimetheus had a daughter, Pyrrha. Their story is told by Ovid. Jupiter tells an assembly of the gods how he, a god, became man to test the truth of the rumors of man's wickedness in the age of iron. There follows an account of Jupiter's anger at the evil of mortals, the flood, the salvation of Deucalion (the Greek Noah) and his wife Pyrrha, and the subsequent repopulation of the earth (*Metamorphoses,* 1.211–421).

"Reports of the wickedness of the age had reached my ears; wishing to find them false, I slipped down from high Olympus and I, a god, roamed the earth in the form of a man. Long would be the delay to list the number of evils and where they were found; the iniquitous stories themselves fell short of the truth. I had crossed the mountain Maenalus, bristling with the haunts of animals, and Cyllene, and the forests of cold Lycaeus; from these ridges in Arcadia I entered the realm and inhospitable house of the tyrant Lycaon, as the dusk of evening was leading night on. I gave signs that a god had come in their midst; the people began to pray but Lycaon first laughed at their piety and then cried: 'I shall test whether this man is a god or a mortal, clearly and decisively.' He planned to kill me unawares in the night while I was deep in sleep. This was the test of truth that suited him best. But he was not content even with this; with a knife he slit the throat of one of the hostages sent to him by the Molossians and as the limbs were still warm with life, some he boiled until tender and others he roasted over a fire. As soon as he placed them on the table, I with a flame of vengeance brought the home down upon its gods, worthy of such a household and such a master. He himself fled in terror, and when he reached the silence of the country he howled as in vain he tried to speak. His mouth acquired a mad ferocity arising from his basic nature, and he turned his accustomed lust for slaughter against the flocks and now took joy in their blood. His clothes were changed to hair; his arms to legs; he became a wolf retaining vestiges of his old form. The silver of the hair and the violent countenance were the same; the eyes glowed in the same way;

[11] For Io's story see pp. 386–387; the name Epaphus means "he of the touch," for he was conceived merely by the gentle touch of the hand of the god.

the image of ferocity was the same.[12] One house had fallen but not only one house was worthy to perish. Far and wide on the earth the Fury holds power; you would think that an oath had been sworn in the name of crime. Let all quickly suffer the penalties they deserve. Thus my verdict stands."

Some cried approval of the words of Jove and added goads to his rage, others signified their assent by applause. But the loss of the human race was grievous to them all and they asked what the nature of the world would be like bereft of mortals, who would bring incense to the altars, and if Jupiter was prepared to give the world over to the ravagings of animals. As they asked these questions the king of the gods ordered them not to be alarmed, for all that would follow would be his deep concern; and he promised a race of wondrous origin unlike the one that had preceded.

And now he was about to hurl his bolts against the whole world, but he was afraid that the holy aether and the long axis of the heavens would catch fire from so many flames. He also remembered that in the decrees of Fate, a time was destined to come when the sea, the earth, and the realm of the sky would be overwhelmed by flames and the complex mass of the universe labor in sore distress.[13] He laid down the weapons forged by the hands of the Cyclopes; a different punishment pleased him more: to send down from every region of the sky torrents of rain and destroy the human race under the watery waves. Straightway he imprisoned the North Wind, and such other blasts as put storm clouds to flight in the caves of Aeolus, and let loose the South Wind who flew with drenched wings, his dread countenance cloaked in darkness black as pitch; his beard was heavy with rain, water flowed from his hoary hair, clouds nestled on his brow, and his wings and garments dripped with moisture. And as he pressed the hanging clouds with his broad hand, he made a crash, and thence thick rains poured down from the upper air. The messenger of Juno, Iris, adorned in varied hues, drew up the waters and brought nourishment to the clouds. The crops were leveled and the farmers'

[12] Ovid provides his version of a tale about a werewolf that appears elsewhere in the Greek and Roman tradition. The name Lycaon itself was taken to be derived from the Greek word for wolf. The story may reflect primitive rites in honor of Lycaean Zeus performed on Mt. Lycaeus.

[13] A reflection of the Stoic doctrine of the Great Year (Magnus Annus) when the sun, moon, and the planets returned to their original positions. At the end of each of these periods came the conflagration, and all was reduced to elemental fire and then born again. A repetition of the pattern and the details of the previous cycle would follow.

hopeful prayers lay ruined and bemoaned, the labor of the long year in vain destroyed.

Nor was the wrath of Jove content with his realm, the sky. His brother Neptune of the sea gave aid with waves as reinforcements. He called together the rivers and, when they had entered the dwelling of their master, said: "Now I cannot resort to a long exhortation. Pour forth your strength, this is the need—open wide your domains, and all barriers removed, give full rein to your streams." This was his command. They went back home and opened wide their mouths for their waters to roll in their unbridled course over the plains. Neptune himself struck the earth with his trident; it trembled and with the quake laid open paths for the waters. The streams spread from their course and rushed over the open fields and swept away, together and at once, the trees and crops, cattle, men, houses, and their inner shrines with sacred statues. If any house remained and was able to withstand being thrown down by so great an evil, yet a wave still higher touched its highest gables, and towers overcome lay submerged in the torrent.

Now earth and sea bore no distinction; all was sea and besides a sea without shores. One occupied a hill, another would sit in his curved boat and ply the oars in the place where he had recently ploughed, another sailed over the crops and the roof of his submerged villa, another caught a fish in the upper branches of an elm. Anchor was dropped in a green meadow, if chance so ordained, or the curved keels scraped the vineyards that stretched below. And now the places where graceful goats had plucked grass were occupied by ugly seals. The Nereids wondered at the groves and cities and homes under water and dolphins possessed the woods and ran into the high branches and shook the oak trees as they swam against them. A wolf swam among sheep, the waves carried along tawny lions and swept away tigers. The power of his lightning thrust was of no advantage to the boar nor his fleet limbs to the deer, as they were carried off. Wandering birds searched long for a spot of land where they could light and with wearied wings fell into the sea. The vast and unrestrained surge of the sea overwhelmed the hills, and billows unknown before beat against the mountain peaks. The greatest part of life was swept away by water; those whom the water spared were overcome by slow starvation because of lack of food.

The territory of Phocis separates the terrain of Thessaly from that of Boeotia, a fertile area when it was land, but in this crisis it had suddenly become part of the sea and a wide field of water. Here a lofty mountain, Parnassus by name, reaches with its two peaks up to the stars, the heights extending beyond the clouds. When Deucalion with his wife was carried in his little boat to this mountain and ran aground (for the deep waters had covered the rest of the land) they offered worship to the Corycian nymphs,[14] the deities of the mountain, and prophetic Themis, who at that time held oracular power there. No man was better than Deücalion nor more devoted to justice, and no woman more reverent towards the gods than his wife Pyrrha. When Jupiter saw the earth covered with a sea of water and only one man and one woman surviving out of so many thousands of men and women, both innocent and both devout worshipers of deity, he dispelled the clouds and, after the North Wind had cleared the storm, revealed the earth to the sky and the upper air to the world below. The wrath of the sea did not endure and the ruler of the deep laid aside his trident and calmed the waves. He summoned the sea god Triton, who rose above the waters, his shoulders encrusted with shellfish; he ordered him to blow into his resounding conch shell and by this signal to recall the waves and the rivers. Triton took up the hollow horn which grows from the lowest point of the spiral coiling in ever widening circles. Whenever he blows into this horn in the middle of the deep its sounds fill every shore to east and west. Now too as the god put the horn to his lips moist with his dripping beard and gave it breath, it sounded the orders of retreat and was heard by all the waves on land and on the sea, and as they listened all were checked. Once more the sea had shores and streams were held within their channels, rivers subsided, and hills were seen to rise up. Earth emerged and the land grew in extent as the waves receded. And after a length of time the tops of the woods were uncovered and showed forth, a residue of mud left clinging to the leaves. The world had been restored. When Deucalion saw the earth devoid of life and the profound silence of its desolation, tears welled up in his eyes as he spoke to Pyrrha thus: "O my cousin, and my wife, the only woman left, related to me by family ties of blood, then joined to me in marriage, now danger itself unites us. We two alone are the host of the whole world from east to west; the sea holds all the rest. Besides assurance of our life is not yet completely certain. Even now the clouds above strike terror in my heart. What feelings would you have now, poor dear, if you had been snatched to safety by the Fates without me? In what way could you have been able to bear your fear alone? Who would have consoled you as you grieved? For I, believe me, would have followed, if the sea had taken you, dear wife, and the sea would have taken me with you. How I wish I might be able

[14] That is, nymphs of the Corycian cave on Mt. Parnassus.

to repopulate the earth by the arts of my father and infuse the molded clods of earth with life. As it is, the race of mortals rests in just us two—thus have the gods ordained—and we remain as patterns of mankind." Thus he spoke and they wept.

They decided to pray to the goddess Themis and seek help through her holy oracles with no delay. Together they approached the waves of the river Cephisus, which, although not yet clear, was cutting its accustomed course. When they had drawn water and sprinkled their heads and clothes, they turned their steps from there to the temple of the goddess; its pediments were discolored with vile moss and its altars stood without fire. As they reached the steps of the temple both fell forward on the ground, and in dread awe implanted kisses on the cold stone. They spoke as follows: "If the divine majesty is won over and made soft by just prayers, if the anger of the gods is turned aside, tell, O Themis, by what art the loss of the human race may be repaired and give help, O most gentle deity, in our drowned world." The goddess was moved and gave her oracle: "Go away from my temple, cover your heads and unloose the fastenings of your garments and toss the bones of the great mother behind your back." For a long time they were stupefied at this; Pyrrha first broke the silence by uttering her refusal to obey the orders of the goddess; with fearful prayer she begged indulgence, for she feared to hurt the shade of her mother by tossing her bones. But all the while they sought another explanation and mulled over, alone and together, the dark and hidden meaning of the obscure words given by the oracle. Then the son of Prometheus soothed the daughter of Epimetheus with pleasing words: "Unless my ingenuity is wrong, oracles are holy and never urge any evil; the great parent is the earth; I believe that the stones in the body of earth are called her bones. We are ordered to throw these behind our backs." Although the Titan's daughter was moved by the interpretation of her husband, her hope was still in doubt; to this extent they both distrusted heaven's admonitions. But what harm would there be in trying? They left the temple, covered their heads, unloosed their garments, and tossed the stones behind their steps as they were ordered. The stones (who would believe this if the antiquity of tradition did not bear testimony?) began to lose their hardness and rigidity and gradually grew soft and in their softness assumed a shape. Soon as they grew, and took on a more pliant nature, the form of a human being could be seen, in outline not distinct, most like crude statues carved in marble, just begun and not sufficiently completed. The part of the stones that was of earth dampened by some moisture was converted into flesh; what was solid and unable to be so transformed was changed into bone; what once had been a vein in the stone remained with the same name; in a short time, through the will of the gods, the stones hurled by the hands of the man assumed the appearance of men, and those cast by the woman were converted into women. Hence we are a hard race and used to toils and offer proof of the origin from which we were sprung.

The earth of her own accord produced other animals of different sorts, after the moisture that remained was heated by the fire of the sun; and the mud and soggy marshes began to swell because of the heat, and fertile seeds of things began to grow nourished by the life-giving earth, as in a mother's womb, and gradually took on a certain form.

Deucalion and Pyrrha had a son Hellen, the eponymous ancestor of the Greek people; for the Greeks called themselves Hellenes and their country Hellas.[15] Hellen had three sons: Dorus, Aeolus, and Xuthus. Xuthus in turn had two sons: Ion and Achaeus. Thus eponyms were provided for the four major divisions of the Greeks on the basis of dialect and geography: Dorians, Aeolians, Ionians, and Achaeans.

[15] The names Greeks and Greece came through the Romans who first met a group of Hellenes called the Graioi, participants in the colonization of Cumae just north of Naples.

CHAPTER 3

The Twelve Olympians; Zeus, Hera, and Their Children

Thus Zeus is established as lord of gods and men. He is supreme but he does share his powers with his brothers. Zeus himself assumes the sky as his special sphere; Poseidon, the sea; and Hades, the underworld. Sometimes the three are said to have cast lots for their realms. Zeus takes his sister, Hera, as his wife; she reigns by his side as his queen and subordinate. His sisters Hestia and Demeter share in divine power and functions; the other major gods and goddesses are also given significant prerogatives and authority as they are born.

And so a circle of major deities (fourteen in number) is evolved: Zeus, Hera, Poseidon, Hades, Hestia, Hephaestus, Ares, Apollo, Artemis, Demeter, Aphrodite, Athena, Hermes, and Dionysus.[1] This list was reduced to a canon of twelve Olympians by omitting Hades (whose specific realm is under the earth) and replacing Hestia with Dionysus, a great deity who comes relatively late to Greece.

Although Hestia is important, her role and function are relatively limited and therefore she may be briefly discussed here. Her mythology is meager. She rejected the advances of both Poseidon and Apollo and vowed to remain a virgin; like Athena and Artemis, then, she is a goddess of chastity. But she is primarily the goddess of the hearth and its sacred fire; her name Hestia is the Greek word for hearth. Among primitive men fire was obtained with difficulty, kept alive, and revered for its basic importance in daily

---

[1] The order is to a large extent arbitrary; the Roman equivalents (Jupiter, Juno, Neptune, Pluto, Vesta, Vulcan, Mars, Apollo, Diana, Ceres, Venus, Minerva, Mercury, and Bacchus) are discussed in pp. 396–415.

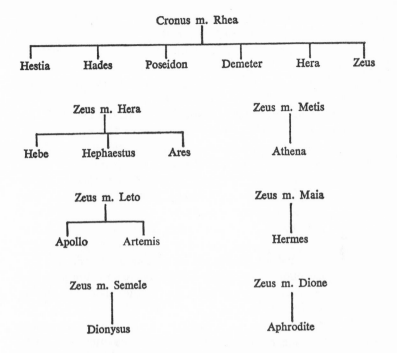

Fig. 3. The lineage of major deities

needs and religious ceremony. The hearth too was the center of the family and then of the larger political units, the tribe, the city, and the state. Transmission of the sacred fire from one settlement to another represented a continuing bond of sentiment and heredity. Thus both the domestic and the communal hearth were designated as holy, and the goddess herself presided over them. Hestia often gained precedence at banquets and in sacrificial ritual, for as the first born of Cronus and Rhea she was considered august, one of the older generation of the gods. But when the other gods went to a feast, she alone stayed at home and eventually it was easy to squeeze her out of the Olympian canon of twelve.

Zeus is an amorous deity; he mates with countless goddesses and mortal women and his offspring are legion. Most genealogies demanded the glory and authority of the supreme god himself as their ultimate progenitor. Along with this necessity emerged the character of a Zeus conceived and readily developed by what may be called a popular mythology. This Zeus belonged to a monogamous society in which the male was dominant; however moral the basic outlook, the standards for the man were different from those for the woman. Illicit affairs were possible and even if not officially sanctioned were at least condoned for the one, but under no circumstances tolerated for the other. Thus Zeus is the glorified image of the husband and father but, as well, the lover; his consort Hera is the wife and mother who with matronly severity upholds the sanctity of marriage. As the picture evolves Zeus's behavior may be depicted as amoral or immoral or merely a joke; the supreme god can stand above conventional standards; at other times he will act in harmony with them and more than once must face the shrewish harangues of his wife and pay at least indirectly through pain and suffering wrought by his promiscuity. Ultimately the depiction depends upon a certain period and the intent and purpose of an individual author. As we shall see, the conception of deity is infinitely varied and complex, and this characterization of Zeus is merely one of many which have, yet to be considered.

We shall not catalogue the gamut of Zeus's conquests here. They will provide a recurrent theme throughout this book. Two of his affairs are pertinent now for the universal significance of their progeny. Zeus mates with the Titaness Mnemosyne (Memory) who gives birth to the Muses, the patronesses of literature and the arts; thus allegorically Memory with divine help produces inspiration. Their home is often located in Pieria in northern Thessaly near Mt. Olympus [2] or about the fountain Hippocrene on Mt. Helicon in Boeotia. The Muses (their name means the Reminders) may originally have been water spirits with the power of prophecy and then inspiration, imagined from the babbling of waters as they flow. They are supreme in their fields and those who dare to challenge them meet with defeat and punishment. In this respect they resemble Apollo, with whom they are often associated.

[2] The Muses are sometimes called the Pierides, but Ovid (*Metamorphoses*, 5.295–678) tells a story of nine daughters of Pierus of Pella in Macedonia who were also called Pierides. They challenged the Muses to a musical contest, lost, and were changed into magpies, birds that imitate sounds and chatter incessantly.

The number of the Muses is not consistent, but later authors usually identify nine of them, with specific functions, although assignments will vary. Calliope presides over epic poetry; Clio, history (or lyre playing); Euterpe, lyric poetry (or tragedy and flute playing); Melpomene, tragedy (or lyre playing); Terpsichore, choral dancing (or flute playing); Erato, love poetry (or hymns to the gods and lyre playing); Polyhymnia, sacred music (or dancing); Urania, astronomy; Thalia, comedy.

Zeus is sometimes said to be the father of the Fates (Moirae) as a result of his union with Themis;[3] or Night and Erebus may be the parents. The Fates are originally birth spirits and often came to be depicted as three old women responsible for the destiny of every individual. Clotho (the Spinner) spins out the thread of life which carries with it the fate of each human being from the moment of birth; Lachesis (the Apportioner) measures the thread; and Atropos (the Inflexible), sometimes characterized as the smallest and most terrible, cuts it off and brings life to an end. On occasion they can be influenced to alter the fate decreed by their labors, but usually the course of the destiny that they spin is irrevocable.

Often Fate is thought of in the singular, Moira, in a conception that is much more abstract and linked closely to a profound realization of the roles played by Luck or Fortune (Tyche) and Necessity (Ananke) in the scheme of human life. The relation of the gods to destiny is variously depicted and intriguing to analyze in the literature. According to some authors Zeus is supreme and controls all, but others portray a universe in which even the great and powerful Zeus must bow to the inevitability of Fate's decrees. The depth of this feeling of the Greeks for the working of Moira or the Moirae cannot be overemphasized. It provides a definite and unique tone and color to the bulk of their writing. One thinks immediately of Homer or Herodotus or the tragedians, but no major author was untouched by fascination with the interrelation

[3] Zeus and Themis also unite to produce the seasons (Horae), goddesses who are two, three, or four in number and closely connected with vegetation. They attend the greater deities and provide attractive decoration in literature and art. Zeus and Themis as sky-god and earth-goddess enact once again the ritual of the holy marriage.

of god, man, and fate and the tantalizing interplay of destiny and free will.[4]

The union of Zeus and Hera represents yet another enactment of the holy marriage between the sky-god and earth-goddess; this is made clear in the lines from Homer (*Iliad,* 14.346–351), which describe their love-making: "The son of Cronus clasped his wife in his arms and under them the divine earth sprouted forth new grass, dewy clover, crocuses and hyacinths, thick and soft, to protect them from the ground beneath. On this they lay together and drew around themselves a beautiful golden cloud from which the glistening drops fell away."

Hera has little mythology of her own and is important mainly as Zeus's consort and queen. She appears in many stories as the vehement wife who will punish and avenge the romantic escapades of her husband. In art she is depicted as regal and matronly often with attributes of royalty. Homer describes her as ox-eyed and white-armed, both epithets presumably denoting her beauty. The peacock is associated with her; this is explained by her role in the story of Io. Argos was a special center for her worship, and a great temple was erected there in her honor in classical times. Hera was worshiped not so much as an earth-goddess but rather as a goddess of women, marriage, and childbirth, functions that she shares with other deities.

We are already familiar with Zeus the god of the sky, the cloud-gatherer of epic. The etymological root of his name means bright (as does that of Jupiter). His attributes are thunder and lightning, and he is often depicted as about to hurl them. The king of gods and men is a regal figure represented as a man in his prime, usually bearded. He bears as well the aegis, a word meaning goat skin which originally designated merely the cloak of a shepherd. For Zeus it is a shield with wonderful and miraculous protective powers.[5] The eagle and the majestic oak tree were sacred to Zeus.

---

[4] The Romans developed this same tragic view of human existence. For them Fate is personified by the Parcae, or more abstractly conceived of as Fatum (Fate).

[5] The warrior-goddess Athena will also carry the aegis on which may be depicted the head of the Gorgon whom she helped Perseus slay. Athena's aegis may be her own or lent by Zeus to his favorite daughter.

Olympia and Dodona were important centers for his worship, and both were frequented in antiquity for their oracular responses.[6]

The traditional methods for eliciting a response from the god were by the observation and interpretation of omens, for example, the rustling of leaves, the sound of the wind in the branches of the oaks, the call of doves, and the condition of burnt offerings. At Olympia inquiries were usually confined to the chances of the competitors in the games. Eventually at Dodona, through the influence of the oracle of Apollo at Delphi, a priestess would mount a tripod and deliver her communications from the god. Here leaden tablets have been found inscribed with all kinds of questions posed by the state and the individual. The people of Corcyra ask Zeus to what god or hero they should pray or sacrifice for their common good; others ask if it is safe to join a federation; a man enquires if it is good for him to marry; another, whether he will have children from his wife. There are questions about purchases, health, and family.

The worship of Zeus at Dodona and Olympia makes it clear that there is more than one facet to the Greeks' conception of their supreme deity. In fact he becomes for them the one god, and his concerns envelop the whole sphere of morality for both gods and men. He is the wrathful god of justice and virtue upholding all that is sacred and holy in the moral order of the universe. This Zeus we shall discuss at greater length in a subsequent chapter.

Zeus and Hera have four children: Eileithyia, Hebe, Hephaestus, and Ares. Eileithyia is a goddess of childbirth, a role she shares with her mother; at times mother and daughter merge in identity.[7]

Hebe is the goddess of youthful bloom (the literal meaning of her name). She is a servant of the gods as well; in the *Iliad*

---

[6] The Panhellenic sanctuary at Olympia was also the site of one of the principal athletic festivals of the ancient world. The games were celebrated every four years and were initiated in 776. One of the many systems of dating for the Greeks was by Olympiads, the years in which the celebrations were held. Among the numerous buildings within the sanctuary was a great temple to Olympian Zeus. Olympia was not as famous for its oracles as was the sanctuary of Apollo at Delphi, which is similar to that at Olympia and is described later in some detail as representative of this facet of Hellenic worship and life. See pp. 135–138.

[7] Artemis and Hera also share this function with Eileithyia.

(5.905) she bathes and clothes Ares after he has been healed of the wounds inflicted by the hero Diomedes. Hebe is primarily known for her services as the cupbearer for the deities on Olympus. When Heracles wins immortality, Hebe becomes his bride. Some versions explain that she resigned from her position to marry. Late authors claim that she was discharged for clumsiness. The Trojan prince Ganymede shares honors with Hebe as cupbearer of the gods; according to some he replaces her. The *Homeric Hymn to Aphrodite* (5.202–217) tells how Zeus carried off Ganymede, the handsome son of Tros.

Indeed Zeus in his wisdom seized and carried off fair-haired Ganymede because of his beauty, so that he might be in the company of the gods and pour wine for them in the house of Zeus, a wonder to behold, esteemed by all the immortals, as he draws the red nectar from a golden bowl. But a lasting sorrow gripped the heart of Tros, for he had no idea where the divine whirlwind had taken his dear son. Indeed he mourned for him unceasingly each and every day and Zeus took pity on the father and gave him as recompense for his son brisk-trotting horses, the kind which carry the gods. These he gave him to have as a gift. And at the command of Zeus, Hermes, · the guide and slayer of Argus, told everything and how Ganymede would be immortal and never grow old, just like the gods. When Tros heard this message from Zeus, he no longer continued his mourning but rejoiced within his heart and joyfully was borne by the horses that were as swift as a storm.

In some accounts an eagle not a whirlwind carries Ganymede away; some too boldly attribute homosexual desire to Zeus, thus having the supreme god mirror yet another human passion.

Hephaestus, the next child of Zeus and Hera to be considered, is a god of creative fire and a divine smith. His workshop is often placed in heaven or on Olympus. Homer (*Iliad,* 18) presents a splendid picture of his house on Olympus when Thetis appeals to Hephaestus to forge new armor for her son Achilles. All that this immortal craftsman produces excites wonder; his major role in mythology is to create things of extraordinary beauty and utility, often elaborately wrought. One of his masterpieces, the shield of Achilles, is described in exquisite detail by Homer. Hephaestus even has attendants fashioned of gold that look like living young women; these robots can move with intelligence and speak with knowledge. He is indeed the master artisan. Sometimes his forge is under the earth, and as he labors all covered with soot and sweat he may be attended by the three Cyclopes, whom we already know as the ones who create the thunder and lightning of Zeus.[8]

The god Hephaestus was a cripple from birth. One story maintains that Hera was ashamed of his deformity and cast him down from Olympus or heaven. But he was rescued and eventually returned home. We are also told that he was hurled to earth on another occasion, this time by Zeus. Hephaestus lands on the island of Lemnos, which in classical times was an important center of his worship. Other volcanic regions (e.g., in Sicily and its environs) were associated with this divine smith; these places bore testimony to the fire and smoke that at times would erupt from his forge.

At the close of Book 1 of the *Iliad,* Hephaestus himself recounts the episode of Zeus's anger against him. We shall excerpt this passage because it illustrates many things: the character of Hephaestus, his closeness to his mother Hera,[9] the tone and atmosphere instigated by an episode in the life of the Olympian family, Zeus as the stern father in his house and his difficult relations with his wife, the uneasy emotions of the children while they witness the quarrel of their parents.

Thetis has come to Zeus on Olympus to ask that he grant victory to the Trojans until the Achaean Greeks honor her son Achilles and give him recompense for the insult that he has suffered. As she clasps his knees and touches his chin in the traditional posture of a suppliant, Zeus agrees to her wishes with these words (*Iliad,* 1.517–611):

"A bad business indeed if you set me at variance with Hera and she reviles me with reproaches. She always abuses me, even as it is, in the presence of the immortal gods and says that I help the Trojans in battle. But you now must withdraw, lest Hera notice anything. These

[8] Vergil (*Aeneid,* 8) locates Vulcan's workshop in a cave on the island of Vulcania near Sicily where he fashions magnificent armor for Venus's son Aeneas.

[9] In fact Hephaestus sometimes is claimed to be the son of Hera alone without Zeus; thus Hera has her own favorite child, just as Zeus has his special daughter Athena, who was born from his head.

things you have asked for will be my concern until I accomplish them. Come now, I shall nod my assent to you so that you may be convinced. For this from me is the greatest pledge among the immortals; for no promise of mine is revocable or false or unfulfilled to which I give assent with the nod of my head."

He spoke and the son of Cronus with his dark brows nodded to her wishes; and the ambrosial locks flowed round the immortal head of the lord and he made great Olympus tremble.[10]

After the two had made their plans, they parted; then she leaped into the deep sea from shining Olympus and Zeus returned to his own house. All the gods rose together from their places in the presence of their father and no one dared to remain seated as he entered but all stood before him. Thereupon he sat down on his throne. But Hera did not fail to observe that silver-footed Thetis, daughter of the old man of the sea, had taken counsel with him. Immediately she addressed Zeus, the son of Cronus, with cutting remarks: "Which one of the gods this time has taken counsel with you, crafty rogue? Always it is dear to you to think secret thoughts and to make decisions apart from me and never yet have you dared say a word openly to me about what you are thinking."

Then the father of men and gods answered her: "Hera, do not hope to know all that I say; it would be difficult for you even though you are my wife. But whatever it is fitting that you should hear, then not anyone either of gods nor of men will know it before you. But do not pry or ask questions about each and every thing to which I wish to give thought apart from the gods."

And then ox-eyed Hera in her majesty replied: "Most dread son of Cronus, what kind of answer is this you have given? I have not pried too much or asked questions before but completely on your own you plan whatever you wish. Yet now I am terribly afraid in my heart that silver-footed Thetis, daughter of the old man of the sea, has won you over; for early this morning she sat by your side and grasped your knees and I believe that you nodded your oath that you would honor Achilles and destroy many by the ships of the Achaeans." The cloud-gatherer Zeus spoke to her in answer: "You always believe something and I never escape you; nevertheless you

[10] The artist Pheidias, responsible for the sculpture on the Parthenon, was also famous for his mighty statue of the seated figure of Zeus in the temple at Olympia; he is said to have claimed that these lines from Homer describing Zeus as he nods provided the model for his conception of the god's majesty rendered in marble, gold, and ivory.

will be able to accomplish nothing, but you will be farther removed from my heart; and this will be all the more chill an experience for you. If what you say is so, its fulfillment is what I desire. But sit down in silence, and obey what I say; for now all the gods in Olympus will be of no avail when I come closer and lay my invincible hands upon you." Thus he spoke and ox-eyed lady Hera was afraid, and she sat down in silence wrenching her heart to obedience, and the gods of heaven were troubled in the house of Zeus. But Hephaestus renowned for his art began to make a speech to them showing his concern for his dear mother Hera of the white arms. "This will be a sorry business indeed and not to be endured any longer, if you two quarrel on account of mortals and bring wrangling among the gods. There will be no further pleasure in the excellent feast when baser instincts prevail. I advise my mother, even though she is prudent, to act kindly towards my dear father Zeus so that he will not be abusive again and disturb our banquet. Just suppose he, the Olympian hurler of lightning, wishes to blast us from our seats. For he is by far the strongest. But you touch him with gentle words; immediately then the Olympian will be kindly towards us." Thus he spoke and springing up he placed a cup with two handles in the hand of his mother and spoke to her: "Bear up, mother dear, and endure, although you are hurt, so that I may not see you struck before my eyes, and then even though you are dear and I am distressed I shall not be able to help. For the Olympian is hard to oppose. Previously on another occasion when I was eager to defend you he grabbed me by the feet and hurled me from the divine threshold. And I fell the whole day and landed on Lemnos when the sun was setting, and little life was left in me. There Sintian men took care of me at once after my fall." Thus he spoke. And the goddess Hera of the white arms smiled and as she smiled she received the cup from his hand. He drew sweet nectar from a mixing bowl and poured it like wine for all the other gods from left to right. Then unquenchable laughter rose up among the blessed gods as they saw Hephaestus bustling about the house.

In this way then the whole day until the sun went down they feasted, nor was anyone's desire for his share of the banquet found wanting nor of the exquisite lyre that Apollo held nor of the Muses, who sang in harmony with beautiful voice. But when the bright light of the sun set they went to bed each to his own home which the re-nowned lame god Hephaestus had built by his skill and knowledge. Olympian Zeus, the hurler of lightning, went to his own bed where he always lay down until sweet sleep would come to him. There he went and took his rest and beside him was Hera of the golden throne.

Hephaestus is a figure of amusement as he hobbles around acting as the cupbearer to the gods on this particular occasion. But he is a deadly serious figure in his art and in his love. His wife is Aphrodite [11] and theirs is a strange and tempestuous marriage: the union of beauty and deformity, the intellectual and the sensual. Aphrodite is unfaithful to her husband and turns to the virile Ares, handsome and whole, brutal and strong. Homer with deceptive simplicity lays bare the psychological implications in a tale about the eternal triangle that remains forever fresh in its humanity and perceptions.

In Book 8 (266–366) of the *Odyssey* the bard, Demodocus, sings of the love affair between Ares and Aphrodite and the suffering of Hephaestus:

He took up the lyre and began to sing beautifully of the love of Ares and Aphrodite with the fair crown: how first they lay together by stealth in the home of Hephaestus. He gave her many gifts and defiled the marriage bed of lord Hephaestus. But soon Helius, the sun, came to him as a messenger, for he saw them in the embrace of love, and Hephaestus when he heard the painful tale went straight to his forge planning evil in his heart. He put his great anvil on its stand and hammered out chains that could not be broken or loosened so that they would hold fast on the spot. When he had fashioned this cunning device in his rage against Ares, he went directly to his chamber where the bed was and spread the many shackles all around the bedposts and hung them suspended from the rafters, like a fine spider's web that no one could see, not even the blessed gods, for they were very cunningly made. When he had arranged the whole device all about the bed, he pretended to journey to the well-built citadel of Lemnos, which of all lands was by far the most dear to him. But Ares of the golden reins was not blind in his watch and as he saw Hephaestus leave he went straight to the house of the craftsman renowned for his art, eager for love with Cytherea of the fair crown. She was sitting having just come from her mighty father, the son of Cronus, when Ares came into the house; he took her hand and spoke out exclaiming: "My love, come let us go to bed and take our pleasure, for Hephaestus is no longer at home but he has gone now, probably to visit Lemnos and the Sintian inhabitants with their barbarous

---

[11] Sometimes Hephaestus's mate is one of the Graces, either the youngest, Aglaea, or Grace herself (Charis), which actually may be but another designation for Aphrodite.

speech." Thus he spoke and to her the invitation seemed most gratifying; they both went and lay down on the bed. And the bonds fashioned by ingenious Hephaestus poured around them and they were not able to raise or move a limb. Then to be sure they knew that there was no longer any escape. The renowned lame god came from close by; he had turned back before he had reached the land of Lemnos, for Helius watched from his lookout and told him the story. Hephaestus made for his home, grieving in his heart, and he stood in the doorway and wild rage seized him; he cried out in a loud and terrible voice to all the gods: "Father Zeus and you other blessed gods who live forever, come here so that you may see something that is laughable and cruel: how Aphrodite the daughter of Zeus always holds me in contempt since I am lame and loves the butcher Ares because he is handsome and sound of limb, but I was born a cripple. I am not to blame for this nor is anyone else except both my parents who I wish had never begotten me. You will see how these two went into my bed where they lay down together in love. As I look at them I am overcome by anguish. I do not think that they will still want to lie here in this way for even a brief time, although they are so very much in love, and very quickly they will no longer wish to sleep side by side, for my cunning and my bonds will hold them fast until her father pays back all the gifts that I gave to him for this hussy because she was his daughter and beautiful, but she is wanton in her passion."

Thus he spoke and the gods assembled at his house with the floor of bronze. Poseidon the earthshaker came, and Hermes the helpful runner, and lord Apollo the far-shooter. But the goddesses in their modesty stayed at home one and all. The blessed gods, dispensers of good things, stood at the door and unquenchable laughter rose up among them as they saw the skill of ingenious Hephaestus. And one would speak to another who was next to him as follows: "Bad deeds do not prosper; the slow overtakes the swift, since now Hephaestus who is slow and lame has caught by his skill Ares, even though he is the swiftest of the gods who inhabit Olympus. Therefore he must pay the penalty for being caught in adultery." This was the sort of thing that they said to one another. And lord Apollo, son of Zeus, spoke to Hermes: "Hermes, son of Zeus, runner and bestower of blessings, would you wish to lie in bed by the side of golden Aphrodite, even though pressed in by mighty shackles?" Then the swift runner Hermes answered: "I only wish it were so, lord Apollo, far-shooter. Let there be three times the number of shackles and you gods looking on and all the goddesses, I still would lie by the side of golden Aphrodite."

Thus he spoke and a laugh rose up among the immortal gods. But Poseidon did not laugh; he relentlessly begged Hephaestus, the renowned smith, to release Ares and addressed him with winged words: "Release him. I promise you that he will pay all that is fitting in the presence of the immortal gods, as you demand." Then the renowned lame god answered: "Do not demand this of me, Poseidon, earthshaker; pledges made on behalf of worthless characters are worthless to have and to keep. How could I hold you fast in the presence of the immortal gods, if Ares gets away and escapes both his debt and his chains?" Then Poseidon the earthshaker answered: "Hephaestus, if Ares avoids his debt and escapes and flees, I myself will pay up." Then the renowned lame god replied: "I cannot and I must not deny your request."

Thus speaking Hephaestus in his might released the chains. And when they both were freed from the strong bonds, they immediately darted away; the one went to Thrace and the other, laughter-loving Aphrodite, came to Paphos in Cyprus where are her sanctuary and altar fragrant with sacrifices. There the Graces bathed her and anointed her with divine oil, the kind that is used by the immortal gods, and they clothed her in lovely garments, a wonder to behold.

A funny story yet a painful one; glib in its sophisticated and ironic portrayal of the gods, but permeated with a deep and unshakable moral judgment and conviction. The Greeks particularly enjoyed the fact that the lame Hephaestus by his intelligence and craft outwits the nimble and powerful Ares.

Ares himself, the god of war, is the last child of Zeus and Hera to be considered. His origins probably belong to Thrace, an area with which he is often linked. Aphrodite is usually named as his cult partner; several children are attributed to them, the most important being Eros. Dawn (Eos) was one of his mistresses and we have already mentioned Aphrodite's jealousy.

In character Ares is generally depicted as a kind of divine swashbuckler. He is not highly thought of and at times he appears as little more than a butcher. The more profound moral and theological aspects of war were taken over by other deities, for example, Zeus or Athena.[12] Zeus's response to Ares after he has been

---

[12] Mars for the Romans had deeper religious and philosophical connotations; see pp. 398–399.

wounded by Diomedes (Ares sometimes gets the worst of things even in battle) is typical of the Greek attitude toward him (*Iliad*, 5.889–891, 895–898).

Do not sit beside me and complain, you two-faced rogue. Of all the gods who dwell on Olympus you are the most hateful to me, for strife and wars and battles are always dear to you. . . . Still I shall not endure any longer that you be in pain, for you are of my blood and your mother bore you to me. But if you were born of some other of the gods, since you are so destructive you would have long since been thrown out of Olympus.

The Greeks felt strongly about the brutality, waste, and folly of war, all of which are personified and deified in the figure of Ares.

CHAPTER 4

Anthropomorphism and Greek Humanism

By now the nature of the anthropomorphic conception of deity evolved by the Greeks and Romans has become evident. The gods are generally depicted as human in form and in character, but although they look and act like men, very often their appearance and their actions are at least to some extent idealized. Their beauty is beyond that of ordinary mortals, their passions more grand and intense, their sentiments more praiseworthy and touching; and they can embody and impose the loftiest moral values in the universe. Yet these same gods too can mirror the physical and spiritual weaknesses of human counterparts: they may be crippled and deformed or conceived as vain, petty, and insincere; they can steal, lie, and cheat, sometimes with a finesse that is exquisitely divine.

The gods usually live in houses on Mt. Olympus or in heaven; an important distinction, however, is to be made between those deities of the upper air and the upper world and those of the earth (i.e., Chthonian) and the realm below. They eat and drink but their food is ambrosia and their wine, nectar. Ichor (a substance clearer than blood) flows in their veins. Just as they can feel the gamut of human emotion, so too they can suffer physical pain and torment. They are worshiped in shrines and temples and sanctuaries; they are honored with statues, placated by sacrifices, and invoked by prayers.

In general the gods are more versatile and more powerful than men. They are able to move with amazing speed and dexterity, appear and disappear in a moment, and change their shape at will, assuming various forms, human, animal, and divine. Their powers are far greater than those of mortals, but they are usually not ómnipotent, except possibly Zeus himself. Yet even Zeus may be made subject to Fate or the Fates, although the conception is by no means always clear or consistent. Their knowledge, too, is superhuman, but on occasion limited. Omniscience is most often reserved as a special prerogative of Zeus and Apollo, who communicate their knowledge of the future to men. Most important of all, the gods are immortal, and this is perhaps the one most consistent divine characteristic that in the last analysis distinguishes them from mortals.

Very often one or more animals are associated with a particular deity, for example, Zeus, the eagle; Ares, the boar; Athena, the owl; Aphrodite, the dove, sparrow, or goose; and so forth. In addition any god can take the form of an animal if he so desires. But there is no concrete evidence to show that the Greeks at an early period ever worshiped animals as sacred, and it is unlikely that any one of the gods was for them ever originally an animal totem.

It is, however, difficult and dangerous, if not impossible, to generalize about the nature of the Greek deities. Many of the preceding remarks apply for the most part only to the highest order of divinity in the Greek pantheon. Such wondrous and terrible creations as the Gorgons or Harpies, who populate the universe to enrich the mythology and saga, obviously represent a different category of the supernatural. Of a similar but different order, too, are the divine spirits who animate nature. These beings are usually depicted as nymphs, beautiful young girls who love to dance and sing; some of them are extremely amorous. Very often they act as attendants for one or more of the major gods or goddesses. The Muses, for example, are a kind of nymph, and so are the Nereids and Oceanids, although some of them assume virtually the stature of deity. Nymphs are more typically rather like fairies, extremely long-lived but not necessarily immortal. They are sometimes classified as follows: the spirits of water, springs, lakes, and rivers are called Naiads; Potamiads are specifically the nymphs of rivers; tree-nymphs are generally called Dryads or Hamadryads, although their name should restrict them as "spirits of oak trees" in particular; Meliae are the nymphs of the ash tree.

Demigods are another class of superhuman beings, or better,

a superior kind of human being, that is, supermen. They are the offspring of mixed parentage, the union of a god with a mortal, although the mortal may bask in the grand aura of the great mythological age of saga and boast of a genealogy that in the not too distant past included at least one divine ancestor. Demigods are, therefore, limited in their powers which are rather less than those of a full-fledged god; and they are, in the last analysis, mortal, often being little more than figures made larger than life because of their tragic and epic environment. Heroes sometimes are demigods, but the terminology is not easy to define precisely. Mortals such as Oedipus and Amphiaraus are not, strictly speaking, demigods, although they are far from ordinary beings. They may be called heroes, and certainly they become so after their death, honored with a cult largely because of the spiritual intensity of their lives and the miraculous nature of their deaths; they thus assume a divine status. Heracles, too, is a hero and a demigod who is accepted (like Oedipus?) among the company of the gods on Olympus because of his glorious attainments in this world. The difficulty in establishing absolute definitions is complicated because of the use of the designation "hero" in the vocabulary of literary criticism. Achilles is a demigod, that is, the son of a mortal Peleus and the nymph-goddess Thetis. His powers are extraordinary, but it is ultimately as a mortal, the dramatic and epic hero of the *Iliad,* that he lives and moves.

Thus it is apparent that a hierarchy of divinities existed in the Greek pantheon. The Olympians along with the major deities of the lower world represent as it were the powerful aristocracy at the higher levels. Although the honors bestowed on individual gods and goddesses may vary to some extent from place to place (e.g., Athena belongs particularly to Athens, Hera to Argos, Hephaestus to Lemnos, Apollo to Delos and Delphi, etc.), in general the power and importance of the major divinities were universally recognized throughout the Greek world. At the top of the pinnacle is Zeus himself, the king, the father of both gods and men, the supreme lord.

We have already seen the popular anthropomorphic conception of Zeus as the father, husband, and lover; and we know too the primary sphere of his power, the sky and the upper air, with their thunder, lightning, and rain. It is important to realize as well that Zeus becomes the god who upholds the highest moral values in the order of the universe—values that he absorbs unto himself or that are divided among and shared by other deities. He is the god who protects the family, the clan, and the state, championing the universal moral and ethical responsibilities that these human associations entail. He protects suppliants, imposes ties of hospitality, upholds the sanctity of oaths; in a word he is the defender of all that is right or just in the mores of advanced civilization. Thus a monotheistic cast in the conception of Zeus is evident from the beginning; as it evolves it may be linked closely to the standard depictions of an anthropomorphic Zeus or imagined in terms of more abstract philosophical and religious theories of a supreme power.

Many selections from many authors could be quoted to bear testimony to the variety and complexity of these conceptions among the Greeks of the nature of the one god. These few examples must suffice.

Hesiod, who preaches a harsh message of righteousness and warns of the terror of Zeus's punishment of the wicked, sounds very much like a severe prophet of the Old Testament. The opening section of his *Works and Days* includes the following lines:

> Through Zeus who dwells in a most lofty home and thunders from on high and by his mighty will, mortals are both known and unknown. renowned and unrenowned; for easily he makes a man strong and easily he brings him low; easily he makes the overweening humble and champions the obscure; easily he makes the crooked straight and strikes down the haughty.

Xenophanes, a poet and philosopher of the pre-Socratic period, was vehement in his attack of the conventional anthropomorphic depictions of the gods.

> Homer and Hesiod have ascribed to the gods all that is shameful and reproachful among men: stealing, adultery, and deception. [fragment 11]
> But mortals think that gods are born and have clothes and a voice and a body just like them. [fragment 14]

The Ethiopians say that their gods are flat-nosed and black and the Thracians that theirs are fair and ruddy. [fragment 16]

But if cattle and horses and lions had hands and could create with their hands and achieve works like those of men, horses would render their conceptions of the gods like horses, and cattle like cattle, and each would depict bodies for them just like their own. [fragment 15]

One god, greatest among gods and men, not at all like mortals, either in body or in mind. [fragment 23]

The chorus of Aeschylus's *Agamemnon* (160–161) calls upon god by the name of Zeus with these words that illustrate beautifully the universality of this supreme deity: "Zeus, whoever he may be, I call on him by this name, if it is pleasing to him to be thus invoked."

It is important to realize that monotheism and polytheism are not mutually exclusive, that the religious experience of mankind usually tends (as Xenophanes observes) to be anthropomorphic. It would be absurd to deny that Christianity in its very essence is monotheistic, but its monotheism too rests upon a hierarchical conception of the spiritual and physical universe, and its standard images are obviously cast in anthropomorphic molds: for example, there is one God in three divine persons, God the Father, the Son, and the Holy Ghost; there are angels, saints, devils, and so on. This does not mean that the Christian philosopher and the practicing layman view the basic tenets of their religion in exactly the same way; ultimately one's vision of deity is personal, as abstract and sublime for one as it is human and compassionate for another. Among Christian sects alone there are significant variations in dogma and ritual, and of course, there are those who do not believe at all. The range from devout belief to agnosticism and atheism was equally diverse and rich in the ancient world. The tendency in a brief survey such as this is to oversimplify and distort.

The anthropomorphism of the Greeks is almost invariably linked to their role as the first great humanists. Humanism (the Greek variety or for that matter any other) can mean many things to many people. Standard interpretations usually evoke a few sublime (although hackneyed) quotations from Greek literature. The sophist Protagoras is said to have proclaimed (presumably challenging absolute values by voicing new relativistic attitudes):

"Man is the measure of all things"; a chorus in Sophocles's *Antigone* sings out exultantly: "Wonders are many but none is more wonderful than man"; and Achilles's judgment of the afterlife in Homer's *Odyssey* (translated in a later chapter) quoted out of context seems to affirm the glories of this life as opposed to the dismal gloom of the hereafter.

I should prefer as a slave to serve another man, even if he had no property and little to live on, than to rule all those dead who have done with life.

With words such as these ringing in one's ears, it seems easy to postulate blindly a Greek worship (even idolatry) of man in a man-centered universe, where man pays the gods the highest (but surely dubious) compliment of being cast in their own image.

Whatever truths this popular view may contain, it is far too one-dimensional and misleading to be genuinely meaningful and fair. Greek literature and Greek thought are shot through with an awesome reverence for the supremacy of god, a tragic realization of the irony of man's dilemma as the plaything of fate, and a profound awareness of the pain and suffering of human existence, however glorious the triumphant heights to which mortals may attain in the face of dreadful uncertainties and terrors.

The historian Herodotus perhaps best represents these human and religious attitudes in their clearest and most succinct form, when he relates the story of Solon, Croesus, and Cyrus. Fortunately, episodes in their drama may be easily excerpted as an entity here, for they illustrate many things. Monotheism and polytheism are shown resting compatibly side by side. The jealous god of Solon is not unlike the wrathful deity of the Old Testament, and this is a god who makes manifest to men that it is better to be dead than alive. The divine is able to communicate with mortals in a variety of ways; one can understand, for example, the simple and sincere belief in Apollo and Delphi possible in the sixth century B.C. Fate or destiny plays a fascinating role in the interplay between its inevitability and the individuality of human character and free will.

There is much that is Homeric in the Herodotean view, not

least of all a compassion tinged with a most profound sadness and pity for the human condition. Homeric and dramatic, too, is the simple elucidation of the dangers of hybris and the irrevocable vengeance of Nemesis—the kernel, as it were, of a theme that dominates Greek tragedy, with multiple and sometimes very sophisticated variations. His conception of god and his message of knowledge through suffering are strikingly Aeschylean. The story of the death of Atys is most Sophoclean in its movement and philosophy, and Croesus like Oedipus fulfills his inevitable destinies in terms of his character; each step that he takes in his blind attempts to avoid his fate brings him closer to its embrace. As Herodotus tells it, we have a complete drama conceived and beautifully executed within the structure of the short story.

But let Herodotus's art speak for itself. He is neither professional theologian nor philosopher, yet he sums up the spiritual essence of an age of faith. By the second half of the fifth century, the seeds of question and doubt sown in the earlier period by men such as Thales will be brought to fruition by the scepticism and agnosticism of the Sophistic movement.

The story of Solon's meeting with Croesus is found in Book 1 of Herodotus (30–46):

And so Solon set out to see the world and came to the court of Amasis in Egypt and to Croesus at Sardis. And when he arrived, Croesus received him as a guest in his palace. Three or four days later at the bidding of Croesus servants took Solon on a tour of his treasuries, pointing out that all of them were large and wealthy. When he had seen and examined them all to suit his convenience, Croesus asked the following question: "My Athenian guest, many stories about you have reached us because of your wisdom and your travels, of how you in your love of knowledge have journeyed to see many lands. And so now the desire has come over me to ask if by this time you have seen anyone who is the happiest of men." He asked this expecting that he was the happiest of men, but Solon did not flatter him at all but following the truth said: "O king, Tellus the Athenian." And Croesus, amazed at this reply, asked sharply: "How do you judge Tellus to be the most happy?" And Solon said: "First of all he was from a city that was faring well and he had beautiful and good children and to all of them he saw children born and all

survive, and secondly his life was prosperous, according to our standards, and the end of his life was most brilliant. When a battle was
fought by the Athenians against their neighbors near Eleusis, he went
to help and after routing the enemy died most gloriously, and the
Athenians buried him at public expense there where he fell and
honored him greatly." Thus Solon provoked Croesus as he listed the
many good fortunes that befell Tellus, and he asked whom he had
seen second to him, thinking certainly that he would at least win
second place. And Solon said: "Cleobis and Biton. They were Argives
by race and their strength of body was as follows; both similarly
carried off prizes at the festivals and as well this story is told. The
Argives celebrated a festival to Hera and it was absolutely necessary
that the mother of these boys be brought by chariot to the temple.[1]
But the oxen had not come back from the fields in time, and the
youths, because it was growing late, yoked themselves to the chariot
and conveyed their mother, and after a journey of five miles they
arrived at the temple. When they had done this deed witnessed by
the whole congregation, the end of life that befell them was the very
best. And thereby god showed clearly how it is better for man to be
dead than alive.[2] For the Argive men crowded around and congratu-
lated the youths for their strength and the women praised their mother
for having such fine sons. And the mother was overjoyed at both
the deed and the praise and standing in front of the statue prayed
to the goddess to give to her sons, Cleobis and Biton, who had honored her greatly, the best thing for man to obtain. After this prayer,
when they had sacrificed and feasted, the two young men went into
the temple itself to sleep and never more woke up but the end of
death held them fast. The Argives had statues made of them and set
them up in Delphi since they had been the best of men.[3]

Thus Solon assigned the second prize of happiness to these two and
Croesus interrupted in anger: "My Athenian guest, is our happiness
so dismissed as nothing that you do not even put us on a par with
ordinary men?" And he answered: "O Croesus, you ask me about

[1] Her name was Cydippe and she was a priestess of Hera, hence the
necessity for her presence at the festival. The temple would be the Argive
Heraeum.

[2] Herodotus here uses the masculine article with the word for god; he is
thinking specifically of one supreme god or generically of the divine power
of deity. But he does not refer to Hera specifically, although subsequently
it is to the goddess Hera that the mother prays on behalf of her sons.

[3] These statues have been excavated and do much to tantalize in the quest
for precise distinctions between myth and history in Herodotus's account.

human affairs, who know that all deity is jealous and fond of causing troubles. For in the length of time there is much to see that one does not wish and much to experience. For I set the limit of a man's life at seventy years; these seventy years comprise 25,200 days, if an intercalary month is not inserted. But if one wishes to lengthen every other year by a month, so that the seasons will occur when they should, the months intercalated in the seventy years will number thirty-five and these additional months will add 1050 days. All the days of the seventy years will total 26,250; and no one of them will bring exactly the same events as another. Thus then, O Croesus, man is completely a thing of chance.[4] To me you appear to be wealthy and king of many men; but I cannot answer the question that you ask me until I know that you have completed the span of your life well. For the one who has great wealth is not at all more fortunate than the one who has only enough for his daily needs, unless fate attend him and, having everything that is fair, he also end his life well. For many very wealthy men are unfortunate and many with only moderate means of livelihood have good luck. Indeed the one who is very wealthy but unfortunate surpasses the lucky man in two respects only, but the man of good luck surpasses the wealthy but unlucky man in many. The latter [wealthy but unlucky] is better able to fulfill his desires and to endure a great disaster that might befall him, but the other man [who is lucky] surpasses him in the following ways. Although he is not similarly able to cope with doom and desire, good fortune keeps these things from him, and he is unmaimed, free from disease, does not suffer evils, and has fine children and a fine appearance. If in addition to these things he still ends his life well, this is the one whom you seek who is worthy to be called happy. Before he dies do not yet call him happy, but only fortunate. Now it is impossible that anyone, since he is a man, gather unto himself all these blessings, just as no country is self-sufficient providing of itself all its own needs, but possesses one thing and lacks another. Whichever has the most, this is the best. Thus too no one human person is self-sufficient, for he possesses one thing but lacks another. Whoever continues to have most and then ends his life blessedly, this one justly wins this name from me, O king. One must see how the end of everything turns out. For to be sure god gives a glimpse of happiness to many and then casts them down headlong.

Solon did not find favor with Croesus by his words. He was sent away as one of no account, since Croesus was very much of the

[4] That is, man is entirely at the mercy of what befalls him.

opinion that a man must be ignorant who sets aside present goods and bids one look to the end of everything.

After the departure of Solon, a great Nemesis from god took hold of Croesus, very likely because he considered himself to be the happiest of all men. Straightway a dream stood before him as he slept, which made clear to him the truth of the evils that were to come about in connection with his son. Croesus had two sons, one of whom was dumb, the other by far the first in all respects among youths of his own age. His name was Atys. The dream indicated to Croesus that this Atys would die struck by the point of an iron weapon. When he woke up he thought about the dream and was afraid; he got his son a wife and although the boy was accustomed to command the Lydian forces he no longer sent him out on any such mission, and javelins and spears and all such weapons that men use in war he had removed from the men's quarters and piled up in the women's chambers, for fear that any that were hanging might fall on his son.

While they had on their hands arrangements for the marriage, there came to Sardis a man seized with misfortune, his hands polluted with blood, a Phrygian by race and of the royal family. This man came to the palace of Croesus and according to the traditions of the country begged to obtain purification, and Croesus purified him. The ritual of cleansing is similar for the Lydians and the Hellenes.[5] When Croesus had performed the customary rites, he asked from where he came and who he was in the following words: "My fellow, who are you and from where in Phrygia have you come to my hearth? What man or woman have you killed?" And he answered: "O king, I am the son of Gordias, the son of Midas, and I am called Adrastus. I killed my brother unintentionally and I come here driven out by my father and deprived of everything." Croesus answered him with these words: "You happen to be from a family of friends and you have come to friends where you will want for nothing while you remain with us. It will be most beneficial to you to bear this misfortune as lightly as possible." So Adrastus lived in the palace of Croesus.

At this very same time a great monster of a boar appeared in Mysian Olympus and he would rush down from this mountain and destroy the lands of the Mysians; often the Mysians went out against him but did him no harm but rather suffered from him. Finally messengers of the Mysians came to Croesus and spoke as follows: "O

[5] The ritual consisted at least in part of slaying a suckling pig and pouring the blood over the hands of the guilty murderer, who sat in silence at the hearth while Zeus was invoked as the Purifier.

king, the greatest monster of a boar has appeared in our country and destroys our lands. We are not able to capture him despite our great effort. Now then we beseech you to send your son to us and with him a picked company of young men and dogs so that we may drive him out of our land." They made this plea, but Croesus remembering the dream spoke the following words: "Do not mention my son further; for I will not send him to you; he is newly married and this now is his concern. I shall, however, send along a select group of Lydians and all my hunting equipment and hounds, and I shall order them as they go to be most zealous in helping you drive the beast from your land."

This was his answer, and the Mysians were satisfied with it when the son of Croesus, who had heard their request, broke in on them. Croesus still refused to send his son along with them and the young man spoke to him as follows: "O father, previously the finest and most noble pursuits were mine—to win renown in war and in the hunt. But now you have barred me from both, although you have not seen any lack of spirit or cowardice in me. Now how must I appear in the eyes of others as I go to and from the agora? What sort of man will I seem to my fellow citizens, what sort to my new bride? What kind of husband will she think she has married? So either let me go to the hunt or explain and convince me that it is better for me that things be done as you wish." Croesus answered with these words: "My child, I do not do this because I have seen in you cowardice or any other ugly trait, but the vision of a dream stood over me in sleep and said that your life would be short; for you will die by means of the sharp point of an iron weapon. And so in answer to the vision I urged this marriage on you and do not send you away on the present enterprise, being on my guard if in any way I might be able to steal you from fate for my own lifetime. For you happen to be my one and only child; for the other boy is deaf and I do not count him as mine." [6] The young man answered: "O father, I forgive you for taking precautions for me since you have seen such a vision. But you do not understand; the meaning of the dream has escaped you and it is right for me to explain. You say that the dream said that I would die by the point of an iron weapon.

[6] These words of Croesus at first strike the modern reader as extremely cruel. But he only means that he cannot consider the other boy as his son in the same way. Since the boy is deaf and dumb Croesus's hopes, both domestic and political, must rest in the son who is not crippled. We are told later in this excerpt that Croesus did everything for the unfortunate boy.

But what sort of hands does a boar have? And what sort of iron point that you fear? For if it said that I would die by a tusk or tooth or some other appropriate attribute, you should do what you are doing. But as it is, the instrument is a weapon's point; and so then let me go since the fight is not against men." Croesus answered: "My child, you have won me over with your interpretation of the dream; and so since I have been won over by you I reverse my decision and let you go to the hunt." After these words Croesus sent for the Phrygian Adrastus; when he arrived he spoke as follows to him: "Adrastus, I did not reproach you when you were struck down by an ugly misfortune, I cleansed you, received you in my palace, and offered you every luxury. Now then since you owe me good services in exchange for those that I have done for you, I ask that you be a guardian of my boy while he hastens out to the hunt, in case some malicious robbers turn up on the journey to do you harm. Furthermore you should go where you will become famous for your deeds, for it is your hereditary duty and you have the strength and prowess besides." Adrastus answered: "Ordinarily I would not go out to this kind of contest, for it is not fitting that one under such a misfortune as mine associate with companions who are faring well, nor do I have the desire and I should hold myself back for many reasons. But now, since you urge me and I must gratify you (for I owe you a return for your good services), I am ready to do this; expect that your boy, whom you order me to guard, will come back home to you unharmed because of his guardian." This was the nature of his answer to Croesus, and afterwards they left equipped with a band of picked young men and dogs. When they came to the mountain Olympus they hunted the wild beast and after they had found him they stood in a circle round about and hurled their weapons. And then the stranger, the guest and friend who had been cleansed of murder, who was called Adrastus, hurled his javelin at the boar, but missed him, and hit the son of Croesus, who, struck by the point of the weapon, fulfilled the prediction of the dream; someone ran as a messenger to Croesus of what had happened, and when he came to Sardis he told him of the battle and the fate of his child.

Croesus was greatly distressed by the death of his son and was even more disturbed because the very one whom he himself had purified had killed him. Overcome by his misfortune Croesus called terribly on Zeus the Purifier, invoking him to witness that he had suffered at the hands of the stranger and guest-friend; he called on him too as god of the hearth and as god of friendship, giving this same god these different names: god of the hearth because he did not realize that he received in his palace and nourished the guest and murderer of his son, and god of friendship because he sent him along as a guardian and found him to be his greatest enemy. Afterwards the Lydians arrived with the corpse and the murderer followed behind. He stood before the dead body and stretching forth his hands surrendered himself to Croesus; he bade Croesus slaughter him over the corpse, telling of his former misfortune and how in addition to it he had destroyed the one who had cleansed him, and life for him was not worth living. Croesus heard and took pity on Adrastus although he was enmeshed in so great a personal evil, and he spoke to him: "I have complete justice from yourself, my guest and friend, since you condemn yourself to death. You are not the one responsible for this evil (except insofar as you did the deed unwillingly), but some one of the gods somewhere who warned me previously of the things that were going to be." Croesus now buried his son as was fitting; Adrastus, the son of Gordias, the son of Midas, this murderer of his own brother and murderer of the one who purified him, when the people had gone and quietness settled around the grave, conscious that he was the most oppressed by misfortune of mankind, slaughtered himself on the tomb.

Croesus's personal and domestic tragedy was compounded by his political downfall. Daily the power of Cyrus the Great and the Persians was growing and as they extended their empire to the west, Croesus's own kingdom of Lydia would eventually be absorbed. In this crisis Croesus consulted various oracles, and by a test he came to believe that the one of Apollo at Delphi could alone speak the truth. He sent magnificent offerings to Delphi and inquired of the oracle whether or not he should go to war with the Persians. The Delphic reply is perhaps the most famous oracle of all time, typically ironic in its simple ambiguity: if Croesus attacked the Persians he would destroy a mighty empire. Croesus, of course, thought he would destroy the empire of the Persians; instead he brought an end to his own. The wisdom of Solon is now confirmed as Croesus learns through his own suffering. But let us allow Herodotus to tell the story of the fall of Sardis (the capital of Lydia) and the fate of Croesus, its king (1.85–88):

Thus Sardis was taken and the whole city was pillaged. With respect to Croesus himself the following happened. He had a son (whom I have mentioned before) in all respects a fine boy except that he could not speak. In the past time of his prosperity Croesus had done everything for him and among the many things that he tried was to send an embassy to Delphi to consult the oracle about him. And the Pythian priestess answered as follows:

O Lydian Croesus, king of many people, childlike in your ignorance,
   do not wish to hear in your house the much prayed for sound of your
   son's voice;
far better for you if it were otherwise;
for you will first hear him speak on the day of your wretchedness.

When the city was taken, one of the Persians made for Croesus to kill him, not knowing who he was; now Croesus saw the man coming but he did not care, since in the present misfortune it made no difference to him if he were struck down and died. But the boy, this one who was dumb, when he saw the Persian attacking, through fear of the terrible evil that was to happen broke into speech and cried: "Soldier, do not kill Croesus." This was the first time that he had uttered a sound but afterwards he could speak for the rest of his life.

The Persians then held Sardis and took Croesus himself captive after he had ruled for fourteen years and been besieged for fourteen days, and as the oracle predicted, he brought to an end his own mighty empire. The Persians took Croesus and led him to Cyrus, who had a great pyre erected and ordered Croesus bound in fetters to mount it and along with him twice seven children of the Lydians. Cyrus intended either to offer them as the first fruits of the booty to some one of the gods, perhaps in a desire to fulfill a vow, or having learned that Croesus was a god-fearing man placed him on the pyre wishing to see if any of the gods would save him from being burnt alive. At any rate this is what Cyrus did, but to Croesus as he stood on the pyre came the realization (even though he was in such sore distress) that the words of Solon had been spoken under god's inspiration: "No one of the living is happy!" As this occurred to him he sighed and groaned and broke the lengthy silence by calling out three times the name of Solon. When Cyrus heard this he bade interpreters ask Croesus who this was whom he invoked, and they came up and asked the question. For a time Croesus did not answer but eventually through compulsion he said: "The man I should like at all costs to converse with every tyrant." Since his words were unintelligible to them, they asked again and again what he meant; annoyed by their persistence, he told how Solon the Athenian first came to him and after having beheld all his prosperity made light of it by the nature of his talk, and how everything turned out for him just as Solon had predicted, with words that had no more reference to Croesus himself than to all mankind and especially those who in their own estimation considered themselves to be happy. As Croesus talked, the fire was kindled and began to burn the outer edges of the pyre. When Cyrus heard from his interpreters what Croesus had said, he changed his mind, reflecting that he too was a human being who was surrendering another human being while still alive to the fire; besides he feared retribution and, realizing how nothing in human affairs is certain and secure, he ordered the burning fire to be quenched as quickly as possible and Croesus and those with him taken down from the pyre. And they made the attempt but were unable to master the flames. Then, according to the Lydian version of the story, when Croesus learned of Cyrus's change of heart as he saw all the men trying to put out the fire but no longer able to hold it in check, he shouted aloud calling on Apollo, if ever he had received from him any gift that was pleasing, to stand by him and save him from the present evil. In tears he called on the god and suddenly out of the clear and calm atmosphere storm clouds rushed together, burst forth in violent torrents of rain, and quenched the fire. Thus Cyrus knew that Croesus was beloved by god and a good man. He brought him down from the pyre and asked: "Croesus, what man persuaded you to march against my land and become my enemy instead of my friend?" And he answered: "O king, these things I have done are to your good fortune but my own misfortune. The god of the Hellenes is responsible since he incited me to war. For no one is so senseless as to prefer war instead of peace. In time of peace sons bury their fathers, but in war fathers bury their sons. But it was somehow the pleasure of the gods that this be so." These were his words, and Cyrus released him and sat him by his side and held him in great respect, and both he and all those around him looked on him with wonder.

Thus Croesus became the wise and benevolent counsellor of Cyrus, who in his gratitude asked (Herodotus, 1.90–91):

"Croesus, since you, a valiant king, are determined to do excellent things in word and in deed, ask straightway for whatever gift you wish to have." And he said: "My master, you would please me if you allow that I ask the god of the Greeks whom I honored most of all whether it is his custom to deceive those who have done him well and send these fetters of mine to him." Cyrus asked what was the complaint that prompted this request. . . . Croesus explained how he felt, telling about the answers from the shrine, and especially the offerings he had made and how he had marched against Persia at the instigation of the oracle. These were his words and he ended by repeating his request that he be allowed to reproach the god. Cyrus replied with a laugh: "I shall grant both requests and any other which you may at any time demand." After Croesus heard this, he sent Lydians to Delphi, enjoining them to place his fetters on the threshold of the temple and ask the god if he were not at all ashamed of having incited Croesus, by his oracles, to march against the Persians as though to bring an end to the power of Cyrus, when these (they were to point to the fetters) were the fruits of the campaign. They were to ask as well if it was customary for the gods of the Hellenes to be ungrateful.

When the Lydians arrived and spoke what they had been told, the Pythian priestess is said to have replied as follows. "It is impossible even for god to escape destined fate. Croesus had fulfilled the payment for the sin of his fifth ancestor, one of the bodyguard of the Heraclidae who, following the guile of a woman, killed his master and assumed the royal power that in no way belonged to him.[7] Apollo was anxious that the fall of Sardis occur in the generation of Croesus's children and not that of Croesus himself, but he was not able to persuade the Fates. As much time as they granted he took and gave as a gift to Croesus. He postponed the capture of Sardis for three years and Croesus should know that he was three years later than had been destined. Besides this, Apollo saved him from burning. And it was not right that Croesus find fault with the oracle that he received. For Apollo warned that if he marched against Persia he would destroy a great empire. He should, if he were going to act wisely with respect to this reply, have sent again to ask whether his own empire or that of Cyrus was meant. If he did not understand the reply and he did not press the question he should see himself as the one to blame. And when he had last consulted the oracle and Apollo had spoken the words about the mule, he did not

[7] This is Gyges, whose story Herodotus has told earlier in Book 1 (7–14). The kingdom of Lydia had belonged to the family of the Heraclidae. Candaules the king was overthrown by his wife and his bodyguard, Gyges. Gyges was of the family of the Mermnadae and an ancestor of Croesus. The Pythian priestess, however, had predicted vengeance for the Heraclidae in the fifth generation; this was fulfilled by Croesus.

understand even this.[8] For Cyrus himself was the mule. He was born of parents of different races and stations, his mother the better, his father the lesser of the two. For she was a Mede, daughter of Astyages, king of the Medes, but he was a Persian and a subject and although inferior in all these ways married his mistress." This was the Pythia's response to the Lydians and they returned to Sardis and told Croesus. When he heard he agreed that it was his own fault and not that of the god.

The Herodotean account gives us a glimpse into the fascinating world of historical myth. How can one possibly with complete confidence isolate the facts from the fiction in the epic and literary context of Herodotus's art? The name of Croesus's son Atys means the one under the influence of Ate (a goddess of doom and destruction), and he has links, too, with Attis and Adonis in cult and in story. Adrastus may be connected to the mythological concept of Nemesis or Adrasteia (Necessity), and the name Adrastus may be translated "the one who cannot escape," that is, "the one who is doomed." Incidents in the tale recall those of the Calydonian boar hunt. Is there anyone today who has enough faith in miracles to believe that Apollo saved Croesus from a fiery death?

But there *are* parts of the myth that perhaps may be true. Despite the chronological problems, Solon could have met Croesus, although not at the time Herodotus imagines; [9] Croesus probably had a son named Atys who died young. But the historian could never be satisfied with this prosaic truth alone. His stories (wrought with exquisite art) must illustrate a different level of emotional and spiritual truth that illuminates character and elucidates philosophy. The life of Tellus the Athenian, the happiest of men, reveals the character and the values of those who fought at Marathon and explains in part (military numbers and strategy will come later)

[8] Croesus's question was if his kingdom would last a long time. Apollo's answer implied that it would last until a mule was king of the Persians (Herodotus, 1.55).

[9] Solon held office in Athens as archon extraordinary in 594 and his travels belong at some time after that date; his death may be placed in the years following 560. Croesus did not become king of Sardis until around 560, and his defeat by Cyrus occurred in 546

why they defeated the Persians. These are truths, too, but of another order, and they are the essence of mythic art.

Finally another word of caution about generalizations concerning Greek religious attitudes. It has been claimed that the Greeks had no bible or strict dogma and (incredible as it may seem) no real sense of sin, or they were innocently free and tolerant in their acceptance of new gods (what difference does one more make to a polytheist?), and so on. One cannot merely repeat stories (many of them from Ovid) and make pronouncement upon the spiritual adequacy or inadequacy of the theological convictions they are supposed to represent. Mythology, philosophy, and religion are inextricably entwined and one must try to look at all the evidence. Homer offered to the Greeks as a people a literary bible of humanism that could on occasion be quoted (as Shakespeare for us) like scripture; the mystery religions provided certain segments with a dogma and ritual of a more exacting nature, whether written or unwritten. Priests and priestesses devoted their lives to the service of the gods. The state (or better the city-states) upheld by custom, tradition, and law strict moral and ethical codes of behavior. If the stories of opposition to the new god Dionysus rest upon any stratum of historical truth, a foreign message of salvation was not always readily or easily accommodated, and one could be put to death (in Athens of all places) on a charge of impiety. The Greeks thought profoundly about god and man, the immortality of the soul, and the meaning and consequences of vice and virtue. The myth of Er (translated in a later chapter) is a terrifying vision of heaven and hell; as such it is a religious document. Along with abundant and varied other evidence it shows that Greek philosophical thought can hold its own with that of any one of the so-called "higher" religions.

CHAPTER 5

Poseidon, Sea Deities, Group Divinities, and Monsters

Poseidon, the great god of waters in general and of the sea in particular, was by no means the first or only such divinity for the Greeks. As we have seen, Pontus (the Sea) was produced by Ge in the initial stages of creation; and the Titans, Oceanus and Tethys, bore thousands of children, the Oceanids. In addition Pontus mated with his mother Ge and begat Nereus, the eldest of his children, who was gentle, wise, and true, an old man of the sea with the gift of prophecy. Nereus in turn united with Doris (an Oceanid) and they had fifty daughters, the Nereids; three of these mermaids should be singled out here: Thetis, Galatea, and Amphitrite.

We have already mentioned that Thetis was destined to bear a son mightier than his father. Zeus learned this secret from Prometheus and avoided mating with Thetis; she married instead a mortal named Peleus, who was hard pressed to catch his bride. For Thetis possessed the power of changing shape and transformed herself into a variety of states (e.g., a bird, tree, tigress) in rapid succession, but eventually she was forced to succumb. Peleus and Thetis celebrated their marriage in great ceremony and they had a son, Achilles, who did indeed become mightier than his father.

Galatea, another Nereid, was loved by the Cyclops, Polyphemus, a son of Poseidon. Ovid's account (*Metamorphoses,* 13.750–897) is perhaps the most famous version of their story, a touching rendition that plays upon the incongruity of the passion of the monstrous and boorish giant for the delicate nymph. She was repelled

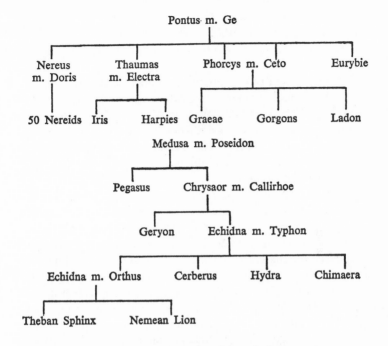

Figs. 4 and 5. Descendants of the sea

by his attentions and loved Acis, a handsome son of Faunus and
a sea-nymph. Polyphemus, overcome by emotion, attempted to
mend his savage ways; he combed his hair with a rake and cut his
beard with a scythe and sang out his heart to the tune of a shepherd's pipe. But his love turned to rage when he found Acis and
Galatea in each other's arms. With a roar he announced that this
would be their last embrace. The lovers were terrified; Galatea
jumped into the sea and Acis took to flight. The Cyclops, in hot
pursuit, picked up a huge rock and hurled it at his rival who was
crushed to death. The trickle of his blood was turned to water as
Acis became transformed into the river that bears his name.

The third Nereid, Amphitrite, is important mainly as the wife
of Poseidon; like her sister Thetis she proved a reluctant bride
but Poseidon finally was able to win her. As husband and wife
they play roles very much like those enacted by Zeus and Hera;
Poseidon has a weakness for women and Amphitrite with good

cause is angry and vengeful. They had a son, Triton, a merman, human above the waist, fish-shaped below. He is often depicted as blowing a conch shell, a veritable trumpeter of the sea; [1] he can change shape at will.

The sea divinity, Proteus, probably another of the older generation of gods, is often named as the attendant of Poseidon or even his son. Like Nereus he is an old man of the sea and can foretell the future; he can also change shape. It is easy to see how the identities of Nereus, Proteus, and Triton could be merged. Confusion among sea divinities and duplication of their characteristics are everywhere apparent.

Poseidon is similar in appearance to his brother Zeus, a majestic bearded figure, but he is generally more severe and rough; besides, he carries the trident, a three-pronged fork resembling a fisherman's spear. By his very nature Poseidon is ferocious. He is called the supporter of the earth but the earthshaker as well, and as a god of earthquakes he exhibits his violence by the rending of the land and the surge of the sea. By a mere stroke of his trident he may destroy and kill. His relentless anger against Odysseus for the blinding of Polyphemus provides a dominant theme in the *Odyssey*.

The origins of Poseidon are much disputed; if his trident represents what was once a thunderbolt, then he was in early times a god of the sky. More attractive is the theory that he began as a male spirit of fertility, a god of earth who sent up springs. This fits well with his association with horses and bulls (he either creates them or makes them appear) and explains the character of some of his affairs. He mates with Demeter in the form of a stallion; he pursued her at the time when she was searching for her daughter and her ruse of changing into a mare to escape him was to no avail. Thus we have the union of the male and female powers of fertility. The result is the birth of a daughter and the wonderful horse Arion who belonged to Adrastus. Similarly he united with Ge and they produced Antaeus, a giant encountered by Heracles. But it should be remembered that standard epithets of the sea are "barren" and "unharvested" as opposed to the fecundity of

[1] Ovid provides a typical description in his version of the flood (see pp. 50–51); it offers as well a vivid characterization of Poseidon under his Roman name of Neptune.

the land. The suggestion that Poseidon's horses are the mythical depiction of the whitecaps of the waves is not convincing, at least in terms of origins.

Poseidon is also violent in his loves. He made advances to Scylla, the daughter of Phorcys and Hecate. Amphitrite was jealous and threw magic herbs into Scylla's bathing place. Thus Scylla was transformed into a terrifying monster, encircled with a ring of dogs' heads; [2] her home was a cave in the straits of Messina between Sicily and Italy. With her was Charybdis, the daughter of Poseidon and Ge, a formidable and voracious ally whom Zeus had cast into the sea by his thunderbolt; three times a day she drew in mountains of water and spewed them out again. Scylla and Charybdis have been rationalized into natural terrors faced by mariners when they sailed through the straits. Certainly many of the tales about the gods of the waters are reminiscent of the yarns spun by fishermen, sailors, and the like, whose lives are involved with the sea and with travel.

A famous story links Poseidon with Athena and the city-state of Athens. Athena and Poseidon were said to have vied for control of Athens and the surrounding territory, Attica. The contest took place on the Acropolis. Poseidon struck the rock with his trident and produced a salt spring, or according to another version a horse, the first that had ever been seen. Athena planted an olive tree, or more dramatically brought one forth from the ground by the touch of her spear. Athena was proclaimed the victor by a jury or judge variously identified as the gods, the people of Athens, or their king, Cecrops. The moment of the goddess's triumph was immortalized in stone on the west pediment of her great temple, the Parthenon. Poseidon, in his anger at losing, flooded the Thriasian plain, but he was appeased and continued to be worshiped in Athens particularly in conjunction with the Athenian hero, Erechtheus. In his beautiful temple on the Acropolis, just across from the Parthenon, it was said that the marks of the blow of

[2] Ovid (*Metamorphoses,* 13.917–968; 14.1–71) tells this same story about Glaucus, a mortal who was transformed into a sea-god. It was he who fell in love with Scylla; when he was rejected, he turned to the sorceress, Circe, for help. But Circe fell in love with him and in her jealousy poisoned the waters of Scylla's bathing place.

his trident could still be seen, and nearby the olive tree that Athena had produced continued to grow. The importance of the olive in Greek and especially Athenian economy and life is symbolized by Athena's victory.

In conclusion let us look at some other descendants of Pontus and Ge. Notice how elements of the fantastic and the grotesque appear again and again in the nature of the progeny associated with the sea and the deep.

In addition to Nereus, Pontus and Ge had two more sons, Thaumas and Phorcys, and two daughters, Ceto and Eurybie. Thaumas mated with Electra (an Oceanid) and produced Iris and the Harpies. Iris is the goddess of the rainbow (her name means rainbow). She is a messenger of the gods as well, sometimes the particular servant of Hera, with Hermes's offices then confined to Zeus. She is fleet-footed and winged, as are her sisters, the Harpies, but they are much more violent in nature; in early sources they are conceived of as strong winds (their name means the snatchers), but later they are depicted in literature and in art as bird-like creatures with the faces of women, often terrifying and a pestilence to mankind.[3]

Phorcys and his sister Ceto produce two groups of children, the Graeae and the Gorgons. The Graeae (Aged Ones) are three sisters, personifications of old age; their hair was gray from birth but in their general aspect they appeared swan-like and beautiful. They had, however, only one eye and one tooth which they were forced to share among themselves. They knew the way to their sisters, the Gorgons, also three in number (Stheno, Euryale, and Medusa), whose hair writhed with serpents. They were of such terrifying aspect that those who looked upon them were turned to stone. Gorgons are a favorite theme in Greek art, especially in the early period; they leer out most disconcertingly with a broad archaic smile, tongue protruding in the midst of a row of bristling teeth. Medusa is the most important Gorgon; Poseidon was her lover. When she was beheaded by Perseus she was pregnant; from her corpse sprang a winged horse, Pegasus, and a son, Chrysaor (He of the Golden Sword).

---

[3] The Harpies are not unlike the Sirens, who lure men to destruction and death by the enticement of their song.

Phorcys and Ceto also bore a dragon named Ladon; he helped the lovely Hesperides (Daughters of Evening) who guarded a wondrous tree that grew golden fruit far away in the West and passed their time in beautiful singing.

Chrysaor mated with an Oceanid, Callirhoe, and produced the monsters, Geryon and Echidna (half nymph and half snake). Echidna united with Typhon and bore Orthus (the hound of Geryon), Cerberus (the hound of Hades), the Lernaean Hydra, and the Chimaera. Echidna and Orthus produced the Theban sphinx and the Nemean lion. These monsters will be encountered later in saga.

CHAPTER 6

Athena

The *Homeric Hymn* (number 28) tells the story of Athena's birth.

I begin to sing about Pallas Athena, renowned goddess, with bright eyes, quick mind, and inflexible heart, chaste and mighty virgin, protectress of the city, Tritogeneia. Wise Zeus himself gave birth to her from his holy head and she was arrayed in her armor of war, all-gleaming in gold, and every one of the immortals was gripped with awe as they watched. She quickly sprang forth from the immortal head in front of aegis-bearing Zeus, brandishing her sharp spear. And great Olympus shook terribly at the might of the bright-eyed goddess and the earth round about gave a dread groan and the dark waves of the deep seethed. But suddenly the sea became calm, and the glorious son of Hyperion halted his swift-footed horses all the while that the maiden Pallas Athena took the divine armor from her immortal shoulders, and Zeus in his wisdom rejoiced. So hail to you, child of aegis-bearing Zeus; I shall remember both you and another song too.

Hesiod (*Theogony*, 886–898) tells how Zeus had swallowed his consort Metis (her name means wisdom) after he had made her pregnant with Athena; he was afraid that Metis would bear a son who would overthrow him.

Zeus, king of the gods, first took as his wife Metis, who was very wise indeed among both gods and men. But when she was about to give birth to the bright-eyed goddess Athena, then Zeus treacherously deceived her with wheedling words and swallowed her down into his belly at the wise instigations of Gaea and starry Uranus. These two gave Zeus this advice so that no other of the eternal gods might rule supreme as king in his place. For Metis was destined to bear exceptional children: first, the keen-eyed maiden, Athena, Tritogeneia, the equal of her father in might and good counsel, and then she was to give birth to a

92

son of indomitable spirit who would become the king of both gods and men.

Variations in the story of Athena's birth have Hephaestus (or sometimes Prometheus or even Hermes) split Zeus's head open with an axe to facilitate the birth; some add to the dread awe of the occasion by having Athena cry out thunderously as she springs to life in full panoply. This myth (whatever its etiology may be in terms of the physical manifestations of the thunderstorm) establishes the close bond of affection between Zeus and his favorite daughter and allegorizes the three basic characteristics of the goddess Athena: her prowess, her wisdom, and the masculinity of her virgin nature, sprung ultimately not from the woman but from the male.

The dramatic moment of the divine birth was immortalized by the genius of the sculptor Pheidias in the east pediment of the goddess's great temple, the Parthenon. (Parthenos, meaning virgin, was a standard epithet of Athena.) The theme of the west pediment was equally appropriate: the victory of Athena (by her token of the olive tree) over Poseidon for control of Athens and Attica (the details of which have been recounted in the previous chapter). The continuous Ionic frieze of the temple also bore testimony to the glory and prestige of the goddess. Frozen in stone the people of Athens move as it were forever in stately procession as they celebrate the splendid festival of the Panathenaea in honor of their patron deity. Each summer, on the very day of Athena's birth (every four years the festivities were especially splendid), an embroidered robe (*peplos*) was brought in ceremonial state to the goddess. Men and women, young and old, on foot or on horseback proceeded along the ordained route through the Agora up onto the Acropolis; with them were animals, implements of sacrifice, and all the paraphernalia of ritual.[1] In the cella of the Parthenon itself stood a monumental statue of the goddess magnificently wrought in gold and ivory.

Athena is often (but not always) represented in art with her

[1] Games and contests were also a part of the festivities; the prize awarded was an amphora, filled with oil. On it was depicted Athena in her war gear with an inscription identifying the vase as Panathenaic.

attributes as a war goddess: helmet, spear, and shield (the aegis, on which the head of the Gorgon Medusa may be depicted).[2] She is beautiful with a severe and aloof kind of loveliness that is striking. One of her standard epithets is *glaukopis,* which may mean gray- or green-eyed, but more probably refers to the bright or keen radiance of her glance rather than to the color of her eyes. Possibly, too, the adjective may be intended to mean owl-eyed, or of owlish aspect or countenance; certainly Athena is at times closely identified with the owl. The snake is also associated with Athena; one may, for example, appear coiled at her feet or on her shield. This association (along with those of the owl and the olive tree) suggests that perhaps Athena originally was (like so many others) a fertility goddess, despite the fact that her character as a virgin dominates the later tradition.

Athena's title, Tritogeneia, is obscure, although conjectural explanations have not been wanting. It would seem to refer to a region sometimes associated with her birth, the river or lake Triton or Tritonis in Boeotia or in Libya. Some scholars see in this link the possibility that Athena was at least in her origins at one time a goddess of waters or the sea. We are told that soon after her birth Athena was reared by Triton (presumably the god of this body of water, wherever it may be). Now Triton had a daughter named Pallas, and Athena and the girl used to practice the arts of war together. But on one occasion they quarreled and as Pallas was about to strike Athena, Zeus intervened on behalf of his daughter by interposing the aegis. Pallas was startled and Athena, taking advantage of her surprise, wounded and killed her. Athena was distraught when she realized what she had done; in her grief she made a wooden image of the girl and decked it with the aegis. This statue, the Palladium, was cast down by Zeus and fell into the territory of the Trojans, who built a temple to house it in honor. This Palladium appears in saga as carrying with it the destiny of the city of Troy. Athena, too, in honor of her friend took the name Pallas for herself. A more likely etiology is that the word Pallas means maiden and is but another designation of Athena's

---

[2] Sometimes she is attended by a winged figure (Nike, Victory) bearing a crown or garland of honor and success. Athena herself as Athena Nike represented victorious achievement in war.

chastity, just as she is called parthenos, virgin, or (like Persephone) Kore, girl.

Athena is a goddess of many specific arts, crafts, and skills (military, political, and domestic), as well as the deification of wisdom and good counsel in a more generic and abstract conception. She is, for example, skilled in the taming and training of horses, interested in ships and chariots, and the inventor of the flute. This latter invention was supposed to have been inspired by the lamentations (accompanied by the hiss of serpents) uttered by the surviving Gorgons after the death of Medusa. But Athena quickly grew to dislike the new instrument because her beautiful features became distorted when she played and so she threw it away in disgust. Marsyas, the satyr, picked up the instrument with dire consequences as we shall see. Athena was worshiped along with Hephaestus in Athens as patroness of all arts and crafts.

The famous story of Arachne bears testimony to the importance of Athena as the patroness of women's household arts, especially spinning and weaving. In Ovid's account (*Metamorphoses,* 6.5–145) Athena has, of course, become the Roman Minerva.

Minerva turned her mind to Arachne's destruction, for she had heard that her fame as a worker in wool equaled her own. Arachne's birth and position brought her no distinction—it was her skill that did. Idmon of Colophon was her father, who dyed the thirsty wool with Ionian purple; her mother, who also was of low birth like her husband, had died. Yet their daughter, Arachne, for all that she was born in a lowly family living at lowly Hypaepa, pursued her quest for fame throughout the cities of Lydia by her work. The nymphs of Tmolus often left their vineyards, the nymphs of Pactolus often left their waters—to see and wonder at Arachne's handiwork. Nor was their pleasure merely in seeing her finished work, but also in observing her at work, such delight was in her skill. Whether at the beginning she gathered the unworked wool into balls, or worked it with her fingers and drew out lengths of fleece like clouds, or with swift-moving thumb turned the smooth spindle, or whether she used her embroidering needle—you would know that Minerva had taught her. Yet she would not admit this; jealous of her great teacher she said, "Let her compete with me; if she wins I deny her nothing."

Minerva disguised herself as an old woman, white-haired and supporting herself upon a stick, and spoke as follows: "Not everything that old age brings is to be avoided; experience comes with the passing years. Do not despise my advice! Let your ambition be to excel mortal women at weaving; give place to the goddess and pray for her forgiveness for your rash words! She will pardon you if you pray." Arachne glowered at her; leaving her half-finished work and with difficulty restraining herself from blows, she openly showed her anger by her expression, as she attacked disguised Minerva with these words: "You old fool, enfeebled by advanced old age. Too long a life has done you no good! Keep your advice for your sons' wives (if you have any) and your daughter. I can think for myself, and you need not think your advice does any good—you will not change my mind. Why does not the goddess herself come? Why does she refuse to compete with me?" Then Minerva cried: "She has come!" and throwing off her disguise she showed herself as she was, the goddess Minerva. The nymphs and women of Lydia worshiped her divine presence; Arachne alone felt no awe. Yet she blushed; a sudden flush stole over her face in spite of herself and as suddenly faded, like the red glow of the sky when Dawn first glows just before the heavens begin to whiten with the sun's rising. Obstinately she holds to her course and rushes to destruction in her foolish desire for the prize. Jupiter's daughter resists no more; she offers her no more advice; no more does she put off the competition.

Ovid goes on to describe the weaving contest. Each weaves a tapestry at her loom with surpassing skill, depicting scenes from mythology. Minerva displays her contest with Neptune for the lordship of Attica and adds four subordinate scenes of mortals who challenged gods and were turned by them into other shapes. The whole was framed by an olive-tree motif—"with her own tree she concluded her work."

Unwarned by the lessons of Minerva's legends, Arachne depicted scenes of the gods' less honorable amorous conquests—where Jupiter, Neptune, Apollo, Bacchus, and Saturn deceived goddesses and mortal women. As she completed her tapestry with a design of trailing ivy, Minerva's anger burst forth. Ovid continues:

Minerva could find no fault with the work, not even Envy herself could. Angered by Arachne's success, the golden-haired goddess tore up the embroidered tapestry with its stories of the gods' shameful deeds. With the boxwood shuttle she beat Arachne's face repeatedly. In grief Arachne strangled herself, stopping the passage of life with a noose.

Minerva pitied her as she was hanging and raised her up with these words: "Stubborn girl, live, yet hang! And—to make you anxious for the future—may the same punishment be decreed for all your descendants."

With these words Minerva sprinkled her with the juice of a magic herb. As the fateful liquid touched her, Arachne's hair dropped off; her nose and ears vanished, and her head was shrunken; her whole body was contracted. From her side thin fingers dangled for legs, and the rest became her belly. Yet still from this she lets the thread issue forth and, a spider now, practices her former weaving art.

This story also illustrates the moral earnestness of this warrior maiden that is often only too apparent. Her character is usually impeccable; unlike another virgin goddess, Artemis, to whom men made advances, although at their dire peril, Athena remained virtually unapproachable sexually. The attempt of Hephaestus on her honor (in the early saga of Athens in which Athena inevitably must play an important role) confirms the purity and integrity of her convictions. It would be a misconception, however, to imagine Athena only as a cold and formidable virago who might easily elicit one's respect but hardly one's love. This Valkyrie-like maiden does have her touching moments, not only in her close and warm relationship with her father Zeus, but also in her devout loyalty and steadfast protection of more than one hero (e.g., Telemachus and Odysseus, Heracles, Perseus, and Bellerophon).

Either alone or coupled with Apollo, Athena can be made the representative of a new order of divinity—the younger generation of the gods championing progress and the advanced enlightenment of civilization. It is Athena as the agent of Zeus who brings the *Odyssey* to a close by answering the primitive demand for blood evoked by the relatives of the suitors and establishing the divine and universal validity of the justice meted out by Odysseus. In Aeschylus's *Oresteia* she is on the side of Apollo for the acquittal of Orestes through the due process of law in Athens before the court of the Areopagus (which the goddess is said to have created), appeasing and silencing, presumably forever, the old social order of family vendetta represented by the Furies.

CHAPTER 7

Aphrodite and Eros

As we have seen, Hesiod describes the birth of Aphrodite after the castration of Uranus and derives her name from the Greek work for foam, *aphros*. Hesiod also links the goddess closely with Cythera and Cyprus; the latter was especially associated with her worship, in its city of Paphos particularly. Thus Aphrodite is called both Cytherea and Cypris. Another version of her birth gives her parents as Zeus and Dione. Dione is little more than a name to us, but a curious one, since it is the feminine form of the name Zeus· (which in another form is Dios).

This double tradition of Aphrodite's birth suggested a basic duality in her character or the existence of two separate goddesses of love: Aphrodite Urania or Celestial Aphrodite sprung from Uranus alone, ethereal and sublime; Aphrodite Pandemos (Aphrodite of all the people or common Aphrodite) sprung from Zeus and Dione and essentially physical in nature. In Plato's *Symposium,* one of the speakers, Pausanias, elaborates upon this distinction and claims that Aphrodite Urania, the older of the two, is stronger, more intelligent, and spiritual, but also being born from the male alone represents the love of one male for another, whereas Aphrodite Pandemos born from both sexes is more base, heterosexual, as well as homosexual and aimed primarily at physical satisfaction.

In general Aphrodite is the goddess of beauty, love, and marriage. Her worship was universal in the ancient world but its facets were many and varied. At Corinth, for example, temple harlots were kept in Aphrodite's honor; at Athens this same goddess was the staid and respectable deity of marriage and married love (one could presumably forget or deny the Aphrodite who betrayed her husband Hephaestus in Homer's story).

The gamut of the conceptions of the goddess of love is reflected in painting and sculpture as well as in literature. Archaic idols are grotesque in their exaggeration of her sexual attributes as with other fertility goddesses. In early Greek art she is rendered as a beautiful woman, usually clothed. By the fourth century she is portrayed in the nude (or nearly so), the idealization of womanhood in all her femininity; the sculptor Praxiteles was mainly responsible for establishing the type—sensuous in its soft curves and voluptuousness. (His mistress, the courtesan Phryne, was said to be his model and some claim that Aphrodite herself asked: "Where did Praxiteles see me naked?") As so often in the ancient world, once a master had captured a universal conception, it was repeated endlessly with or without significant variations. Everyone knows the Venus di Milo or one of the many other extant copies, although Praxiteles's originals have not survived.

The Graces (Charites) and the Seasons (Horae), whose birth and nature have already been mentioned, are often associated with Aphrodite as decorative and appropriate attendants. The goddess herself possessed a magic girdle having special powers of enticement that were irresistible. In the *Iliad* Hera borrows it with great effect upon her husband Zeus.

The more elemental and physical aspects of Aphrodite's nature are seen in the offspring attributed to her; her union with Hermes produced Hermaphroditus, whose story is told elsewhere. Priapus is another son of Aphrodite; the father is variously named. He may be Hermes again, or Dionysus, Pan, Adonis, and even Zeus. Priapus is a fertility-god, generally depicted as deformed and bearing a huge and erect phallus. He is found in gardens and at the doors of houses. He is part scarecrow, part bringer of luck, and part guardian against thieves; therefore he has something in common with his father Hermes. He resembles Dionysus and Pan (two of his reputed fathers) and sometimes is confused with them or their retinues. Whatever the origins of Priapus in terms of sincere and primitive reverence for the male powers of generation, stories about him usually came to be comic and obscene. In the jaded society of later antiquity his worship meant little more than a cult of sophisticated pornography.

There are many stories that illustrate the mighty power of Aphrodite; the following one has provided a potent theme in subsequent literature.

Ovid tells how Aphrodite (Venus in his version) was enraged with the women of Cyprus because they dared to deny her divinity; the goddess in her wrath caused them to be the first women to prostitute themselves and as they lost all their sense of shame it was easy to turn them into stone. Ovid goes on to relate the story of Pygmalion and the result of his disgust for these women (*Metamorphoses,* 10.243–297).

Pygmalion saw these women leading a life of sin and was repelled by the many vices which nature had implanted in the feminine mind. And so he lived alone without a wife for a long time doing without a woman to share his bed. Meanwhile he fashioned happily a statue of ivory, white as snow, and gave it a beauty surpassing that of any woman born; and he fell in love with what he had made. It looked like a real maiden who you would believe was alive and willing to move, had not modesty prevented her. To such an extent art concealed art; Pygmalion wondered at the body he had fashioned and the flames of passion burned in his breast. He often ran his hands over his creation to test whether it was real flesh and blood or ivory. And he would not go so far as to admit that it was ivory. He gave it kisses and thought that they were returned; he spoke to it and held it and believed that his fingers sank into the limbs that he touched and was afraid that a bruise might appear as he pressed her close. Sometimes he enticed her with blandishments, at other times he brought her gifts that please a girl: shells and smooth pebbles, little birds, flowers of a thousand colors, lilies, painted balls, and drops of amber, the tears wept by Phaethon's sisters who had been changed into trees. He also clothed her limbs with garments, put rings on her fingers, draped long necklaces around her neck, dangled jewelry from her ears, hung adornments on her breast. All was becoming but she looked no less beautiful naked. He placed her on his bed with covers dyed in Tyrian purple and laid her down, to rest her head on soft pillows of feathers as if she could feel them.

The most celebrated feast day of Venus in the whole of Cyprus arrived; heifers, their crooked horns adorned with gold, were slaughtered by the blow of the axe on their snowy necks and incense smoked. When he had made his offering at the altar, Pygmalion stood and timidly prayed: "If you gods are able to grant everything, I desire for my wife. . . ." He did not dare to say "my ivory maiden." Golden Venus herself was present at her festival and understood what his prayers meant. As an omen of her kindly will a tongue of flame burned bright and flared up in the air. When he returned home Pygmalion grasped the image of his girl and lay beside her on the bed and showered her with kisses. She seemed to be warm. He touched her with his lips again and felt her breasts with his hands. At his touch the ivory grew soft, and its rigidity gave way to the pressure of his fingers; it yielded just as Hymettan wax when melted in the sun is fashioned into many shapes by the working of the hands and made pliable. He is stunned but dubious of his joy and fearful he is wrong. In his love he touches this answer to his prayers. It was a body; the veins throbbed as he felt them with his thumb. Then in truth Pygmalion was full of prayers in which he gave thanks to Venus. At last he presses his lips on lips that are real and the maiden feels the kisses she is given and as she raises her eyes to meet his she sees both her lover and the sky. The goddess is present at the marriage that she has made, and now when the crescent moon had become full nine times Pygmalion's wife gave birth to Paphos, and from him the place got its name.

Galatea is the name given to Pygmalion's beloved in later modern versions of the tale.

Many of Aphrodite's characteristics are Oriental in tone and specific links can be found that are clearly Phrygian, Syrian, and Semitic in origin. In the most famous of her myths she is confused with the great Phoenician goddess, Astarte; they have in common as their love a young and handsome youth named by the Greeks Adonis. Perhaps the best-known version of the story of Aphrodite and Adonis is told by Ovid. Paphos (the son of Pygmalion and Galatea) had a son, Cinyras. Myrrha, the daughter of Cinyras, fell desperately in love with her own father. Tormented by her sense of shame and guilt, the poor girl was on the point of suicide but she was rescued just in time by her faithful nurse, who eventually wrenched the secret from her. Although the old woman was horrified by what she learned, she preferred to help satisfy the girl's passion rather than to see her die. It was arranged that the daughter should go to the bed of her father without his knowing her identity, and their incestuous relations continued for some time until Cinyras in dismay found out with whom he had been sleeping. In terror Myrrha fled from the wrath of her father. As he pursued her she prayed for deliverance and was changed into a myrrh tree which continually drips with her tears. Myrrha had become pregnant by her father and from the tree was born a beautiful son named Adonis, who grew up to be a most handsome youth and keen hunter. At the sight of him Aphrodite fell desperately in love. She warned Adonis against the dangers of the hunt telling him to be especially wary of any wild beasts that would not turn and flee but stood firm. Ovid's story continues as follows (*Metamorphoses,* 10.708–739):

These were the warnings of Venus and she rode away through the air in her chariot yoked with swans. But Adonis's courageous nature stood in the way of her admonitions. By chance his dogs followed the clear tracks of a wild boar and frightened it from its hiding place. As it was ready to come out of the woods, the son of Cinyras hit a glancing blow on its side. With its crooked snout the savage beast immediately dislodged the blood-stained spear and made for the frightened youth as he fled for safety. The boar buried its tusk deep within his groin and brought him down on the yellow sand, dying. As Venus was being borne through the air in her light chariot on the wings of swans (she had not yet reached Cyprus), she heard the groans of the dying boy from afar and turned the course of her white birds toward them. When she saw from the air above his lifeless body lying in his own blood, she rushed down, and rent her bosom and her hair and beat her breast with hands not meant to do such violence. She complained against the Fates, crying: "But still everything will not be subject to your decrees; a memorial of my grief for you, Adonis, will abide forever. The scene of your death will be recreated annually with the ritual of my grief performed. But your blood will be transformed into a flower. O Persephone, you were allowed at one time to change the limbs of the maiden Mentha into the fragrant mint—will I be begrudged then the transformation of my hero, the son of Cinyras?" With these words she sprinkled fragrant nectar on his blood which, at the touch of the drops, began to swell just like a gleaming bubble in the rain. In no longer than an hour's time a flower sprang from the blood, red as the thick skin of the fruit of the pomegranate that hides the seeds within. Yet the flower is of brief enjoyment for the winds (which give it its name, anemone) blow upon it; with difficulty it clings to life and falls under the blasts and buffeting.

Ovid's story predicts the rites associated with the worship of Adonis involving ceremonial wailing and the singing of dirges over the effigy of the dead youth. Obviously we have here once again a rendition of a recurrent theme: the Great Mother and her lover, who dies as vegetation dies and comes back to life again. Another version of the myth makes this even clearer. When Adonis was an infant, Aphrodite put him in a chest and gave it to Persephone to keep. Persephone looked inside and once she saw the beauty of the boy she refused to give him back. Zeus settled the quarrel that ensued by deciding that Adonis would stay with Persephone below one part of the year and with Aphrodite in the upper world for the other part. It is possible to detect similarities between Easter celebrations of the dead and risen Christ in various parts of the world and those in honor of the dead and risen Adonis. Christianity, too, absorbed and transformed the ancient conception of the sorrowing goddess with her lover dying in her arms to that of the sad Virgin holding in her lap her beloved Son.

Parallels to the figures of Aphrodite and Adonis may be found in the Assyrio-Babylonian myth of Ishtar and Tammuz and more readily and obviously in the Phrygian story of Cybele [1] and Attis. The Oriental touches are apparent in the myth of the Great Mother and her lover. Cybele was sprung from the earth, originally a bi-sexual deity but then reduced to a female. From the severed organ an almond tree arose. Nana, the daughter of the god of the river Sangarios, picked a blossom from the tree, and put it in her bosom; the blossom disappeared and Nana found herself pregnant. A son, Attis, was born and exposed, but a he-goat attended him. Attis grew up to be a handsome youth and Cybele fell in love with him; however, he loved another and Cybele in her jealousy drove him mad. In his madness Attis castrated himself and died.[2] Cybele repented and obtained Zeus's promise that the body of Attis would never decay.

In her worship Cybele was followed by a retinue of devotees who worked themselves into a frenzy of devotion that could lead

---

[1] Her worship was introduced into Rome in 204. Lucretius (*De Rerum Natura*, 2.600–651) presents a hostile but vivid account of the orgiastic nature of her worship; for Lucretius the very nature of deity is that it exists forever tranquil and aloof, untouched by the human condition and immune to human prayers.

[2] Catullus (63) makes the anguish, love, and death of Attis the stuff of great poetry.

to self-mutilation. The orgiastic nature of her ritual is suggested by the frantic music that accompanied her: the beating of drums, the clashing of cymbals, and the blaring of horns. The myth explains why her priests (called Galli) were eunuchs. It is also easy to see how the din that attended Cybele could be confused with the ritual connected with another mother-goddess Rhea, whose attendants long ago hid the cries of the infant Zeus from his father Cronus by the clash of their music.

Attis, then, like Adonis is another resurrection-god, and their personalities become merged in the tradition. Like Adonis, Attis may die not through his self-inflicted wounds but by the tusk of a boar. Furthermore Attis, like Adonis, comes back to life with the rebirth of vegetation.

We have evidence of springtime ceremonies at which the public mourned and rejoiced for the death and rebirth of Attis. We can ascertain, too, the nature of the secret and mystic rites that were also a part of his worship. Frazer provides a compelling reconstruction.

Our information as to the nature of these mysteries and the date of their celebration is unfortunately very scanty, but they seem to have included a sacramental meal and a baptism of blood. In the sacrament the novice became a partaker of the mysteries by eating out of a drum and drinking out of a cymbal, two instruments of music which figured prominently in the thrilling orchestra of Attis. The fast which accompanied the mourning for the dead god may perhaps have been designed to prepare the body of the communicant for the reception of the blessed sacrament by purging it of all that could defile by contact the sacred elements. In the baptism the devotee, crowned with gold and wreathed with fillets, descended into a pit, the mouth of which was covered with a wooden grating. A bull, adorned with garlands of flowers, its forehead glittering with gold leaf, was then driven on to the grating and there stabbed to death with a consecrated spear. Its hot reeking blood poured in torrents through the apertures, and was received with devout eagerness by the worshiper on every part of his person and garments, till he emerged from the pit, drenched, dripping, and scarlet from head to foot, to receive the homage, nay the adoration, of his fellows as one who had been born again to eternal life and had washed away his sins in the blood of the bull. For some time afterwards the fiction of a new birth was kept up by dieting him on milk like a newborn babe. The regeneration of the worshiper took place at the same time as the regeneration of his god, namely at the vernal equinox.[3]

These were the practices as far as we can know in the East and at Rome; they are not Greek. But we are obviously, once again, in the exotic realm of the mystery religions; this one, like the others, rests upon a common fundamental belief in immortality.

The myth of Aphrodite and Adonis, like that of Cybele and Attis, depicts the destruction of the subordinate male in the grip of the eternal and all-dominating female through whom resurrection and new life may be attained. An important variation on the same theme is illustrated by the story of Aphrodite and Anchises. In this instance the possibility of the utter debilitation of the male as he fertilizes the female is very real; Anchises is in dread fear that he will be depleted and exhausted as a man because he has slept with the immortal goddess. As the story is told in the *Homeric Hymn to Aphrodite* (number 5) we are given ample evidence of the mighty power of the goddess in the universe and a rich and symbolic picture of her devastating beauty. Here Aphrodite is a fertility goddess and mother as well as a divine and enticing woman, epitomizing the lure of sexual and romantic love.

The *Homeric Hymn* begins by telling us that there are only three hearts that the great goddess of love is unable to sway: those of Athena, Artemis, and Hestia. All others, both gods and goddesses, she can bend to her will. And so great Zeus caused Aphrodite herself to fall in love with a man, because he did not want her to continue her boasts that she in her power had joined the immortal gods and goddesses in love with mortals to beget mortal children but had experienced no such humiliating experience herself. The *Hymn* continues (53–201):

Zeus put into Aphrodite's heart sweet longing for Anchises, who at that time was tending cattle on the high ranges of Mt. Ida with its many streams. In beauty he was like the immortals and so when laughter-loving Aphrodite saw him, she fell in love and a terrible longing

[3] *The New Golden Bough, a New Abridgement of the Classic Work* (by James G. Frazer), ed. Theodor H. Gaster (New York: Criterion Books, 1959), pp. 313–314.

seized her being. She went to Paphos in Cyprus and entered her fragrant temple. For her precinct and fragrant altar are there. And after she went in she closed the shining doors; inside the Graces (Charites) bathed her and rubbed her with ambrosial oil, the kind used by the eternal gods, and she emerged perfumed in its heavenly sweetness. After she was beautifully clothed in her lovely garments and adorned with gold, laughter-loving Aphrodite left fragrant Cyprus and hastened to Troy, pressing swiftly on her way, high among the clouds. And she came to Ida, the mother of beasts, with its many springs and crossed the mountain straight for the hut of Anchises. Gray wolves, bright-eyed lions, bears, and swift panthers, ravenous after deer, followed her, fawning. When she saw them, she was delighted within her heart and filled their breasts with desire; and they all went together in pairs to their beds, deep in their shadowy lairs.

She came to the well-built shelter and found him in his hut, left alone by the others, the hero Anchises, who had in full measure the beauty of the gods. All the rest were out following the cattle in the grassy pastures, but he, left alone by the others, paced to and fro playing a thrilling melody on his lyre. The daughter of Zeus, Aphrodite, stood before him, assuming the form of a beautiful young virgin, so that Anchises might not be afraid when he caught sight of her with his eyes. After Anchises saw her, he pondered as he marveled at her beautiful form and shining garments. For she wore a robe that was more brilliant than the gleam of fire, and she was adorned with intricate jewelry and radiant flowers and about her soft throat were exquisite necklaces beautifully ornate and of gold. The raiment about her tender breasts shone like the moon, a wonder to behold.

Desire gripped Anchises and he addressed her: "Hail to you, O lady, who have come to this dwelling, whoever of the blessed gods you are, Artemis or Leto or golden Aphrodite or well-born Themis or gleaming-eyed Athena; or perhaps you who have come here are one of the Graces who are the companions of the gods and are called immortal or one of the nymphs who haunt the beautiful woods or inhabit this beautiful mountain, the streams of rivers, and the grassy meadows. I shall build an altar for you on a high mound in a conspicuous spot and I shall offer you beautiful sacrifices in all seasons. Be kindly disposed towards me and grant that I be a pre-eminent hero among the Trojans; make my offspring flourish in the time to come and allow me myself to live well for a long time and see the light of the sun, happy among my people, and reach the threshold of old age."

Then Aphrodite, the daughter of Zeus, answered him: "Anchises, most renowned of earth-born men, I tell you that I am not any one of the gods. Why do you compare me to the immortals? No, I am a mortal and my mother who bore me was a mortal woman; my father Otreus, who rules over all Phrygia with its fortresses, has a famous name; perhaps you have heard of him. But I know your language as well as I know our own, for a Trojan nurse reared me in my home in Phrygia; she took me from my mother when I was a very little child and brought me up. And so to be sure I readily understand your language. Now Hermes, the slayer of Argus, with his golden wand, snatched me away from the choral dance in honor of Artemis, the goddess of the golden arrows, who delights in the sounds of the hunt. We were a group of many nymphs and virgins such as suitors pursue, and in a vast throng we circled round about. From here the slayer of Argus with his golden wand snatched me away and whisked me over many places, some cultivated by mortal men, others wild and unkempt, through which carnivorous beasts stalk from their shadowy lairs. I thought that I should never set foot again on the life-giving earth. But he told me that I should be called to the bed of Anchises as his lawful wife and that I should bear splendid children to you. And when he had explained and given his directions, then indeed he, the mighty slayer of Argus, went back again among the company of the gods. But I have come to you and the force of destiny is upon me. I implore you, by Zeus and by your goodly parents (for they could not be base and have such a son as you), take me, pure and untouched by love, as I am, and present me to your father and devoted mother and to your brothers who are born from the same blood. I shall not be an unseemly bride in their eyes but a fitting addition to your family. And send a messenger quickly to Phrygia, home of swift horses, to tell my father and worried mother. They will send you gold enough and woven raiment; accept their many splendid gifts as their dowry for me. Do these things and prepare the lovely marriage celebration which both men and immortal gods cherish."

As she spoke thus, the goddess struck Anchises with sweet desire and he cried out to her: "If, as you declare, you are mortal and a mortal woman is your mother and Otreus is your renowned father, and you have come here through the agency of Hermes and are to be called my wife all our days, then no one of the gods or mortal men will restrain me from joining with you in love right here and now, not even if the archer god Apollo himself were to shoot his grief-laden shafts from his silver bow. After I have once gone up into your bed, O maiden, fair as a goddess, I should even be willing to go below into the house of Hades."

As he spoke he clasped her hand and laughter-loving Aphrodite turned away and with her beautiful eyes downcast crept into his bed, with its fine coverings, for it had already been made with soft blankets; on it lay the skins of bears and loud-roaring lions that Anchises had slain in the lofty mountains. And then when they went up to his well-wrought bed, Anchises first removed the gleaming ornaments, the intricate brooches and flowers and necklaces; and he loosened the belt about her waist and took off her shining garments and set them down on a silver-studded chair. Then by the will of the gods and of fate he, a mortal man, lay with an immortal goddess, without knowing the truth.

At the time when herdsmen turn their cattle and staunch sheep back to their shelter from the flowery pastures, Aphrodite poured upon Anchises a sleep that was sound and sweet, and she dressed herself in her lovely raiment. When the goddess of goddesses had clothed her body beautifully, she stood by the couch and her head reached up to the well-wrought beam of the roof, and from her cheeks shone the heavenly beauty that belongs to Cytherea of the beautiful crown. She roused Anchises from sleep and called out to him with the words: "Get up, son of Dardanus; why do you sleep so deeply? Tell me if I appear to you to be like the person whom you first perceived with your eyes."

Thus she spoke, and he immediately awoke and did as he was told. When he saw the neck and the beautiful eyes of Aphrodite he was afraid and looked down turning his eyes away and he hid his handsome face in his cloak and begged her with winged words: "Now from the first moment that I have looked at you with my eyes, O goddess, I know you are divine; and you did not tell me the truth. But I implore you, by aegis-bearing Zeus, do not allow me to continue to dwell among men, still alive but enfeebled; have pity, for no man retains his full strength who sleeps with an immortal goddess."

Then Aphrodite, the daughter of Zeus, replied: "Anchises, most renowned of mortal men, be of good courage and do not be overly frightened in your heart. For you need have no fear that you will suffer evil from me or the other blessed ones; indeed you are beloved by the gods. And you will have a dear son who will rule among the Trojans; and his children will produce children in a continuous family succession. His name will be Aeneas since I am gripped by a dread anguish [4] because I went into the bed of a man, although among

---

[4] The name Aeneas is here derived from the Greek *ainos* which means dread.

mortals those of your race are always most like the gods in beauty and in stature."

Aphrodite is upset because she can no longer taunt the gods with the boast that she has caused them to love mortals while she alone has never succumbed. As the *Hymn* proceeds she continues to try to justify her actions by glorifying the family of Anchises. She tells the story of Ganymede, who was beautiful and made immortal by Zeus, and relates the sad tale of handsome Tithonus, also of the Trojan royal family, who was beloved by Eos, and granted immortality. Aphrodite's son Aeneas, of course, emerges eventually as the great hero of the Romans.

Eros, the male counterpart of Aphrodite, shares many of her characteristics. He too had a dual tradition for his birth. He may be the early cosmic deity in the creation myths of Hesiod and the Orphics or the son of Aphrodite, his father being Ares. At any rate he is often closely associated with the goddess as her attendant. Eros, like Aphrodite, may represent all facets of love and desire, but often he is the god of male homosexuality, particularly in the Greek classical period. He is depicted as a handsome young man, the embodiment and idealization of masculine beauty. The *Symposium* of Plato provides a most comprehensive and profound analysis of the manifold nature and power of love, especially in terms of a conception of Eros, although Aphrodite is not excluded. The dialogue tells of a select gathering at the house of Agathon, a dramatic poet, on the day after the customary celebration with the members of his cast in honor of his victory with his first tragedy. The topic at this most famous of dinner parties was that of love. Each guest in turn was asked to expound on the subject. The speeches of Aristophanes and Socrates, both of whom were present, are by far the most rewarding in their universal implications.

Aristophanes's speech [Plato, *Symposium*, 14–16 (189A–193E)] follows that of Pausanias and Eryximachus, two of the other guests.

Men seem to me to have failed completely to comprehend the power of Eros, for if they did comprehend it, they would have built to him the greatest altars and temples and offered the greatest sacrifices, whereas he is given none of these honors, although he should have them most of all. For he is the most friendly to man of all the gods, his helper and physician in those ills, which if cured, would bring about the greatest happiness for the human race. Therefore I shall try to initiate you into the nature of his power and you will be the teachers of others.

But first you must understand the nature of mankind and what experiences it has suffered. For our nature long ago was not the same as it is now but different. In the beginning mankind had three sexes, not two, male and female, as now; but there was in addition, a third, which partook of both the others; now it has vanished and only its name survives. At that time there was a distinct sex, the androgynous both in appearance and in name partaking of the characteristics of both the male and the female, but now it does not exist, except for the name which is retained as a term of reproach. Furthermore every human being was in shape a round entity, with back and sides forming a circle; he had four hands, an equal number of feet, one head, with two faces exactly alike but each looking in opposite directions, set upon a circular neck, four ears, two sets of genitals and everything else as one might imagine from this description. He walked upright just as we do now in whichever direction (backwards or forwards) he wished. When they were anxious to run they made use of all their limbs (which were then eight in number) by turning cart wheels just like acrobats and quickly carried themselves along by this circular movement. The sexes were three in number and of such a kind for these reasons; originally the male was sprung from the sun, the female from the earth, and the third, partaking of both male and female, from the moon, because the moon partakes of both the sun and the earth, and indeed because they were just like their parents their shape was spherical and their movement circular. Their strength and might were terrifying; they had great ambitions and they made an attack on the gods. What Homer relates about Ephialtes and Otus and their attempt to climb up to heaven and assail the gods is told also about these beings as well.

Zeus and the other gods took counsel about what they should do and they were at a loss. They could not bring themselves to kill them (just as they had obliterated the race of the giants with blasts of thunder and lightning), for they would deprive themselves of the honors and sacrifices which they received from men, nor could they allow them to continue in their insolence. After painful deliberation Zeus declared that he had a plan. "I think that I have a way," he said, "whereby men may continue to exist but will cease from their insolence by being made weaker. For I shall cut each of them in two and they will be at the same time both weaker and more useful to us because of their greater numbers, and they will walk upright on two legs. If they still seem to be insolent and do not wish to be quiet, I shall split them again and they will hop about on one leg."

With these words he cut men in two, just as one splits fruit which is to be preserved or divides an egg with a hair. As he bisected each one, he ordered Apollo to turn the face with the half of the neck attached around to the side that was cut, so that man by being able to see the signs of his bisection might be better behaved; and he ordered him to heal the marks of the cutting. Apollo turned the face around and drew together the skin like a pouch with drawstrings on what is now called the belly and tied it in the middle making a single knot which is called the navel. He smoothed out the many other wrinkles and molded the chest using a tool like that of cobblers when they smooth out the wrinkles in the leather on their last. But he left a few on their bellies around the navel as a reminder of their experience of long ago. And so when their original nature had been split in two, each longed for his other half and when they encountered it they threw their arms about one another and embraced in their desire to grow together again and they died through hunger and neglect of the other necessities of life because of their wish to do nothing separated from each other. Whenever one of a pair died, the other that was left searched out and embraced another mate, either the half of a whole female (which we now call woman) or of a male. Thus they perished, and Zeus in his pity devised another plan: he transferred their genitals to the front; for until now they had been on the outside and they begot and bore their offspring not in conjunction with one another but by emission into the earth, like grasshoppers. And so Zeus moved their genitals to the front and thereby had them reproduce by intercourse with one another, the male with the female. He did this for two reasons: if a man united with a woman they would propagate the race and it would survive, but if a male united with a male, they might find satisfaction and freedom to turn to their pursuits and devote themselves to the other concerns of life. From such early times then love for one another has been implanted in the human race, a love that unifies in his attempt to make one out of two and to heal and restore the basic nature of man.

Each of us therefore is but a broken tally, half a man, since we have been cut just like the side of a flatfish and made two instead of one.

All who are a section halved from the beings of the common sex (which was at that time called androgynous) are lovers of women; many adulterers come from this source including women who love men and are promiscuous. All women who are a section halved from the female do not pay any attention to men but rather turn to women; lesbians come from this source. All who are a section halved from the male pursue males and all the while they are young, since they are slices, as it were, of the male, they love men and take delight in lying by their side and embracing them; these are the best of boys and youths because they are the most manly in nature. Some say that they are without shame but they do not tell the truth. For they behave the way they do not through shamelessness but through courage, manliness, and masculinity as they cling to what is similar to them. Here is a great proof of what I say. Only men of this sort proceed to politics when they grow up. Once they are men they love boys and do not turn their thoughts to marriage and procreation naturally but are forced to by law or convention; it is enough for them to spend their lives together unmarried. In short then a man like this is a lover of men as a boy and a lover of boys as a man, always clinging to what is akin to his nature. Therefore whenever anyone of this sort and every other kind of person encounters the other half that is actually his, then they are struck in an amazing way with affection, kinship, and love, virtually unwilling to be separated from each other for even a short time. These are the ones who spend their whole life together, although they would not be able to tell what they wish to gain from each other. No one would imagine that it is on account of their sexual association that the one enjoys intensely being with the other; clearly the soul of each desires something else which it cannot describe but only hint at obscurely. Suppose Hephaestus, his tools in hand, were to stand over them as they lay together and ask: "O mortals, what is it that you wish to gain from one another?" Or when they were at a loss for an answer he were to ask again: "Is this what you desire, to be together always as much as possible so as never to be separated from each other night and day? If this is what you desire I am willing to fuse and weld you together so that the two of you may become one and the same person and as long as you live, you may both live united in one being, and when you die, you may die together as one instead of two united even in the realms of Hades. Just see if this would be enough to satisfy your longing." We know that there is not one person who after hearing these words would deny their truth and say that he wanted something else, but he would believe that he had heard exactly what he had desired for a long time—namely to be melted in unison with his beloved and the two of them become one. The reason is that our ancient nature was thus and we were whole. And so Love is merely the name for the desire and pursuit of the whole. Previously, as I have said, we were one, but now because of our wickedness we have been split by the god (just as the Arcadians have been split up by the Spartans).[5] There is too the fear that if we do not behave properly towards the gods we may again be bisected just as dice that are divided as tallies and go around like the figures cut in profile on steles, split right along their noses. For this reason all men must be urged to pay reverence to the gods so that we may avoid suffering further bisection and win what Eros has to give as our guide and leader. Let no one act in opposition to him—whoever does incurs the enmity of the gods. For if we are reconciled and friendly to the god of love we shall find and win our very own beloved, an achievement few today attain. Eryximachus is not to suppose in ridicule of my speech that I am referring only to Pausanias and Agathon since they perhaps happen to be of the class of those who love males by nature. I am referring rather to all men and women when I say that the happiness of our race lies in the fulfillment of love; each must find the beloved that is his and be restored to his original nature. If this ancient state was best, of necessity the nearest to it in our present circumstances must be best—namely to find a beloved who is of one and the same mind and nature. It is right to praise Eros as the god responsible; he helps us most in our present life by bringing us to what is kindred to us and offers us the greatest hopes for the future. If we pay reverence to the gods, he will restore us to our ancient nature and with his cure make us happy and blessed.

Aristophanes concludes by again imploring Eryximachus not to ridicule his speech and indeed, in the last analysis, we cannot help but take it very seriously. The invention, the wit, and the absurdity are all typical of the comic playwright, but so is the insight that they so brilliantly elucidate. We do not know how much belongs to the genius of Plato, but it would be difficult to imagine anything more in character for Aristophanes. If we omit the outspoken glorification of love between males (inspired perhaps by the com-

---

[5] This reference to the dispersion of the inhabitants of Mantinea (an Arcadian city) by the Spartans in 385 is an anachronism since the dramatic date of the speech is purportedly 416.

pany present and certainly preliminary to Plato's own message in Socrates's subsequent speech), we have a most contemporary vision of the basic need of one human being for another. Who can ever forget Hephaestus as he stands before the two lovers and asks what they hope to gain from each other? And who can deny that the complex nature of this most fundamental physical and psychological drive is here laid bare, with a ruthless penetration that is disconcertingly contemporary, however much the scientific quest for precise definition and vocabulary since the time of Freud has replaced the symbols of mythic art?

In Socrates's speech which provides the dramatic and philosophical climax of the dialogue, we move from the conception of love that is elemental and essentially physical to a sublime elucidation of the highest spiritual attainments that Eros can inspire. Another myth is evoked, this time to establish the true nature of the divine being, in opposition to the misconceptions of the previous speakers. Socrates tells how he was instructed in the true nature of Eros by a woman of Mantinea called Diotima. She makes him realize that Eros is not good or beautiful nor bad and ugly, but in nature lies somewhere between the two. Therefore he is not a god. Socrates continues his argument quoting from his conversation with Diotima [*Symposium,* 23 (202D–204 C)]:

"What then might love be," I said, "a mortal?" "Not in the least," she replied. "But what is he then?" "As I told you earlier, he is not mortal or immortal but something between." "What then, O Diotima?" "A great spirit, O Socrates; for every spirit is intermediate between god and man." "What power does he have?" I asked. "He interprets and conveys exchanges between gods and men, prayers and sacrifices from men to gods, and orders and gifts in return from gods to men; being intermediate he fills in for both and serves as the bond uniting the two worlds into a whole entity. Through him proceeds the whole art of divination and the skill of priests in sacrifice, ritual, spells, and every kind of sorcery and magic. God does not have dealings with man directly, but through Love all association and discourse between the two are carried on, both in the waking hours and in time of sleep. The one who is wise in such matters as these is a spiritual man, and he who is wise in other arts and crafts is his inferior. These spirits are many and of every kind and one of them is Eros."

"Who were his father and mother?" I asked. "Although it is a rather long story, I shall tell you," she replied. "When Aphrodite was born the gods held a feast and among them was Resourcefulness (Poros), the son of Cleverness (Metis), and while they were dining, Poverty (Penia) came and stood about the door to beg, since there was a party.[6] Resourcefulness became intoxicated with nectar (for wine did not yet exist) and went into the garden of Zeus where, overcome by his condition, he fell asleep. Then Poverty, because of her own want and lack of resourcefulness, contrived to have a child by Resourcefulness and she lay by his side and conceived Eros. And so Eros became the attendant and servant of Aphrodite, for he was begotten on her birthday and he is by nature a lover of beauty and Aphrodite is beautiful. Since Eros then is the son of Resourcefulness and Poverty he is fated to have the following kind of character. First of all he is continually poor and, far from being soft and beautiful as many believe, he is hard and squalid, without shoes, without a home, and without a bed; he always sleeps on the ground, in doorways, and on the street. Thus he has his mother's nature with want as his constant companion. On the other hand, like his father, he lays his plots to catch the beautiful and the good; being vehement and energetic, he is a dread hunter, always weaving some scheme; full of resource he has a passion for knowledge and is a lover of wisdom during all his life, a clever wizard, sorcerer, and sophist. He is not immortal nor is he mortal, but at one time he flourishes and lives whenever he is successful, and at another he dies all in the same day, but he will come back to life again because of his nature inherited from his father—what he acquires slips away from him again, and so Eros is never either poor or rich and he is in a state between wisdom and ignorance. This is the way he is. No one of the gods loves wisdom and longs to become wise because he is wise, and so with any other who is wise—he does not love wisdom. On the other hand the ignorant do not love wisdom nor long to become wise. Ignorance is a difficult thing for this very reason that the one who is neither beautiful or good or wise is completely satisfied with himself. The one who does not think he is lacking in anything certainly does not desire what he does not think that he lacks."

"O Diotima," I asked, "who are those who love wisdom if not the wise or the ignorant?" "By now certainly it would be clear even to a child," she replied, "that they are those who are in a state between desire and wisdom, one of whom is Eros. To be sure wisdom is among

[6] It is difficult to find one word that expresses adequately the abstract conceptions personified. The name Poros also suggests contrivance; Metis, wisdom or invention; and Penia, need.

the most beautiful of things and Eros is love of beauty; and so Eros must be a lover of wisdom, and being a lover of wisdom he lies between wisdom and ignorance. The nature of his birth is the reason for this. He springs from a wise and resourceful father and a mother who is not wise and without resources. This then, my dear Socrates, is the nature of this spirit. The conception you had of Eros is not surprising. You believed, to infer from what you said, that Love was the beloved (the one who is loved) and not the lover (the one who loves). For this reason, I think, Love appeared to you to be all beautiful. For that which is loved is that which actually is beautiful and delicate, perfect and most happy, but that which loves has another character, of the kind that I have described."

Diotima goes on to explain the function, purpose, and power of Eros in the life of man. Love and the lover desire what they do not possess, namely, the beautiful and the good, and the ultimate goal of their pursuit is happiness. Love finds particular expression in the procreation of what is beautiful both physically and spiritually, and all men in their quest to bring forth in beauty are thereby touched by a divine harmony with the immortal. Procreation is the closest means by which the human race can attain to perpetuity and immortality; love, then, is a love of immortality as well as of the beautiful and the good.

Animals as well as men seek to perpetuate themselves and thereby become immortal. But for man there are various stages in the hierarchy of love. The lowest is that of the animal inspired by the desire for children of the body, but as one ascends there is the realization of the possibility of producing children of the mind. Who would not prefer the poetic offspring of a Homer or a Hesiod and the more lasting glory and immortality that they have achieved? Just as on the rungs of a ladder so we proceed from one step to another, initiates into the mysteries of love from the lower to the higher.

Love begins with the physical and sensual desire for the beautiful person or the beautiful thing. From the specific object one moves to the generic conception of beauty which is wondrous, and pure, and universal. It is the love of this eternal beauty (and with it the goodness and wisdom it entails) that inspires the pursuit of philosophy in the philosopher.

AURORA AND CEPHALUS by Nicholas Poussin (1594–1665), London, National Gallery. Reproduced by courtesy of the Trustees, the National Gallery, London.

CYBELE *from Vincenzo Cartari's* IMAGINI DELLI DELI DELGI' ANTICHI (*edition of 1647*).

JUPITER AND JUNO *by Annibale Carracci (1560–1609), Rome, Farnese Palace. Reproduced by permission of the French Ambassador to Italy.*

JUPITER AND THETIS by J.A.D. Ingres (1780–1867), Aix-en-Provence, France, Musée Granet.

Nereid by Georges Braque (b. 1882), Paris, Galeries Maeght. Reproduced by permission of A.D.A.G.P. 1970 by French Reproduction Rights, Inc.

NEREIDS, mosiac by Aspasius (ca. 200 A.D.), Lambèse, Algeria, Museum.

APHRODITE RISING FROM THE SEA (marble relief, ca. 460 B.C.), Rome, Museo Nazionale delle Terme.

VENUS DRAWN BY DOVES (ca. 1815), *artist unknown, Williamsburg, Virginia, Abby Aldrich Rockefeller Folk Art Collection. Reproduced by permission.*

VENUS AND ADONIS by Titian (ca. 1477–1576), Washington, D.C., National Gallery of Art, Widener Collection. Reproduced by permission of the National Gallery of Art.

THE DEATH OF ADONIS by Jusepe de Ribera (1591–1652), The Cleveland Museum of Art, Mr. and Mrs. William H. Marlatt Fund. Reproduced by permission of the Cleveland Museum of Art.

Diotima sums up by describing the final stages of initiation and revelation sustaining the vocabulary of the mysteries [28 (210A–C)]:

It is necessary for the one proceeding in the right way toward his goal to begin, when he is young, with physical beauty, and first of all, if his guide directs him properly, to love one person and in his company to beget beautiful ideas and then to observe that the beauty in one person is related to the beauty in another. If he must pursue physical beauty, he would be very foolish not to realize that the beauty in all persons is one and the same. When he has come to this conclusion, he will become the lover of all beautiful bodies and will relax the intensity of his love for one and think the less of it as something of little account. Next he will realize that beauty in the soul is more precious than that in the body, so that if he meets with a person who is beautiful in his soul, even if he has little of the physical bloom of beauty, this will be enough and he will love and cherish him and beget beautiful ideas that make young men better, so that he will in turn be forced to see the beauty in morals and laws and that the beauty in them all is related.

This then is the Platonic Eros, a love that inspires the philosopher to deny himself in the cause of his fellow man and in the pursuit of true wisdom. Whatever the physical roots, the spiritual import is universal, kindred to the passionate love of God that pervades all serious religious devotion. Aristotle too thinks in Platonic terms when he describes his god as the unmoved mover, the final cause in the universe, who moves as a beloved moves the lover.

How far we have come from the traditional depiction of Eros as the handsome young athlete who attends Aphrodite! Even more remote is the image that evolved of Eros as Cupid, a chubby mischievous little darling with wings and a bow and arrow. He still attends Aphrodite and although the wounds he inflicts can inspire a passion that is serious and even deadly, too often he becomes little more than the cute and frivolous *deus ex machina* of romantic love.

It is impossible to survey the mythological concepts of love without including the poetic vision of Sappho of Lesbos, the poetess of love in antiquity. Only a little of her work has survived but the critical acclaim of her artistry glows undiminished. We know practically nothing with certainty about her life and career. She was devoted to Aphrodite and to the girls with whom she was associated. But we cannot even confidently speak about a cult of the goddess, and her relations with her loved ones can only legitimately be imagined from the meager remains of her poetry. Her circle has been interpreted as everything from a finishing school for girls in the Victorian manner to a hotbed of sensuality.

Sappho's invocation to Aphrodite has real meaning for us in this context because it illustrates beautifully the passionate intensity that infuses so much of Greek art within the disciplined control of artistic form. It reminds us too of the sincerity of the conception of the goddess that was possible in the seventh and sixth centuries. Too often our sensibilities are numbed by the later artificial and conventional stereotypes to which the gods are reduced, once all genuine belief is gone. There can be no question about the intense reality of Aphrodite in the following lines— which even a prose translation cannot obliterate completely.

Exquisitely enthroned, immortal Aphrodite, weaver of charms, child of Zeus, I beg you, reverend lady, do not crush my heart with sickness and distress. But come to me here, if ever once before you heard my cry from afar and listened and, leaving your father's house, yoked your chariot of gold. Beautiful birds drew you swiftly from heaven over the black earth through the air between with the rapid flutter of their downy wings.

Swiftly they came and you, O blessed goddess, smiling in your immortal beauty asked what I was suffering this time, why I was calling again, what I wished to happen most of all in my frenzied heart. "Who is it this time you desire that Persuasion entice to your love? Who, O Sappho, has wronged you? For if she runs away now, soon she will follow; if she rejects your gifts, she will bring gifts herself; if she does not now, soon she will love you, even though she does not wish it."

Come to me now too and free me from my harsh anxieties; all that my heart longs for, accomplish. You, your very self, stand with me in my conflict.

CHAPTER 8

Artemis

The *Homeric Hymn to Artemis* (number 27) draws the essential features of her character.

I sing about Artemis of the golden arrows, chaste virgin of the noisy hunt, who delights in her shafts and strikes down the stag, the very own sister of Apollo of the golden sword. She ranges over shady hills and windy heights, rejoicing in the chase as she draws her bow, made all of silver, and shoots her shafts of woe. The peaks of the lofty mountains tremble, the dark woods echo terribly to the shrieks of wild beasts, and both the earth and fish-filled sea are shaken. But she with dauntless heart looks everywhere to wreak destruction on the brood of animals. But when the huntress, who takes delight in her arrows, has had her fill of pleasure and cheered her heart, she unstrings her curved bow and makes her way to the great house of her dear brother, Phoebus Apollo, in the rich land of Delphi, where she supervises the lovely dances of the Muses and the Graces. After she has hung up her unstrung bow and arrows, she takes first place and exquisitely attired leads the dance. And they join in a heavenly choir to sing how Leto of the beautiful ankles bore two children who are by far the best of the immortals in sagacious thought and action. Hail, children of Zeus and Leto of the lovely hair; I will remember you and another song too.

The goddess Leto mated with Zeus and bore the twin deities, Artemis and Apollo. The story of Apollo's birth on the island of Delos is recounted in the next chapter in the version given by the *Homeric Hymn to Apollo,* but there are variants. Traditionally Artemis is born first at a place called Ortygia (the name means Quail Island), which cannot be identified with certainty. In some accounts it is clearly not merely another name for Delos; in others, it is. At any rate, Artemis either immediately or very soon after

119

her birth is able to help with the delivery of her brother Apollo, thus performing one of her primary functions as a goddess of childbirth early in her career (a role she shares with Hera and Eileithyia, as we have seen).

On other occasions Artemis can be closely linked with her brother Apollo, both appearing as vehement and haughty agents of destruction with their shafts of doom. Sudden death (particularly of the young) was often attributed to these two deities, Artemis striking down the girls, Apollo the boys. One of their most famous exploits concerns Niobe and her children, told at length by Ovid (*Metamorphoses,* 6.148–315). The women of Thebes bestowed great honor upon Leto and her twin children, crowning their heads with laurel and offering up incense and prayers in obedience to an injunction by the goddess herself. Niobe, however, was enraged by the whole proceedings and rashly boasted that she was more deserving of tribute than Leto. After all she was rich, beautiful, and the wife of Amphion, ruling by his side as the queen of Thebes in the royal palace of Cadmus. As the daughter of Tantalus and the granddaughter of Atlas, her lineage was much more splendid than that of Leto, the daughter of an obscure Titan, Coeus. In addition to everything else, Leto bore only two children, whereas she was the mother of seven sons and seven daughters. Indeed Niobe was so confident in the abundance of her blessings that she felt that she could afford to lose even a part of them without serious consequences.

Leto was enraged at such hybris and complained bitterly to her children, Artemis and Apollo. Together the two deities swiftly glided down to the palace of Thebes to avenge the insulted honor of their mother. Apollo struck down all the sons of Niobe with his deadly and unerring arrows and Artemis in turn killed all her daughters. Just as Artemis was about to shoot the last child, Niobe in desperation shielded the girl and pleaded that this one, her youngest, be spared. While she was uttering this prayer she was turned to stone and a whirlwind whisked her away to her homeland, Phrygia, where she was placed on a mountain top. Tears continue to trickle down from her face of marble, as she wastes away. A rock on Mt. Sipylus in Asia Minor was identified in antiquity as the figure of Niobe.

There are several stories that illustrate the hallowed purity of the goddess Artemis. A famous one is told about Actaeon (the son of Aristaeus and Autonoe), an ardent hunter who lost his way and by accident (or was it fate?) had the misfortune to see Artemis (Diana in Ovid's version) naked (*Metamorphoses,* 3.138–255):

Actaeon first tinged with grief the happiness of his grandfather, Cadmus. A stag's horns grew on his head, and his hounds feasted on their master's flesh. Yet, if you look closely, you will find that his guilt was misfortune, not a crime: what crime indeed lies in an innocent mistake?

There was a mountain on which had fallen the blood of beasts of many kinds. It was midday, when shadows are at their shortest and the sun is midway in his course. Young Actaeon calmly called his fellow huntsmen as they tracked the game through the depths of the pathless forest: "My friends, our nets and spears are wet with the blood of our prey; we have had luck enough today! Dawn's saffron-wheeled chariot will bring another day tomorrow and then we will renew the chase. The Sun now stands midway 'twixt east and west and with his hot rays parches the earth. Stop now the hunt, and take in the knotted nets!" His men obeyed and halted from their labors.

A vale there was called Gargaphie, sacred to the huntress Diana; clothed with a dense growth of pine and pointed cypress it had at its far end a woodland cave which no human hand had shaped. Nature had imitated man's work by her own skill. She had created a natural arch of unwrought pumice and porous tufa; on the right from a murmuring spring issued a stream of clearest water, and around the pool was a grassy bank. Here would the woodland goddess rest when weary from the hunt and bathe her virgin body in the clear water.

That day she came there and to one of her nymphs handed her hunting spear, her quiver and bow, and the arrows that were left. Upon another's waiting arms she cast her cloak and two more took off her sandals, while Theban Crocale, more skilled than they, knotted her flowing hair, although her own was unbound. Nephele, Hyale, Ranis, Psecas, and Phiale [1] fetched water and poured it from the ample urns. And while Diana thus was being bathed, as she had been many times before, Actaeon, Cadmus's grandson, his labors left unfinished, came to the grotto uncertain of his way and wander-

---

[1] The nymphs' names are all Greek words suggestive of cool, crystal-clear water.

ing through the unfamiliar wood; so fate carried him along. Into
the dripping cave he went, and the nymphs, when they saw a man,
beat their breasts and filled the forest with their screams. Surrounding
Diana they shielded her with their bodies, but the goddess was taller
than they and her head o'ertopped them all. Just as the clouds are
tinged with color when struck by the rays of the setting sun, or like
the reddening Dawn, Diana's face flushed when she was spied naked.
Surrounded by her nymphs she turned and looked back; wishing that
her arrows were at hand she used what weapons she could and flung
water over the young man's face and hair with these words, foretelling
his coming doom: "Now you may tell how you saw me naked—
if you can tell!" And with this threat she made the horns of a long-
lived stag [2] rise on his head where the water had struck him; his neck
grew long and his ears pointed, his hands turned to hooves, his arms
to legs, and his body she clothed with a spotted deerskin. And she
made him timid; Autonoe's valiant son ran away in fear and as he
ran wondered at his speed. He saw his horned head reflected in a
pool and tried to say "Alas"—but no words would come. He sobbed;
that at least was a sound he uttered, and tears flowed down his new-
changed face. Only his mind remained unchanged. What should he do?
Go home to the royal palace? Or hide in the woods? Shame prevented
him from the one action, fear from the other.

While he stood undecided his hounds saw him. Blackfoot and clever
Tracker first raised the hue and cry with their baying, the latter a
Cretan hound, the former of Spartan pedigree. Then the rest of the
pack rushed up, swifter than the wind, whose names it would take
too long to give.[3] Eager for the prey they hunt him over rocks and
cliffs, by rough tracks and trackless ways, through terrain rocky and
inaccessible. He fled, by ways where he had often been the pursuer;
he fled, pursued by his own hounds! He longed to cry out "Actaeon
am I; obey your master!" He longed—but could utter no words; and
the heavens echoed to the baying hounds. First Blackie gored his back;
then Hunter followed, while Hill-hound gripped Actaeon's shoulder
with his teeth. These three had been slower to join the chase, but
had outstripped the pack along mountain short cuts; while they held
back their master the pack came up and all sank their teeth into his
body. His whole body was torn by the hounds; he groaned, a sound
which was not human nor yet such as a stag could make. The hills

[2] A stag was commonly believed to live nine times as long as a man.

[3] Ovid gives thirty-one more names, however, that we have omitted in the
translation.

he knew so well echoed with his screams; falling on his knees, like a man in prayer, he dumbly looked at them in entreaty, for he had no human arms to stretch out to them. But the huntsmen, ignorant of the truth, urge on the pack with their usual cries; they look round for Actaeon and loudly call his name as if he were not there. At the sound of his name he lifts his head; they think it a pity that he is not there, too slow to see the sight of the stag at bay. He could indeed wish he were not there! But he is; he could wish to be the spectator, not the victim, of his hounds' cruel jaws. Completely encircling him, with jaws biting deep, they tear in fact their master's flesh when he seems to be a stag. Only when his life has ebbed out through innumerable wounds was it said that the vengeance was satisfied of the huntress Diana.

Opinions varied about the deed. Some thought the goddess had been more cruel than just; others approved, and said that her severity was worthy of her virgin chastity. Each view had good reasons to support it.

The same insistence on purity and chastity, the same vehemence against defilement of any sort appear again in the story of Callisto, one of the followers of Artemis (or Diana, as Ovid tells it, *Metamorphoses,* 2.409–507):

As Jupiter journeyed back and forth to Arcadia he saw the Arcadian girl Callisto, and the fires of love were kindled in his bones. She did not care to draw out the unworked wool nor to change her hair's style. She would pin her dress with a brooch, keep her hair in place with a white ribbon; with a smooth spear in her hand or a bow she marched in Diana's troops. No other girl who trod the Arcadian hills was dearer to the goddess—but no one's power can last for long! High in the heaven rode the sun beyond the middle of his course when Callisto came to a wood that no one throughout the years had touched. Here she took off the quiver from her shoulder and unstrung the pliant bow; she lay upon the grassy ground, her head resting upon the painted quiver. Jupiter saw her, tired and unprotected. "My wife," said he, "will never discover this affair, and if she does—well, the prize is worth her anger." So he disguised himself to look like Diana and said: "Dear girl, my follower, upon which mountain did you hunt?" Callisto sprung up from the turf. "Hail, goddess," said she, "greater in my opinion than Jupiter—and let him hear my words!" Jupiter smiled as he heard this, glad that Diana was preferred to himself;

he kissed the girl, more warmly than a maiden should. He cut short Callisto's tale of the forest hunt with an embrace and as he forced her showed who he really was. Callisto fought against him with all a woman's strength—Juno's anger would have been lessened could she have seen her—but what god is weaker than a girl, and what god can overcome Jupiter? He won; to the heavens he flies and she hates the wood that knows her shame; as she fled from it she almost forgot to take her quiver and arrows and the bow that she had hung up.

Diana saw her as she moved with her followers along the heights of Maenalus, flushed with pride at the beasts she had killed, and called her. Callisto hid, afraid at first that Jupiter in disguise was calling her. But as she saw the nymphs and goddess go on together she knew it was no trick, and joined the band. Poor Callisto! How hard it is not to show one's guilt in one's face! She could hardly lift her eyes from the ground; no longer did she stay close to Diana's side nor be the first of all her followers. In silence she blushed and showed her shame; if Diana had not been a maiden she could have known Callisto's guilt by a thousand signs. They say that the nymphs realized it.

The horned moon was waxing for the ninth time when Diana, weary from the chase and tired by the sun, her brother's flaming heat, reached a cool wood; here flowed a babbling stream, gliding over its smooth and sandy bed. She praised the place; she dipped her feet into the water and it pleased her. "No man is here to spy on us," she cried: "let us bathe naked in the stream!" Callisto blushed; the others took off their clothes, she alone held back. And as she delayed, they stripped her, and then her naked body and her guilt were plain to see. She stood confused, trying to hide her belly with her hands; but Diana cried "Be off from here! Do not defile these sacred waters!" and expelled her from her band.

Long before Juno had known the truth and had put off revenge until the time was ripe. She saw no cause to wait now; Callisto's son Arcas (his very name caused Juno pain) had been born, and when Juno's cruel gaze fell on him she cried: "So only this was left, you whore; for you to be pregnant and by this birth make known the wrong I suffer and my husband's shameful act! But I will have my revenge! I will take away the beauty that pleases you so much and gives my husband, you flirt, such pleasure." And as she spoke she seized Callisto's hair and threw her to the ground. Callisto spread her arms in suppliant prayer; her arms began to bristle with black hair, her hands to be bent with fingers turning to curved claws; she used her hands as feet and the face which once delighted Jupiter grew ugly with grinning jaws. Her power of speech was lost, with no prayers or entreaties could she win pity, and a hoarse and frightening growl was her only utterance. Yet her human mind remained even when she had become a bear; with never-ceasing moans she made known her suffering; lifting what once had been her hands to heaven she felt Jupiter's ingratitude, although she could not with words accuse him. Poor thing! How often was she afraid to sleep in the solitary forest before her former home; how often did she roam in the lands that once were hers! How often was she pursued over the rocky hills by the baying hounds; how often did the huntress run in fear from the hunters! Often she hid herself (forgetting what she was) and though a bear, shrunk from the sight of bears; wolves scared her, although her father, Lycaon, had become one.

One day Arcas, now nearly fifteen years old and ignorant of his parentage, was out hunting; as he picked a likely covert and criss-crossed the forests of Mt. Erymanthus with knotted nets, he came upon his mother. She saw him and stood still like one who sees a familiar face. He ran away, afraid of the beast who never took her gaze from him (for he knew not what she was); he was on the point of driving a spear through her body, eager as she was to come close to him. Then almighty Jupiter prevented him; he averted Arcas's crime against his mother and took them both on the wings of the wind to heaven and there made them neighboring stars.

Callisto became the Great Bear (Arctus or Ursa Major); Arcas the "Bear Warden" (Arctophylax or Arcturus or Böotes). Ursa Major was also known as Hamaxa (the Wain).

The story of Callisto is typical of a group of myths that provides etiology for individual stars or constellations. These stories (most of which belong to late antiquity) are told about various figures in mythology and several of them, in one way or another, cluster about Artemis herself. One such story concerns Orion, a composite figure, about whom many tales are related with multiple and intricate variations.

Orion sometimes appears as the son of Earth; in other accounts his father is Poseidon. He is traditionally a mighty hunter and he is, as well, involved in several love affairs. He amorously pursued Artemis (or Opis, a follower of Artemis, if, indeed, she is not the goddess herself) and attempted to rape her; he was run through by her arrows.

Several stories concern Orion and the island of Chios and his adventures with the king of the island, Oenopion (the name means wine-face; Chios was famous for its wines). The many versions play upon the following themes. Orion woos the daughter of Oenopion, Merope; he becomes drunk and is blinded by the king, and he regains his sight through the rays of the sun-god, Helius. In some versions, while he is clearing the island of wild beasts as a favor for Oenopion, he encounters Artemis and tries to ravish her. In her anger the goddess produced a scorpion out of the earth that stung Orion to death. Both can be seen in the heavens. Some say that Orion pursued the Pleiades (daughters of the Titan, Atlas, and Pleione, an Oceanid), and they were all transformed into constellations; with Orion was his dog, Sirius, who became the dog star.

The origins of Artemis are obscure. Although she is predominantly a virgin goddess in the classical period, certain aspects of her character suggest that at some time she may have had fertility connections. Several of the nymphs associated with her (e.g., Callisto and Opis) were probably once goddesses in their own right and may actually represent various manifestations of Artemis's own complex nature. One of them, Britomartis, is closely linked to Crete, and certain aspects of her character could imply that she was once a traditional mother-goddess type. Artemis's interest in childbirth and in the young of both men and animals seems to betray concerns that are not entirely virginal. At Ephesus in Asia Minor, a statue of Artemis depicts her in a robe of animal heads, which in its upper part exposes what appears to be a ring of multiple breasts. We should remember too that Artemis became a goddess of the moon in classical times. As in the case of other goddesses worshiped by women (e.g., Hera), this link with the moon may be associated with the monthly cycle and women's menstrual period.

As a moon-goddess, Artemis is sometimes closely identified with Selene and Hecate. Hecate is clearly a fertility deity with definite chthonian characteristics. She can make the earth produce in plenty and her home is in the depths of the Underworld. She is a descendant of the Titans, and, in fact, a cousin of Artemis: Asterie, her mother, is Leto's sister; her father is Perses. Hecate is a goddess of roads in general and crossroads in particular, the latter being considered the center of ghostly activities, particularly in the dead of night. Thus the goddess developed a terrifying aspect; triple-faced statues depicted the three manifestations of her multiple character as a deity of the moon—Selene in heaven, Artemis on earth, and Hecate in the realm of Hades. Offerings of food (known as Hecate's suppers) were left to placate her, for she was terrible both in her powers and in her person—a veritable Fury, armed with a scourge and blazing torch and accompanied by terrifying hounds. Her skill in the arts of black magic made her the patron deity of sorceresses (like Medea) and witches. How different is the usual depiction of Artemis, young, vigorous, wholesome, and beautiful! In the costume of the huntress she is ready for the chase, armed with her bow and arrow; an animal often appears by her side and crescent moon-like horns rest upon her head; the torch that she holds burns bright with the light of birth, life, and fertility. Whatever the roots of her fertility connections, the dominant conception of Artemis in the classical period is that of the virgin huntress. She becomes, as it were, the goddess of nature itself, not always in terms of its teeming procreation, but instead often reflecting its cool, pristine, and virginal aspects. As a moon-goddess too (despite the overtones of fecundity) she can appear as a symbol, cold, white, and chaste.

In her role as a goddess of chastity, Artemis provides a ready foil for the voluptuous sensuality of Aphrodite. Artemis in this view becomes at one and the same time a negative force, representing the utter rejection of love and also a positive compulsion towards purity and asceticism. No one has rendered the psychological and physiological implications of this contrast in more human and meaningful terms than the poet Euripides in his play *Hippolytus*. The full story of the tragedy belongs in another context, but the essential nature of the conflict in terms of Artemis and Aphrodite will prove revealing here. Aphrodite is enraged (and she tells us so in a typical Euripidean prologue); her power is great and universal, yet she is vehemently spurned by Hippolytus who will have absolutely nothing to do with her. The young man must certainly pay for this hybris, and the goddess uses his stepmother Phaedra to make certain that he will. Phaedra is the second wife of Theseus, the father of Hippolytus, and Aphrodite impels the poor woman to fall desperately in love with her stepson. Phaedra's nurse wrests the fatal secret of her guilty love from her sick and distraught mistress and makes the tragic mistake of taking it upon herself to inform the unsuspecting Hippolytus. The boy is horrified; the thought of physical love for any woman is for him traumatic enough; an incestuous relationship with the wife of his beloved father would be an abomination. Phaedra in her disgrace commits suicide after leaving a note that falsely incriminates Hippolytus, whose death is brought about by the curse of his enraged father, Theseus. Artemis appears to her beloved follower, Hippolytus, as he lies dying. She promises him, in return for a lifetime of devotion that has brought about his martyrdom, that she will get even by wreaking vengeance upon some favorite of Aphrodite, and she will establish a cult in honor of Hippolytus as well—virgin maidens will pay tribute to him by dedicating their shorn tresses and lamenting his fate by their tears and their songs.

Theseus realizes his error too late; what has he done to suffer the deaths of both his wife and his son? At the close of the play we are left with a fascinating chain of enigmas in the Euripidean manner. Is Hippolytus a saint or a foolish and obstinate prig? Has he destroyed himself through the dangerous, if not impossible, rejection of the physical? Are men at the mercy of ruthless and irrational forces inherent in their very nature, which they deify in terms of ruthless and vindictive women? Certainly the two goddesses play upon the basic character of the human protagonists. Aphrodite uses the essentially sensual Phaedra, and Artemis responds to the purity of Hippolytus's vision. Each man is created in his god's image, or each creates his own god according to his own nature.

At any rate, the prayer with which Euripides introduces us to Hippolytus defines the essential nature of the young man and of Artemis; he stands before a statue of the goddess offering her a diadem of flowers (*Hippolytus,* 73–87):

"For you, my mistress, I bring this garland which I have fashioned of flowers plucked from a virgin meadow untouched by iron implements, where no shepherd has ever presumed to graze his flock—

indeed a virgin field which bees frequent in spring. Purity waters it like a river stream for those who have as their lot the knowledge of virtue in everything, not through teaching but by their very nature. These are the ones for whom it is right to pluck these flowers, but those who are evil are forbidden. My dear lady, accept from my holy hand this garland to crown your golden hair. I alone of mortals have this privilege: I am with you and converse with you, for I hear your voice, although I do not see your face. As I have begun life in your grace, may I so keep it to the end."

CHAPTER 9

Apollo

As has been told in the previous chapter, Zeus mated with Leto and she conceived the twin gods, Artemis and Apollo. The *Homeric Hymn to Apollo* (number 3), which concentrates in its first part on the details of Apollo's birth, begins as follows (1–18):

I shall not forget far-shooting Apollo but remember him before whom the gods tremble when he comes to the home of Zeus. They all spring up from their seats as he approaches and draws his shining bow, and Leto alone remains beside Zeus, who delights in thunder. But then she unstrings his bow and closes his quiver and taking them from his mighty shoulders hangs them on a column of his father's house from a golden peg. She leads him to a chair and sits him down and his father welcomes his dear son by giving him nectar in a gold cup. Then the other deities sit down in their places and the lady Leto rejoices because she has borne a son who is a mighty archer. Rejoice, O blessed Leto, since you have borne splendid children, lord Apollo and Artemis who take delight in arrows; Artemis you bore in Ortygia and Apollo in rocky Delos as you leaned against the great and massive Cynthian hill, right next to the palm tree near the stream of the Inopus.

Leto had roamed far and wide in her search for a refuge where she might give birth to Apollo. The *Hymn* provides a long and impressive list of cities and islands visited by the goddess and then goes on to explain (45–161):

Leto approached these many places in labor with the far-shooting god in the hope that some land might want to make a home for her son. But they all trembled and were very much afraid and not one of

130

them, even the more rich, dared to receive the god Phoebus,[1] until lady Leto came to Delos and asked with winged words: "Delos, if you would like to be the home of my son, Phoebus Apollo, and to establish for him a rich temple—do not refuse, for no one else will come near you, as you will find out, and I do not think that you will be rich in cattle and sheep or bear harvests or grow plants in abundance—if you would then have a temple of Apollo, the far-shooter, all men will congregate here and bring hecatombs and the aroma of rich sacrifices will rise up incessantly and your inhabitants will be nourished by the hands of foreigners."

Thus she spoke; Delos rejoiced and said to her in answer: "Leto, most renowned daughter of great Coeus, I should receive your son, the lord who shoots from afar, with joy, for the terrible truth is that I have a bad reputation among men, and in this way I should become greatly esteemed. But I fear this prediction (and I shall not keep it from you): they say that Apollo will be someone of uncontrollable power, who will mightily lord it over both the immortal gods and mortal men on the fruitful earth. And so I am dreadfully afraid in the depths of my heart and soul that when he first looks upon the light of the sun he will be contemptuous of me (since I am an island that is rocky and barren) and overturn me with his feet and push me down into the depths of the sea where the surge of the great waves will rise mightily above me. And he will come to another land that pleases him where he will build his temple amidst groves of trees. But sea monsters will find their dens in me and black seals will make me their home without being disturbed, since I will be without human inhabitants. But if, O goddess, you would dare to swear to me a great oath that he will build here first of all a very beautiful temple to be an oracle for men, then after he has done this let him proceed to extend his prestige and build his sanctuaries among all mankind; for to be sure his wide renown will be great."

Thus Delos spoke. And Leto swore the great oath of the gods: "Now let Gaea and wide Uranus above bear witness and the flowing waters of the Styx (this is the greatest and most dread oath that there is for the blessed gods), in truth a fragrant altar and sacred precinct

---

[1] In later accounts Hera by various schemes tries to prevent Leto from finding a place to bear her children, and it is through fear of Hera that the whole earth rejects Leto's pleas. Hera also is said to have decreed that Leto's children could not be born in any place where the sun shone, so Poseidon kept the island of Delos (which in this early time was afloat) covered by his waves from the sun's rays during the birth of the twins.

of Apollo will be established here forever, and he will honor you above all."

When she had ended and sworn her oath, Delos rejoiced greatly in the birth of the lord who shoots from afar. But Leto for nine days and nine nights was racked by desperate pains in her labor. All the greatest of the goddesses were with her—Dione, Rhea, righteous Themis, and sea-moaning Amphitrite—and others too except for white-armed Hera; for she sat at home in the house of Zeus the cloud gatherer. Eileithyia, the goddess of pangs of childbirth, was the only one who had not heard of Leto's distress, for she sat on the heights of Olympus beneath golden clouds through the wiles of white-armed Hera, who kept her there because she was jealous that Leto of the beautiful hair was about to bear a strong and noble son.

But the goddesses on the well-inhabited island sent Iris away to fetch Eileithyia, promising her a great necklace strung with golden threads, over thirteen feet long. They ordered her to call Eileithyia away from white-armed Hera so that Hera might not be able to dissuade the goddess of childbirth from going. When Iris, swift-footed as the wind, heard her instructions, she ran on her way, and quickly traversed all the distance between. And when she came to sheer Olympus, home of the gods, immediately she called Eileithyia out of the house to the door and addressed her with winged words, telling her everything just as the goddesses who have their homes on Olympus had directed. And thus she moved Eileithyia to the depths of the heart in her breast, and like timid doves they proceeded on their journey. As soon as Eileithyia, goddess of the pangs of childbirth, came to Delos, the pains of labor took hold of Leto and she was anxious to give birth. And she threw her arms about the palm tree and sank on her knees in the soft meadow, and the earth beneath her smiled. The baby sprang forth to the light and all the goddesses gave a cry. There, O mighty Phoebus, the goddesses washed you with lovely water, holily and purely, and wrapped you in white swaddling clothes, splendid and new, fastened round about with a golden cord. And his mother did not nurse Apollo of the gold sword, but Themis from her immortal hands gave him nectar and delicious ambrosia. And Leto rejoiced because she had borne a strong son who carries a bow.

But after you had tasted the divine food, O Phoebus, then no longer could golden cords hold you in your restlessness nor bonds keep you confined, but they all were undone. And straightway Phoebus Apollo exclaimed to the immortal goddesses: "Let the lyre and curved bow be dear to my heart, and I shall prophesy to men the unerring will of Zeus." With these words Phoebus, the far-shooter with unshorn hair, strode on the ground that stretches far and wide; all the goddesses were amazed, and the whole of Delos blossomed laden with gold like the top of a mountain with woodland flowers, as she beheld the son of Zeus and Leto, in her joy that the god had chosen her among all islands and mainland sites to be his home, and loved her most of all in his heart.

And you yourself, O lord Apollo, far-shooter, of the silver bow, come at times to the steep Cynthian hill of Delos, and on other occasions you wander among other islands and other peoples; indeed many are your temples and wooded groves and every vantage point, highest peak of lofty mountains, and river flowing to the sea, is dear to you. But, O Phoebus, your heart is delighted most of all with Delos, where the long-robed Ionians gather with their children and their revered wives. In commemoration of you they will take pleasure in boxing and dancing and song when they celebrate your festival. And anyone who might encounter the Ionians while they are thus assembled together would say that they were immortal and ageless, for he would perceive grace in them all and be delighted in his heart as he beheld the men and the beautifully robed women, the swift ships, and the abundant possessions. In addition to this there would be the maidens who serve the far-shooting god, the Deliades, a great and wondrous sight, whose renown will never perish. They sing their hymn to Apollo first of all and then to Leto and Artemis, who delights in her arrows, and they remember the men and women of old and enchant the assembled throng with their songs.

The second part of the *Hymn* (which is considered by some scholars to have been originally a separate composition) deals with Pythian Apollo, the god of Delphi. It tells how he descended from Mt. Olympus and made his way through northern and central Greece, finally discovering the proper spot for the foundation of his oracle among mankind at Crisa under snow-capped Parnassus. Apollo laid out his temple and then slew a she-dragon by the fair-flowing stream nearby. The name of the site was henceforth called Pytho (and Apollo, the Pythian) because the rays of the sun made the monster rot. (The verb *pytho,* in Greek, means "I rot.") [2]

[2] In later accounts the dragon or serpent is sometimes masculine with the name Python (as in Ovid's story of Apollo and Daphne translated later).

Other accounts (mainly those of Aeschylus in the prologue to his *Eumenides* and of Euripides in a chorus from his *Iphigenia in Tauris*) provide additional although conflicting evidence for the early history of Delphi.[3] A cogent historical reconstruction maintains that originally (perhaps as early as 1500) the site was occupied by an oracle of the great mother-goddess of the Minoan-Mycenaean period, sometimes known as Ge-Themis. The slaying of the dragon (the traditional manifestation of a deity of earth), therefore, represents the subsequent conquest by Hellenic or Hellenized Apollo. The Omphalos, an archaic stone shaped like an egg, which was kept in the temple during the classical period, seems to confirm an early habitation of the site. Legend has it that this Omphalos (the word means navel) signified that Delphi actually occupied the physical center of the earth (certainly it was in many ways the spiritual center of the ancient world). Zeus was said to have released two eagles who flew from opposite ends of the earth and met exactly at the site of Apollo's sanctuary—a spot marked out for all to see by the stone Omphalos with two birds perched on either side.

For the murder of the dragon, Apollo was forced by Zeus to suffer exile in Thessaly for a period of nine years (his punishment presumably mirrors the religious dictates of ancient society). A festival (called the Stepteria) was celebrated every ninth year at Delphi; the festival was believed to commemorate these events in the early history of the sanctuary. The ritual went as follows: [4] a hut was constructed in an open space and a handsome and noble youth, especially chosen, played the role of Apollo in a pantomime that consisted of the actual burning of the hut by attendants carry-

---

It may also be described as the hostile opponent of Leto before the birth of her children. Some versions stress the great prowess of Apollo early in his life and career (as in the case of the wondrous childhood of Hermes and Heracles) to the extent of having him, while still a child, kill the dragon.

[3] A good scholarly survey of the problems with a reconstruction of the origins and procedures of the oracle is provided by H. W. Parke and D. E. W. Wormell, *The Delphic Oracle*, 2 vols. (Oxford: Basil Blackwell, 1956).

[4] The details of this festival apply to the ceremonies performed in the time of Plutarch (second century A.D.).

ing lighted torches. The group then fled on a prescribed journey to the Vale of Tempe in northern Thessaly where the boy was ritually purified and returned, crowned with Apollo's sacred laurel, amidst honors and ceremonies.

To return to the *Homeric Hymn,* the curious and interesting story that concludes the poem is worth paraphrasing. After he had established his sanctuary at Crisa, Apollo was concerned about recruiting attendants to his service. He noticed a ship passing, manned by Cretans from Cnossus, on its way to sandy Pylos. Phoebus Apollo, transformed into a dolphin, immediately sprang aboard. At first the men tried to throw the monster into the sea, but such was the havoc it created that they were awed to fearful submission. The ship, speeded on by a divine wind, would not obey the efforts of the crew to bring it to land. Finally after a lengthy course, Apollo led them to Crisa, where he leaped ashore and revealed himself as a god amidst a blaze of fiery brightness and splendor. He addressed the Cretan men ordering them to perform sacrifices and pray to him as Apollo Delphinius, and he led them to his sanctuary, accompanying them on the lyre as they chanted a paean in his honor. The *Hymn* ends with the god's prediction of the prestige and wealth that is to come for his sanctuary as he instructs the Cretan band, who are placed in charge.

The story links the early cult of Apollo with Crete, explains the epithet Delphinius in terms of the Greek word for dolphin and provides an etymology for Delphi as the name of the sanctuary. Apollo as the god of sailors and colonization (his oracle played a primary role as the religious impetus for the sending out of colonies) was worshiped under the title Delphinius.

The *Hymn* confirms the universality of the worship of Apollo and the importance of his outstanding cult centers at Delos and above all at Delphi. The sanctuary of Apollo at Delphi (excavated by the French) is representative of the nature and character of other panhellenic sites elsewhere.[5] The sacred area (temenos) was built on the lower slopes of Mt. Parnassus, about two thousand feet above the Corinthian Gulf. It is an awe-inspiring spot to this

---

[5] The other major panhellenic festivals were those at Olympia and Nemea, both in honor of Zeus, and the Isthmian games at Corinth, dedicated to Poseidon.

day. As one traces one's steps along the Sacred Way up to the great temple of the god, it is not too difficult to sense the feelings of reverence and exaltation that filled the heart and the soul of the ancient believer. The excavations have laid bare the foundations of the many and varied types of monuments along the winding path that were set up by individuals and city-states in honor and gratitude. Small temples (called treasuries) were a particularly imposing type of dedication, erected to house expensive and precious offerings. Among the major buildings of the sanctuary were a stadium, a theater, and, of course, the great temple of Apollo himself.

The Pythian games, which were celebrated every four years, included (after 582) both physical and intellectual competitions. Foot races, chariot races, musical, literary, and dramatic presentations were among the events that combined to make the festival second only to that of Zeus at Olympia. The sanctuary and the celebrations reflect much that is characteristic of Greek life and thought. The numerous dedications of triumphant victory in war mirror the narrow particularism and vehement rivalry among individual city-states, while the fact of the festivals themselves, to which *all* Greeks might come to honor gods common to their race, reveals the strivings toward a wider and more humane vision. Certainly the sense of competition in both athletics and the arts was vital to the Greek spirit. The importance of the physical as well as the aesthetic also suggests a fundamental duality made one and whole in the prowess and intellectuality of the god Apollo himself. The *Odes* of Pindar written to celebrate the glorious victors in the athletic competitions have proven to be among the most sublime lyrical outpourings of the human spirit. Physical excellence intensified a sense of physical beauty that inspired Greek artists to capture in sculpture and in painting the realism and idealism of the human form. The crystallization of the Doric, Ionic, and Corinthian orders of architecture in the construction of sublime and eternal architectural forms was also inspired by religious as well as civic devotion. The spiritual and human impetus to great feats of the body and the mind is among the most wondrous achievements wrought by the Greek religious experience.

The panhellenic sanctuary of Delphi was above all an oracle in the classical period. People from all over the Greek world (and even beyond) came to Apollo with questions of every sort, both personal and political. Herodotus's story of Solon and Croesus translated in Chapter 4 bears testimony to the prestige of the god, already well-established in the sixth century, and provides primary evidence for the nature and form of his responses as well.

The exact oracular procedures followed cannot be determined precisely. Not that they were secrets (like the details of dogma and ritual of the mystery religions), but because our sources are inadequate, often taking for granted an exact knowledge of Delphic practices. From all the evidence (literary, epigraphical, and archaeological) the following reconstruction may be pieced together with some degree of confidence. We cannot, however, always be sure that some of the rituals that are described by later authors belong to the earlier period. The assumption, rightly or wrongly, is that procedures became standardized early and remained essentially the same.

The Pythia (prophetess of Apollo) uttered the responses of the god. Her seat of prophecy was the tripod, a bowl supported by three metal legs. A tripod was a utensil of everyday life; a fire could be lit beneath or inside the bowl and it could be used for many obvious practical purposes. The tripod at Delphi was both a symbol and a source of divine prophetic power. Ancient pottery depicts Apollo himself seated on the bowl; his Pythian priestess who does likewise becomes his mouthpiece. In a frenzy of inspiration she utters her incoherent ravings. A priest or prophet nearby will transcribe them into intelligible prose or verse (usually dactylic hexameters) to be communicated to the enquirer.

Preliminary to the Pythia's response was the elicitation of the proper auspices for prophecy. A goat, which was subsequently sacrificed, had to display signs of trembling in all its limbs (the sprinkling of cold water on the animal was an inducement), just as later the Pythia would be racked in the same way during her prophetic ecstasies. The Pythia herself underwent certain initial ceremonies to ensure purification and inspiration, among them a ritual cleansing with the sacred water of the famous Castalian spring.

Some of our sources maintain that the Pythia's inspiration came from the vaporous outpourings from a chasm or cave and depict the priestess seated on the tripod above some such cleft or opening. Unfortunately, the west end of Apollo's temple (where she uttered her responses) is so badly preserved in the excavations that it cannot be reconstructed with certainty. Here in the innermost shrine (the adyton) are we to imagine stairs descending to a crypt below and perhaps as well a cleft (it would have to be small) from which vapors arose?

On the seventh day of each month (except for three months in the winter) the oracle was open.[6] The enquirer who came to the temple with his question for the god had to go through certain prescribed ceremonies that were in the nature of a fee.[7] First he must offer an expensive sacred cake on the altar outside the temple, and once he had entered he was required to sacrifice a sheep or goat, a portion of which went to the Delphians. After these preliminaries he could enter the holy of holies, the innermost shrine of the temple, where he would take his seat. The sequence depended on the prestige of the enquirer and the lot. The chief priest or prophet addressed the questions to the Pythia and, as we have already mentioned, interpreted her answers. The Pythia herself may have been in a room separated from the enquirers or perhaps (as we have seen) even in a crypt on a lower level. The adyton proper was decked with impressive religious objects: the sacred lyre and armor of Apollo, the Omphalos set upon a rectangular base, a golden statue of Apollo himself, and the tomb of Dionysus.[8]

---

[6] There is some evidence that the practice of oracular response by lot was also followed at Delphi, perhaps on other days of the month. A bean (possibly providing only a simple yes or no answer) would be drawn.

[7] One could enquire on one's own behalf or on the behalf of someone else. Often enquiries came from state representatives. Both the question and the answer were usually set down in writing.

[8] The omphalos found in the excavations and originally identified as the archaic sacred stone has subsequently been labeled a fraud. The tomb of Dionysus is a reminder that the god Dionysus was welcomed and worshiped alongside Apollo in the sanctuary (perhaps as early as the sixth century). The prophetic madness of the Pythia has much in common with Dionysiac frenzy.

According to tradition the Pythia was a young virgin in early times. But on one occasion an enquirer fell in love with one and seduced her. From then on only mature women (probably over fifty years old) could become priestesses; whatever the nature of their previous life (they could have been married), purity was required once they had been appointed for life to serve the god. At times one from among at least three women could be called upon to prophesy, and there were probably more in reserve. The first Pythia who is named Phemonoe (Prophetic Mind) is a poetic figure; we have from Herodotus the names of later ones (Aristonice and Periallus), historically much more real.

Inevitably one must wonder about the religious sincerity of the priests and the priestesses at Delphi. Was it all a fraud? There is no good reason to think so. Many peoples have believed in the possibility of god communicating with man in marvelous ways. And belief in a medium, a person with special mantic gifts, is by no means unique to the Greeks. The Pythia presumably was chosen because of her special nature and religious character—she was susceptible to supernatural callings. It is true that often the oracle was on the side of political expediency and that the ambiguity of the responses was notorious. Apollo's obscure epithet, Loxias, was thought to bear testimony to the difficult and devious nature of his replies. But one has only to glance at the life and career of a Socrates to realize the sincere and inner religious meaning that the intellectually devout is able to wrest from the material trappings of established institutions in any society. Socrates's friend Chaerephon went to Delphi to enquire who was the wisest of men. The answer was "Socrates," and when the philosopher was informed he could not rest until he had determined the meaning of the response and proved the god right. If we are to take the *Apology* at all literally and historically (and why not?), this message from Apollo provided a turning point for Socrates in his divine missionary-like zeal to make men think of eternal moral and ethical values in terms of their immortal souls.

The Pythia is the specific title given to the priestess of Apollo at Delphi. A more generic term for prophetess was Sibyl, and many Sibyls were found at various places in various periods in the ancient world. Originally the title was probably the proper name

(Sibylla) of an early prophetess. At any rate the Sibyls at Cumae
were among the most famous mediums of antiquity.

The description of the Cumaean Sibyl as she prophesies to
Aeneas helps us understand the nature of the communication of
a prophetess with her god, even though we must allow for poetic
imagination. This Sibyl is Deiphobe, daughter of Glaucus, priestess
of the temple of Phoebus Apollo and Diana. The innermost shrine
of the temple is a cavern from which the responses issue (Vergil,
Aeneid, 6.42–51):

> The vast end of the temple built in Euboean stone is cut out into
> a cavern; here are a hundred perforations in the rock, a hundred
> mouths from which the many utterances rush, the answers of the
> Sibyl. They had come to the threshold, when the virgin cried: "Now
> is the time to demand the oracles, the god, behold, the god!" She
> spoke these words in front of the doors and her countenance and
> color changed; her hair shook free, her bosom heaved, and her heart
> swelled in wild fury; she seemed of greater stature and her cries were
> not mortal as she was inspired by the breath of the god drawing nearer.

Later follows the metaphor of a wild horse trying to throw its
rider (77–82):

> Not yet willing to endure Apollo, the prophetess raged within the
> cavern in her frenzy, trying to shake the mighty god from her breast;
> all the more he wore out her ravings, mastering her wild heart and
> fashioning her to his will by constraint. Now the hundred mouths of
> the cavern opened wide of their own accord and bore the responses
> of the prophetess to the breezes.

After her prophecies are reported the metaphor is continued
(98–101):

> With such words the Cumaean Sibyl chants her terrifying riddles
> and from the innermost shrine of the cavern truth resounded enveloped
> in obscurity, as Apollo applied the reins to her raving and twisted
> the goad in her breast.

Earlier in the *Aeneid* (3.445) the seer Helenus had warned
Aeneas that the Sibyl wrote her prophecies on leaves that were

carefully arranged. But when the doors of the cavern were opened, these leaves were scattered by the wind so that those who had come for advice left without help and hated the dwelling of the Sibyl. Thus Aeneas asks (6.74–76) that the Sibyl utter the prophecies herself and not entrust them to the leaves. All this may be an oblique reference to some characteristic of the Sibylline books (collections of prophecies of the Sibyls that the Romans consulted) and the way in which they were interpreted.[9]

Ovid has the Sibyl tell Aeneas the story of her fate (*Metamorphoses* 14.132–153): [10]

Eternal life without end would have been given me if I had yielded my virginity to Phoebus Apollo who loved me. He hoped that I would and desired to bribe me with gifts, so he said: "Virgin maid of Cumae, choose what you desire; you will attain whatever it is." I picked up a heap of sand, showed it to him and asked for the vain wish that I might have as many birthdays as the individual grains in my hand. I forgot to ask for continuous youth along with the years. He would have given me both, long life and eternal youth, if I had succumbed to his love. But I despised Phoebus's gift and I remain unmarried. And now the happier time of youth is gone and sick old age has come with its feeble steps and I must endure it for a long time. For now as you see I have lived through seven generations; there remain for me to witness three hundred harvests, three hundred vintages [11] in order to equal in years the number of grains of sand. The time will be when length of days will have reduced me from my former stature and make me small and my limbs consumed by age will be diminished to the tiniest weight. And I shall not seem like one who was pleasing to a god and loved by him. Even Phoebus himself perhaps either will not recognize me or will deny that he once desired me; I shall be changed to such an extent that I shall be visible to no one but I shall be recognized by my voice; the Fates will leave me my voice.

Another version (Petronius, *Satyricon,* 48, 8) has it that the

[9] Vergil's works themselves were consulted as oracles in later times as the *Sortes Vergilianae.*

[10] The Sibyl's story appears to be late in its reminiscences of Cassandra and Tithonus.

[11] A total of one thousand years counting the generations (*saecula*) as one hundred years each.

tiny thing the Sibyl became was suspended in a bottle. Boys asked: "Sibyl, what do you want?" Her answer was: "I want to die."

Priam's daughter, Cassandra, a pathetic figure in the Trojan saga, was another of Apollo's loves and a prophetess. She agreed to give herself to Apollo and as a reward the god bestowed upon her the power of prophecy. But Cassandra changed her mind and rejected his advances. Apollo asked for one kiss and spat in her mouth. He did not revoke his gift but thereafter Cassandra was doomed to prophesy in vain, for no one would believe her.

Nearly all Apollo's affairs (and they are numerous) are in one way or another tragic; he is perhaps the most touchingly human and the most terrifyingly sublime of all the Greek gods. A notable exception is his success with Cyrene, an athletic nymph, with whom Apollo fell in love as he saw her wrestling with a lion. He whisked her away in his golden chariot to Libya, to the very site of the city that would be given her name, and she bore to him a son, Aristaeus.[12]

The story of Apollo's love for Daphne explains why the laurel (Daphne is the Greek word for laurel) was sacred to him. Ovid's version is the best known (*Metamorphoses,* 1.452–567):

Daphne, daughter of Peneus, was the first object of Apollo's love. It was not blind fate who brought this about, but Cupid's cruel anger. Apollo, flushed with pride at his victory over Python, had seen Cupid drawing his bow and taunted him: "What business of yours are brave men's arms, young fellow? The bow suits *my* shoulder; *I* can take unerring aim at wild animals or at my enemies. I it was who laid low proud Python, though he stretched over wide acres of ground, with uncounted arrows. You should be content with kindling the fires of love in some mortal with your torch; do not try to share my glory!" To him Cupid replied: "Although your arrows pierce every target, Apollo, mine will pierce you. Just as all animals yield to you, so your glory is inferior to mine." And as he spoke he quickly flew to the peak of shady Parnassus and from his quiver drew two arrows. Different were their functions, for the one, whose point was dull and leaden,

---

[12] This is the Aristaeus who will become the husband of Autonoe, and father of Actaeon; he too is the one who made advances to Eurydice. He is particularly linked with agricultural pursuits, especially bee keeping.

repelled love; the other, golden, bright, and sharp, aroused it. Cupid shot the leaden arrow at Peneus's daughter, while he pierced Apollo's inmost heart with the golden one.

Straightway Apollo loved, and Daphne ran even from the name of "lover." Companion of Diana, her joy was in the depths of the forests and the spoils of the chase; a headband kept her flowing hair in place. Many suitors courted her, while she cared not for love or marriage; a virgin she roamed the pathless woods. Her father often said, "My daughter, you owe me a son-in-law and grandchildren;" she, hating the marriage torch as if it were a disgrace, blushed and embraced her father saying, "Allow me, dearest father, always to be a virgin. Jupiter granted this to Diana." Peneus granted her prayer; but Daphne's beauty allowed her not to be as she desired and opposed her wish.

Apollo loved her; he saw her and desired to marry her. He hoped to achieve his desire, misled by his own oracle. Even as the stubble burns after the harvest, or a hedge catches fire from a careless traveler's embers, so the god burned with all-consuming fire and fueled his love with fruitless hope. He sees her hair lying unadorned upon her neck and says, "What if it were adorned?" He sees her flashing eyes like stars; he sees her lips—and merely to see is not enough. He praises her fingers, hands and arms, and shoulders half-bared; those parts which are covered he thinks more beautiful. Swifter than the wind Daphne runs from him and stays not to hear him call her back: "Stay, nymph! Stay, daughter of Peneus, I pray! I am not an enemy who pursue you. Stay, nymph! A lamb runs like this from the wolf, a hind from the lion, doves with fluttering wings from the eagle. Each kind runs from its enemy: love makes me pursue! Oh, take care you do not fall; let not the thorns scratch those legs that never should be marred and I be the cause of your hurt! Rough is the place where you run; run more slowly, I beg, and I will pursue more slowly. Yet consider who loves you; I am not a mountain peasant; I am not an uncouth shepherd who watches here his flocks and herds. Unheeding you know not whom you try to escape, and therefore do you run. I am lord of Delphi, of Claros, Tenedos, and royal Patara; Jupiter is my father! I show the future, the past, the present; through me came the harmony of lyre and song! Unerring are my arrows, yet one arrow is yet more unerring and has wounded my heart, before untouched. The healing art is mine; throughout the world am I called the Bringer of Help; the power of herbs is mine to command. Ah me! for no herb can remedy love; the art which heals all cannot heal its master!"

Even as he spoke Daphne fled from him and ran on in fear; then too she seemed lovely—the wind laid bare her body and her clothes fluttered as she ran and her hair streamed out behind. In flight she was yet more beautiful. Yet the young god could not bear to have his words of love go for nothing; driven on by love he followed at full speed. Even as a Gallic hound sees a hare in an empty field and pursues its prey as it runs for safety—the one seems just to be catching the quarry and expects each moment to have gripped it; with muzzle at full stretch it is hot on the other's tracks; the other hardly knows if it has been caught and avoids the snapping jaws—so the god chased the virgin: hope gave him speed; her speed came from fear. Yet the pursuer gains, helped by the wings of love; he gives her no respite; he presses hard upon her and his breath ruffles the hair upon her neck.

Now Daphne's strength was gone, drained by the effort of her flight, and pale she saw Peneus's waters. "Help me, Father," she cried, "if a river has power; change me and destroy my beauty which has proved too attractive!" Hardly had she finished her prayer when her limbs grew heavy and sluggish; thin bark envelops her soft breasts; her hair grows into leaves, her arms into branches. Her feet, which but now had run so swiftly, held fast with clinging roots. Her face was the tree's top; only her beauty remains.

Even in this form Apollo loves her; placing his hand on the trunk he felt the heart beating beneath the new-formed bark. Embracing the branches, as if they were human limbs, he kisses the wood: yet the wood shrinks from his kisses. "Since you cannot be my wife," said he, "you shall be my tree. Always you shall wreathe my hair, my lyre, my quiver. You shall accompany the Roman generals when the joyous Triumph hymn is sung and the long procession climbs the Capitol . . . and as my young locks have never been shorn, so may you forever be honored with green leaves!" Apollo's speech was done: the new-made Laurel nodded her assent and like a head bowed her topmost branches.

Apollo attempted to win Marpessa, the daughter of Evenus, a son of Ares. She was wooed as well by Idas, one of the Argonauts. He carried her off in his chariot against the will of her father, who unsuccessfully pursued the pair and in his anger and heartbreak committed suicide. Subsequently Apollo, who had also been a suitor for Marpessa's hand, stole her away from Idas in similar fashion. The outcome was that the two rivals met face to face in conflict over the girl. At this point Zeus intervened and ordered

Marpessa to choose between her lovers. She chose Idas because he was a mortal, for she was afraid that the undying and eternally handsome god Apollo would abandon her when she grew old.

Apollo was also susceptible to the love of boys. His devotion to Hyacinthus, a handsome Spartan youth from Amyclae, is well-known because of Ovid's account; the great god neglected his other duties in order to be in the company of his beloved (*Metamorphoses,* 10.174–219):

The Titan sun was almost midway between the night that had passed and the one to come—equidistant from both—when Apollo and the boy took off their garments and glistening with rich olive oil began to compete with the broad discus. Phoebus made the first throw. He poised the discus and hurled it so far into the air that the clouds were scattered by its course and only after a long time, because of its own sheer weight, did it fall back again to solid earth. His throw exhibited great skill combined with great strength. Straightway Hyacinthus under the impulse of his enthusiasm, heedless of all but the game, made a dash to pick up the discus. But it bounced back, O Hyacinthus, as it hit the hard earth and struck you full in the face.[13] The god turned as pale as the boy himself. He took up the limp body in his attempt to revive him, frantically staying the flow of blood from the sad wound and applying herbs to sustain the life that was ebbing away. His arts were to no avail; the wound was incurable. Just as when someone in a garden breaks off violets or brittle poppies or lilies that cling to their tawny stems, and suddenly these flowers droop and fade and cannot support the tops of their heavy heads which look down to the ground, so dropped the head of the dying boy and his neck, once strength was gone, gave way to the burden of its weight and sank on his shoulder. Phoebus cried: "You slip away, cheated of your youthful prime. Your wound that I look upon accuses me. You are my grief and my guilt—my own hand is branded with your death! I am the one who is responsible. But what fault was mine? Can it be called a fault to have played a game with you, to have loved you? O that I could give you my life as you deserve or die along with you. But we are bound by fate's decree. Yet you will always be with me, your name will cling to my lips, forever remembering. You will be my

---

[13] Ovid puts the story in the mouth of Orpheus. Other accounts have Zephyrus (the West Wind) deliberately divert the course of the discus because of his jealous love for Hyacinthus.

theme as I pluck my lyre and sing my songs and you, a new flower, will bear markings in imitation of my grief; and there will come a time when the bravest of heroes will be linked to this same flower and his name will be read on its petals." While Apollo spoke these words from his unerring lips, lo and behold, the blood that had poured upon the ground and stained the grass ceased to be blood and a flower arose, of a purple more brilliant than Tyrian dye; it took the shape of a lily and differed only in color, for lilies are silvery white. Apollo, although responsible for so honoring Hyacinthus, was not yet satisfied. The god himself inscribed his laments upon the petals and the flower bears the markings of the mournful letters *AI AI*.[14] Sparta was proud to claim Hyacinthus as her son and his glory endures to this day; every year a festival, the Hyacinthia, is celebrated in his honor with ceremonies ancient in their traditions.

Several of these stories emphasize Apollo's role as a god of medicine, which is taken over in large part by his son, Asclepius. And this brings us to Apollo's affair with Coronis, the last we shall tell. Coronis (in Ovid's version) was a lovely maiden from Larissa in Thessaly whom Apollo loved; in fact she was pregnant with his child. Unfortunately the raven, Apollo's bird, saw Coronis lying with a young Thessalian and told all to the god (*Metamorphoses, 2.600–634*):

When Apollo heard this charge against Coronis, the laurel wreath slipped from his head, his expression changed, and the color drained from his cheeks. As his heart burned with swollen rage, he took up his accustomed weapons and bent his bow to string it; with his unerring arrow he pierced the breast which he had so often embraced. She gave a groan as she was struck and, when she drew the shaft from her body, red blood welled up over her white limbs. She spoke: "You could have exacted this punishment and I have paid with my life, after I had borne your child; as it is, two of us die in one." With these words her life drained away with her blood; the chill of death crept over her lifeless corpse.

[14] These marks not only reproduce Apollo's moans of grief but they are also the initial letters of the name of the hero of the Trojan saga, the great Ajax (Greek, *Aias*), son of Telamon, as Apollo indicates in his prophetic words above. When Ajax committed suicide, the same flower, the hyacinth, sprang from his blood (Ovid, *Metamorphoses*, 13.391–398).

Too late, alas, the lover repented of his cruel punishment. He hated himself because he had listened to the charge against her and had been so inflamed. He hated his bow and his arrows and his hands that had so rashly shot them. He fondled her limp body and strove to thwart the Fates but his efforts came too late, and he applied his arts of healing to no avail. When he saw that his attempts were in vain and the pyre was being built and saw her limbs about to be burnt in the last flames, then truly (for it is forbidden that the cheeks of the gods be touched by tears) Apollo uttered groans that issued from the very depths of his heart, just as when a heifer sees the mallet that is poised above the right ear of her suckling calf shatter the hollow temples with a crashing blow. He poured perfumes upon her unfeeling breast, clasped her in his embrace, and performed the proper rites so just and yet unjust. Phoebus could not bear that his own seed be reduced to the same ashes, but he snatched his son out of the flames from the womb of his mother and brought him to the cave of the centaur Chiron. The raven, who hoped for a reward for the truth of his utterances, Apollo forbade evermore to be counted among white birds. Meanwhile the centaur was happy to have the divine infant as a foster child and delighted in such an honorable task.

Thus, like many another mythological figure, Asclepius was trained by the wise and gentle Chiron, and he learned his lessons well, particularly in the field of medicine. When he grew up, he refined this science and raised it by transforming it into a high and noble art (just as the Greeks themselves did in actual fact, particularly in the work of the great fifth century physician, Hippocrates, with his medical school at Cos). Asclepius married and had several children, among them doctors such as Machaon (in the *Iliad*), or more shadowy figures such as Hygeia (Health).

So skilled a physician was Asclepius (he was worshiped as both a hero and a god) that, when Hippolytus died, Artemis appealed to him to restore her devoted follower to life. Asclepius agreed and was successful but incurred the wrath of Zeus for such a disruption of nature. Asclepius was hurled into the lower world by a thunderbolt.

Apollo was enraged by the death of his son; he did not, of course, turn against Zeus, but killed the Cyclopes who had forged the lethal thunderbolt. Because of his crime he was sentenced (following once again the pattern of the human social order and its codes concerning blood-guilt) to live in exile for a year under the rule of Admetus, the benificent king of Pherae in Thessaly. Apollo felt kindly towards his master and when he found out that Admetus had only a short time to live, he went to the Moirae and induced them, with the help of wine, to allow the king a longer life. But they imposed the condition that someone must die in his place. Admetus, however, could find no one willing to give up his life for him (not even his aged parents) except his devoted wife, Alcestis; and he accepted her sacrifice. Euripides, in his fascinating and puzzling play, the *Alcestis* (it is difficult to find general agreement on the interpretation of this tragi-comedy), presents a touching and ironic portrait of the devoted wife. She is, however, rescued from the tomb in the nick of time by the good services of Heracles, who happened to be a visitor in the home of Admetus and wrestled with Death himself (*Thanatos*) for the life of Alcestis.

Apollo's skill as a musician has already been attested. But two stories which concentrate more exclusively upon the divine excellence of his art and the folly of inferiors who challenged it remain to be told. The first concerns Marsyas; he was the satyr (as we have previously mentioned) who picked up the flute after it had been invented and then discarded by Athena. The goddess gave Marsyas a thrashing for taking up her instrument, but he was not deterred by this and became so proficient that he dared to challenge the great Apollo himself to a contest. The condition imposed by the god was that the victor could do what he liked with the vanquished. Of course Apollo won and it was his decision to flay Marsyas alive. Ovid describes the anguish of the satyr (*Metamorphoses,* 6.385–400):

Marsyas cried out: "Why are you stripping me of my very self? Oh no, I am sorry; the flute is not worth this torture!" As he screamed, his skin was ripped off all his body and he was nothing but a gaping wound. Blood ran everywhere, his nerves were laid bare and exposed, and the pulse of his veins throbbed without any covering. One could make out clearly his pulsating entrails and the vital organs in his chest that lay revealed. The spirits of the countryside and the fauns who haunt the woods wept for him; and so did his brothers, the satyrs, and nymphs and all who tended woolly sheep and horned cattle on those mountains—and Olympus, dear to him now, wept as well. The fertile earth grew wet as she received and drank up the tears that fell and became soaked to the veins in her depths. She formed of them a stream which she sent up into the open air. From this source a river, the clearest in all Phrygia, rushes down between its sloping banks into the sea. And it bears the name of Marsyas.

Apollo was involved in another musical contest, this time with the god Pan, and King Midas of Phrygia acted as one of the judges (Ovid, *Metamorphoses,* 11.146–193):

Midas, in his loathing for riches, found a retreat in the woods and the country and worshiped Pan, the god who always inhabits mountain caves.[15] But his intelligence still remained limited, and his own foolish stupidity was going to harm him once again as it had before. There is a mountain, Tmolus, that rises high in its steep ascent with a lofty view to the sea; on one side it slopes down to Sardis, on another to the little town of Hypaepa. Here while he was singing his songs to his gentle nymphs and playing a dainty tune on his pipes made of reeds and wax, Pan dared to belittle the music of Apollo as compared with his own. And so he engaged in an unequal contest, with Tmolus as judge. This elderly judge took his seat on his own mountain and freed his ears of trees; only the oak remained to wreathe his dark hair and acorns hung down around his hollow temples. He turned his gaze upon the god of flocks and said: "Now the judge is ready."

---

[15] This is the famous Midas of the golden touch (Ovid's version of his story, *Metamorphoses,* 11.85–145 is well-known). Phrygian peasants had captured Silenus and brought him to their king, Midas, who recognized the satyr at once as a follower of Dionysus. So Midas returned Silenus to Dionysus and the god was so delighted that he gave the king the right to choose any gift he would like for himself. Midas foolishly asked that whatever he should touch might be turned into gold. At first Midas was delighted with his new power when he saw that he could transform everything into gleaming riches by the mere touch of his hand. But the blessing quickly became a curse, for he could no longer eat or drink; any morsel or drop that he brought to his lips became a solid mass of gold. Midas's greed turned to loathing; in some accounts even his beloved daughter was transformed. He begged the god's forgiveness for his sin and release from his accursed power. Dionysus took pity and ordered the king to cleanse himself of the remaining traces of his guilt in the source of the river Pactolus, near Sardis. Midas obeyed and the power of transforming things into gold passed from his person into the stream, whose sands forevermore were sands of gold.

Pan began to blow on his rustic pipes, and Midas, who happened to be nearby as he played, was charmed by the tune. When Pan had finished, Tmolus, the sacred god of the mountain, turned around to face Phoebus, and his forests followed the swing of his gaze. The golden head of Apollo was crowned with laurel from Parnassus, and his robe dyed in Tyrian purple trailed along the ground. His lyre was inlaid with precious stones and Indian ivory; he held it in his left hand with the plectrum in his right. His very stance was the stance of an artist. Then he played the strings with knowing hand; Tmolus was captivated by their sweetness and ordered Pan to concede that his pipes were inferior to the lyre. The judgment of the sacred mountain pleased everyone except Midas; he alone challenged the verdict and called it unjust. At this the god of Delos could not bear that such stupid ears retain their human shape. He made them longer, covered them with white shaggy hair, and made them flexible at their base so that they could be twitched. As for the rest of him he remained human; in this one respect alone he was changed, condemned to be endowed with the ears of a lumbering ass. Midas of course wanted to hide his vile shame and he attempted to do so by covering his head with a purple turban. But his barber, who regularly trimmed his long hair, saw his secret. He wanted to tell about what he had seen but he did not dare reveal Midas's disgrace. But it was impossible for him to keep quiet and so he stole away and dug a hole in the ground. Into it, with the earth removed, he murmured in a low whisper that his master had ass's ears. Then he filled the hole up again, covering up the indictment he had uttered and silently stole away from the scene. But a thick cluster of trembling reeds began to grow on the spot; in a year's time, as soon as they were full grown, they betrayed the barber's secret. For, as they swayed in the gentle south wind, they echoed the words that he had buried and revealed the truth about his master's ears.

Thus if one listened carefully to the wind whistling in the reeds he could hear the murmur of a whisper: "King Midas has ass's ears." [16]

The many and complex facets of Apollo's character have by now become evident. He sums up in his very nature the multiple con-

---

[16] Elements of folktale appear dominant in this story, particularly in the traditional depiction of the garrulous barber. In some versions Midas plays this same role in the contest between Apollo and Marsyas. Thus he favors the satyr against Apollo and suffers the same humiliation.

tradicions in the tragic dilemma of human existence. He is gentle and vehement, compassionate and ruthless, guilty and guiltless, healer and destroyer. The extremes of his emotion are everywhere apparent. He acts swiftly and surely against Tityus, who dared to attempt to rape Leto and for this crime was punished (as we shall see later) in the realm of Hades. Apollo shot down Tityus with his arrows; he acts in the same way against Niobe, only this time in conjunction with his sister, Artemis (the story has been told in the previous chapter). Can one ever forget Homer's terrifying picture of the god as he lays low the Greek forces at Troy with a plague in response to the appeal of his priest Chryses (*Iliad,* 1.43–52)?

Phoebus Apollo . . . came down from the peaks of Olympus, angered in his heart, wearing on his shoulders his bow and closed quiver. The arrows clashed on his shoulders as he moved in his rage, and he descended just like night. Then he sat down apart from the ships and shot one of his arrows; terrible was the clang made by his silver bow. First he attacked the mules and the swift hounds but then he let go his piercing shafts against the men themselves and struck them down. The funeral pyres with their corpses burned thick and fast.

Yet this very same god is the epitóme of Greek classical restraint, championing the proverbial Greek maxims, "Know thyself" and "Nothing too much." He knows by experience the dangers of excess. From a sea of blood and guilt, Apollo brings enlightenment, atonement, and purification, wherever he may be, but especially in his sanctuary at Delphi.

The origins of Apollo are obscure. It is not unlikely that he was in the beginning one of the gods brought into Greece by the northern invaders of 2000; if not, at any rate, he was probably very soon absorbed by them in the period 2000–1500. Some scholars imagine Apollo as originally the prototype of the Good Shepherd with his many protective powers and skills, especially those of music and medicine.[17] It is not until the classical period that he becomes a sun-god and usurps the power of Helius.

[17] Apollo's epithet, Lykios, was believed by the Greeks to refer to him as a "Wolf-god," whatever this may mean. Was he at one time a god of nomadic hunters, who later settled down?

For many Apollo appears as the most characteristically Greek god in the whole pantheon—a gloriously conceived anthropomorphic figure, perhaps epitomized best of all in the splendid depiction of the west pediment of the great temple of Zeus at Olympia. Here Apollo stood with calm intelligent strength, his head turned to one side, his arm upraised against the raging turmoil of the battle between the Centaurs and Lapiths by which he is surrounded.

By stressing certain aspects of his character, Apollo may be presented as the direct antithesis of the god Dionysus; in the persons of these two deities the rational (Apollonian) and irrational (Dionysiac) forces in human psychology, philosophy, and religion are pitted dramatically, one against the other. Some go so far as to maintain that it is Apollo who represents the true and essential nature of the Greek spirit as reflected in the poetry of Homer, in opposition to the later foreign intrusion of the mysticism of Dionysus. Whatever kernel of truth this view may hold, it is important to realize that by the sixth and fifth centuries Dionysus has become an integral part of Greek civilization. He is, therefore, in the classical period as characteristically Greek as Apollo, and *both* deities actually reflect a basic duality inherent in the Greek conception of things. We have already detected in Chapter 1 this same dichotomy in the union of the mystical and mathematical that was mirrored in the amalgamation of two cultures (the Nordic and the Mediterranean) in the Minoan and Mycenaean period.

Just as Apollo may be made a foil for Dionysus, so he may be used as a meaningful contrast to the figure of Christ. Each in his person and his life represents, physically and spiritually, two quite different concepts of meaning and purpose both in this world and in the next. Apollo and Christ do indeed afford a startling and revealing antithesis.

CHAPTER 10

Hermes

The *Homeric Hymn to Hermes* (number 4) tells the story of his birth with delightful charm and disarming candor.

Sing, O Muse, of the son of Zeus and Maia,[1] lord of Cyllene and Arcadia rich in flocks, the messenger of the gods and bringer of luck, whom Maia of the beautiful hair bore after uniting in love with Zeus. She in her modesty shunned the company of the blessed gods and lived within a shadowy cavè; here the son of Cronus joined in love with this nymph of the beautiful hair in the dark of night without the knowledge of immortal gods and mortal men, while sweet sleep held white-armed Hera fast. But when the will of Zeus had been accomplished and her tenth month was fixed in the heavens, she brought forth to the light a child and a remarkable thing was accomplished; for the child whom she bore was devious, winning in his cleverness, a robber, a driver of cattle, a guide of dreams, a spy in the night, a watcher at the door, who soon was about to make manifest renowned deeds among the immortal gods. Maia bore him on the fourth day of the month. He was born at dawn, by midday he was playing the lyre, and in the evening he stole the cattle of far-shooting Apollo. After he leaped forth from the immortal limbs of his mother he did not remain lying in his sacred cradle, but he sprang up and looked for the cattle of Apollo. When he crossed the threshold of the high-roofed cave, he found a tortoise and obtained boundless pleasure from it. Indeed Hermes was the very first to make the tortoise a minstrel. He happened to meet it in the very entranceway, waddling along as it ate the luxurious grass in front of the dwelling. When Zeus's son, the bringer of luck, saw it he laughed and said at once: "Already a very good omen for me; I shall not be scornful. Greetings; what a delight you appear to me, lovely in shape, graceful in movement, and a good

[1] Maia was one of the Pleiades, the daughters of Atlas and Pleione.

dinner companion. Where did you, a tortoise living in the mountains, get this speckled shell that you have on, a beautiful plaything? Come, I shall take you and bring you inside. You will be of some use to me and I shall do you no dishonor. You will be the very first to be an advantage to me, but a better one inside, since the out-of-doors is harmful to you. For while you are alive you will be a charm against evil witchcraft, but if you were dead, then you would make very beautiful music.[2] Thus he spoke and lifted the tortoise in both hands and went back into his dwelling carrying the lovely plaything. Then he cut up the mountain-dwelling tortoise and scooped out its life-marrow with a knife of gray iron. As swiftly as a thought darts through the mind of a man whose cares come thick and fast or as a twinkle flashes from the eye, thus glorious Hermes devised his plan and carried it out simultaneously. He cut to size stocks of reeds, extended them across the back and through the tortoise shell and fastened them securely. In his ingenuity he stretched the hide of an ox all around and affixed two arms to which he attached a bridge and then he extended seven tuneful strings of sheep gut. When he had finished he took up the lovely plaything and tried it by striking successive notes. It resounded in startling fashion under his hand, and the god accompanied his playing with a beautiful song, improvising at random just as young men exchange banter on a festive occasion. He sang about Zeus, the son of Cronus, Maia with the beautiful sandals, and their talk in the intimacy of their love, and proclaimed aloud the renown of his birth. He honored too the handmaids of the nymph, her splendid home, and the tripods and the ample cauldrons it contained.

He sang of these things but his heart was set on other pursuits. He took the hollow lyre and set it down in his sacred cradle; for he craved for meat and leaped out of the fragrant hall to a place where he could watch, since he was devising in his heart sheer trickery such as men who are thieves plan in the dead of black night.

Helius, the sun, with his horses and chariot was descending to earth and the stream of ocean, when Hermes came hurrying to the shady mountains of Pieria where the immortal cattle of the blessed gods have their home, grazing on the lovely untouched meadows. The sharp-sighted son of Maia, the slayer of Argus, cut off from the herd fifty loud-bellowing cattle and drove them over sandy ground reversing their tracks as they wandered. For he did not forget his skill at trickery and made their hoofs go backwards, the front ones last and the

---

[2] The live tortoise was believed to be a tabu against harm and sorcery.

back ones first; he himself walked straight ahead. For he quickly wove sandals of wicker by the sea sand, a wonderful achievement, beyond description and belief; he combined twigs of myrtle and tamarisk, and fastened together bundles of the freshly sprouting wood which he bound, leaves and all, under his feet as light sandals. The glorious slayer of Argus made them so, as he left Pieria, improvising since he was hastening over a long journey.[3]

But an old man, who was working in a luxuriant vineyard, noticed him coming to the plain through Onchestus with its beds of grass. The renowned son of Maia spoke to him first: "Old man, digging about with stooped shoulders, you will indeed have much wine when all these vines bear fruit, if you listen to me and earnestly remember in your heart to be blind to what you have seen and deaf to what you have heard and to keep silent, since nothing of your own has been harmed in any way." He said only this much and pushed the sturdy head of cattle on together. Glorious Hermes drove them over many shady mountains, echoing hollows, and flowery plains.

The greater part of divine night, his dark helper, was over, and the break of day that calls men to work was soon coming on, and bright Selene, daughter of lord Pallas, the son of Megamedes, had climbed to a new watchpost, when the strong son of Zeus drove the broad-browed cattle of Phoebus Apollo to the river Alpheus. They were unwearied when they came to the lofty shelter and the watering places that faced the splendid meadow. Then, when he had fed the loud-bellowing cattle well on fodder, he drove them all together into the shelter, as they ate lotus and marsh plants covered with dew. He gathered together a quantity of wood and pursued with diligent passion the skill of producing fire. He took a good branch of laurel and trimmed it with his knife, and in the palm of his hand he grasped a piece of wood; and the hot breath of fire rose up.[4] Indeed Hermes was the very first to invent fire-sticks and fire. He took many dry sticks which he left as they were and heaped them up together in a pit in the ground. The flame shone forth, sending afar a great blaze of burning fire.

While the power of renowned Hephaestus was kindling the fire,

[3] Hermes as he walks along makes the cattle walk backwards. Thus the hoof prints of the cattle will seem to be going towards the meadow and not out of it. Hermes's own tracks will be obscured by his sandals.

[4] The text is corrupt at this point; apparently Hermes used the laurel branch to rub against a piece of wood grasped in the palm of his hand, thus creating the friction to produce fire.

Hermes dragged outside near the blaze two horned cattle bellowing, for much strength went with him. He threw them both panting upon their backs onto the ground and bore down upon them. Rolling them over, he pierced through their life's marrow; he followed up this work with more, cutting the meat rich in fat, and spearing the pieces with wooden spits, and roasted all together, the flesh, choice parts from the black, and the bowels that enclosed the back blood. He laid these pieces on the ground and stretched the hides on a rugged rock and thus still even now they are there continually long afterward, despite the interval of time. Next Hermes in the joy of his heart whisked the rich bundles away to a smooth flat rock and divided them into twelve portions that he allotted, adding a choice piece to each, making it wholly an honorable offering. Then glorious Hermes longed for the sacred meat of the sacrifice, for the sweet aroma made him weak, even though he was an immortal. But his noble heart did not yield, although his desire was overwhelming to gulp the offering down his holy throat.[5] But he quickly put the fat and all the meat away in the cave with its lofty roof, setting them up high as a testimony of his recent childhood theft, and he gathered up wood for the fire and destroyed all the hoofs and the heads in the blaze. When the god had accomplished all that he had to do he threw his sandals into the deep-eddying stream of the Alpheus; he put out the embers and hid the black ashes in the sand. Thus he spent the whole night as the beautiful light of Selene shone down on him. Swiftly then he went back to the divine peaks of Cyllene and encountered no one at all (neither blessed gods nor mortal men) on his long journey, and dogs did not bark.

And Hermes, the luck-bringer, son of Zeus, slipped sideways past the lock into his house, like the gust of a breeze in autumn, and went directly through the cave to his luxurious inner chamber, stepping gently on his feet, for he did not make a sound as he walked over the threshold. Glorious Hermes quickly got into his cradle and wrapped the blankets about his shoulders like a helpless baby and lay toying with his fingers at the covers on his knees; at his left side he kept his beloved lyre close by his hand.

But the god did not escape the notice of his goddess mother, who spoke to him: "You devious rogue, in your cloak of shameless guile, where in the world have you come from in the nighttime? Now I am

---

[5] Hermes offers a portion to each of the twelve gods and, according to sacrificial ritual, he as one of them must not eat his portion or those of the other gods but merely savor the aroma.

convinced that either Apollo, son of Leto, by his own hands will drag you with your sides bound fast right out the door or you will prowl about the valleys, a robber and a cheat. Be gone then! Your father begat you as a great trouble for mortal men and immortal gods!"

Hermes answered her with clever words: "Mother, why do you throw this up at me, as to a helpless child who knows in his heart very little of evil, a fearful baby, frightened of his mother's chiding? But I shall set upon whatever work is best to provide for me and you together. We two shall not endure to stay here in this place alone, as you bid, apart from the immortals without gifts and prayers. Better all our days to live among the gods, rich and full in wealth and plenty, than to sit at home in the shadows of this cave! And I shall go after divine honor just as Apollo has. And if my father does not give it to me, to be sure I shall take my honor myself (and I can do it) which is to be the prince of thieves. And if the glorious son of Leto search me out I think he will meet with another even greater loss. For I shall go to Pytho and break right into his great house and I shall seize from within plenty of very beautiful tripods and bowls and gold and gleaming iron and an abundance of clothing. You will be able to see it all, if you like." Thus they conversed with each other, the son of aegis-bearing Zeus and the lady Maia.

As Eos, the early-born, sprang up from the deep-flowing waters of Ocean bringing light to mortals, Apollo was on his way and came to Onchestus, a very lovely grove sacred to loud-roaring Poseidon, who surrounds the earth. There he found the old man, who on the path within was feeding the animal that guarded his vineyard. The glorious son of Leto spoke to him first: "Old man, who pull the weeds and briars of grassy Onchestus, I have come here from Pieria looking for some cattle, all cows, all with curved horns, from my herd. The bull, which was black, fed alone away from the others; keen-eyed dogs followed behind, four of them, of one mind like humans. They were left behind, both the dogs and the bull—a truly amazing feat. But just as the sun had set, the cows went out of the soft meadow away from the sweet pasture. Tell me this, old fellow, have you seen a man passing along the road with these cows?"

The old man spoke to him in answer: "My friend, it is hard to tell everything that one sees with one's eyes. For many wayfarers pass along the road; some travel intent on much evil, others on much good. To know each of them is difficult. But, good sir, the whole day long until the sun set I was digging about in my fruitful vineyard and I thought that I noticed a child, I do not know for sure; whoever the child was, he, an infant, tended the fine-horned cattle and he had a stick. He walked from side to side as he drove them backwards and kept their heads facing him."

Thus the old man spoke; after Apollo had heard his tale, he went more quickly on his way. He noticed a bird with its wings extended and from this sign knew at once that the thief was a child born of Zeus, the son of Cronus. So lord Apollo, the son of Zeus, eagerly hastened to holy Pylos in search of his shambling cows, his broad shoulders enshrouded in a dark cloud. When the archer-god spied the tracks he cried out: "Why, indeed, here is a great marvel that I see with my eyes. These are definitely the tracks of straight-horned cows, but they are turned backwards towards the asphodel meadow. And these here are not the prints of a man or a woman or gray wolves or bears or lions; nor are they, I expect, those of a shaggy-maned centaur or whoever makes such monstrous strides with its swift feet. On this side of the road the tracks are strange but on the other side they are even stranger." With these words lord Apollo, the son of Zeus, hurried on and came to the forest-clad mountain of Cyllene and the deeply shaded cave in the rock where the immortal nymph bore the child of Zeus, the son of Cronus. A lovely odor pervaded the sacred mountain and many sheep ranged about grazing on the grass. Then the archer-god, Apollo himself, hurried over the stone threshold down into the shadowy cave.

When the son of Zeus and Maia perceived that far-shooting Apollo was in a rage about his cattle, he sank down into his fragrant blankets. As ashes hide a bed of embers on logs of wood, so Hermes buried himself in his covers when he saw the archer-god. He huddled head and hands and feet tightly together as though just bathed and ready for sweet sleep, but he was really wide awake, and under his arm he held his lyre. The son of Zeus and Leto knew both the beautiful mountain nymph and her dear son, the little boy enveloped in craft and deceit, and he was not fooled. He looked in every corner of the great house. He took a shining key and opened three chambers full of nectar and lovely ambrosia, and in them too lay stored much silver and gold and many of the nymph's garments, rich in their hues of purple and silver, such as are found in the sacred dwellings of the blessed gods. Then, when the son of Leto had searched every nook in the great house, he addressed glorious Hermes with these words: "You, O child, lying in the cradle, inform me about my cattle and be quick or soon the two of us will be at variance and it will not be nice. For I shall take hold of you and hurl you down into the terrible and irrevocable darkness of murky Tartarus; neither your mother or your father will release you to the light above but you will wander under the earth, a leader among little men." Hermes answered him craftily: "Son of Leto, what are these harsh words you have spoken? Have you come here looking for cattle of the field? I have not seen a thing, I do not know a thing, I have not heard a word from anyone. I cannot give information nor can I win the reward. Do I look like a man of brawn, a cattle rustler? That is not my line; I am interested rather in other things: sleep, milk from my mother's breast, baby blankets about my shoulders, and warm baths. Do not let anyone find out how this dispute came about. It would indeed be a source of great amazement among the immortals that a newborn child should bring cattle of the field right through the front door of his house. What you say is pretty unlikely. I was born yesterday, my feet are tender and the ground is rough beneath them. If you wish, I shall swear a great oath by the head of my father; I pledge a vow that I am not guilty myself and that I have not seen anyone else who might be the one who stole your cows—whatever cows are, for I have only heard about them now for the first time." Thus Hermes spoke, his eyes twinkling and his brows raised as he looked all about, and gave a long whistle to show how fruitless he considered Apollo's quest.

But far-shooting Apollo laughed softly and spoke to him: "Oh splendid, you sly-hearted cheat; from the way that you talk I am sure that many a time you have broken into the better homes during the night and reduced more than one poor fellow to extremities by grabbing everything in the house without a sound. And you will distress many a shepherd in the mountain glens, when greedy after meat you come upon their herds of cattle and their woolly sheep. But come on now, if you do not want to sleep your last and longest sleep, get down out of your cradle, you comrade of black night. For this then you will have as your prerogative hereafter among the gods: you will be called forevermore the prince of thieves."

Thus Phoebus Apollo spoke and took hold of the child to carry him away. At that very moment the mighty slayer of Argus had an idea; as he was being lifted in Apollo's hands he let go an omen, a bold and servile messenger from his belly, a hearty blast and right after it he gave a violent sneeze. And when Apollo heard, he dropped glorious Hermes out of his hands to the ground and sat in front of him; even though he was eager to be on his way he spoke with taunting words: "Rest assured, son of Zeus and Maia, in your swaddling clothes, with these omens I shall find my sturdy head of cattle by and by, and furthermore you will lead the way." Thus he spoke and Cyllenian Hermes gave a start and jumped up pushing the blanket away from both his ears with his hands, and clutching it around his shoulders he cried out: "Where are you taking me, O far-shooter, most vehement of all the gods? Is it because of the cows that you are so angry and assault me? Oh, oh, how I wish the whole breed of cattle might perish! For I did not steal your cows and I have not seen anyone else who has —whatever cows are, for I have only heard about them now for the first time. Let us have the case decided before Zeus, the son of Cronus."

Thus as they quarreled over each and every point, Hermes, the shepherd, and the splendid son of Leto remained divided. The latter spoke the truth and not without justice seized upon glorious Hermes because of the cattle; on the other hand the Cyllenian wished to deceive the god of the silver bow by tricks and by arguments. But when he in his ingenuity found his opponent equally resourceful, he hastened to walk over the sandy plain in front with the son of Zeus and Leto behind. Quickly these two very beautiful children of Zeus came to their father, the son of Cronus, on the top of fragrant Olympus. For there the scales of justice lay ready for them both. A happy throng occupied snow-capped Olympus, for the deathless gods had assembled with the coming of golden-throned Dawn.

Hermes and Apollo of the silver bow stood before the knees of Zeus and he who thunders from on high spoke to his glorious son with the question: "Phoebus, where did you capture this delightful booty, a child newly born who has the appearance of a herald? This is a serious business that has come before the assembly of the gods."

Then lord Apollo, the archer, replied: "O father, you, who scoff at me for being the only one who is fond of booty, are now going to hear a tale that is irrefutable. After journeying for a long time in the nountains of Cyllene I found a child, this out and out robber here; as sharp a rogue I have not seen either among gods or men who cheat their fellows on earth. He stole my cows from the meadow in the evening and proceeded to drive them along the shore of the loud-sounding sea making directly for Pylos. The tracks were of two kinds, strange and marvelous, the work of a clever spirit. The black dust retained the prints of the cattle and showed them leading into the asphodel meadow. But this rogue I have here, an inexplicable wonder, did not cross the sandy ground on his feet or on his hands; but by some other means he smeared the marks of his amazing course as though someone had walked on oak saplings. As long as he followed the cattle across the sandy ground the tracks stood out very clearly in the dust. But when he had covered the great stretch of sand, his own course and that of the cows quickly became inperceptible on the hard ground. But a mortal man noticed him driving the herd of cattle straight for Pylos. When he had quietly penned up the cows and slyly confused his homeward trail by zigzagging this way and that, he nestled down in his cradle, obscure as the black night, within the darkness of the gloomy cave, and not even the keen eye of an eagle would have spied him. He kept rubbing his eyes with his hands as he devised his subtle wiles, and he himself immediately maintained without a qualm: 'I have not seen a thing, I do not know a thing, and I have not heard a word from anyone. I cannot give information nor can I win the reward.' "

Thus Phoebus Apollo spoke and then sat down. And Hermes in answer told his side of the story, directing his words pointedly to Zeus, the ruler of all the gods. "Father Zeus, I shall indeed tell you the truth. For I am honest and I do not know how to lie. He came to our house today as the sun was just rising, in search of his shambling cattle. He brought none of the blessed gods as witnesses or observers and with great violence ordered me to confess; he made many threats of hurling me down into wide Tartarus, since he is in the full bloom of his glorious prime, while I was born only yesterday (as he too well knows himself) and do not look at all like a cattle rustler or a man of brawn. Believe me (for you claim to be my own dear father too) that I did not drive his cows home nor even cross the threshold— so may I prosper, what I tell you is the truth. I deeply revere Helius and the other gods; I love you and I am in dread of this fellow here. You know yourself that I am not guilty—I shall swear a great oath besides—no, by these beautifully ornate portals of the gods. Somehow, someday, I will pay him back, even though he is mighty, for his ruthless behavior. Be on the side of a defenseless baby." Thus the Cyllenian slayer of Argus spoke, blinking in innocence, and he held his baby blanket on his shoulder and would not let it go.

Zeus gave a great laugh as he saw the devious child knowingly and cleverly make his denials about the cattle. He ordered the two of them to act in accord and make a search; Hermes, in his role of guide, was to lead without any malicious intent and point out the spot where he had hidden away the mighty herd of cattle. The son of Cronus nodded his head and splendid Hermes obeyed, for the will of aegis-bearing Zeus easily persuaded him.

The two very beautiful sons of Zeus hastened together to sandy Pylos, crossed the river Alpheus, and came to the lofty cave where the animals were sheltered in the nighttime. Then, while Hermes went into the rocky cavern and drove the mighty head of cattle out into the light, the son of Leto looked away and noticed the cowhides on the steep rock and immediately asked glorious Hermes: "O sly rogue, how were you, a new born infant, able to skin two cows? I do indeed wonder at the strength that will be yours in the future; there is no need to wait for you to grow up, O Cyllenian, son of Maia."

Thus he spoke and fashioned with his hands strong bonds out of willow.[6] But they grew up in that very spot on the ground under their feet, and twisting and twining together they readily covered over all the cattle of the field at the will of the trickster Hermes, while Apollo watched in wonder. Then the mighty slayer of Argus looked away to the ground, fire flashing from his eyes, in his desire to get out of his predicament. But it was very easy for him, just as he wished, to soften the far-shooting son of Leto, even though he was strong; he took up the lyre in his left hand and tried it by striking successive notes. The instrument resounded in startling fashion and Phoebus Apollo laughed with delight as the lovely strains of the heavenly music pierced his being, and sweet yearning took hold of his heart while he listened. The son of Maia, growing bold as he played so beautifully, took his stand on the left side of Phoebus Apollo and began to sing a song—and lovely was the ensuing sound of his voice—fashioned on the theme of the immortal gods and the dark earth and how in the beginning they came into being and how each was allotted his due. Of the gods he honored first of all Mnemosyne, mother of the Muses, for she honored him, the son of Maia, as one of her own. The splendid son of Zeus paid tribute to each of the other immortal gods according to age and birth, mentioning all in the proper order, as he played the lyre on his arm. But an irresistible desire took hold of Apollo, heart and soul, and he spoke up, interrupting with winged words: "Cattle slayer, contriver, busy worker, good companion at a feast, this skill of yours is worth fifty cows—I think that we soon will be peacefully reconciled. Come now, tell me, ingenious son of Maia, was this wonderful achievement yours from birth or did one of the gods or mortal men give you this noble gift and teach you inspired song? For this newly uttered sound I hear is wonderful, and I tell you that no one, either man or god who dwells on Olympus, has ever before known it, except you, you trickster, son of Zeus and Maia. What skill! What Muse's art! What salve for sorrow and despair! It gives the choice of three blessings together all at once: joy and love and sweet sleep. I follow the Olympian Muses who delight in dancing, the swelling beat of music and the lovely tune of flutes, yet never have I been as thrilled by such clever delights as these at young men's feasts.

---

[6] Presumably Apollo intends to bind Hermes or the cows.

I marvel, O son of Zeus, at your charming playing. Since you know such a glorious skill, even though you are little, sit down, my boy, and listen to what I intend. For you yourself and your mother will have renown among the immortal gods. And I shall vow this to you truly: By this spear of cornel wood, I shall make you a renowned and prosperous guide among the immortal gods, and I shall give you splendid gifts and to the end I shall not deceive you."

And Hermes answered him with clever words: "Archer-god, your questions are well-considered; I do not begrudge your taking up my art. You will know it this very day. I want us to be friends, alike in what we think and what we say. You know all things in your heart, for you, son of Zeus, sit in the first place among the immortals, brave and strong. Zeus in his wisdom loves you as he rightly should and has granted you splendid gifts. And they say that you have acquired from the mouth of Zeus honors and, O archer-god, from him too every kind of divine oracular power. I know then that you are very rich in these gifts and you have only to make the choice of whatever you desire to learn. So, since your heart is set on playing the lyre, sing and play and be merry; accept this gift from me and you, my dear friend, bestow glory upon me. With this clear-voiced companion in your hands,[7] sing beautifully and well, knowing the art of proper presentation. Then with confidence take it to a luxurious feast and lovely dance and splendid revel, a thing of joy both night and day. Whoever makes demands of it after acquiring skill and knowledge is informed with sounds of every sort to delight the mind, for it is played by gentle familiarity and refuses to respond to toilsome drudgery. And whoever through lack of skill is from the first vehement in his demands is answered in return with wild and empty notes that clang upon the air. But you have only to make the choice of learning whatever you desire. To you I give this gift, splendid son of Zeus, and we both will feed the cattle of the field on the pastures in the mountain and the plain where horses also graze. Even you, shrewd bargainer that you are, ought not to be violently angry."

With these words he held out the lyre and Phoebus Apollo accepted it. And he entrusted to Hermes the shining whip that he had and put him in charge of cattle herds. The son of Maia accepted this with joy.

---

[7] The lyre is referred to as a beloved companion, that is, a girl friend, and in the next few lines Hermes sustains the metaphor, which reads naturally in Greek, but is difficult to render in English. Thus she will accompany Apollo to the feast and the dance and she will behave and respond as a beloved should, only if she is treated in the right way.

The far-shooting lord Apollo, the glorious son of Leto, took the lyre in his left hand and tried it by striking successive notes. It sounded in startling fashion at his touch and the god sang a beautiful song in accompaniment.

Afterwards the two of them turned the cows out into the sacred meadow and they, the very beautiful sons of Zeus, hastened back to snow-capped Olympus, all the while taking delight in the lyre. Zeus in his wisdom was pleased and united them both in friendship; Hermes has loved the son of Leto steadfastly and he still does even now, as is evident from the pledges made when Hermes entrusted his lovely lyre to the archer-god and Apollo took it on his arm and learned how to play. But Hermes himself fashioned another instrument and learned another art, producing the sound of pipes [8] that are heard from afar.[9]

This hymn to Hermes has been much admired for its content and its art. Shelley himself was one of its translators. The glib and playful treatment of both Hermes and Apollo is often labeled typically Greek.[10] It is typically Greek only if we mean by typical *one* of the many brilliant facets of Hellenic genius and a suggestion of the wide variety and scope in the conception of deity. Sincere profundity in religion and philosophy are as typically Greek as wit and facetious sophistication.

Many of Hermes's characteristics and powers are evident from the poem. The Greek admiration for cleverness is readily apparent; it is this same admiration that condones the more dubious traits in the hero Odysseus. Anthropomorphism and liberalism are both pushed to their extremes in the depiction of the god, Hermes, as a thief, and in the implication that thieves too must have their patron deity.

The similarities between Hermes and Apollo are equally obvious. They share many attributes; the origins of both gods were probably rooted in the same pastoral society of shepherds with

[8] These are shepherds' pipes of reed also called Pan pipes, since they are often said to be the invention of the god Pan. Hermes sometimes is named as the father of Pan, whom he resembles in certain respects.

[9] The *Hymn* is translated here virtually complete. The last section (513–580) adds little to the artistic whole and is extremely difficult both in its text and its meaning.

[10] The tone and mood is not unlike the story of Aphrodite, Ares and Hephaestus in Homer.

their interest in flocks, music, and fertility. The two are alike in appearance, splendid examples of vigorous and handsome masculinity. But Hermes is the younger and more boyish, the idealization and patron of youths in their late teens; his statue belonged in every gymnasium.

Hermes is perhaps best known as the divine messenger, often delivering the dictates of Zeus himself; as such he wears a traveler's hat (petasus) and carries a herald's wand (caduceus), which sometimes bears two snakes entwined. Wings may be depicted on his hat, his sandals, and even his wand. Thus he is also the god of travelers and roads. As the guide of souls (*psychopompos*) to the realm of Hades under the earth, he provides another important function, which reminds us once again of his fertility connections.

Statues of Hermes, called Herms (singular, Herm), are common in the ancient world; they also suggest fertility. They were square pillars with the male genitals depicted; on top of each pillar was the head of Hermes. These phallic statues probably marked areas that were regarded as sacred or designated, at least originally, the bounds of one's home or property, hopefully to bring prosperity and luck. At any rate, in the classical period a Herm might be found in front of any house.

A historical incident in the fifth century concerning Herms warns us to be wary of facile generalizations about Greek religious attitudes. In 415, on the eve of the great Athenian expedition against Sicily, the Herms of the city of Athens were mutilated during the night. The incident was very likely the exploit of a gang of spirited men flushed with wine, perhaps members of one of the political clubs. Alcibiades, the general who most ardently advocated the Sicilian expedition, was incriminated; nevertheless he was allowed to set sail. The religious scandal that ensued became a political football, and in his absence Alcibiades was charged not only with the mutilation of the Herms, but also with the parody and desecration of the Eleusinian mysteries of Demeter in a private home. He refused to face charges and fled to Sparta. As far as we can know he was not guilty, at least of the sacrilege of the disfigurement of the Herms. Arrests were made and charges brought, but the whole episode remains to this day shrouded in mystery. This seems quite a fuss over statues of a god whom some

would describe as essentially amoral or nonmoral in conception.[11]
The incident itself occurred in a period fraught with Sophistic
scepticism, agnosticism, and atheism, echoed by the questions posed
in the plays of the iconoclast Euripides.

Among the adventures and affairs of Hermes his union with
Aphrodite is important for their offspring, Hermaphroditus, whose
story is told by Ovid (*Metamorphoses,* 4.285–388):

Let me tell you how the fountain Salmacis got its bad reputation
and why it weakens and softens limbs touched by its enervating
waters.[12] This power of the fountain is very well known; the reason
for it lies hidden. A son was born to Mercury and Venus and Naiads
brought him up in the cave of Mount Ida. You could recognize his
mother and father in his beauty and his name also came from them.
As soon as he reached the age of fifteen, he left the hills of his homeland. When he had departed from Ida, the mountain that had nur-
tured him, he took delight in wandering over unknown lands and
in seeing unknown rivers; his zeal made the hardships easy. Then
he came to the cities of the Lycians and their neighbors the Carians.
There he saw a pool of water that was clear to the very bottom with
no marsh reeds, barren sedge, or sharp-pointed rushes to be seen.
The water was transparent in its clarity and the edge of the pool was
surrounded by fresh turf and grass that was always green. A nymph
lived here; but one who was not inclined to hunt and not in the
habit of bending the bow or contending in the chase. She alone of the
Naiads was unknown to swift Diana. It is told that her sisters often
said to her: "Salmacis, take up a javelin or a lovely painted quiver;
vary the routine of your idleness with the strenuous exercise of the
hunt." She did not take up the javelin or the lovely painted quiver
and did not vary the routine of her idleness with the strenuous exercise of the hunt. Instead she would only bathe her beautiful limbs in
her fountain and often comb out her hair with a comb of boxwood
and look into the water to see what suited her best; and then she
would clothe her body in a transparent garment and recline on the
soft leaves or the soft grass. Often she picked flowers. She was picking

[11] Alcibiades was charged with mimicking the mysteries of Demeter at
Eleusis and revealing them to his companions in his home; he wore a robe
like that of the Hierophant when he shows the holy secrets to the initiates.

[12] In context Alcithoe is telling the story to her sisters. The spring
Salmacis was at Halicarnassus.

flowers as it happened when she saw the boy, Hermaphroditus. As soon as she saw him she desired to have him. Although she was anxious to hasten to him she did not approach until she had composed herself, arranged her garment, and assumed a beautiful countenance. When she looked as attractive as she ought, she began to speak as follows: "Lovely boy, most worthy to be believed a god; if you are a god, you could be Cupid; if a mortal, blessed are your parents, and happy your brother and fortunate indeed your sister, if you have one, and the nurse who gave you her breast. But by far the most blessed of all is your betrothed, if she exists, whom you will consider worthy of marriage. If you have such a beloved, let my passion be satisfied in secret but if you do not, let me be the one and let us go together to our marriage bed." With this the nymph was silent. A blush flared up in the boy's face, for he did not know what love was. But the flush of red was becoming; his was the color of apples hanging in a sunny orchard or of tinted marble or of the moon, a reddish glow suffusing its whiteness when bronze resounds with vain attempts to help in its eclipse.[13] To the nymph, as she demanded without end at least the kisses of a sister and brought her hand to touch his ivory neck, he exclaimed: "Are you going to stop or am I to flee and leave you and your abode?" Salmacis was frightened and replied: "I give over to you free access to this place, my guest and friend." She turned her step away and pretended to depart, though still with a glance back. She concealed herself in a hidden grove of bushes dropping on bended knees. But he moved on the deserted grass from one spot to another, confident that he was not being watched and gradually dipped his feet as far as the ankles in the playful waves. Taken by the feel of the captivating waters, with no delay he threw off the soft clothes from his young body. Then to be sure Salmacis was transfixed, enflamed with desire for his naked form. Her eyes too were ablaze just as if the radiant orb of the glowing sun were reflected in their mirror. With difficulty she endured the agony of waiting, with difficulty she held off the attainment of her joy. Now she longed to embrace him, now in her frenzy she could hardly contain herself. He swiftly struck his hollow palms against his sides and plunged into the pool and as he moved one arm and then the other he glistened in the limpid water like an ivory statue or a lily that one has encased within clear glass. The nymph cried out: "I have won, he is mine!" And she flung off all her clothes and threw herself into the middle of the waves. She held him as he fought and snatched kisses as he struggled; she grasped

---

[13] A reference to superstitious rituals in the time of an eclipse.

him with her hands and touched his chest and now from this side and now from that enveloped the youth. Finally she encircled him as he strove against her in his desire to escape, like a serpent which the king of birds has seized and carried aloft, and which as it hangs binds the eagle's head and feet and with its tail enfolds the spreading wings, even as ivy is wont to weave around tall trunks of trees or as the octopus grabs and holds fast its enemy in the deep with tentacles let loose on every side. Hermaphroditus, the descendant of Atlas, endured and denied the nymph the joys that she had hoped for. She continued her efforts and her whole body clung to him as though they were glued together. She cried: "You may fight, cruel villain, but you will not escape. May the gods so ordain and may we never be separated in future time, you from me nor me from you." The gods accepted her prayer. For their two bodies were joined together as they entwined and in appearance they were made one, just as when one grafts branches on a tree and sees them unite in their growth and become mature together; thus, when their limbs united in their close embrace, they were no longer two but a single form that could not be called girl or boy and appeared at the same time neither one, but both. And so, when he saw that the limpid waters into which he had gone as a man had made him half a man and in them his limbs had become enfeebled, Hermaphroditus stretched out his hands and prayed in a voice that was no longer masculine: "Father and mother, grant this gift to your son who bears both your names. Let whatever man who enters this pool come out half a man and let him suddenly become soft when touched by its waves." Both parents were moved and granted the wish of their child who was now of a double nature and they tainted the waters with this foul power.

Statutes of Hermaphroditus and hermaphrodites became common in the fourth century and in the following Hellenistic period, when Greek masters strove to vary their repertoires with fascinating and brilliantly executed studies in the realistic, and erotic, and bizarre.

CHAPTER 11

Dionysus, Pan, Echo, and Narcissus

The traditional account of the birth of Dionysus runs as follows.[1] Semele, the daughter of Cadmus, was loved by Zeus.[2] Hera found out and was jealous; she appeared to Semele disguised as an old woman and convinced her rival that she should ask her lover to appear in the full magnificence of his divinity. Semele first persuaded Zeus to swear that he would grant whatever she might ask of him and then she made known her demand. Zeus was unwilling but was forced to comply, and Semele was consumed by the splendor of his person and the fire of his lightning flash. But the unborn child was not destroyed in the conflagration; Zeus saved his son from the ashes of his mother and sewed him up in his own thigh, from which the god was born again at the proper time.[3]

---

[1] He is often also called Bacchus by the Greeks, the name for the god that the Romans preferred.

[2] The genealogy for the house of Cadmus is given on p. 267. For the purposes of this chapter it is necessary to know the following relationships and to realize that Pentheus and Dionysus are cousins:

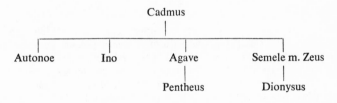

Cadmus

Autonoe   Ino   Agave   Semele m. Zeus

Pentheus   Dionysus

[3] The word *dithyrambos,* an epithet of Dionysus and the name of a type of choral poetry that included hymns sung in the god's honor, was in ancient times believed to refer etymologically to his double birth.

Various nurses are associated with the infant Dionysus, in particular certain nymphs of Nysa, a mountain of legendary fame located in various parts of the ancient world. Ino, Semele's sister, is also commonly singled out as one who cared for the god when he was a baby.[4] When Dionysus reached manhood he carried the message of his worship far and wide, bringing happiness and prosperity to those who would listen and madness and death to those who dared oppose. The tradition of his arrival in Greece makes clear that he is a late-comer to the Olympian pantheon. His origins lie in Thrace (note, for example, the Dionysiac aspects of Orpheus's missionary zeal) and ultimately Phrygia. The date for the introduction of the worship of the god into Hellas is difficult to establish; it probably belongs to the obscure period of transition after the Dorian invasion (ca. 1100). But it is foolhardy to be dogmatic, especially if the recent decipherment of a Linear B tablet is correct and the name Dionysus (whether that of the god or not) can be identified as belonging to the Mycenaean Age.

Dionysus is basically a god of vegetation in general, and in particular of the vine, the grape, and the making and drinking of wine. But his person and his teaching eventually embrace very much more. The best source for the profound meaning of his worship and its most universal implications is found in Euripides's tragedy the *Bacchae* (*The Bacchic Women*). Whatever one makes of his depiction of the rites in a literal sense, the sublimity and terror of the spiritual message for all mankind are inescapable and timeless. The play opens with Dionysus himself who has come in anger to Thebes; his mother's integrity has been questioned by her own relatives and the magnitude and power of his very godhead have been challenged and repudiated (1–63).

[4] The career of Ino is extremely confusing because of multiple versions of her story. She was the second wife of Athamas (whom we shall meet again in the Argonautic saga) and they had two sons, Learchus and Melicertes. Hera, angry with Ino because of her care for Dionysus, drove both Ino and her husband, Athamas, mad. Athamas killed his son, Learchus, and pursued Ino, who escaped with their other son, Melicertes, in her arms. She leaped from a cliff into the sea and was transformed into the sea-goddess, Leucothea; Melicertes also became deified under the new name of Palaemon.

I, Dionysus, the son of Zeus, have come to this land of the Thebans;
my mother, Semele, the daughter of Cadmus, gave birth to me, delivered by a fiery blast of lightning. I am here by the stream of Dirce
and the waters of the Ismenus, not as a god but in disguise as a man.
I see here near the palace the shrine that commemorates my mother,
who was struck dead by the lightning blast and the ruins of her home,
smoldering yet from the flame of Zeus's fire that still lives—the everlasting evidence of Hera's outrage against my mother. I am pleased
with Cadmus for setting this area off as a holy sanctuary dedicated
to his daughter, and I have enclosed it round about with the fresh
greenery of the clustering vine.

I left the fertile plains of gold in Lydia and Phrygia and made my
way across the sunny plateaus of Persia, the walled towns of Bactria,
the grim land of the Medes, rich Arabia, and the entire coast of Asia
Minor, where Hellenes and non-Hellenes live together in teeming
cities with beautiful towers. After having led my Bacchic dance and
established my mysteries in these places, I have come to this city of the
Hellenes first.

And I have raised the Bacchic cry and clothed my followers in the
fawn skin and put into their hands the thyrsus—my ivy-covered shaft
—here in Thebes first of all of Greece, because my mother's sisters
claim (as least of all they should) that I, Dionysus, was not begotten
of Zeus, but that Semele became pregnant by some mortal man
and through the clever instigations of Cadmus laid the blame on Zeus;
they gloatingly proclaim that Zeus because of her deception struck
her dead. And so these same sisters I have stung with madness, driving
them from their homes, and they inhabit Mt. Cithaeron bereft of sense;
I have compelled them to take up the symbols of my rituals, and all
the women of Thebes—the entire female population—I have driven
from their homes in frenzy. Together with the daughters of Cadmus
they sit out in the open air on rocks under the evergreens. For although it does not wish to, this city must learn full well that it is still
not completely schooled in my Bacchic mysteries and I must defend
the reputation of my mother, Semele, by showing myself to mortals as
the god whom she bore to Zeus.

Cadmus has handed over the prerogatives of his royal power to
his daughter's son, Pentheus, who fights against my godhead, thrusting
me aside in sacrifices and never mentioning my name in prayers. Therefore I shall show myself as a god to him and all the Thebans. And
when I have settled matters here I shall move on to another place
and reveal myself. If the city of Thebes in anger tries by force to

drive the Bacchae down from the mountains, I shall join them in their madness as their war commander. This then is why I have assumed a mortal form and changed myself into the likeness of a man.

O you women whom I have taken as companions of my journey from foreign lands, leaving the Lydian mountain Tmolus far behind, come raise the tambourines, invented by the great mother, Rhea, and by me, and native to the land of Phrygia.

Come and surround the royal palace of Pentheus and beat out your din so that the city of Cadmus may see. I will go to my Bacchae on the slopes of Cithaeron, where they are, and join with them in their dances.

The chorus of women that follows reveals the exultant spirit and mystic aura surrounding the celebration of their god's mysteries (64–167):

Leaving Asia and holy Mt. Tmolus, we run in sweet pain and lovely weariness with ecstatic Bacchic cries in the wake of the roaring god, Dionysus. Let everyone, indoors or out, keep his respectful distance and hold his tongue in sacred silence as we sing the appointed hymn to Bacchus.

Happy is the one who, blessed with the knowledge of the divine mysteries, leads a life of ritual purity and joins the holy group of revellers, heart and soul, as they honor their god Bacchus in the mountains with holy ceremonies of purification. He participates in mysteries ordained by the great mother, Cybele herself, as he follows his god, Dionysus, brandishing a thyrsus.

Run, run, Bacchae, bringing the roaring god, Dionysus, son of a god, out of the Phrygian mountains to the spacious streets of Hellas.

Once when his mother carried him in her womb, the lightning bolt flew from the hand of Zeus and she brought the child forth prematurely with the pains of a labor forced on her too soon, and she gave up her life in the fiery blast. Immediately Zeus, the son of Cronus, took up the child and enclosed him in the secret recess of his thigh with fastenings of gold, and hid him from Hera thus in a second womb.

When the Fates had so decreed, Zeus bore the bull-horned god and wreathed his head with a crown of serpents, and so the Maenads hunt and catch wild snakes and twine them in their hair.

O Thebes, crown yourself with ivy, burst forth luxuriant in verdant leaves and lovely berries; join the Bacchic frenzy with branches torn from trees of oak or fir and consecrate your cloak of dappled fawnskin with white tufts of purest wool. Be reverent with the violent powers of the thyrsus. Straightway the whole land will dance its way (whoever leads the sacred group represents the roaring god himself) to the mountain, to the mountain where the crowd of women waits, driven from their labors at the loom by the maddening sting of Dionysus.

O secret chamber on Crete, holy cavern where Zeus was born attended by the Curetes! Here the Corybantes [5] with their three-crested helmets invented this drum of hide stretched tight for us and their ecstatic revels mingled its tense beat with the sweet alluring breath of the Phrygian flutes, and they put it into the hand of mother Rhea, so that she might beat an accompaniment to the cries of her Bacchic women. The satyrs in their frenzy took up the drum from the mother-goddess and added it to the music of their dances during the festivities in which Dionysus delights.

How sweet it is in the mountains, when, out of the rushing throng, the priest of the roaring god falls to the ground in his quest for blood and with a joyful cry devours the raw flesh of the slaughtered goat. The plain flows with milk and wine and the nectar of bees; but the Bacchic celebrant runs on, brandishing his pine torch and the flame streams behind with smoke as sweet as Syrian frankincense. He urges on the wandering band with shouts and renews their frenzied dancing, as his delicate locks toss in the breeze. Amidst the frantic shouts is heard his thunderous cry: "Run, run, Bacchae, you the pride of Tmolus with its streams of gold. Celebrate the god Dionysus on your thundering drums, honoring this deity of joy with Phrygian cries and shouts of ecstasy, while the melodious and holy flute sounds its sacred accompaniment as you throng, to the mountain, to the mountain."

Every Bacchanal runs and leaps in joy, just like a foal that frisks beside her mother in the pasture.

The scene that follows (215–313) is fraught with tragic humor and bitter irony. Cadmus (retired king) and Tiresias (priest of the traditional religion) welcome the new god with motives that are startling in their blatant pragmatism. These two old men, experienced realists, present in their joyous rejuvenation just the right foil for the introduction of the doomed Pentheus, who in his mortal blindness dares to challenge the god.

---

[5] The Curetes, as we have seen, are the attendants of Rhea, who hid the cries of the infant Zeus from his father, Cronus. In this passage Euripides associates them with the Corybantes, the ministers of Cybele.

Tiresias: Who attends at the gate? Summon Cadmus from the house, the son of Agenor, who came from Sidonia and fortified the city of the Thebans. Let someone go and announce that Tiresias wants to see him. He already knows for what reason I have come. I made an agreement with him, even though I am old and he is even older, to make myself a thyrsus, wear a fawn skin, and crown my head with shoots of ivy.

Cadmus: My dearest friend, I knew your voice from inside the palace, and recognized the wise words of a wise man. I have come ready with the paraphernalia of the god. For since Dionysus, who has revealed himself to men as a god, is the son of my daughter, I must do everything in my power to magnify his greatness. Where should we go to join the others in the dance, shaking our gray heads in ecstasy? Tell me, an old man, Tiresias, for you are old too and wise. I shall never grow tired by night or by day as I strike the ground with my thyrsus. It will be a sweet pleasure to forget that we are old.

Tiresias: You experience the same sensations as I do, for I feel young again and I shall attempt the dance.

Cadmus: Shall we not proceed to the mountain by chariot?

Tiresias: No, the god would not have as appropriate an honor.

Cadmus: I will lead the way for you, two old men together.

Tiresias: The god will lead the two of us there without any difficulty.

Cadmus: Are we to be the only men of the city to dance in honor of Bacchus?

Tiresias: We are the only ones who think the way one should; the others are wrong and perverse.

Cadmus: We delay too long; give me your hand.

Tiresias: Here it is, take hold and join our hands together.

Cadmus: Being a mere mortal, I am not scornful of the gods.

Tiresias: About the gods we have no new wise speculations. The ancestral beliefs which we hold are as old as time and they cannot be destroyed by any argument or clever subtlety invented by profound minds. How could I help being ashamed, one will ask, as I am about to join in the dance, at my age, with an ivy wreath on my head? The god does not discriminate whether young or old must dance in his honor, but he desires to be esteemed by all alike and wishes his glory to be magnified, making no distinctions whatsoever.

Cadmus: Since you are blind, Tiresias, I shall be a prophet for you, and tell you what I see. Pentheus, the son of Echion, to whom I have given my royal power in Thebes, comes in haste to this palace. How excited he is; what news has he to tell us?

Pentheus: Although I happened to have been away from Thebes, I have heard of the new evils that beset the city; the women have abandoned our homes on the pretense of Bacchic rites, and gad about on the dark mountainside honoring by their dances the new god, Dionysus, whoever he is. Bowls full of wine stand in the midst of each group, and they sneak away one by one to solitary places where they satisfy the lust of males. Their pretext is that they are Maenad priestesses, but they put Aphrodite ahead of Bacchus. All those I have caught are kept safe with their hands tied by guards in the state prison. The others, who still roam on the mountain, I shall hunt out including my own mother, Agave, and her sisters, Ino and Autone, the mother of Actaeon. And when I have bound them fast in iron chains, I shall soon put an end to this evil Bacchism.

They say too that a stranger has come here from Lydia, some wizard and sorcerer, with scented hair and golden curls, who has the wine-dark charms of Aphrodite in his eyes. He spends both night and day in the company of young girls, enticing them with his Bacchic mysteries. If I catch him here in my palace, I'll cut off his head and put a stop to his thyrsus-pounding and head-tossing. That fellow is the one who claims that Dionysus is a god, who was once sewn up in the thigh of Zeus, when he was in fact destroyed by the fiery blast of lightning along with his mother, because she lied and said that Zeus had been her husband. Whoever this stranger may be, does he not deserve to hang for such hybris?

But here is another miracle—I see the prophet Tiresias in a dappled fawnskin and my mother's father, a very funny sight, playing the Bacchant with a wand of fennel reed. I refuse, sir, to stand by and see you behave so senselessly in your old age. You are my grandfather, won't you toss away your garland of ivy and rid your hand of the thyrsus?

You persuaded him, Tiresias. Why? By introducing this new divinity among mankind do you hope that he will afford you an additional source of income from your omens and your sacrifices? If it were not for your gray hairs, you would not escape being bound and imprisoned along with the Bacchae for initiating evil rites.

As far as women are concerned, I maintain that whenever the gleam of wine is in their feasts, there can be nothing further that is wholesome in their ceremonies.

Chorus: What sacrilege, sir! Do you not have respect for the gods and Cadmus, who sowed the seeds from which the earth-born men arose; are you the son of Echion, who was one of them, bringing shame on your own family?

Tiresias: Whenever a wise man takes a good theme for his argument, it is no great task to speak well. You seem to be a man of intelligence from the glibness of your tongue, but there is no good sense in your words. A headstrong man who is powerful and eloquent proves to be a bad citizen because he is wanting in intelligence.

This new divinity whom you laugh at—I could not begin to tell you how great he will become throughout Hellas. For, young man, there are two divinities who are foremost among mankind: the goddess Demeter (she is the Earth, call her whatever name you wish), who provides mortals with the nourishment of dry and solid food; and Dionysus, the son of Semele, who comes next and who discovered and brought to men the moist and liquid drink of the grape, as a counterpart to the food of Demeter. His blessing releases suffering mortals from their pain, when they take their fill of the juice of the vine; he gives them sleep and makes them forget their daily troubles, and they have no other cure for their cares. He, being a god, is poured in libation to the gods, and so through him mankind receives all good things.

Do you laugh at the legend that this god was sewn up in the thigh of Zeus? I shall instruct you in its basic truths. When Zeus snatched Dionysus out of the fiery lightning and brought the infant to Olympus as a god, Hera wished to throw him out of heaven, but Zeus opposed her and devised a plan that was worthy of a god. He broke off a portion of the sky that surrounds the earth and formed a likeness of the child and gave it to Hera as a hostage; he gave the real Dionysus to nymphs to bring up. Thus Zeus saved the child from the jealousy of Hera. Now the word for hostage [*homeros*] and the word for thigh [*meros*] are similar, and so men confused the two words and instead of telling how the likeness of the god was given as a hostage to Hera, they invented the story about Zeus's thigh.

And this god is a prophet, for Bacchic frenzy and madness hold a great deal of prophetic power. Whenever the god enters wholly into a person's body, he makes the one possessed capable of foretelling the future. This god also shares in a certain portion of the power of Ares, for when an army, in battle dress and formation, flees through fear before ever lifting a spear, this too is a madness that comes from Dionysus. Furthermore, some day you will see him on the rocks of Delphi, leaping over the plateau between the two mountain peaks amid torches, brandishing and striking the Bacchic wand, a great god throughout Hellas.

Pentheus, believe me: do not be overly confident that force is all-powerful in human affairs, and do not think that you are wise when the attitude that you hold is sick. Receive the god into the city, pour him libations, crown your head, and celebrate his worship.

Tiresias goes on to argue that self-control is a question of one's own nature and character. Dionysus is not immoral but rather nonmoral; he cannot corrupt a chaste woman or restrain a lewd one. Besides, the god (just like Pentheus himself) is happy to receive the homage of his people. Cadmus reinforces Tiresias's appeal for reason and control. Pentheus must be sick to defy the god, and, even if he were right and Dionysus were an impostor, he should be willing to compromise and lie in order to save the honor of Semele and the whole family.

But Pentheus is young and adamant; he accuses his peers of folly and madness and directs one of his henchmen to smash Tiresias's place of augury (after all has he not himself desecrated his own priestly office?) and to hunt down the effeminate foreigner who has corrupted the women of Thebes.

A guard brings in the exotic stranger who has come with his new religion (in reality he is Dionysus himself), and Euripides presents the first of three interviews between the god and the man which turn upon the ironic reversal of their positions. Pentheus, believing himself triumphant, is gradually but inevitably caught in the net prepared for him by Dionysus. The calm and sure strength of the god plays beautifully upon the neurotic impulsiveness of the mortal (433–518):

Guard: Pentheus, here we are, having hunted the quarry you sent us after, and our efforts have not been unsuccessful. But we found this wild beast tame—he did not attempt to flee, but gave me his hands willingly; he did not even turn pale but kept the flush of wine in his cheeks. With a smile he bade me tie him up and lead him away and waited for me, thus making my task easy. I was taken aback and said: "O stranger, I do not arrest you of my own free will but at the orders of Pentheus who has sent me."

About the Bacchae whom you seized and bound and imprisoned—they are freed and have gone and dance about the glens calling on their god, Bacchus. The bands fell from their feet of their own accord and the locks on the door gave way untouched by mortal hands. This man who has come to our city of Thebes is full of many miraculous wonders—and what else will happen is your concern, not mine.

Pentheus: Untie his hands. Now that he is in my trap, he is not nimble enough to escape me. Well, stranger, you are not unattractive physically—at least to women—and, after all, your purpose in Thebes is to lure them. Your flowing locks that ripple down your cheeks so seductively prove that you are no wrestler. Your fair complexion too is cultivated by avoiding the rays of the sun and by keeping in the shade so that you may ensnare Aphrodite with your beauty. But first tell me where you come from.

Dionysus: I can answer your question easily and simply. I am sure you have heard of the mountain of Tmolus with its flowers.

Pentheus: I have; its range encircles the city of Sardis.

Dionysus: I am from there; Lydia is my fatherland.

Pentheus: How is it that you bring these mysteries of yours to Hellas?

Dionysus: Dionysus, the son of Zeus, has directed me.

Pentheus: Is there a Zeus in Lydia who begets new gods?

Dionysus: No, he is the same Zeus who wedded Semele here in Thebes.

Pentheus: Did he bend you to his service, an apparition in the night, or did you really see him with your own eyes?

Dionysus: We saw each other face to face and he gave me his secrets.

Pentheus: What is the nature of these secrets of yours?

Dionysus: It is not lawful for the uninitiated to know them.

Pentheus: What advantage is there for those who do participate?

Dionysus: It is not right for you to learn this, but the knowledge is worth much.

Pentheus: Your answer is clever, designed to make me want to hear more.

Dionysus: An impious man is abhorred by the god and his mysteries.

Pentheus: You say that you saw the god clearly; well then what did he look like?

Dionysus: He looked as he wished; I had no control over his appearance.

Pentheus: Once again you have sidetracked me cleverly with an answer that says nothing.

Dionysus: The words of the wise seem foolish to the ignorant.

Pentheus: Have you come here first of all to introduce your god?

Dionysus: Every foreigner already dances his rituals.

Pentheus: Yes, of course, for they are far inferior to Hellenes.

Dionysus: Customs differ, but in these rituals the foreigners are superior.

Pentheus: Do you perform your holy rites by night or by day?

Dionysus: By night for the most part; darkness adds to the solemnity.

Pentheus: For women it is treacherous and corrupt.

Dionysus: One may find, if one looks for it, shameful behavior by daylight too.

Pentheus: You must be punished for your evil sophistries.

Dionysus: And you for your ignorance and blasphemy against the god.

Pentheus: How bold our Bacchant is and how facile his retorts.

Dionysus: What punishment must I suffer? What terrible thing will you do to me?

Pentheus: First I shall cut your pretty locks.

Dionysus: My hair is sacred; it belongs to the god.

Pentheus: Hand over your thyrsus then.

Dionysus: Take it away from me yourself. I carry it for Dionysus; it really belongs to him.

Pentheus: I shall close you up in a prison.

Dionysus: The god himself will free me, whenever I wish.

Pentheus: As you call on him when you take your stand amidst your Bacchic women, I suppose.

Dionysus: Even now he is near at hand and sees what I endure.

Pentheus: Where is he? My eyes cannot see him.

Dionysus: Here with me. But you in your blasphemy cannot perceive him for yourself.

Pentheus: Guards, seize him; he is making a fool of me and of all Thebes.

Dionysus: I tell you not to bind me—I am the sane one, not you.

Pentheus: My orders are to bind you and I have the upper hand.

Dionysus: You do not know what life you live, what you do, or who you are.

Pentheus: I am Pentheus, the son of Agave; my father is Echion.

Dionysus: Your name, Pentheus, which means sorrow, is appropriate for the doom that will be yours.

Pentheus: Get out of here—Guards, imprison him in the neighboring stables where he may find his secret darkness—do your mystic dances there. And the women you have brought with you as accomplices in your evil I shall either keep as slaves myself to work the loom or sell them to others—this will stop their hands from beating out their din on tambourines.

Dionysus: I will go, since what is not destined to be, I am not destined to suffer. But Dionysus, who you say does not exist, will exact vengeance for your insolence. For as you do me wrong and imprison me, you do the same to him.

Pentheus confidently follows Dionysus into the prison. But the god miraculously frees himself amidst fire, earthquake, and the destruction of the entire palace. He explains to the chorus how he has escaped from Pentheus's evil clutches, maintaining throughout the fiction of his role as the god's disciple. Quite typically Dionysus is associated with or transformed into an animal (616–636):

Dionysus: I have made a fool of Pentheus—he thought that he was tying me up, yet he did not so much as lay a finger on me but fed on empty hopes. In the chamber where he led me a prisoner, he found a bull. It was the knees and hoofs of this animal that he tried to bind, fuming and raging, biting his lips, and dripping with sweat, while I sat calmly close by his side and watched. In this crisis Bacchus arrived and made the building shake and raised a flame up from the tomb of his mother. When Pentheus saw it he thought that the palace was on fire and rushed this way and that, calling on the servants to bring water. The entire household joined in the work but their toil was for nothing. Pentheus, thinking that I had got away, abandoned his efforts and seized a dark sword and rushed inside the palace in pursuit. Then Dionysus created an illusion in the courtyard (I am telling you what I believe happened) and Pentheus made a dash for it, jabbing and stabbing at the sunny air, imagining he was butchering me. Bacchus had even greater humiliation for him than this. He razed the whole palace to the ground; all lies shattered for him as he beholds the most bitter results of my imprisonment. Worn out and exhausted, he has dropped his sword; a mere mortal, he dared to go to battle against a god.

As Dionysus coolly finishes his account, Pentheus appears, bewildered, angry, and, despite his experience, still relentlessly aggressive. A brief exchange between the two is interrupted by the arrival of a messenger, who reports what he and others have seen of the Bacchic women and their worship in the mountains; at first a calm, peaceful scene full of miracles, then madness and bloodshed when the interlopers are detected—a grim foreshadowing of what is in store for Pentheus (678–774):

Messenger: I had just reached the hill country with my pasturing herds by the time that the sun had risen and was warming the earth with its rays. And I saw the women, who had arranged themselves in three groups; Autonoe led one, your mother Agave, the second, and Ino, the third. All were stretched out asleep, some reclined on beds of fir, others rested their heads on oak leaves, having flung themselves down at random but with modesty and they were not, as you said they would be, intoxicated with wine and the music of the flute, bent on satisfying their lust in solitary places. When your mother heard the sounds of our horned cattle she stood up in the midst of the Bacchae, and cried out to rouse them from their sleep, and they threw off the heavy slumber from their eyes and jumped up—amazing in their orderliness, young and old (many still unwed). The first thing they did was to loosen their hair to their shoulders and tie up their fawn skins if any of the fastenings had come loose; and they made a belt for the dappled fur with snakes that licked their cheeks. Some held in their arms the young of the wild, a gazelle or wolf cubs, and those who had left their newborn babes at home gave them white milk from breasts that were still full. And they put on crowns of ivy, oak, and flowering vine. One took her thyrsus and struck it against a rock, and from it a gush of dewy water welled up; another hit the solid earth with her wand and from the spot the god sent forth a spring of wine. Those who thirsted for milk scraped the earth with their finger tips and produced white streams; and from each thyrsus, wreathed in ivy, dripped sweet drops of honey. And so, if you had been there to see these things, you would have invoked with prayers the god whom you now blame.

We herdsmen and shepherds gathered together to discuss and argue about the strange and wondrous actions. One of the group, who always goes into town and has a way with words, spoke to us all: "You who inhabit the sacred mountain heights, how would you like to hunt down Agave, the mother of Pentheus, in her revels and do the king a favor?" What he said seemed good to us, so we hid ourselves in a leafy thicket and waited in ambush. At the appointed time they began their Bacchic revels, shaking their thyrsus and calling on the god, the son of Zeus, with one voice, "Iacchus, Bromius!" The whole mountain and animals joined in their ecstasy and there was nothing that remained unmoved by the dance.

It happened that Agave as she leaped and ran came close to me, and I leaped out of the ambush where I had hidden myself, bent on seizing her. But she cried aloud: "Oh, my swift-running hounds, we are being hunted by these men; so follow me, follow, armed with your thyrsus in your hands."

And so we fled and escaped being torn into pieces by the Bacchae, but with their bare hands they attacked our cattle grazing on the grass. You could see one of them wrenching apart a bellowing cow, its udders full. Others ripped apart the calves and you could see ribs and cloven hoofs being scattered high and low, and from the pines the pieces hung dripping with blood. Bulls, arrogant before as they raged with their horns, were laid low, dragged bodily to the ground by the countless hands of girls, and their flesh was stripped from their bodies more quickly than you, O king, could wink your eyes. Like birds propelled aloft by the speed of their course, the Bacchae ranged across the stretch of plain along the stream of the Asopus, which affords the Thebans a rich harvest. Like a hostile army they descended upon the villages of Hysiae and Erythrae, nestled low on the slopes of Cithaeron, and devastated them. They snatched children from their homes and all the booty (including bronze and iron) that they carried off on their shoulders did not fall onto the dark earth, although it was not fastened. They bore fire on their hair and it did not burn. The villagers, enraged by the plundering of the Bacchae, rushed to arms. Then, my king, there was a terrifying sight to behold. The weapons that the villagers threw did not draw any blood, but when the Bacchae hurled the thyrsus from their hands they inflicted wounds on many. Women routed men—a feat not to be accomplished without the power of some god. Back they came to where they sallied forth, to the very streams which the god made gush for them. They washed their hands of blood and snakes licked the stains from their cheeks.

And so, my lord, receive into the city this god, whoever he is. He is great in many respects but especially in his reputed gift to mortals, about which I have heard, the grape, our remedy for pain and sorrow. With no more wine there could be no more love and no other pleasure for mankind besides.

Pentheus refuses to listen to the pleas of the messenger and is determined to rush to arms for an assault on the Bacchae. But the stranger, Dionysus, finds a way to restrain him by appealing to Pentheus's basic nature and psychology—in general, the complex neurosis that stems from his repressions, in particular, his prurient preoccupation with sex and his desire to see the orgies that he insists are taking place (811–861):

Dionysus: Would you like to see the women banded together in the mountains?
Pentheus: Yes, indeed. I would give a ton of gold for that.
Dionysus: Why are you driven by such a great desire to see them?
Pentheus: Actually, it would pain me to see them drunk.
Dionysus: Nevertheless you would be pleased to see what is painful to you?
Pentheus: To be sure, if I watched in silence crouched beneath the firs.
Dionysus: But they will track you down, even if you go in secret.
Pentheus: Then I shall go openly; what you say is right.
Dionysus: You will undergo the journey, then? Let me lead you.
Pentheus: Come, as quickly as possible; I begrudge you this delay.
Dionysus: Then dress up in a fine linen robe.
Pentheus: What is this? Am I to change from a man to a woman?
Dionysus: If you are seen there as a man, they will kill you.
Pentheus: Again, what you say is right. You are like some sage of long ago.
Dionysus: Dionysus gives me this inspiration.
Pentheus: In the garb of a woman? But shame holds me back!
Dionysus: You are no longer interested in watching the Maenads?
Pentheus: What dress did you say that you would put on me?
Dionysus: I shall set on your head a long flowing wig.
Pentheus: And what is the next feature of my outfit?
Dionysus: A robe that falls to your feet, and a band around your head.
Pentheus: What else will you give me?
Dionysus: A thyrsus in your hand and a dappled fawn skin cloak.
Pentheus: I cannot bring myself to put on the costume of a woman.
Dionysus: But if you attack the Bacchae in battle, you will shed blood.
Pentheus: This is true; I must first go as a spy.
Dionysus: To be sure, it is wiser than to hunt out evil by evil.
Pentheus: How shall I get out of the city without being seen?
Dionysus: We shall take a deserted route, and I shall lead the way.
Pentheus: Anything, rather than have the Bacchae laugh at me. I shall go into the house and make preparations that are for the best.
Dionysus: So be it, and I am at your side ready for everything.

Pentheus: I am going inside, I shall either proceed with arms or follow your instructions.

Dionysus: Women, this man is ready to be caught in the net. He will go to the Bacchae and he will pay the penalty with his life. Dionysus, now do your work; for you are not far away. We shall exact our retribution. First we shall inflict upon him delirious madness and drive him out of his wits; in his right mind he would not want to dress up in the costume of a woman, but once driven from reason he will put it on. My desire is to make him the laughingstock of the Thebans as they see him led in a woman's garb through the city in return for the terrible threats that he uttered before. I go now to deck out Pentheus in the dress with which he will go down to the realm of Hades, slaughtered by the hands of his mother. He will know Dionysus as the son of Zeus and a deity of his own right, among mankind most dread and most gentle.

The dressing of Pentheus in the garb of the Bacchae suggests the ceremonial decking out of the sacrificial victim. Pentheus, by the ritual donning of his costume, falls under the spell and the power of the god and eventually will be offered up to him. The chorus sings of the joys of their worship and the justice of their triumph over impiety, and at the end of their song Dionysus exerts final and complete mastery over Pentheus, who is delirious (912–970):

Dionysus: Pentheus, I call on you, the one who desires to see what he should not see and hastens upon what he should not do. Come forward out of the house, let me behold you dressed in the garb of a woman, a Bacchic Maenad, about to go as a spy on your mother and her group.

Pentheus: I think that I see two suns, and the image of Thebes with its seven gates appears double. You look like a bull as you lead me forward, with horns growing out of your head. Were you then an animal? Now, indeed, you have become a bull.

Dionysus: The god walks with us; he is on our side although he was not kindly disposed before. Now you see what you should see.

Pentheus: Tell me how I look. Do I not have the carriage of Ino or my mother, Agave?

Dionysus: Looking at you I seem to see those very two. But this lock here that I had fixed under your hairband has fallen out of place.

Pentheus: I shook it loose indoors while I was tossing my head back and forth like a Bacchic reveller.

Dionysus: Well, we, whose concern is to serve you, shall put it back in place. Bend your head.

Pentheus: Fine, you deck me out properly, for I am now dedicated to you.

Dionysus: Your belt is loose and the folds of your dress do not hang straight to your ankles.

Pentheus: They are not straight at the right foot but here on the left the dress hangs well at the heel.

Dionysus: You will, I am sure, consider me the best of your friends, when contrary to your expectation you witness the temperance of the Bacchae.

Pentheus: Shall I be more like one of the Bacchae if I hold my thyrsus in my right or my left hand?

Dionysus: You should hold it in your right hand, and raise it and your right foot at the same time.

Pentheus: Will I be able to lift up on my shoulders Mt. Cithaeron with its glens full of Bacchae?

Dionysus: You will, if you wish; before your mind was not sound, but now it is as it ought to be.

Pentheus: Let us take crowbars, or shall I thrust my shoulder or my arm under the peaks and crush them with my hands?

Dionysus: Do not destroy the haunts of the nymphs and the places where Pan does his piping.

Pentheus: Your words are right; women must not be overcome by force; I will hide myself among the firs.

Dionysus: You will find the hiding place that you should, coming upon the Maenads as a crafty spy.

Pentheus: Indeed I can see them now in the bushes like birds held fast in the enticing coils of love.

Dionysus: Yes, of course, you go on a mission to guard against this very thing. Maybe you will catch them, if you yourself are not caught first.

Pentheus: Take me through the middle of Thebes, for I am the only man among them who dares this deed.

Dionysus: You alone bear the burden of toil for this city—you alone. And so the struggle which must be awaits you. Follow me, I shall lead you there in safety, but another will lead you back.

Pentheus: My mother.

Dionysus: A spectacle for all.

Pentheus: It is for this I am going.
Dionysus: You will be carried home.
Pentheus: What luxury you are suggesting.
Dionysus: In the hands of your mother.
Pentheus: You insist upon pampering me.
Dionysus: Pampering of sorts.
Pentheus: Worthy of such deserts I follow you.

Pentheus imagines he will return in a splendid carriage, with his mother by his side. This terrifying scene is built on more than this one irony and laden with a multiplicity of ambiguities. How bitter now appear the earlier taunts of Pentheus against Cadmus and Tiresias. In his delirium, does Pentheus really see the god in his true and basic character—a beast? Or does his vision spring from his own warped interpretation of the bestial nature of the worship?

A messenger arrives to tell of Pentheus's death (1043–1152):

Messenger: When we had left the town of Thebes behind and crossed the stream of the Asopus, we made our way up the slopes of Cithaeron, Pentheus and I (for I followed with my master) and the stranger who led us to the scene.

First we took a position in a grassy glen, with silent footsteps and not a word, so that we might see and not be seen. It was a valley surrounded by cliffs, watered by streams, and shaded by pines; here Maenads sat, their hands occupied in their joyous tasks. Some were restoring a crown of ivy on a thyrsus that had lost its foliage, others, happy as fillies let loose from their painted yokes, were singing Bacchic hymns in answering refrains. But poor Pentheus, who could not see this crowd of women, said: "My friend, from where we stand I am too far away to see these counterfeit Maenads clearly, but if I climbed up a towering pine on the hill side, I could properly behold the orgies of the Maenads."

Then and there I saw the stranger do wondrous things. He took hold of the very top branch of a pine that reached up to the sky and pulled it down, down, down, to the black earth. And it was bent like a bow or the curving line of the circle of a wheel. Thus the stranger grabbed the mountain pine with his hands and bent it to the ground, a feat no mortal could accomplish. He sat Pentheus on the topmost branches and let the tree go, sliding it through his hands until it was upright again, slowly and carefully so that he might not dislodge him. It towered straight to towering heaven, with our king perched on top. He could be seen more clearly by the Maenads than he could see them. He was just becoming visible, seated aloft, when the stranger was no longer to be seen and from heaven a voice (I imagine that of Dionysus) cried aloud: "Oh women, I bring the man who made a mockery of you and me and our mysteries; now take vengeance on him." As the voice spoke these words, a blaze of holy fire flashed between heaven and earth.

The air grew still, every leaf in the wooded glen stood silent, and no sound of a beast was to be heard. The women had not made out the voice clearly and they stood up straight and looked around. He called again and when the daughters of Cadmus understood the clear command of Bacchus, they rushed forth as swift as doves in their relentless course, his mother, Agave, her sisters, and all the Bacchae. With a madness inspired by the breath of the god they darted over the glen with its streams and rocks. When they saw the king seated in the pine tree, they first climbed on the rock cliff that towered opposite and hurled stones at him with all their might and pelted him with branches of pines. Others hurled the thyrsus through the air at Pentheus, a pitiable target. But they were unsuccessful, for the poor wretch sat trapped and helpless, too high for even their fanaticism. Finally with a lightning force they ripped off oak branches and tried to use them as levers to uproot the tree. But when these efforts too were all in vain, Agave exclaimed: "Come, O Maenads, stand around the tree in a circle and grab hold of it, so that we may catch the climbing beast and prevent him from revealing the secret revels of the god." And they applied a thousand hands and tore up the tree out of the earth. And from his lofty seat Pentheus fell hurtling to the ground with endless cries; for he knew what evil fate was near.

His mother as priestess was the first to begin the slaughter. She fell on him and he ripped off the band from his hair so that poor Agave might recognize him and not kill him, and he cried out as he touched her cheek: "Mother, it is your son, Pentheus, whom you bore in the home of Echion. Have pity on me for my sins and do not kill me, your son."

But Agave was not in her right senses; her mouth foamed and her eyes rolled madly as the god Bacchus held her in his power. And Pentheus could not reach her. She seized his left arm below the elbow and placing her foot against the ribs of her ill-fated son, wrenched his arm out of his shoulder. It was not done through her own strength but the god made it easy for her hands. From the other side, Ino clawed and tore at his flesh and Autonoe and the whole pack converged on him. All shouted together, he moaning with what breath remained, they screaming in triumph. One carried an arm, another a foot with the boot still on; his ribs were stripped clean and they all with blood-drenched hands tossed the flesh of Pentheus among them like a ball.

His body lies scattered, some pieces under hard rocks, others in the shady depths of the woods—not easy to find. His mother has taken his poor head and affixed it on the point of her thyrsus; she carries it like that of a mountain lion through the depths of Cithaeron, leaving her sisters and their Maenad bands. She comes within these walls, exulting in her ill-fated prey and calling on Bacchus, her partner in the hunt, her comrade in the chase, her champion of victory, who gave her tears as her reward.

And so I am leaving now, before Agave reaches the palace, to get away from this misfortune. Temperance and reverence for the gods are best, the wisest possessions, I believe, that exist for mortals who will use them.

Agave returns and awakens to the horror of her deed; the concluding scenes affirm the divine power of Dionysus. There are serious textual problems in the last section of the play and a medieval work, the *Christus Patiens,* which drew upon Euripides is of some help—an interesting fact that rivets our attention to the parallels between Dionysus and Christ.

The pathos and the horror of the butchering of Pentheus have helped some in their sympathetic view of the rash king as an ascetic martyr, who is killed in his crusade against the irrational tide of religious fanaticism. But too much in the make-up of this young man suggests the myopic psychopath, who, unable to accept human nature as it is, foolishly tries to suppress it. The basic impulses toward both the bestial and sublime are terrifyingly and wondrously interrelated; Dionysus is after all the god of mob fury and religious ecstasy and anything in between. Was the celebration of his worship a cry for release from the restraints of civilized society and a return to the mystic purity and abounding freedom of nature, or was it merely a deceptive excuse for self-indulgence in an orgy of undisciplined passion?

The essential characteristics of Dionysiac religion are the possession by the god of his followers, the rending apart of the sacrificial animal, and the eating of the raw flesh (a kind of ritual communion, since the god was believed to be present in the victim). The religious congregation (the holy thiasus) was divided into groups often with a male leader for each, who played the role of the god. The Bacchae or Maenads are the female devotees, mortal women who become possessed. In mythology they are more than human, nymphs rather than mere mortals. Their mythological male counterparts are satyrs, who are, like them, spirits of nature; they, however, are not completely human but part man and part animal, possessing various attributes of a horse or a goat, for example, a horse's tail and ears, a goat's beard and horns (although in the later periods they are often depicted as considerably more humanized). Satyrs dance and sing and love music; they make wine and drink it and they are perpetually in a state of sexual excitement. One of their favorite sports is to chase Maenads through the woods. Animal skins and garlands are traditional attributes of Bacchic revelers (although satyrs are usually nude); Maenads in particular carry the thyrsus, a pole wreathed with ivy or vine leaves, pointed at the top to receive a pine cone. As we have seen, it is a magic wand that evokes miracles, but if necessary it can be converted into a deadly weapon.

Sileni also attend Dionysus; they often cannot be distinguished from satyrs, although some of them are older (*papposileni*) and even more lecherous. Yet others are old and wise, like Silenus himself, the tutor of Dionysus. A story tells how once one of them was made drunk by adding wine to the water of a spring; when he was brought to king Midas, this Silenus philosophized that the best fate for man was not to be born at all, the next best to die as soon as possible after birth, a typical example of Greek pessimism and wisdom reminiscent of Solon and Herodotus.[6] Dionysus and his retinue are favorite subjects in Greek art.

Dionysus, the male god of vegetation, was, as we should expect, associated with a fertility-goddess; his mother, Semele, was a full-fledged earth deity in her own right before she became Hellenized.

---

[6] A famous adaptation of this legend was made by Vergil in his sixth *Eclogue,* in which the utterance of the Silenus is cosmogonical and mythological.

The story of Zeus's birth on Crete, with the attendants who drowned out his infant cries by their frenzied music, suggests contamination with Dionysiac ritual. Certainly Euripides associates Bacchic mysticism with the ritual worship of both Rhea and Cybele. In some accounts Dionysus married Ariadne after she was deserted by Theseus, another enactment of the union of the male and female powers of fertility.

Dionysus represents the sap of life, the coursing of the blood through the veins, the throbbing excitement of nature; thus he is a god of ecstasy and mysticism. Another myth was told about his birth which even more clearly established him in this role.

Zeus mated with his daughter, Persephone, who bore a son, Zagreus, which is another name for Dionysus. Hera in her jealousy aroused the Titans to attack the child. These monstrous beings, their faces whitened with chalk, attacked the infant as he was looking in a mirror, or they beguiled him with toys and cut him to pieces with knives. After the murder, the Titans devoured the dismembered corpse.[7] But the heart of the infant god was saved and brought to Zeus by Athena, and Dionysus was born again— swallowed by Zeus and begotten on Semele. Zeus was angry with the Titans and destroyed them with his thunder and lightning. But from their ashes mankind was born.

Surely this is one of the most significant myths in terms of the philosophy and religious dogma that it provides. By it man is endowed with a dual nature—a body, gross and evil (since he is sprung from the Titans), and a soul that is pure and divine (for after all the Titans had devoured the god). Thus basic religious concepts (which lie at the root of all mystery religions) are accounted for: sin, immortality, resurrection, life after death, reward, and punishment. It is no accident that Dionysus is linked with Orpheus and Demeter and the message that they preached. He is in his person a resurrection god; the story is told that he went down into the realm of the dead and brought back his mother, who in this account is usually given the name, Thyone.

In the emotional environment of Dionysiac ecstasy are to be

---

[7] Variations in the story are obviously etiological attempts to account for elements of Bacchic ritual. Later ceremonies enacted the passion, death, and resurrection of the god in all its details.

found the essence and spirit of Greek drama. Theories concerning the origins of this genre in its relationship to Dionysus are legion. But it is a fact that tragedy and comedy were performed at Athens in a festival in his honor. It is difficult to agree with those who feel that this connection was purely accidental. Certainly Aristotle's treatise dealing with the nature of tragedy in terms of a catharsis of pity and fear takes for granted emotions and excitement that are essentially Bacchic. Frederick Nietzsche has provided the most imaginative and influential modern analysis of the Dionysiac experience, particularly in its antithetical relationship to the Apollonian.

Other stories of opposition to Dionysus less famous than that of Pentheus convey the same terrifying message. In Argos, the daughters of Proetus, king of Tiryns, refused to accept the god and were driven mad, but the famous seer, Melampus, knew of certain therapeutic dances or herbs to cure them. In Orchomenus, a city of Boeotia, the daughters of Minyas refused to participate in Bacchic worship but instead remained at home to weave. Dionysus, in the guise of a girl, warned them of their folly to no avail and they also were driven mad; one of them, Leucippe, had a son, Hippasus, who (like Pentheus) was torn to pieces. The women eventually were turned into bats.

The story of Lycurgus of Thrace is given a brief and affecting version in Homer (*Iliad,* 6.130–140). He pursued the nurses of Dionysus with an ox goad, and Dionysus himself in terror jumped into the sea and was rescued and comforted by Thetis. The gods were angry with Lycurgus and Zeus struck him with blindness; he did not live long after that.

Dionysus, however, can be received amidst peace and joy. In Attica, in the days of King Pandion, a man named Icarius was most hospitable to the god and as a reward he was given the gift of wine. But when the people first felt the effects of this blessing they thought they had been poisoned and they turned upon Icarius and killed him. Erigone, his devoted daughter, accompanied by her dog, Maira, searched everywhere for her father. When she found him she hanged herself in grief. Suffering and plague ensued for the people until, upon Apollo's advice, they initiated a festival in honor of Icarius and Erigone.

The *Homeric Hymn to Dionysus* (number 7) offers a splendid picture of the god's power and majesty and reminds us of fundamental elements in the nature of his character and worship: miracles, bestial transformation, violence to enemies, and pity for those who understand.

I shall sing of how Dionysus, the son of renowned Semele, appeared as a man in the first bloom of youth on a projecting stretch of shore by the sea that bears no harvest. His hair, beautiful and dark, flowed thickly about his head, and he wore on his strong shoulders a purple cloak. Before long foreign pirates, led on by evil fate, appeared swiftly over the sea, dark as wine, in a ship with fine benches of oars. As soon as they saw him they nodded one to the other and, quickly jumping out, seized him at once and put him on board ship, delighted in their hearts. For they thought that he was the son of kings, who are cherished by Zeus, and wanted to bind him in harsh bonds. But the bonds fell far from his hands and feet and did not hold him as he sat with a smile in his dark eyes. When the steersman saw this he called aloud to his comrades: "Madmen, who is this mighty god whom you have seized and attempt to bind? Not even our strong ship can carry him, for this is either Zeus or Apollo of the silver bow or Poseidon, since he is not like mortal men but like the gods who have their homes on Olympus. But come, let us immediately set him free on the dark shore; do not lay hands on him for fear that he become angered in some way and rouse up violent winds and a great storm." So he spoke, but the commander of the ship rebuked him scornfully: "Madman, check the wind and while you are at it seize the tackle and hoist the sail. I expect that he will come with us to Egypt or Cyprus or the northern Hyperboreans or farther. But at his destination he will eventually tell us about his friends and all his possessions and his brothers, since a divine power has put him in our hands." When he had spoken, the mast and sail were hoisted on the ship; the wind breathed into the midst of the sail and the men made the ropes tight all around. But soon deeds full of wonder appeared in their midst. First of all a sweet and fragrant wine flowed through the black ship and a divine ambrosial odor arose. Amazement took hold of all the sailors as they looked, and immediately a vine spread in all directions up along the very top of the sail, with many clusters hanging down; dark ivy, luxuriant with flowers, entwined about the mast and lovely fruit burst forth, and all the oar pins bore garlands. When they saw this they ordered the helmsman to bring the ship to land. But then the god became a terrifying lion in the upper part of the ship and roared loudly and in the middle of the ship he created a shaggy-necked bear, thus manifesting his divine credentials. The bear stood up raging, while on the upper deck the lion glared and scowled. The sailors fled into the stern and stood in panic around the helmsman who had shown his right sense. The lion sprang up suddenly and seized the commander, but the sailors when they saw this escaped an evil fate and leaped all together into the shining sea and became dolphins. The god took pity on the helmsman and saved him and made him happy and fortunate in every way, saying: "Be of good courage, you who have become dear to my heart. I am loud-crying Dionysus, whom my mother Semele, daughter of Cadmus, bore after uniting in love with Zeus." Hail, son of Semele of the beautiful countenance; it is not at all possible to forget you and compose sweet song.

The interior of a drinking cup (*cylix*) in black-figure technique by the artist Exekias shows Dionysus sailing across the sea. In its feeling and detail this masterpiece has much in common with the *Homeric Hymn,* although no direct link can be established.[8]

The god Pan has much in common with the satyrs and sileni of Dionysus. He is not completely human in form but part man and part goat—he has horns, and the ears and the legs of a goat; he will join in Bacchic revels and he is full of spirit, impulsive, and amorous. His parents are variously named: his mother is usually some nymph or other; his father is very often Hermes or Apollo. Like them he is a god of shepherds, who is a musician.

Pan is credited with the invention of his own instrument, the Pan pipe (or in Greek, *syrinx*); Ovid tells the story with brevity and charm (*Metamorphoses,* 1.689–712). Syrinx was once a lovely nymph, who was devoted to Artemis and rejected the advances of predatory satyrs and woodland spirits. Pan caught sight of her, and as he pursued her she was transformed into a bed of marsh reeds. The wind blowing through them produced a sad and beautiful sound and Pan was inspired to cut two of the reeds, fasten them together with wax, and thus fashion a pipe on which he could play.

[8] The story as told by Ovid (*Metamorphoses,* 3.597–691) provides an interesting comparison in artistic method and purpose.

Pan's haunts are the hills and the mountains, particularly those of his homeland, Arcadia. Here, according to Herodotus (6.106), he was encountered by the runner, Phidippides, who had been sent to Sparta by the Athenians to ask for help when they were about to fight the Persians at Marathon in 490. Phidippides claimed that Pan called him by name and asked why the Athenians ignored him although he was a deity friendly to them. The Athenians believed Phidippides and later built a shrine to Pan and honored him with annual sacrifices and torch races.

Pan had other loves besides Syrinx. Another nymph he pursued was turned into a tree that bore her name, Pitys (the Greek word for pine). His passion for the nymph, Echo, also ended tragically. She fled from his advances and Pan spread such madness and "panic" among a group of shepherds (a particular feat to which he was prone) that they tore her to pieces. All that remained was her voice. A more famous story about Echo concerns her love for Narcissus. Ovid's version is as follows (*Metamorphoses,* 3.342–510):

The river-god, Cephisus, once embraced the nymph, Liriope, in his winding stream and enveloping her in his waves took her by force. When her time had come, the beautiful Liriope bore a child with whom even as a baby the nymphs might have fallen in love. And she called him Narcissus. She consulted the seer, Tiresias, asking whether her son would live a long time to a ripe old age; his answer was: "Yes, if he will not have come to know himself." For a long time this response seemed to be an empty prophecy, but as things turned out, its truth was proven by the unusual nature of the boy's madness and death.

The son of Cephisus had reached his sixteenth year and could be looked upon as both a boy and a young man. Many youths and many maidens desired him, but such a firm pride was coupled with his soft beauty that no one (either boy or girl) dared to touch him. He was seen once as he was driving the timid deer into his nets by the talkative nymph, who had learned neither to be silent when another is speaking nor to be the first to speak herself, namely the mimic Echo.

At that time Echo was a person and not only a voice, but, just as now, she was garrulous and was able to use her voice in her customary way of repeating from a flood of words only the very last. Juno brought this about because, when she might have been able to catch the nymphs lying on the mountain with her Jove, Echo knowingly detained the goddess by talking at length until the nymphs could run away. When Juno realized the truth, she exclaimed: "The power of that tongue of yours, by which I have been tricked, will be limited and most brief will be the use of your voice." She made good her threats; Echo only gives back the words she has heard and repeats the final phrases of utterances.

And so she saw Narcissus wandering through the secluded country-side and burned with passion; she followed his footsteps furtively, and the closer she pursued him, the nearer was the fire that consumed her, just like the tops of torches, smeared with sulphur, that catch fire and blaze up when a flame is brought near. O how often she wanted to approach him with blandishments and tender appeals. Her very nature made this impossible for she was not allowed to speak first. But she was prepared to wait for his utterances and to echo them with her own words—this she could do.

By chance the boy became separated from his faithful band of companions and he cried out: "Is there anyone there?" Echo replied "There!" He was dumbfounded and glanced about in all directions; then he shouted at full voice: "Come!" She called back to him with the same word. He looked around but saw no one approaching; "Why do you run away from me?" he asked. She echoed his words just as he spoke them. He was persistent, beguiled by the reflection of the other's voice, and exclaimed: "Come here and let us get together!" Echo replied, "Let us get together" and never would she answer any other sound more willingly. She emerged from the woods, making good her very words and rushed to throw her arms about the neck of her beloved. But he fled and in his flight exclaimed, "Take your hands off me, I would die before I let you possess me." She replied with only the last words "Possess me." Thus spurned she hid herself in the woods where the trees hide her blushes, and from that time on she has lived in solitary caves. Nevertheless her love clung fast and grew with the pain of rejection. Wakeful cares wasted away her wretched body, her skin became emaciated, and the bloom and vigor of her whole being slipped away on the air. Her voice and her bones were all that was left. Then only her voice remained; her bones, they say, were turned into stone. From that time on she has remained hidden in the woods; she is never seen on the mountains but she is heard by everyone. The sound of her echo is all of her that still lives.

Narcissus had played with her so, just as he had previously rejected other nymphs sprung from the waves or the mountains, and as well males who had approached him. Thereupon one of those scorned raised up his hands to the heavens and cried: "So may he himself fall in love, so may he not be able to possess his beloved!" The prayer was a just one and Nemesis heard it. There was a spring, its clear waters glistening like silver, untouched by shepherds, mountain goats, and other animals, and undisturbed by birds, wild beasts, and falling tree branches. Grass grew round about, nourished by the water nearby, and the woods protected the spot from the heat of the sun. Here the boy lay down, tired out by the heat and his quest for game, and attracted by the pool and the beauty of the place. While he was trying to quench his thirst, it kept coming back again and again, and as he continued to drink, he was captivated by the reflection of the beauty that he saw. He fell in love with a hope insubstantial, believing what was only an image to be real and corporeal. He gazed in wonder at himself, clinging transfixed and emotionless to what he saw, just like a statue formed from Parian marble. From his position on the ground he looked at his eyes, twin stars, and his hair, worthy of both Bacchus and Apollo, and his smooth cheeks, his ivory neck, and the beauty of his face, a flush of red amidst snowy whiteness. He marveled at all the things that others had marveled at in him. Unwise and unheeding he desired his very self, one and the same person approving and being approved, seeking and being sought, inflaming and being inflamed. How many times he bestowed vain kisses on the deceptive pool! How many times he plunged his arms into the midst of the waters to grasp the neck that he saw! But he could not catch hold of himself in their embrace. He did not understand what he was looking at, but was inflamed by what he saw, and the same illusion that deceived his eyes aroused his passion. Poor deluded boy, why do you grasp at your fleeting reflection to no avail? What you seek is not real; just turn away and you will lose what you love. What you perceive is but the reflection of your own image; it has no substance of its own. With you it comes and stays, and with you it will go, if you can bear to go. No concern for food or rest could drag him away from his post, but stretched out on the shady grass he looks at this deceptive beauty with insatiable gaze and destroys himself through his own eyes. He raised himself up a little and stretching out his arms to the surrounding woods exclaimed: "Has there ever been anyone smitten by more cruel a love? Tell me, O trees, for you know since you have provided opportune haunts for countless lovers. In the length of your years, in the many ages you have lived, can you remember anyone who has wasted away like me? I behold my beloved, but what I see and love I cannot have; such is the frustration of my unrequited passion. And I am all the more wretched because it is not a vast sea or lengthy road or impregnable fortress that separates us. Only a little water keeps us from each other. My beloved desires to be held, for each time that I bend down to kiss the limpid waters he in return strains upward with his eager lips. You would think that he could be touched; it is such a little thing that prevents the consummation of our love. Whoever you are, come out to me here. Why, incomparable boy, do you deceive me? When I pursue you, where do you go? Certainly you do not flee from my youthful beauty, for nymphs loved me too. You promise me some kind of hope by your sympathetic looks of friendship. When I stretch forth my arms to you, you do the same in return. When I laugh, you laugh back, and I have often noted your tears in response to my weeping. And as well you return my every gesture and nod and, as far as I can surmise from movements of your lovely mouth, you answer me with words that never reach my ears. I am you! I realize it; my reflection does not deceive me; I burn with love for myself, I am the one who fans the flame and bears the torture. What am I to do? Should I be the one to be asked or to ask? What then shall I ask for? What I desire is with me; all that I have makes me poor. O how I wish that I could escape from my body! A strange prayer for one in love, to wish away what he loves! And now grief consumes my strength; the time remaining for me is short and my life will be snuffed out in its prime. Death does not weigh heavily upon me, for death will bring an end to my misery. I only wish that he whom I cherish could live a longer time. As it is, we two who are one in life shall die together!" He finished speaking and, sick with longing, turned back again to his own reflection. His tears disturbed the waters and caused the image in the pool to grow less distinct. When he saw it disappearing he screamed: "Where are you going? Stay here, do not desert me, your lover. I cannot touch you—let me look at you, give me this nourishment at least in my misery and madness. As he grieved, he tore his garment in its upper part and beat his bare chest with his marble-white hands. And his chest when struck took on a rosy tinge, as apples usually have their whiteness streaked with red or grapes in various clusters when not yet ripe are stained with purple. As soon as he beheld himself thus in the water that was once again calm, he could endure it no further but, as yellow wax is wont to melt under the touch of fire and the gentle frost under the warmth of the sun, so he was weakened and destroyed by love, gradually being consumed in its hidden flame. His beautiful complexion, white touched with red, no longer remained nor his youthful strength, nor all that he had formerly looked upon with such pleasure. Not even his body, which Echo had once loved, was left.

When Echo saw what he had become, she felt sorry, even though she had been angry and resentful. Each time that the poor boy exclaimed "Alas," she repeated in return an echoing "Alas." And as he struck his shoulders with his hands, she gave back too the same sounds of his grief. This was his last cry as he gazed into the familiar waters: "Alas for the boy I cherished in vain!" The place repeated these very same words. And when he said "Farewell," Echo repeated "Farewell," too. He relaxed his weary head on the green grass; night closed those eyes that had so admired the beauty of their owner. Then too, after he had been received in the home of the dead below, he gazed at himself in the waters of the Styx. His sister Naiads wept and cut off their hair and offered it to their brother; the Dryads wept and Echo sounded their laments. Now the pyre and streaming torches and the bier were being prepared but the corpse was nowhere to be seen. They found instead a yellow flower with a circle of white petals in its center.

This tragic story of self-love and self-destruction has cast a particularly potent spell upon subsequent literature and thought.[9]

[9] See Louise Vinge, *The Narcissus Theme in Western European Literature up to the Early 19th Century* (Lund: Gleerup, 1967).

CHAPTER 12

Demeter and the Eleusinian Mysteries

The *Homeric Hymn to Demeter* (number 2) tells the story of Demeter and her daughter, Persephone, as follows:

I begin to sing about the holy goddess, Demeter of the beautiful hair, about her and her daughter, Persephone of the lovely ankles, whom Hades snatched away; loud-thundering Zeus, who sees all, gave her to him.

Alone, away from Demeter of the golden scepter and goodly crops, Persephone was playing with the deep-bosomed daughters of Oceanus and picking flowers along a soft meadow: beautiful roses, crocuses, violets, irises, and hyacinths; and Earth at the will of Zeus to please Hades, the host of many, produced as a snare for the fair maiden a wonderful and radiant narcissus, an awesome sight to all, both immortal gods and mortal men. From its stem a hundred blossoms sprouted forth and their odor was most sweet. All wide heaven above, the whole earth below, and the swell of the salt sea laughed. The girl was astounded and reached out with both her hands together to pluck the beautiful delight. And the wide-pathed Earth yawned in the Nysaean plain and the lord and host of many, who goes by many names, the son of Cronus, rushed at her with his immortal horses. And he snatched her up in his golden chariot and carried her away in tears. She shouted with shrill cries and called on father Zeus, the son of Cronus, the highest and the best, but no one of the immortals or of mortals—not even the olive trees laden with their fruit—heard her voice except for the daughter of Persaeus, Hecate, her hair brightly adorned, who listened from her cave as she thought kindly thoughts, and lord Helius, the splendid son of Hyperion. These two heard the maid call on the son of Cronus, father Zeus, but he sat apart, away from the gods, in his temple with its many suppliants, receiving beautiful holy offerings from mortal men. By the counsel of Zeus, his brother

199

and her uncle Hades, the son of Cronus, who bears many names, the lord and host of many, led her off with his immortal horses against her will.

As long as the goddess could behold the earth, starry heaven, the deep flowing sea full of fish, the rays of the sun, and still hoped to see her dear mother and the race of everlasting gods, hope soothed her great heart, although she was distressed. But the peaks of the mountains and the depths of the sea echoed with her immortal voice and her lady mother heard her.

Sharp pain seized Demeter's heart and she tore the headdress about her ambrosial hair with her own dear hands and threw off the dark covering from both her shoulders, and she rushed in pursuit just like a bird over land and water. But no one—either of gods or mortal men— wished to tell what had really happened—not even a bird came to her as a messenger of truth. For nine days then lady Demeter roamed over the earth holding burning torches in her hands and in her grief did not eat any ambrosia or drink sweet nectar, nor did she bathe her body. But when dawn brought on the light of the tenth day, Hecate, a torch in hand, met her and gave her some news as she exclaimed: "Lady Demeter, bringer of goodly gifts in season, who of the heavenly gods or mortal men carried off Persephone and troubled your dear heart? For I heard her voice but did not see with my eyes who it was. I am telling you the whole truth quickly."

This Hecate spoke, and the daughter of Rhea of the beautiful hair did not answer but swiftly rushed away with her, holding burning torches in her hands. They came to Helius, the lookout for both gods and men, and stood before his horses, and the goddess of goddesses spoke: "Helius, do at least have respect for me, a goddess, if I have ever by word or by deed gladdened your heart and your spirits. Through the barren air I heard the piercing cry of the girl whom I bore, a sweet daughter, illustrious in her beauty, as though she were being violated; yet I saw nothing with my eyes. But since you look down from the divine aether with your rays on all the earth and sea, tell me truthfully if you have seen my dear child at all and who either of gods or mortal men has seized her alone, away from me, by force against her will and made away."

Thus she spoke. And the son of Hyperion answered her: "Demeter, regal daughter of Rhea of the beautiful hair, you will know the truth. For indeed I revere you greatly and I pity you in your grief for your daughter of the lovely ankles. No other of the immortals is to blame except the cloud-gatherer Zeus, who gave her to his own brother, Hades, to be called his lovely wife. And he seized her and with his horses carried her away to the gloomy depths below as she cried aloud. But, O goddess, desist from your great lament; you should not thus bear an unrelenting anger to no avail. Indeed Hades, the ruler over many, is not an unseemly husband for your daughter; he is your own brother and born from the same blood and as for honor, when at the first power was divided three ways, his lot was to be made the lord of all those with whom he dwelt."

Thus he spoke and called out to his horses. And at his cry they nimbly bore the swift chariot, just like long-winged birds. But a more dread and terrible grief possessed Demeter's heart, and thereafter she was angry with the son of Cronus, Zeus, enwrapped in clouds; she kept away from the gatherings of the gods and high Olympus, and for a long time she went among the cities and rich fields of men, disguising her beautiful form. No one of men or deep-bosomed women who saw her recognized her until she came to the home of wise Celeus, who at that time was ruler of fragrant Eleusis. Grieving in her dear heart she sat near the road by the Maiden Well, from which the people drew their water; she was in the shade, for an olive tree grew overhead. Her appearance resembled that of a very old woman who was long past her days for childbearing and the gifts of garland-loving Aphrodite; she was like the nurses for the children of law-pronouncing kings or the housekeepers in their echoing halls. The daughters of Celeus, of the family of Eleusis, saw her there as they came after the easily drawn water so that they might bring it in their bronze pitchers to the dear home of their father. There were four of them, just like goddesses in their youthful bloom, Callidice and Cleisidice and lovely Demo and Callithoe, who was the oldest of them all. They did not know Demeter, for it is difficult for mortals to recognize the gods, and standing near they spoke winged words: "Who are you, old woman, of those born long ago? Where are you from? Why have you come away from the city and not approached the houses there, in whose shadowy halls dwell women just like you and younger, who would welcome you in word as well as in deed."

Thus they spoke. And she, the queenly goddess, answered with these words: "Dear children, whoever you are of women, I bid you greeting, and I shall tell you my tale. To be sure it is not inappropriate to relate the truth to you who have asked. My name is Doso, for my lady mother gave it to me. Now then I have come from Crete over the broad back of the sea—not willingly but against my wishes, for by force pirates carried me away. Then they put in at Thoricus, where the women and the men together disembarked; they were busy with their meal beside the cables of the ship, but my heart had no desire

for the delicious food. I hastened away over the black land and
escaped from my overbearing masters so that they might not sell me,
whom they had not bought, and reap a profit from me. And so I have
come here after my wanderings, and I have no idea at all what land
this is or who inhabit it. But may all those who dwell in homes of
Olympus grant that you have husbands and bear children just as
parents desire. But you maidens pity me now and show concern until,
dear children, I come to the home of a man and woman to perform
for them zealously the tasks appropriate for an elderly woman like
me; I could hold a newborn child in my arms and care for him well,
make my master's bed in the recess of his well-built chambers, and
teach the women their tasks."

Thus spoke the goddess and at once the virgin maiden, Callidice,
the most beautiful of the daughters of Celeus, answered: "Good
woman, we mortals even though we suffer must bear what the gods
bestow, for indeed they are much the stronger. I shall help you with
the following advice and I shall tell you the names of the men who
have great honor and power here and who are foremost among the
people and guard the battlements of our city by their counsels and
firm judgments. There is clever Triptolemus and Dioclus and
Polyxeinus and noble Eumolpus and Dolichus and our own brave
father. All of these have wives who take care of their homes, and no
one of them at the very first sight of your person would dishonor
you or turn you out of their house, but they will welcome you, for
to be sure you are like one of the gods. But if you wish, stay here,
so that we may go to our father's house and tell our mother, the
deep-bosomed Metaneira, the whole story in the hope that she will
bid you come to our place and not search for the homes of the others.
She cherishes in our well-built house an only son, born late, a darling
long prayed for. If you were to bring him up and he attained the
measure of his youth, you would easily be the envy of any woman
who saw you. Such are the great rewards that would be yours for your
care."

Thus she spoke and Demeter nodded her head in agreement. And
the girls filled their shining pitchers with water and carried them away
happy. Quickly they came to the great house of their father and
told their mother at once what they had seen and heard. She enjoined
them to go with all speed and to hire the woman at any price. Just
as deer or heifers bound along the meadow when in the springtime
they have had their fill of pasture, thus they hurried along the hollow
wagon path, holding up the folds of their lovely garments, and their
hair, which was like the flower of the crocus, danced about their shoul-

ders. And they found the illustrious goddess where they had left her earlier and thereupon led her to the dear house of their father; she followed behind with her head veiled, distressed at heart, and the dark robe grazed the slender feet of the goddess.

Soon they arrived at the house of Celeus, a man cherished by Zeus, and passed through the vestibule to where their lady mother sat by the pillar that supported the sturdy roof, holding her son, just a baby, in her lap. Her daughters ran to her, but the goddess stood at the threshold; her head reached up to the beams and she filled the doorway with a divine radiance. Then awe and reverence and fear seized Metaneira and she sprang up from her couch and bade her guest be seated, but Demeter, the giver of goodly gifts in season, did not wish to sit on the splendid couch but waited in silence with her beautiful eyes downcast, until Iambe in her wisdom set out for her a chair, artfully made, and threw a silvery fleece over it; then Demeter sat down holding her veil over her face with her hands. For a long time she remained seated without a sound, grieving; she did not by word or action acknowledge anyone but without a smile, not touching food or drink, she sat wasted with longing for her deep-bosomed daughter, until Iambe in her wisdom resorted to many jests and jokes and brought the holy lady around to smile and laugh and bear a happy heart (thereafter too Iambe was to cheer her in her anguish). And Metaneira filled a cup with wine as sweet as honey and offered it, but she refused saying that it was not right for her to drink red wine. But she ordered them to mix meal and water with tender mint and give it to her to drink. Metaneira mixed the potion and gave it to the goddess as she had ordered. And the great lady Demeter took it for the sake of the holy rite.[1]

Beautifully robed Metaneira was the first to speak among them: "Greetings, O lady, I expect that you are not born of base parents but of noble ones. Majesty and grace shine clearly in your eyes as though from the eyes of royalty who mete out justice. But we mortals, even though we suffer, must bear what the gods bestow, for the yoke

---

[1] That is, "to initiate and observe the holy rite or sacrament." The appears to be a lacuna after this sentence. The words translated "for the sake of the holy rite" are difficult and their precise meaning disputed. The reference must be to an important part of the ceremony of the Eleusinian mysteries, namely the partaking of a drink called the *kykeon*. But the nature and significance of the ritual are unknown: was this in any real sense the sharing of a sacrament, an act of communion fraught with mystic significance, or was it merely a token remembrance of these hallowed actions of the goddess?

lies on our necks. Yet now since you have come here, as much as I have will be yours. Nurse this child whom the immortals gave to me late in life, fulfilling my desperate hopes and endless prayers. If you were to bring him up and he attained the measure of his youth, you would easily be the envy of any woman who saw you. Such are the great rewards that would be yours for your care."

Then Demeter of the beautiful crown replied to her: "Sincere greetings to you, also, O lady, and may the gods afford you only good. I shall take the boy gladly, as you bid, and tend to him, and I have good hopes that he will not be harmed or destroyed by any evil charms, for I know much more potent remedies and effective antidotes for harmful spells."

Thus she spoke and with her immortal hands she took the child to her fragrant bosom. And his mother rejoiced in her heart. Thus she nursed in the house the splendid son of wise Celeus, Demophoon, whom beautifully robed Metaneira bore. And he grew like a god, not nourished on mortal food but anointed by Demeter with ambrosia, just as though sprung from the gods, and she breathed sweetness upon him as she held him to her bosom. At night she would hide him in the might of the fire, like a brand, without the knowledge of his dear parents. It was a source of great wonder to them that he grew and flourished before his time, for he was like the gods to look upon. And she would have made him never grow old and immortal, if beautifully robed Metaneira in her foolishness had not seen what was happening, as she watched in the night from her fragrant chamber. Great was her dismay and she gave a shriek and struck both her thighs, terrified for her child. Amidst her groans she uttered winged words: "Demophoon, my child, this stranger buries you within the blazing fire to my anguish and grievous pain."

Thus she spoke in agony, and the goddess of goddesses, Demeter of the beautiful crown, grew angry as she listened; with her immortal hands she snatched from the fire the dear son whom Metaneira had borne in her house, blessing beyond hope, and threw him down on the floor. Demeter was dreadfully angry in her heart as she spoke with beautifully robed Metaneira: "Mortals are ignorant and stupid who cannot foresee the fate both good and bad that is in store. Thus you in your foolishness have done a thing that cannot be remedied. I call to witness by the relentless waters of the river Styx, the oath of the gods, that I would have made your dear child immortal and never grow old all his days and I would have granted him imperishable honor, but now as it is he will not be able to escape death and the Fates. Yet imperishable honor will always be his because he has lain on my knees and slept in my arms. But when the years go by and he has reached his prime, the new generation of Eleusinians will continually engage in dread wars and battles all their days. I am Demeter, esteemed and honored as the greatest benefit and joy **to** mortals and immortals. Now then let all the people build to me **a** great temple and an altar with it, below the town and its steep **wall,** on the rising hill above the well, Kallichoron. And I myself shall teach my rites, so that performing them with reverence you may propitiate my heart."

Thus the goddess spoke and cast aside her old age, transforming her size and appearance. Beauty breathed around and about her and a delicious odor was wafted from her fragrant garments. The radiance from the immortal person of the goddess shone far and wide and her golden hair flowed down on her shoulders. The sturdy house was filled with her brilliance as though with a lightning flash. She disappeared from the room and at once Metaneira's knees gave way; for a long time she was speechless and did not even remember at all to pick up her late-born son from the floor. But his sisters heard his pitiful cries and sprang down from their beds, spread well with covers; one of them then picked up the child in her arms and took him to her bosom; another stirred the fire and a third hastened on her delicate feet to rouse their mother from her fragrant chamber. They gathered around the frantic child and bathed him with loving care. But his spirits were not soothed, for the nurses who tended him now were indeed inferior. The whole night long, trembling with fear, they made their supplication to the illustrious goddess, and as soon as dawn appeared they told the truth to Celeus whose power was great, just as Demeter the goddess of the beautiful crown had commanded. Then Celeus called the many people to an assembly and bade them build a splendid temple to Demeter of the lovely hair and an altar on the rising hill. They listened to him as he spoke and immediately complied and did as they were told. And the child flourished by divine destiny.

When they had finished and ceased from their labor, each made his way homeward. But golden Demeter remained sitting there quite apart from all the blessed gods, wasted with longing for her deep-bosomed daughter. And she caused men a most terrible and devastating year on the fruitful land. The earth would not send up a single sprout, for Demeter of the lovely crown kept the seed covered. In vain the oxen dragged the many curved ploughs through the fields and much white barley was sown in the earth to no avail. Now she would have destroyed the entire human race by cruel famine and deprived those who have their homes on Olympus of their glorious prestige from their gifts and sacrifices, if Zeus had not noticed and taken thought in his heart. First he roused golden-winged Iris to summon Demeter of the lovely hair, desirable in her beauty. Thus he ordered. And Iris obeyed Zeus, the dark-clouded son of Cronus, and on swift feet traversed the interval between. She came to the citadel of fragrant Eleusis and found dark-robed Demeter in her temple. She spoke to her, uttering winged words: "Demeter, father Zeus whose knowledge is imperishable, commands you to join the company of the eternal gods. Come now, let not the word I bring from Zeus be unaccomplished."

Thus she spoke in supplication, but Demeter's heart was unswayed. Thereupon father Zeus sent down to her all the blessed gods who exist forever, and they came one by one calling out her name and offering her many very beautiful gifts and whatever honors she would like to choose for herself among the immortals. But no one was able to sway her mind and her heart from her anger and she stubbornly rejected all appeals. She maintained that she would never set foot on fragrant Olympus nor allow fruit to sprout from the earth until she saw with her own eyes her lovely daughter.

Then loud-thundering Zeus, who sees all, sent the slayer of Argus, Hermes, with his golden wand to Erebus to appeal to Hades with gentle words and bring chaste Persephone up from the murky depths to the light, so that her mother might desist from anger when she saw her daughter with her own eyes. Hermes did not disobey, and straightway he left the realms of Olympus and swiftly rushed down to the depths of the earth. He encountered the lord Hades within his house, sitting on a couch with his modest wife, who was very reluctant because of her longing for her mother. And Demeter far away brooded over her designs to thwart the actions of the blessed gods. The mighty slayer of Argus stood near and said: "Hades of the dark hair, ruler of the dead, father Zeus has ordered me to bring to him from Erebus august Persephone, so that her mother may see her with her own eyes and desist from her wrath and dread anger against the immortals. For she is devising a great scheme to destroy the feeble tribes of earth-born men by keeping the seed hidden under earth and ruining the honors that are bestowed on the immortals. She clings to her dire wrath and does not associate with the gods but remains on the rocky citadel of Eleusis, sitting apart within her fragrant temple."

Thus he spoke. And Hades, the lord of those below, smiled with furrowed brows and did not disobey the commands of Zeus the king and he hastily ordered wise Persephone: "Go, Persephone, to the side of your dark-robed mother, with a gentle and loving heart in your breast. Be not distraught. I among the immortals shall not be an unworthy husband for you, since I am the full brother of your father Zeus. While you are here with me you will rule over all that lives and moves and you will hold the greatest honors among the immortals. Those who wrong you and do not propitiate your power by performing holy rites and sacrifices and offering appropriate gifts will find eternal retribution."

Thus he spoke. And wise Persephone was delighted and jumped up quickly in her joy. But her husband secretly gave her the honey-sweet fruit of the pomegranate to eat, taking thought for himself that she should not remain all her days above with august, dark-robed Demeter. Hades, host of many, then yoked his immortal horses to the front of his golden chariot which Persephone mounted; the mighty slayer of Argus, Hermes, took the reins and whip in his hands and drove them up and away from the palace; the pair of horses readily sped along and easily covered their long journey. Neither the sea nor streams of rivers nor grassy glens nor mountain tops impeded the onrush of the immortal horses as they cut through the deep air above them in their course. The charioteer brought them to a halt in front of the fragrant temple where Demeter of the lovely crown waited. At the sight of her daughter she rushed out like a Maenad down a mountain thick with woods. When Persephone on the other side saw the beautiful eyes of her mother, she leaped down from the chariot with its horses and ran, throwing her arms about her neck in an embrace. But while Demeter still had her dear child in her arms, suddenly her heart sensed some treachery; trembling with dread she let go her loving embrace and asked quickly: "My child, have you eaten any food while you were below? Speak up, do not hide anything so that we both may know. If you have not then, even though you have been in the company of loathsome Hades, you will live with me and your father, Zeus the cloud-gatherer, son of Cronus, in honor among all the immortals. But if you have eaten anything, you will return again beneath the depths of the earth and live there a third part of each year; the other two-thirds of the time you will spend with me and the other immortals. When the spring blooms with all sorts of sweet-smelling flowers, then again you will rise from the gloomy region below, a great wonder for gods and mortal men. But tell me, too, by what trick the strong host of many deceived you?"

The very beautiful Persephone then said in answer: "To be sure, mother, I shall tell you the whole truth. When Hermes, the bringer of luck and swift messenger, came from my father, the son of Cronus, and the other gods of the sky, saying that I was to come up from Erebus in order that you might see me with your own eyes and desist from your wrath and dread anger against the immortals, I immediately jumped up in my joy. But Hades swiftly put in my mouth the fruit of the pomegranate, a honey-sweet morsel, and compelled me to eat it by force against my will. I shall tell you too how he came and carried me down to the depths of the earth through the shrewd plan of my father, the son of Cronus, going through it all as you ask. We were all playing in a lovely meadow . . . and gathering lovely flowers in our hands, a mixed array of soft crocuses, irises, hyacinths, roses in full bloom, and lilies, wonderful to behold, and a narcissus, which the wide earth produced, in color yellow of a crocus. I plucked it joyously, but the earth beneath opened wide and thereupon the mighty lord, the host of many, leaped up and carried me away in his golden chariot beneath the earth despite my violent protests—my cries were loud and shrill. I tell you the whole truth, although the story gives me pain."

Thus they then in mutual love and tender embraces greatly cheered each other's heart and soul the whole long day. Their grief was assuaged as they exchanged their joys. Hecate, her hair brilliantly arrayed, approached them and frequently embraced the holy daughter of Demeter. From that time on, regal Hecate became the lady and attendant of Persephone.

Loud-thundering Zeus, who sees far and wide, sent as a messenger to them Rhea of the lovely hair to lead dark-robed Demeter among the company of the gods, and he promised to grant her the honors that she would choose among the immortal gods, and he consented that her daughter live a third part of the revolving year in the gloomy depths below and the other two-thirds by the side of her mother and the other immortals. Thus he ordered, and the goddess Rhea did not disobey the message of Zeus. She quickly rushed down from the heights of Olympus and came to the Rharian plain, previously very fertile, but now not fertile at all, standing leafless and barren. The white seed was hidden through the machinations of Demeter of the lovely ankles. But thereafter soon, with the burgeoning of spring, long ears of grain would be luxuriant and the rich furrows too along the ground would be laden with grain, some already bound in sheaves. Rhea came from the barren air to this place first of all and the goddesses beheld each other gladly and rejoiced in their hearts. Rhea, her hair brilliantly arrayed, spoke to Demeter thus: "Come here, my daughter; loud-thundering Zeus, who sees far and wide, summons you to join the company of the gods, and he has promised to grant you whatever honors you would like among the immortals, and he has consented that your daughter live a third part of the revolving year in the gloomy depths below and the other two-thirds with you and the other gods. Thus he said it would be accomplished and nodded his head in assent. But come, my child, and be obedient; do not persist in your relentless anger against Zeus, the dark-clouded son of Cronus. But quickly make grow for men the life-bringing fruit in abundance."

Thus she spoke, and Demeter of the lovely crown obeyed. Quickly she caused fruit to spring up from the fertile plains, and the whole wide land was laden with leaves and flowers. She went to the kings who minister justice (Triptolemus, Diocles, the rider of horses, the mighty Eumolpus, and Celeus, the leader of the people) and showed them the performance of her holy rites and taught her mysteries to them all, Triptolemus and Polyxeinus and Diocles besides—holy mysteries which one may not by any means violate or question or express. For the great reverence due to the gods restrains one's voice. Happy is the one of men on earth who has seen these things. But the one who is uninitiated into the holy rites and has no part never is destined to a similar joy when he is dead in the gloomy realm below.

But when the goddess of goddesses had ordained all these things, they made their way to Olympus among the company of the other gods. There they dwell beside Zeus, who delights in the thunder, august and holy goddesses. Greatly happy is the one of men on earth whom they dearly love; straightway they send, as a guest to his great house, Plutus, who gives wealth to mortal men.

Come now you who hold power over the land of fragrant Eleusis, sea-girt Paros, and rocky Antron, lady and queen Demeter, the giver of good things in season, both yourself and your daughter, very beautiful Persephone, kindly grant me a pleasing substance in reward for my song. And I shall remember both you and another song as well.

The myth of Demeter and Persephone represents another variation of a fundamental and recurring theme—the death and rebirth of vegetation. This time the allegory is rendered in terms of the touching emotions of mother and daughter; more often the symbols and metaphors involve the relationship between a fertility-goddess and her male partner, either lover or son (e.g., Aphrodite and Adonis, Cybele and Attis, Semele and Dionysus). Demeter is often imagined as the goddess of the ripe grain; Persephone then is the deity of the budding tender shoots. They are invoked together as the "two goddesses." Persephone (who is often called merely Kore, a name meaning girl) is the daughter of Demeter and

Zeus, who enact once again the holy marriage between earth-goddess and sky-god.

The *Homeric Hymn to Demeter* illustrates the grim character of Hades, his methods of obtaining a wife, and provides the mythological reasons for Hecate's prominence as a goddess of the underworld. Hades's basic character as a fertility god is evident from the location of his realm, the violence of his nature, and his link with horses. He is thus a god of agricultural wealth (compare his names, Pluto, or Dis for the Romans) but he should not be confused with Plutus (Wealth) mentioned in the last lines of the hymn, another deity of agricultural plenty and prosperity (and then wealth in general), the offspring of Demeter and Iasion.

Triptolemus, who also appears in the concluding lines of the *Hymn,* is generally depicted as the messenger of Demeter when she restored fertility to the ground. He is the one who taught and spread her arts of agriculture to new lands at that time and later, often traveling in a magical car drawn by winged dragons, a gift of Demeter. He is sometimes merged in identity with the infant Demophoon (variant spelling is Demophon) of the *Hymn* or said to be his brother; in Plato, Triptolemus is a judge of the dead.

This hymn to Demeter is of major importance, not only for its intrinsic artistic value, its general elucidation of a myth, and its illustration of the character of the deities involved. It provides in addition the most significant evidence that we have for the nature of the worship of Demeter at Eleusis. Eleusis is a town about fourteen miles west of Athens; the religion and ceremony that developed in honor of Demeter and her daughter had its center here, but the city of Athens too was intimately involved. This religion was of a special kind, not the general prerogative of everyone, but open only to those who wished to become initiates; these devotees were sworn to absolute secrecy and faced dire punishments if they revealed the secret rites.[2] This does not imply that initiation was confined to a select few. In early times membership was inevitably limited only to the people of Eleusis and Athens, but soon participants came from all areas of the Hellenic

[2] The charges against Alcibiades mentioned earlier are indicative of the seriousness of the consequences if the sacred ceremonies were divulged in any way.

world and eventually the Roman Empire as well. This religion was not restricted to men only; women, children, and even slaves could participate. But an understanding of Greek was required, presumably for the necessary comprehension of the higher ceremonies.

Appropriately the religious celebration that was evolved was given the name of the Eleusinian mysteries. Demeter then, along with other Hellenic deities, is the inspiration for a kind of worship that is generally designated as the mystery religions (compare Dionysus and Apollo in the religion of Orpheus, or aspects of the devotion to Aphrodite and Adonis or Cybele and Attis). In fact Orpheus himself is credited with originating the mysteries. Although there must have been differences among the various mystery religions (some of them probably quite marked) obvious to the ancient world, we have difficulty today in distinguishing among them precisely. It seems fairly certain that the one major common denominator is the belief in man's immortal soul and future life.

The mysteries at Eleusis were kept secret, and scholars are by no means agreed about what we can say with any certainty, particularly about the highest and most profound elements of the worship. The sanctuary at Eleusis has been excavated and buildings connected with the ceremonies have been found, most important among them being a Telesterion, the temple of Demeter, where the final revelation of the mysteries was celebrated.[3] But no evidence has been unearthed that might dispel the secrecy with absolute certainty once and for all. The priests in charge of the rites presumably transmitted orally what Demeter was said to have taught.

It is impossible to know just how much of the ritual is revealed in the *Homeric Hymn*. It would be presumptuous to imagine that the most profound secrets are here for all to read, and we cannot be sure how much may be inferred from what is directly stated. That elements of the ceremonies are indicated cannot be denied, but presumably these are only the elements that were witnessed

---

[3] See in particular George E. Mylonas, *Eleusis and the Eleusinian Mysteries* (Princeton: Princeton University Press, 1961); this provides the best general survey of all the evidence and the inherent archaeological, historical, religious, and philosophical problems.

or revealed to all, not only to the initiated. Thus we have prescribed by the text such details as an interval of nine days, fasting, the carrying of torches, the exchange of jests, the partaking of the drink, *Kykeon,* the wearing of a special dress, for example, the veil of Demeter; even precise geographical indications (e.g., the Maiden Well, and the site of the temple) are designated. The emotional tone of the poem too might set the key for a mystic performance in connection with the celebrations. The anguish of Demeter, her frantic wanderings and search, the traumatic episode with Demophoon, the miraculous transformation of the goddess, the ecstatic reunion between mother and daughter, the blessed return of vegetation to a barren earth, are some of the obvious emotional and dramatic highlights.

The literary, epigraphical, and archaeological evidence yields the following tentative outline of the basic procedures in the celebration of the Eleusinian mysteries; ultimate revelation and meaning are matters of more tenuous conjecture and dispute. Two major compulsory stages had to be undertaken: (1) participation in the Lesser Mysteries involving preliminary steps in initiation; (2) advancement to the Greater Mysteries (the *teletai* proper), which entailed full initiation into the cult. A third stage, the highest of all, not required but possible, entailed participation in rites known as the *Epopteia.* It is immediately apparent that these mysteries are basically different from the festivals celebrated in the panhellenic sanctuaries, such as that of Apollo at Delphi, which were open to all, without secrecy or initiation or a fundamental mystic philosophy, however religious the tone that oracular response and devotion to a god might set.

Two major priestly families were connected with Eleusis: the Eumolpids, whose ancestor Eumolpus, according to the *Hymn,* received the mysteries from Demeter herself, and the Kerykes. Among the many important priesthoods and assistant officials, the highest was that of the Hierophant; this priest alone could reveal to the worshipers the ultimate mysteries which entailed the showing of the sacred objects (the *Hiera*)—his title means "he who reveals the *Hiera.*" Prominent too was the priestess of Demeter who lived in a sacred house. Many of the priests received a fixed sum of money from each initiate as a fee for their services. The initiate

ATHENA from an Attic amphora, ca. 520 B.C.,
Berlin, Staatliches Museum.

ARTEMIS AND APOLLO SHOOTING THE CHILDREN OF NIOBE from a calyx-crater by the Niobid Painter (ca. 450 B.C.), Paris, Louvre Museum. Reproduced by permission of the Louvre Museum.

APOLLO, from the west pediment of the Temple of Zeus at Olympia (456 B.C.), Olympia Museum.

APOLLO AND DAPHNE by Antonio Pollaiuolo (1429–98) or a follower,
London, National Gallery. Reproduced by courtesy of the Trustees, National
Gallery, London.

APOLLO AND DAPHNE by G. L. Bernini (1598–1680), Rome, Borghese Gallery. Reproduced by permission of the Borghese Gallery.

DIONYSUS, cylix by Exekias (ca. 530 B.C.), Munich, Museum Antikes Kleinkunst. Reproduced by permission of Hirmer Publishing House, Munich.

DIONYSUS WITH SATYRS AND MAENADS, from a sixth-century vase in The British Museum. Reproduced by permission of the Trustees of The British Museum.

SATYRS AND MAENADS, from an amphora by the Celophrades Painter (ca. 500 B.C.), Munich, Staatliche Antikensammlung.

HADES AND PERSEPHONE, terracotta plaque from Locri (ca. 460 B.C.), Reggio, Museum.

SATYR AND MAENAD from an amphora by Phintias (ca. 520 B.C.), Tarquinia Museum.

ORPHEUS, EURYDICE AND HER-
MES, marble relief (ca. 450 B.C.),
Naples, Museo Nazionale.

THE RAPE OF EUROPA, metope
from Temple C at Selinus (ca. 540
B.C.), Palermo, National Museum.

THE RAPE OF EUROPA by Titian (ca. 1477–1576), Boston,
Isabella Stewart Gardner Museum. Reproduced by permission.

*THE JUDGMENT OF PARIS by Lucas Cranach, the Elder (1472–1553),
Karlsruhe, Germany, Staatliche Kunsthalle. Reproduced by permission of
Staatliche Kunsthalle.*

(the *mystes*) was sponsored and directed by a patron called the *mystagogos*.

The Lesser Mysteries were held in Athens usually once a year, in early spring. Precise details are unknown, but the general purpose was certainly the preliminary preparation of the initiate for subsequent advancement to higher things. Ceremonies probably focused upon ritual purification, involving sacrifices, prayer, fasting, and cleansing by water.

The Greater Mysteries were held during the months of September and October annually (every fourth year the celebration was particularly splendid). A holy truce was declared for a period of fifty-five days and heralds were sent to issue invitations to states, which would respond with tithes and special delegations. Both Athens and Eleusis were involved in the festivities. Preliminary to the festival proper was the day on which the *Hiera* were taken out of the Anactoron of the Telesterion (i.e., the holy of holies of the temple of Demeter) in Eleusis and brought to Athens amidst great pomp and ceremony. The splendid procession, headed by the priests and priestesses who carried the *Hiera* in sacred caskets bound by ribbons, was met officially in Athens and escorted in state to the Eleusinion, the sanctuary of Demeter in the city. The next day following these preliminaries was the first of the formal celebration of the Greater Mysteries which continued through eight days, the ceremonies culminating in Eleusis, with a return to Athens on the ninth.

The first day saw the people summoned to an assembly in the Stoa Poikile (the Painted Colonnade) in the Athenian agora; those who were pure and knew Greek were invited by proclamation to participate in the Mysteries. On the second day all participants were ordered to cleanse themselves in the sea; the initiates rushed into the water with cries of "To the sea, O Mystai." Each carried a little pig that also needed to be purified and which was subsequently sacrificed. The following day (the third) was probably devoted to sacrifices and prayers on behalf of the individuals participating as well as for the various states involved, including the city of Athens. The fourth day was spent in honoring Asclepius, who according to tradition had in previous times arrived late for initiation. So on this day other late-comers could enroll and make up the requirements they had missed. The festivities in Athens culminated on the fifth day in a brilliant procession back to Eleusis. Priests and laymen wended their prescribed way, crowned with myrtle and carrying the mystic *bacchus* (myrtle branches tied with wool strands).[4] Clothes and supplies for the stay in Eleusis were borne on staffs and on pack animals. Heading the procession was a wooden statue of Iacchus (very likely another name for the god Dionysus) escorted in a carriage. At some stages of the journey abuse, jests, insults, and scurrilous language were exchanged, perhaps in part to instill humility in the throng. Similar practices may have been part of the subsequent ceremony at Eleusis.

Prayers were chanted and hymns sung; torches were carried and lit as night fell, and the sacred procession reached the sanctuary of Demeter in Eleusis. Here the participants would find rest in hostels or camps or the homes of friends. Perhaps singing and festivities went on far into the night upon arrival in Eleusis; it has been suggested that at this time the women danced with the mystic *kernoi* (sacred vessels) on their heads. Certainly the sixth and seventh days brought the initiates to the secret core of the mysteries, and it seems safe to assume that much of the ritual was performed in remembrance of the episodes described in the *Homeric Hymn.* Thus there was a fast (certain foods, such as pomegranates, beans, and some kinds of fish, were prohibited) and a vigil; probably the fast was ended by the drinking of the prescribed drink, the *Kykeon,* whatever its significance. The heart of the ceremonies apparently involved three stages: a dramatic enactment (*dromena*); the revelation of sacred objects (*deiknymena*), and the uttering of certain words (*legomena*). The center of these activities was the Telesterion proper and the inner sanctuary (Anactoron) of the temple.

What were the themes of the dramatic pageant? Probably it focused upon incidents from the story of Demeter and her wanderings and other episodes recorded in the *Hymn,* all designed to elicit a religious catharsis. Some have suggested scenes of an Orphic character involving a simulated trip to the Underworld with fabricated apparitions of terror and sublimity as the action moved from Hell (Tartarus) to Paradise (Elysium). That no underground

---

[4] Aristophanes, *Frogs,* 340ff., gives us some idea of this procession.

chambers have been found in the excavations does not necessarily invalidate this theory. We do not know whether the initiates merely witnessed the drama or actually participated in it. Eventually the culmination was the awesome exhibition (*deiknymena*) by the Hierophant himself of the holy objects, bathed in a radiant light in front of the Anactoron as he delivered his mystic utterances (*legomena*). The *Epopteia,* the highest stage of all, was not required for full initiation; it entailed further revelation of some sort. The eighth day concluded the ceremonies; the ninth brought the return to Athens, this time with no organized procession. The following day the Athenian council of five hundred heard a full report on the conduct of the ceremonies.

Conjecture about the exact nature of the highest mysteries in terms of the literary, epigraphical, and archaeological evidence has been legion. Comments by the Church Fathers have been brought to witness but their testimony has been rightly viewed with the gravest suspicion as rooted in prejudice stemming from ignorance and hostility. No one of them had ever been initiated into the mysteries and surprisingly enough Christian converts who had been initiated seem to have continued to take their pledges of secrecy very seriously.

The ultimate revelation has been claimed to be connected with the transformation of the Eleusinian plain into a field of golden grain (as in the *Hymn*); the heart of the mysteries consisted of the showing of an ear of grain to the worshipers. Thus we actually do know the secrets, or, if you like, they are really not worth knowing at all in terms of serious religious thought. Others insist upon an enactment of the holy marriage in connection with the ceremonies, imagining not a spiritual but a literal sexual union between the Hierophant and the Priestess of Demeter. The *Hiera* too might be the female pudenda, and, since Dionysus may be linked with Demeter and Kore, the male phallus as well. These holy objects were witnessed or even manipulated by the initiates in the course of the ritual. But there is no good reason to argue for such orgiastic procedures, however much they may belong to other cults in other places. The *Hiera,* as has been conjectured, could be merely sacred and antique relics handed down from the Mycenaean Age.

It is difficult, however, to agree with those who would exclude

Dionysus completely from the worship of Demeter at Eleusis. Iacchus has good claims to be Dionysus. And the myth of Zagreus-Dionysus that provides the biblical authority for Orphism has Persephone as his mother. Any spiritual message in the cult at Eleusis must have in common with Dionysiac belief the immortality of the soul and redemption. If a doctrine similar to that of Orphism then is also involved it need not spring directly from Orphism. The confusion arises because all the mystery religions did in fact preach certain things in common, whatever the precise interrelation.[5] The Eleusinian mysteries need not have remained uncontaminated by similar religions in the ancient world, nor for that matter must any of the others have remained pure.

The death and rebirth of vegetation as defied in Demeter and Kore surely suggest a belief in the afterlife. After all this is the promise of the *Hymn:* "But the one who is not initiated into the holy rites and has no part never is destined to a similar joy when he is dead in the gloomy realm below." If at some future time only obscure evidence remained for the ritual of the Christian Mass, scholars might imagine all sorts of things and miss completely the religious and spiritual doctrine upon which it rests. The words uttered by the Hierophant could have ordained spiritual direction and hope. But there was no church body as such for the followers of Demeter in the sense that they must return each year; we know of no sacred writings like those, say, of Orphism. Mylonas's conclusions after years of study and thought are worthy of the deepest respect (pp. 284–285):

Whatever the substance and meaning of the Mysteries was, the fact remains that the cult of Eleusis satisfied the most sincere yearnings and the deepest longings of the human heart. The initiates returned from their pilgrimage to Eleusis full of joy and happiness, with the

[5] Herodotus (8.65) tells a tale about a mysterious cloud arising from Eleusis amidst the strains of the mystic hymn to Iacchus that provided a true omen of future events; in the context the worship of the mother and the maiden is mentioned. This miracle sets the right tone for elements common to the worship and myths of both Demeter and Dionysus. It is not impossible that the passion of this resurrection-god played some role in the mysteries; Dionysus too is close to drama and drama lies at the essence of the emotional aspects of Eleusinian ritual.

fear of death diminished and the strengthened hope of a better life in the world of shadows: "Thrice happy are those of mortals, who having seen those rites depart for Hades; for to them alone is it granted to have true life there; to the rest all there is evil," Sophocles cries out exultantly. And to this Pindar with equal exultation answers: "Happy is he who, having seen these rites goes below the hollow earth; for he knows the end of life and he knows its god-sent beginning." When we read these and other similar statements written by the great or nearly great of the ancient world, by the dramatists and the thinkers, when we picture the magnificent buildings and monuments constructed at Eleusis by great political figures like Peisistratos, Kimon, Perikles, Hadrian, Marcus Aurelius and others, we cannot help but believe that the Mysteries of Eleusis were not an empty, childish affair devised by shrewd priests to fool the peasant and the ignorant, but a philosophy of life that possessed substance and meaning and imparted a modicum of truth to the yearning human soul. That belief is strengthened when we read in Cicero that Athens has given nothing to the world more excellent or divine than the Eleusinian Mysteries.

Let us recall again that the rites of Eleusis were held for some two thousand years; that for two thousand years civilized humanity was sustained and ennobled by those rites. Then we shall be able to appreciate the meaning and importance of Eleusis and of the cult of Demeter in the pre-Christian era. When Christianity conquered the Mediterranean world, the rites of Demeter, having perhaps fulfilled their mission to humanity, came to an end. The "bubbling spring" of hope and inspiration that once existed by the Kallichoron well became dry and the world turned to other living sources for sustenance. The cult that inspired the world for so long was gradually forgotten, and its secrets were buried with its last Hierophant.

Finally a word of caution about the usual generalizations put forth concerning the dichotomy between the mystery religions and the state religions of antiquity. The argument runs something like this. The formal state religions were sterile or very soon became so; the hope and faith of men lay only in the very real experience offered by the mysteries. Whatever the general truth of this view, it must be noted that for classical Greece, at any rate, the lines are not so distinct. Ceremonies connected with Demeter at Eleusis are tied securely to the policies of the Athenian state. The *archon basileus* (an Athenian official in charge of religious matters in general) directed the celebrations for Demeter in Athens. The

Athenian council as a political body was very much concerned about the festival. The pomp and procession involved are startlingly similar to the pageant connected with the Panathenaic festival in honor of Athena, a civic function, whatever its spiritual import. The "church" at Eleusis and the Athenian state were, to all intents and purposes, one.

CHAPTER 13

Views of the Afterlife;
The Realm of Hades

The earliest account that we have of the realm of Hades is in Book 11 of the *Odyssey*. Homer's geographical and spiritual depiction is fundamental to subsequent elaborations and thus deserves to be excerpted at some length. Odysseus is telling the Phaeacians and their king, Alcinous, of his visit to the Underworld where he must consult the seer Tiresias about how to reach Ithaca, his homeland (12–99):

> Our ship came to the farthest realm of deep-flowing Oceanus, where the country of the Cimmerians lies shrouded in cloud and mist. Bright Helius never looks down on them with his rays either when he ascends to starry heaven or returns to earth but dire night covers these poor mortals. Here we beached our ship and after putting the animals ashore we went along the stream of Oceanus until we came to the place that Circe had indicated. Here two of my men, Perimedes and Eurylochus, held the sacrificial victims, and I drew my sharp sword from my side and dug a pit about eighteen inches square. Around it I poured a libation to all the dead, first with a mixture of honey and milk, then with sweet wine, and a third time with water; over this I sprinkled white barley. I then supplicated the many strengthless spirits of the dead, promising that once I had come to Ithaca I should sacrifice, in my own halls, a barren heifer, the very best I had, and heap the sacrificial pyre with the finest things and offer separately to Tiresias alone a jet-black sheep that was outstanding among my flocks.[1] When I had finished entreating the host of the dead with

---

[1] Tiresias is the famous seer of the Theban cycle, who holds special prerogatives in the world of the dead; his wits are intact and to him alone in death Persephone has left a mind for reasoning; all others are mere shadows (*Odyssey*, 10.492–495).

prayers and supplications, I seized the victims and cut their throats and their dark blood flowed into the pit. Then the souls of the dead who had departed swarmed up from Erebus: [2] young brides, unmarried boys, old men having suffered much, tender maidens whose hearts were new to sorrow, and many men, wounded by bronze-tipped spears and wearing armor stained with blood. From one side and another they gathered about the pit in a multitude with frightening cries. Pale fear took hold of me and then I urgently ordered my companions to flay the animals which lay slaughtered by the pitiless bronze and burn them and pray to the gods, to mighty Hades and dread Persephone. But I myself drew my sword from my side and took my post and did not allow the strengthless spirits of the dead to come near the blood before I had questioned Tiresias.

But first the soul of my comrade, Elpenor, came up. For he had not yet been buried in the wide earth.[3] We had left his body in Circe's palace, unwept and unburied, since other toil had oppressed us. I wept at seeing him and pitied him and calling out addressed him with winged words: "Elpenor, how have you come to this gloomy realm? You arrived on foot sooner than I in my black ship." Thus I spoke; and he replied with a groan:

"Royal son of Laertes, clever Odysseus, a divine and evil destiny and too much wine were my undoing. When I went to sleep in Circe's palace I forgot to climb down the long ladder and fell headlong from the roof; my neck was severed from my spine and my soul came down to the realm of Hades.[4] Since I know that when you leave this house of Hades you will stop with your fine ship at Circe's island of Aeaea, I beseech you by those whom you left behind far away, by your wife and father who took care of you as a child, and by Telemachus, your only son whom you left at home in your palace, do not turn away and go back leaving me unwept and unburied for future time, or I may become the cause of wrathful vengeance from the gods upon you. But burn my body with all the armor that I have and pile up a mound for me on the shore of the gray sea, the grave of an unfortunate man, so that posterity too may know. Do these things for me and plant on the mound the oar with which I rowed alongside my companions

[2] Another name for Hades's realm or a part of it.

[3] Elpenor can address Odysseus first without drinking the blood because his corpse has not been cremated.

[4] As we learn in Book 10, 551–560, Elpenor got drunk, and, wanting fresh air, left his companions in Circe's palace. He fell asleep on the roof; in the morning he was awakened suddenly and forgot where he was.

while I was alive." Thus he spoke. And I addressed him in answer: "My poor friend, I shall accomplish to the full all your wishes." So we two faced each other in sad conversation, I holding my sword over the blood and on the other side the shade of my companion recounting many things. The soul of my dead mother came up next, daughter of great-hearted Autolycus, she who was alive when I went to sacred Ilium. I cried when I saw her and pitied her in my heart. Still even though I was deeply moved I did not allow her to come near the blood before I had questioned Tiresias.

Then the soul of Theban Tiresias came up, bearing a golden scepter. He knew me and spoke: "Royal son of Laertes, clever Odysseus, why, why, my poor fellow, have you left the light of the sun and come to see the dead and their joyless land? But step back from the pit, and hold aside your sharp sword so that I may drink the blood and speak the truth to you." So he spoke; and I drew back my silver-studded sword and thrust it into its sheath. After he had drunk the dark blood, then the noble seer spoke to me.[5]

Tiresias proceeds to tell Odysseus what destiny has in store for him; after the seer has prophesied, Odysseus asked (141–159):

"I see there the soul of my dead mother and she stays near the blood in silence and has not dared to look at her own son face to face nor speak to him. Tell me, O prince, how may she recognize that I am her son?" Thus I spoke. And he addressed me at once with the answer: "I shall tell you simple directions which you must follow. Any one of the dead you allow to come near the blood will speak to you clearly, but anyone you refuse will go back away from you." With these words the soul of prince Tiresias went into the home of Hades, after he had uttered his prophecies. But I remained steadfast where I was until my mother came up and drank the dark blood. Immediately then she knew me and in her sorrow spoke winged words: "My son, how have you come, while still alive, below to this gloomy realm which is difficult for the living to behold? For great rivers and terrible waters lie between, first Oceanus which, if one does not have a sturdy ship, he cannot in any way cross on foot."

---

[5] Tiresias does not have to drink the blood before he can speak but he needs to drink it in order to express his prophetic powers to the full. He may also be drinking it as a mortal would drink wine, or refreshment, and thus he establishes as well ties of hospitality and friendship with Odysseus.

Anticlea and Odysseus continue their conversation questioning each other. Finally she reveals to her son that it was heartache and longing for him that brought her life to an end. At this Odysseus cannot restrain himself (204–234):

Troubled in spirit I wished to embrace the soul of my dead mother; three times I made the attempt, as desire compelled me, three times she slipped through my hands like a shadow or a dream. Sharp pain welled up from the depths of my heart and speaking I addressed her with winged words: "O my mother, why do you not stay for me so eager to embrace you, so that we both may throw our arms about each other, even in Hades's realm, and take comfort in chill lamentation? Or has august Persephone conjured up this phantom for me so that I may groan still more in my grief?" Thus I spoke, and she my lady mother answered at once: "O my poor child, ill-fated beyond all men, Persephone, daughter of Zeus, does not trick you at all, but this is the doom of mortals when they die, for no longer do sinews hold bones and flesh together, but the mighty power of blazing fire consumes all, as soon as the life breath leaves our white bones and the soul like a dream flutters and flies away. But as quickly as possible make your way back to the light, but understand all these things so that you may in the future tell them to your wife." Thus we two exchanged words; then women came up (for august Persephone compelled them), all of whom were the wives or daughters of noble men. And they gathered all together about the dark blood. But I deliberated how I might speak to each one individually and upon reflection this seemed to me the best plan. I drew my sharp sword from my sturdy side and did not allow them to drink the dark blood all at the same time. And they came up one by one and each explained her lineage and I questioned them all.

The parade of beautiful women that follows is packed with mythological and genealogical information that has little meaning for us in this context. At the end Persephone drives away the souls of these illustrious ladies. A lengthy interview follows between Odysseus and Agamemnon, who embittered tells of his murder at the hands of his wife, Clytemnestra, and her lover, Aegisthus, and remains suspiciously hostile toward all women. Then the souls of Achilles and Patroclus and the greater Ajax appear. The soul of Achilles addresses Odysseus next (Patroclus does not speak).

We must excerpt two portions of their conversation to establish more completely the tone and humanity of Homer's conception. Achilles says (473–491):

"Royal son of Laertes, clever and indomitable Odysseus, what still greater exploit have you ingeniously devised? How have you dared to come down to Hades's realm where spirits without body of sense dwell, shadows of mortals worn out by life?" Thus he spoke, and I addressed him in answer: "O Achilles, son of Peleus, by far the mightiest of the Achaeans, I came down to Hades's realm to ask the seer Tiresias if he might tell me some way by which I might return to rocky Ithaca. For I have not yet come near Achaea nor yet reached my homeland but I always have misfortunes. But no man either before or after is more fortunate than you, Achilles. Previously while you lived we Argives heaped honors on you equal to those of the gods, and now being in this place you have great power among these shades. So, Achilles, do not be at all distressed, even though you are dead." Thus I spoke, and he at once addressed me in answer: "Do not speak to me soothingly about death, glorious Odysseus; I should prefer as a slave to serve another man, even if he had no property and little to live on, than to rule over all these dead who have done with life."

Achilles goes on to inquire about his son, Neoptolemus, and when Odysseus has given details of how the boy has proven himself a man worthy of his father, Achilles in his pride feels a surge of joy illumine his gloomy existence (538–544):

"The soul of swift-footed Achilles [Odysseus goes on to relate] made its way in great strides over the plain full of asphodel, rejoicing because I said that his son was a renowned hero. Other souls of the dead stood grieving, and each recounted his sorrows. Only the soul of Ajax, son of Telamon, stood apart."

Ajax, who had committed suicide because Odysseus and not he had been awarded the armor of Achilles, will not respond to Odysseus's appeals (563–600):

Instead he went after the dead spirits into Erebus, where perhaps he might have spoken to me or I to him. But desire in my breast wished to see the souls of the other dead.
There I saw Minos, the splendid son of Zeus, sitting with a gold

scepter in his hand and pronouncing judgments for the dead, and they sitting and standing asked the king for his decisions within the wide gates of Hades's house.

And I saw next the giant hunter, Orion, driving together on the plain of asphodel the wild beasts which he himself had killed on the lonely mountains, having in his hand a bronze club that was always unbreakable. And I saw Tityus, son of revered Earth, lying on the ground covering a vast area. Two vultures sitting on either side of him tore into his body and ate at his liver and his hands could not keep them off. For he had assaulted Leto, the renowned consort of Zeus, as she was going through Panopeus, a city of beautiful dancing places, to Pytho.[6]

And also I saw Tantalus enduring harsh sufferings as he stood in a pool which splashed to his chin. He strained to quench his thirst but was not able, for every time the old man leaned eagerly to take a drink, the water was swallowed up and gone and about his feet the black earth showed, dried up by some divine power. Tall and leafy trees dangled fruit above his head: pears, pomegranates, apples, sweet figs, and olives, growing in luxuriant profusion. But whenever he reached out to grasp them in his hands, the wind snatched them away to the shadowy clouds.[7]

And also I saw Sisyphus enduring hard sufferings as he pushed a huge stone; exerting all his weight with both his hands and feet he kept shoving it up to the top of the hill. But just when he was about to thrust it over the crest then its own weight forced it back and once again the pitiless stone rolled down to the plain. Yet again he put forth his strength and pushed it up; sweat poured from his limbs and dust rose up high about his head.

Odysseus next sees the phantom of Heracles—the real Heracles is with his wife, Hebe, among the immortal gods. Heracles tells how he too was ill-fated while he lived, performing labors for an inferior master.

Homer's Book of the Dead ends with the following description by Odysseus (628–640):

[6] An early name of Delphi.

[7] Tantalus's crime is variously described in later writers; whatever its specific nature, it is a crime against the gods, often identified as some abuse of their trust or hospitality. The verb "tantalize" comes from his name and his punishment.

After the departure of Heracles I remained steadfast in my place in case any other heroes who had previously died might still come; now I should have seen men, whom I wanted to see, of earlier times. Theseus and Pirithous, renowned sons of the gods, but countless hordes of the dead swarmed together with frightening shrieks; pallid fear took hold of me that dread Persephone might send from Hades a Gorgon head of terrible portent. Immediately then I went to my ship and ordered my comrades to board and release the mooring cables. They obeyed at once and took their places at the oars. As they started to row a fair breeze sprang up.

Countless difficulties beset any interpretation of the Homeric view of the afterlife, many of which are linked to the nature of the composition of the *Odyssey* as a whole and this book in particular. Discrepancies are apparent and explanations must finally hinge upon one's views on the much wider problems of the Homeric question. Does the Book of the Dead reflect different attitudes and concepts put together by one man or several, at one time or over a period of years and even centuries? Basic to the account perhaps is a cult of the dead seen in the sacrificial ceremonies performed at the trench and in the serious note of moral compulsion to provide burial for one who has died. But as the description proceeds there is much that is puzzling. Odysseus apparently should remain at his post while the souls come up; if so, does he witness the torments of the sinners and the activities of the heroes described with them as a vision from the pit of blood, or is this episode an awkward addition from a different treatment that had Odysseus actually tour the realm of Hades? Certainly the section listing the women who come up in a group conveys strongly the feelings of an insertion, written in the style of the Boeotian epic of Hesiod. As the book begins the stream of Oceanus seems to be the only barrier, but later Anticlea speaks of other rivers to be crossed.

Thus the geography of the Homeric underworld is vague and similarly the classification of those who inhabit it obscurely defined, particularly in terms of the precision that is evident in subsequent literature. Elpenor, among those who first swarm up, may belong to a special group in a special area, but we cannot be sure. Heroes like Agamemnon and Achilles are together but they do not clearly occupy a separate paradise; the meadow of asphodel which they inhabit seems to refer to the whole realm and not an Elysium such as we shall have described by Vergil. One senses rather that all mortals end up together pretty much in the same place without distinction. Since Odysseus thinks that Achilles has as great power among the shades as he had among the living, perhaps some prerogatives are assigned or taken for granted. A special hell for sinners may be implied (at least they are listed in a group), but it is noteworthy that these sinners are extraordinary indeed, great figures of mythological antiquity who dared great crimes against the gods. Apparently ordinary mortals do not suffer so for their sins. Homer does not seem to present an afterlife of judgment and reward and punishment, and Minos presumably acts as a judge among the dead, settling their disputes there very much as he did in real life.

The tone and mood of the Homeric afterlife is generally more consistent. Vague and fluttering spirits with pursuits, passions, and prejudices they had while alive drift aimlessly and joylessly in the gloom; the light and hope and vigor of the upper world are gone. Philosophical and religious thought, shot through with moral earnestness and righteous indignation, will soon bring about sublime and terrifying variations in this picture.

Plato concludes the last book of his great dialogue, the *Republic,* with the myth of Er. This vision of the afterlife is steeped in religious and philosophical concepts and, although figures from mythology are incorporated, the symbolic and spiritual world depicted is far removed from that of Homer. Socrates, addressing Glaucon, makes this clear as he begins (614B):

I shall not tell a tale like that of Odysseus to Alcinous but instead my story is of a brave man, Er, the son of Armenius, a Pamphylian, who at one time died in war; after ten days, when the bodies by now decayed were taken up, his alone was uncorrupted. He was brought home and on the twelfth day after his death placed on a funeral pyre in preparation for burial. But he came back to life and told what he had seen in the other world. He said that after his soul had departed it traveled with many and came to a divine place, in which there were two openings in the earth next to each other, and opposite were two others in the upper region of the sky. In the space between these four openings sat judges who passed sentence: the just they ordered

to go to the right through one of the openings upwards in the sky
after they had affixed their judgments in front of them; the unjust
they sent to the left through one of the downward openings, bearing
on their backs indications of all that they had done; to Er when he
approached they said that he must be a messenger to men about the
afterlife and commanded him to listen and watch everything in this
place. To be sure he saw there the souls after they had been judged
going away through the opening either in the heaven or in the earth,
but from the remaining two openings he saw some souls coming up
out of the earth, covered with dust and dirt, and others descending
from the second opening in the sky, pure and shining. And they kept
arriving and appeared as if they were happy indeed to return after
a long journey to the plain that lay between. Here they encamped
as though for a festival, and mutual acquaintances exchanged greetings; those who had come from the earth and those from the sky
questioned one another. The first group recounted their experiences,
weeping and wailing as they recalled all the various things they had
suffered and seen in their journey under the earth, which had lasted
one thousand years; the others from the sky told in turn of the happiness they had felt and sights of indescribable beauty. O Glaucon,
it would take a long time to relate everything. But he did say that the
essential significance was this: everyone had to suffer an appropriate
penalty for each and every sin ten times over, in retribution for the
number of times and the number of persons he had wronged; that is,
he must make one full payment once every hundred years (since
this is considered the span of human life) so that he might pay in
full for all his wrongs, tenfold in one thousand years. For example,
if any were responsible for the deaths of many or betrayed and en-
slaved cities or armies or were guilty of any other crime, they would
suffer torments ten times over for all of these sins individually, but on
the other hand, if they had done good deeds and were just and holy,
in the same proportion they were given a worthy reward. About those
who died immediately after birth and those who had lived a short
time he said other things not worth mentioning.

He described still greater retribution for honor or dishonor toward
gods and parents and for murder. He told how he was near one
spirit who asked another where Ardiaeus the Great was. This Ardiaeus
had been tyrant in a city of Pamphylia a thousand years before this
time and he was said to have killed his aged parents and older brother
and to have committed many other unholy deeds. The reply was that
he had not and would not come back to the plain. For to be sure this
was one of the terrifying sights that we witnessed. When we were near

the mouth and about to come up, after experiencing everything else, we suddenly saw Ardiaeus and others, most of whom were tyrants, but there were also some ordinary persons who had committed great wrongs. They all thought that they would at last ascend upwards but the mouth would not let them; instead it gave forth a roar, whenever any who were so incurable in their wickedness or had not paid suffi- cient penalty attempted to come up. Then indeed wild men, fiery of aspect, who stood by and understood the roar, seized some of them and led them away, but they bound Ardiaeus and the others, head, hand, and foot, threw them down, and flayed them; they dragged them along the road outside the mouth combing their flesh like wool with thorns, making clear to others as they passed the reason for the pun- ishment and that they were being led away to be hurled down to Tartarus. Of all the many and varied terrors that happened to them there, by far the greatest for each was that he might hear the roar as he came up, and when there was silence each ascended with the utmost joy. The judgments then were such as these: punishments for some and again rewards for others in due proportion.

The next section of the myth is extremely difficult. It presents a cosmological explanation of the universe; problems arise from the astronomical terminology and metaphorical imagery in terms of a spindle with its fly or whorl, a commonplace item in the ancient world but relatively unfamiliar today. A paraphrase and with it inevitably an interpretation follow for the sake of brevity and clarity. We have taken the liberty of adding the metaphor of an open umbrella, held upside down, to that of the spindle with its shaft and at one end a fly or whorl.

The souls who have completed their cycle of one thousand years spend seven days on the plain and then proceed on another jour- ney accompanied by Er. Four days later they arrive at a place from which they behold a beam of light that extends like a pillar through all of heaven and earth. After another day's journey they can see that this light provides as it were a bond or chain to hold the universe together; from this chain of light extends the spindle (or umbrella) of Necessity (*Ananke*) made for the most part of adamantine steel, by which all the revolving spheres are turned. The fly or whorl of the spindle (open end of an inverted umbrella) is hollow and filled with eight concentric circular rings which fit into one another like a set of bowls; the shaft pierces the middle of the central eighth ring. The lips or rims of these circular rings (which vary in width) revolve and carry with them the fixed stars and all the planets; the order, beginning from the outside of the circle, is: fixed stars, Saturn, Jupiter, Mars, Mercury, Venus, the sun, the moon. The whole spindle (or umbrella) revolves in one direction while the seven inner circles turn individually at various speeds in the opposite direction. Thus is explained the apparent daily revolution of the stars and planets; earth is at the center.

Let us return directly to Plato's account of Er as Socrates relates it.

The spindle turned on the knees of Necessity. A Siren was perched aloft each of the circles and borne along with it, uttering a single sound on one musical note; from all eight came a unified harmony. Round about at equal distances sat three others, each on a throne, the Fates (*Moirae*), daughters of Necessity, in white robes with garlands on their heads, Lachesis, Clotho, and Atropos, singing to the music of the Sirens: Lachesis of the past, Clotho of the present, and Atropos of the future. Clotho touches with her right hand the outside circle of the spindle and helps turn it; with her left Atropos moves the inner circles in the same way, and Lachesis touches and moves both, alternating with each hand.

Immediately after the souls arrived they had to approach Lachesis. First of all a prophet arranged them in order and then, after taking from the knees of Lachesis lots and examples of lives, he mounted a lofty platform and spoke: "Hear the word of Lachesis, maiden daughter of Necessity. Ephemeral souls, this is the beginning of another cycle of mortal life fraught with death. A divinity will not allot himself to you, but you will choose your divinity.[8] Let one who has drawn the first lot choose a life, which will be his by necessity. Virtue is without master; each man has a greater or lesser share, insofar as he honors or dishonors her. The blame belongs to him who makes the choice; god is blameless." With these words he cast the lots among them all, and each picked up the one that fell near him. Only Er was not allowed to participate. It was clear to each when he had picked up his lot what number he had drawn. Next he placed the examples of lives on the ground in front of them, many more than those present and of every kind; lives of all living creatures and all

[8] This divinity (*daimon*) is the destiny that accompanies each soul through its life on earth, its good or bad *genius*.

mankind. Among them lives of tyrants, some complete, others cut short and ending in poverty, exile, and destitution. There were lives of illustrious men, renowned for form and beauty or strength and physical achievement, others for family and the virtues of their ancestors; in the same way were lives of unknown or disreputable men; and so it was for women. But the disposition of the soul was not included, because with its choice of another life it too of necessity became different, but the other qualities were mixed with one another, wealth and poverty, sickness and health, and intermediate states. Herein to be sure, as it seems, my dear Glaucon, lies all the risk; therefore each one of us must see to it most particularly that he forsake all other learning and seek to find and understand this crucial knowledge; he must search if he can hear of and discover one who will make him capable of knowing; he must distinguish the good life from the wicked and choose always in every situation from the possibilities the better course, taking into account all that has now been said. He must know how these qualities individually or combined affect virtue in a life, what beauty mixed with poverty or wealth achieves in terms of good and evil along with the kind of state of soul that it inspires, and what high and low birth, private status, public office, strength, weakness, intelligence, stupidity, and all such qualities, inherent or acquired, achieve in combination with one another, so that after deliberation he may be able to choose from all of these between the worse and better life, looking only to the effect upon the nature of his soul. By the worse life I mean that leading the soul to become more unjust, by the better, that leading it to become more just. All other considerations he will ignore. For we have seen that this is the most crucial choice for a man living or dead. Indeed one must cling to this conviction even when he comes to the realm of Hades, so that here just as in the other world he may not be overwhelmed by wealth and similar evils and succumb to acts like those of a tyrant, committing many incurable evils and besides suffering still greater ones himself, and so that he may know how to choose a life that follows the mean in such circumstances, and to avoid the excesses in either direction both in this life and in every future life, as far as he is able. For in this way a man becomes most fortunate and blessed.

Then indeed Er, the messenger from the afterlife, reported that the prophet spoke as follows: "Even for the one who comes last there lies a life that is desirable and not evil, if he chooses intelligently and lives it unflinchingly. Let not the one who chooses first be careless, nor the last discouraged." After he had spoken, the one who had drawn the first lot immediately went up and chose the most extreme tyranny and he made his choice out of senselessness and greed and did not look closely at everything, and he did not notice that his life entailed the fate of eating his own children and other evils. And when he examined his choice at leisure he beat his breast and lamented that he had not abided by the warnings of the prophet. For he did not accept the responsibility for these evils but he blamed fate and the gods and everything rather than himself. He was one of those who had come down from the sky and had lived his previous life in a city with an orderly political constitution and adopted virtue through habit rather than wisdom. Generally speaking the number of those who came down from the sky and were caught in this kind of predicament was not small, since they were untrained in suffering. But many of those from earth, since they had themselves suffered and seen others suffer, did not make their choice on impulse. Because of this and because of the chance of the lot, for many souls there occurred a change from an evil or a good fate or the reverse. For if one always pursues wisdom with all his strength each time he takes a life in the world and if the lot of choosing does not fall to him among the last, it is likely from all that has been reported that not only will he be happy in life but also his journey after death from the plain and back will not be under the earth and hard, but easy and upward to the sky. Er said that to watch each soul as he chose his life was a worthwhile sight, piteous, laughable, and wondrous. For the most part they made their choice on the basis of their experiences in their previous life. He saw the soul that had been that of Orpheus choose the life of a swan through hatred of the female sex because of his death at their hands, not wishing to be born again of woman. And he saw the soul of Thamyras select the life of a nightingale, and a swan decide to change to the life of a human, and other musical creatures make similar decisions. The soul that drew the twentieth lot chose the life of a lion; this was the soul of Ajax, son of Telamon, avoiding a human life because he remembered the judgment concerning Achilles's armor. After him came the soul of Agamemnon; he too through hatred of the human race because of his sufferings changed to the life of an eagle. The choice of the soul of Atalanta fell in the middle of the proceedings; she saw great honors attached to the life of a male athlete and took it, not being able to pass it by. He saw after her the soul of Epeus, the son of Panopeus, assuming the nature of a craftswoman, and far away among the last the soul of the ridiculous Thersites taking the form of an ape. In his fated turn the soul of Odysseus, who had drawn the last lot, went to choose; remembering his former toils he sought to be free from ambition; he looked a long time and with difficulty found the quiet life of an ordinary man lying somewhere disregarded by the others, and when he saw it he made his choice gladly and said that he would have done the same thing even if the first lot had fallen to him. In the same way souls of wild animals exchanged forms or entered human beings, the unjust changing to savage beasts, the just to tame ones and all kinds of combinations occurred. When all the souls had chosen lives, they proceeded in order according to their lots to Lachesis. She gave to each the divinity (*daimon*) he had chosen to accompany him as a guardian for his life and to fulfill his choices. This divinity first led the soul to Clotho, under her hand as it turned the revolving spindle, to ratify the fate each had chosen after drawing his lot. He touched her and then led the soul to the spinning of Atropos, thus making the events on the thread of destiny unalterable. From here without turning back they went under the throne of Necessity and passed beyond it. When all the souls and their guardian divinities had done this, they proceeded together to the plain of the river of forgetfulness (Lethe) through a terrible and stifling heat. For it was devoid of trees and all that the earth grows. Now that it was evening they encamped by the river of forgetfulness, whose water no container can hold. It is necessary for all to drink a fixed amount of the water, but some do not have the wisdom to keep from drinking more than this amount. As one drinks one becomes forgetful of everything. In the middle of the night when they were asleep there was thunder and an earthquake, and then suddenly just like shooting stars they were borne upward each in a different direction to his birth. Er himself was prevented from drinking the water. He does not know where and how he returned to his body but suddenly opening his eyes he saw that he was lying on the funeral pyre at dawn. Thus, O Glaucon, the myth has been preserved and has not perished and we should be saved if we heed it and we shall cross the river of forgetfulness well and not contaminate our souls. But if we all agree in believing the soul is immortal and capable of enduring all evils and all good, we shall always cling to the upward path and in every way pursue justice with wisdom, so that we may be in loving reconciliation with ourselves and the gods and so that when we carry off the prizes of justice, just like victors in the games collecting their rewards, both while we are here and in the thousand-year journey we have described, we may fare well.

This vision of an afterlife written in the fourth century comes from various sources about which we can only conjecture, and of course we must allow for the inventive genius of Plato himself in terms of his own philosophy. The numerical intervals (e.g., the journey of a thousand years) are reminiscent of Pythagoras and the belief in the transmigration of the soul; reward and punishment with ultimate purification is usually identified as Orphic. Problems abound in connection with the precise interpretation of this myth of revelation that concludes the *Republic* with proof of divine immortality. How much was intended to be accepted literally? Is Er's story an allegory filled with profound symbols hiding the universal truths it wishes to disclose? For the purposes of our sketch of the development of the Greek and Roman depiction of the afterlife, it is important to stress the fact that a heaven and a hell are clearly depicted for the soul of every mortal, and in addition to the upward and downward path that must be traversed, special tormentors exist and a special place of torment (Tartarus) in which the greatest sinners are placed forever.[9] In such a conception lies the mythical and biblical basis for the mystery religions of antiquity, whether their god be Demeter or Dionysus and their prophet, Orpheus or Plato.[10] Ties with Christian sentiments are not hard to see, despite the obvious differences. More specific links are provided by the identification of Er as an ancestor of St. Joseph and the fact that the early Christians in their championship of free will seized upon the admonition of Lachesis: "The blame belongs to him who makes the choice; god is blameless."

In Book 6 of the *Aeneid,* Vergil paints his sad and prophetic picture of the Underworld in shadowy halftones fraught with tears

---

[9] In Hesiod (*Theogony*, 713–814) Tartarus is a dark place in the depths of the earth into which Zeus hurled the Titans after he had defeated them. It is surrounded by a fortification of bronze and inside dwell Night and her children, Sleep and Death. The house of Hades and Persephone is guarded by a terrifying hound. The river of Tartarus is the Styx, by whose water the gods swear dread oaths; if they break these oaths they must suffer terrible penalties for a full nine years.

[10] In graves in southern Italy and Crete have been found thin plates of gold on which religious verses have been inscribed, which were presumably intended to help the mystic believer in the afterlife; some of the sentiments reflect the eschatology found in Plato, especially concerning the drinking of the waters of Lethe.

and pathos. His sources are eclectic but his poetic vision is personal and unique. Despite the centuries of oral and written tradition and the Roman chauvinistic cast of his depiction, Homeric and Platonic elements are often still distinctly evident. At Cumae in Italy, the Sibyl, prophetess of Apollo, tells Aeneas what the requirements are to visit his father in the realm of Hades. He must get a golden bough, sacred to Proserpine, and bury his comrade, Misenus. It is easy to descend to the Underworld; the task is to retrace one's steps to the upper air; only a special few have managed this. While his men are preparing a funeral pyre for Misenus, Aeneas goes in search of the bough (186–204):

As Aeneas gazed at the vast woods, it happened that he uttered a prayer: "If only the golden bough would show itself to me in so immense a forest. For the priestess told all that was true—alas, too true—about your need for burial, Misenus." At that moment, as it happened, twin doves came flying from the sky under his very eyes and settled on the green ground. Then the great hero recognized his mother's birds and in his joy prayed: "Be leaders, if there is some way, and direct your course to the grove where the branch rich in gold shades the fertile earth; O goddess mother do not fail me in this crisis." Thus he spoke and stopped in his tracks, watching what sign they gave and what course they took. They would stop to feed and then fly ahead always permitting Aeneas as he followed to keep them in sight. When they approached the foul odor coming up from Lake Avernus they quickly flew higher and gliding through the liquid air the doves settled down together on the longed-for tree, where the tawny gleam of gold flickered through the branches.

Aeneas eagerly breaks off the golden bough; after the funeral rites for Misenus have been completed he takes it to the Sibyl (237–322):

There was a deep and rocky cave with a huge yawning mouth sheltered by the black lake and the darkness of the forest; no birds at all were able to wing their way overhead, so great and foul an exhalation poured up to the vault of heaven from the lake. Its name, Avernus, deriving from the Greek, means birdless. Here first of all the priestess set four black bullocks and poured wine over their heads; between their horns she cut the tips of bristles and placed them on the sacred fire as first libations, calling aloud on Hecate, who holds power both in the sky above and in the depths of Erebus. Attendants applied their knives and caught the warm blood in bowls. Aeneas himself slaughtered with his sword a black-fleeced lamb for Night, the mother of the Eumenides, and her great sister, Earth, and for you, Proserpine, a barren cow; then he built an altar in the night for the Stygian king and placed on the flames the whole carcasses of bulls, pouring rich oil over their entrails. Lo, at the first rays of the rising sun, the ground rumbled and the wooded ridges began to move and she-dogs appeared howling through the gloom as the goddess approached from the Underworld. The Sibyl cried: "Keep back, keep back, you who are unhallowed; withdraw completely from this grove. But you, Aeneas, enter the path and seize your sword from its sheath. Now there is need for courage and a stout heart." This much she spoke and threw herself furiously into the cave. Aeneas, without fear, matched the steps of his leader as she went.

You gods who rule over spirits, silent shades, depths of Chaos, Phlegethon, and vast realms of night and silence, let it be right for me to speak what I have heard; by your divine will let me reveal things buried deep in earth and blackness.

They went, dim figures in the shadows of the lonely night, through the empty homes and vacant realms of Dis, as though along a road in woods by the dim and treacherous light of the moon, when Jupiter has clouded the sky in darkness and black night has taken color from things. At the entrance itself, in the very jaws of Orcus, Grief and avenging Cares have placed their beds; here dwell pale Diseases, sad Old Age, Fear, evil-counseling Hunger, foul Need, forms terrible to behold, and Death and Toil; then Sleep, the brother of Death, and Joys evil even to think about, and opposite on the threshold, death-dealing War, the iron chambers of the Eumenides, and insane Discord, her hair entwined with snakes and wreaths of blood. In the middle a huge and shady elm spreads its boughs, aged arms in which empty Dreams are said to throng and cling beneath all the leaves. There were besides many different forms of beasts and monsters: Centaurs had their haunt in the doorway, Scyllas with two-fold form, hundred-handed Briareus, the creatures of Lerna, hissing dreadfully, the Chimaera armed with flames, Gorgons, Harpies, and the shade of triple-bodied Geryon. Suddenly Aeneas startled by fear snatched his sword and threatened them with his drawn blade as they approached. If his wise companion had not warned that these insubstantial lives without body flitted about with but the empty shadow of a form, he would have rushed in and smitten the shades with his weapon for nothing.

From here is a path that leads to the waters of Acheron, a river of Tartarus, whose seething flood boils turbid with mud in vast eddies and pours all its sand into the stream of Cocytus.[11] A ferryman guards these waters, Charon, horrifying in his terrible squalor; a mass of white beard lies unkempt on his chin, his eyes glow with a steady flame, and a dirty cloak hangs from his shoulders by a knot. He pushes his boat himself by a pole, tends to the sails, and conveys the bodies across in his rusty craft; he is now older but for a god old age is vigorous and green. Here a whole crowd poured forth and rushed down to the bank: mothers and men, the bodies of great-souled heroes finished with life, boys and unmarried girls, young men placed on the pyres before the eyes of their parents, as many as the leaves that drop and fall in the forest at the first cold of autumn or as the birds that flock to land from the stormy deep, when winter puts them to flight across the sea and sends them to sunny lands. They stood pleading to be the first to cross and stretched out their hands in longing for the farther shore. The grim boatman accepted now these and now those, but he drove others back and kept them at a distance from the sandy shore. Aeneas, who was moved by the tumult, asked in wonder: "Tell me, O virgin Sibyl, the meaning of this gathering at the river? What do these souls seek? By what distinction do some retire from the bank, while others are taken across the murky stream?" The aged priestess answered him briefly as follows: "Son of Anchises, and most certainly a descendant of the gods, you see the deep pools of Cocytus and the marshes of the Styx, the river by which the gods fear to swear falsely. This one group here consists of those who are poor and unburied.[12] The ferryman is Charon. The others whom he takes across are those who have been buried. Charon is not allowed to transport them over the hoarse-sounding waters to the dread shore if their bones have not found rest in proper burial; but a hundred years they wander and flit about this bank before they come back at last to the longed for waters and are admitted to the boat." The son of Anchises stopped in his tracks and stood thinking many thoughts, pitying in his heart the inequity of man's fate.

---

[11] Vergil's conception of the rivers of the Underworld is far from clear. Charon seems to ferry the souls across Acheron, although Cocytus is mentioned in the immediate context; the Styx is identified by Vergil later. Tradition often has Charon cross the river Styx.

[12] By poor, Vergil probably means that they do not have the fare to pay Charon. A coin was placed between the lips of the dead for passage to the Underworld.

Among those who have not received burial Aeneas sees his helmsman, Palinurus, who had fallen overboard on their voyage from Africa; he managed to reach the coast of Italy but once ashore tribesmen killed him. The interview is reminiscent of the exchange between Odysseus and Elpenor in human emotion and religious sentiment. The Sibyl comforts Palinurus with the prediction that he will be buried by a neighboring tribe. The book continues (384–449):

Aeneas and the Sibyl proceed on their way and approach the river. When the ferryman spied them from his post by the river Styx coming through the silent grove and turning their steps toward the bank, he challenged them first with unprovoked abuse: "Whoever you are who approach our river in arms, explain why you have come but answer from there, do not take another step. This is the place of the shades, of sleep and drowsy night; it is forbidden to carry living bodies in my Stygian boat. To be sure I was not happy to have accepted Heracles and Theseus and Pirithous when they came to these waters, although they were of divine descent and invincible strength. Heracles by his own hand sought and bound in chains the guardian dog of Tartarus and dragged it away trembling from the throne of the king himself. The other two attempted to abduct the queen from the chamber of Dis." The priestess of Apollo answered briefly: "No such plots this time; be not dismayed; our weapons bear no violence; let the huge doorkeeper howl forever and strike terror into the bloodless shades; let Proserpine remain safe and pure within the house of Pluto, her uncle. Trojan Aeneas, outstanding in goodness and valor, descends to the shades below to his father. If the sight of such great virtue and devotion does not move you, at least recognize this bough." She revealed the bough which lay hidden in her robe and at this his heart that was swollen with anger subsided. Not a word more was uttered. He marveled at the hallowed gift of the fateful branch which he had not seen for a long time, turned his dark-colored boat around to approach the shore. Then he drove away the souls that were sitting on the long benches, cleared the gangway, and at the same time took the mighty Aeneas aboard; the leaky seams groaned under his weight and let in much of the swampy water. At last Charon disembarked the seer and the hero safe and sound on the further shore amid shapeless mud and slimy sedge.

Huge Cerberus, sprawling in a cave facing them, made these regions echo with the howling from his three throats. When the prophetess saw his necks bristling with serpents she threw him a cake of meal and honey drugged to make him sleep. He opened wide his three throats in ravenous hunger and snatched the sop; his immense bulk went limp and spread out on the ground filling the whole of the vast cavern. With the guard now buried in sleep Aeneas made his way quickly over the bank of the river of no return.

Immediately, on the very threshold, voices were heard and a great wailing and the souls of infants weeping who did not have a full share of sweet life but a black day snatched them from the breast and plunged them into bitter death. Next to them were those who had been condemned to die by a false accusation. To be sure their abode has not been assigned without an allotted jury, and a judge, Minos, is the magistrate; he shakes the urn and draws lots for the jury, summons the silent court, and reviews the lives and the charges. Right next is an area occupied by an unhappy group who were guiltless, but sought death by their own hand and hating the light abandoned their lives. How they wished now even for poverty and hard labor in the air above! But fate stands in the way and the hateful marsh binds them with its gloomy waters and the Styx flowing round nine times imprisons them.

Not far from here spread out in all directions were the Fields of Mourning, as they are named. Here those whom relentless and cruel love had wasted and consumed hide themselves in secret paths in the woods of myrtle; even in death itself their anguish does not leave them. In this place he saw Phaedra, Procris, and unhappy Eriphyle displaying the wounds inflicted by a cruel son, and Evadne, Pasiphae, and with them Laodamia and Caeneus, who had been changed into a boy and now once again was a woman.

Here Aeneas meets Dido, queen of Carthage, who recently has committed suicide because of her love for Aeneas and his betrayal. He addresses her in sad, piteous, and uncomprehending tones, but she refuses to answer and turns away to join the shade of her former husband, Sychaeus.

From here Aeneas and his guide move on to the last group and farthest fields reserved for those renowned in war, who had been doomed to die in battle and were much lamented by those on earth. Tydeus, Parthenopaeus, Adrastus, and many, many others come to meet Aeneas. Trojan heroes crowd around him but the Greek warriors from Troy fled in terror. Aeneas converses with Deiphobus, the son of Priam who married Helen after the death

of Paris. Deiphobus tells the story of his death at the hands of
Menelaus and Odysseus through the treachery of Helen. Their
talk is interrupted by the Sibyl, who complains that they are
wasting the brief time that they have; it is now already past midday
on earth and night is coming on (540–543):

This is the place where the road divides and leads in two directions:
our way is to the right and extends under the ramparts of Dis to
Elysium, but the left path leads to the evil realms of Tartarus, where
penalties for sin are exacted.

We must look at Vergil's conception of hell, Tartarus, and
paradise, Elysium or the Elysian Fields (548–579):

Suddenly Aeneas looked back to the left and saw under a cliff lofty
fortifications enclosed by a triple wall around which flowed Phlegethon, the swift stream of Tartarus, seething with flames and rolling
in its torrent clashing rocks. He saw in front of him a huge door,
with columns of solid adamant that no human force nor even the
gods who dwell in the sky would have the power to attack and break
through. Its tower of iron stood high against the winds and one of
the furies, Tisiphone, clothed in a bloody robe, sat guarding the
entrance, sleepless day and night. From within he heard groans and
the sound of savage lashes, then the grating of iron and the dragging
of chains. Aeneas stood in terror absorbed by the din. "Tell me, virgin
prophetess, what is the nature of their crimes? What penalties are
imposed? What is this great wail rising upward on the air?" Then she
began to speak: "Renowned leader of the Trojans, it is not permitted
for anyone who is pure to cross the threshold of the wicked. But
when Hecate put me in charge of the groves of Avernus she herself
taught me the penalties exacted by the gods and went through them
all. Cretan Rhadamanthus presides over this pitiless kingdom; he
punishes crimes and recognizes treachery, forcing each to confess the
sins committed in the world above, atonement for which each had
postponed too long, happy in his futile stealth, until Death. At once
the avenging fury, Tisiphone, armed with a whip, leaps on the guilty
and drives them with blows; as she threatens with her fierce serpents
in her left hand, she summons the phalanx, her savage sisters. Then
at last the sacred gates open wide, turning with strident horror on
their creaking hinges. Do you see what kind of sentry sits at the
entrance? What forms are watching in the threshold? The monstrous

Hydra more fierce than the Furies with its fifty black and gaping throats has its home within. Then Tartarus itself yawns deep under the shades, extending straight down twice as far as the view upward to the sky and celestial Olympus.

In Tartarus Vergil places the Homeric sinners Tityus, Sisyphus, and possibly Tantalus, but there is difficulty in the text and its interpretation; Tityus is the only one of the three named directly. Other criminals identified by Vergil are the Titans, who were hurled to the very bottom of Tartarus by the thunderbolts of Jupiter; the sons of Aloeus, Otus and Ephialtes,[13] who tried to storm heaven and seize Jupiter himself; Salmoneus, who was foolish enough to play the role of Jupiter and claim divine honors; Theseus and Pirithous; Phlegyas; [14] and Ixion. Ixion is one of the more famous sinners condemned to Tartarus; he is punished by being bound to a wheel that eternally revolves.[15]

Vergil's Tartarus is not a hell just for heroic sinners of mythological antiquity; in it all men who are guilty suffer punishment. It is important to realize fully the ethical standards that he applies. The nature of sin is clearly summed up by the Sibyl as she continues; just as clear is the moral conviction that assigns happiness to the good in the paradise of Elysium (608–751):

"Here are imprisoned and await punishment those who hated their brothers while they were alive or struck a parent and devised guile against a dependent or who hovered over their acquired wealth all alone and did not share it with their relatives (these misers were the greatest throng), and those who were killed for adultery or took up arms in an impious cause and were not afraid to betray the pledges made to their masters. Do not seek to learn the nature of the crime and fate of each and every sinner and the punishment in which he is submerged. Some roll a huge rock, others hang stretched on the spokes

[13] The mother of the Aloadae was Iphimedeia, who said that their real father was Poseidon, according to the Greek version. These twins grew to be giants and their attack on Zeus was made by piling Mt. Ossa upon Olympus, and then Mt. Pelion upon Ossa. For this presumption they were both killed while still young by Apollo.

[14] In some accounts Phlegyas is the father of Ixion; he burned the temple of Apollo at Delphi because of Apollo's affair with his daughter Coronis.

[15] Sometimes the wheel is on fire.

of a wheel; Theseus sits in his misery and he will remain sitting forever; wretched Phlegyas admonishes all as he bears testimony in a loud voice among the shades: 'Be warned! Learn justice and not to despise the gods.' This one sold his country for gold, set up a tyrannical despot, made laws, and revoked them for a price. This one invaded the bedroom of his daughter in forbidden incestuous marriage. All dared enormous crime, and were successful in the attainment of their daring. I should not be able to recount all the forms of wickedness or enumerate all the names of the punishments if I had a hundred tongues and a hundred mouths." After the aged priestess of Phoebus had uttered these words, she continued: "But come now, proceed on your way and accomplish the task you have undertaken. Let us hurry. I see opposite fortifications of Pluto's palace erected by the forges of the Cyclopes and the vaulted arch of its door where we have been ordered to lay down this gift!" She had spoken and making their way together through the gloom of the path they hurried over the space between, and approached the gates. Aeneas reached the entrance, sprinkled himself with fresh water and placed the bough on the threshold.

When this had been done and the gift had been given to the goddess, then at last they came to the happy places, the pleasant green glades of the Woods of the Fortunate, the home of the blessed. Here air that is more pure and abundant clothes the plains in soft-colored light and they have their own sun and their own stars. Some exercise their limbs on the grassy wrestling grounds, vie in sport, and grapple on the yellow sand. Others dance in a chorus and sing songs and the Thracian priest, Orpheus, in his long robe, accompanies their measures on the seven strings of his lyre, plucking them now with his fingers, now with an ivory quill. Here is the ancient Trojan line of king Teucer, a most beautiful race, great-souled heroes born in better years, and Ilus, Assaracus, and Dardanus, the founder of Troy. Aeneas marvels at the unreal arms of the heroes and their chariots nearby. The spears stand fixed in the ground, and horses browse freely everywhere on the plain. The same pleasure that they had in their chariots and arms and in tending their sleek horses follows them after they have been laid in the earth. Behold he sees others feasting to the right and to the left on the grass and singing a happy paean in a chorus amidst a fragrant grove of laurel, from which the full stream of the Eridanus river rolls through the woods in the upper world.[16] Here in a group were those

[16] The Po River near its source flowed for some distance underground, and the legendary river of the Underworld, Eridanus, was identified with it.

who suffered wounds while fighting for their country, and the priests who remained pure while they lived, and the poets who were devout in their art and whose words were worthy of their god, Phoebus Apollo, or those who made life better by their discoveries in the arts and the sciences and who through merit made others remember them. All of these wore around their temples a snowy white garland; the Sibyl spoke to them as they surrounded her, singling out Musaeus especially: "Tell my happy souls and you, O illustrious poet, what region, what place does Anchises inhabit? We crossed the great rivers of Erebus and have come on his account." Musaeus replied in these few words: "No one has a fixed abode; we inhabit shady groves living in meadows fresh with streams along whose banks we recline. But if the desire in your heart so impells you, cross over this ridge; I shall show you an easy path." He spoke and walked ahead of them pointing out the shining fields below; then they made their way down from the height.

Father Anchises was eagerly contemplating and surveying souls that were secluded in the depths of a green valley and about to enter upon the light of the upper air. It happened that he was reviewing the whole number of his own dear descendants; the fate, fortune, character, and exploits of Roman heroes. When he saw Aeneas coming towards him over the grass, he quickly extended both his hands and a cry escaped his lips as the tears poured down his cheeks: "At last you have come and your long awaited devotion to your father has overcome the hard journey. Is it granted to me to see your face, to hear your voice, to speak to you as of old? I have been pondering your visit, thinking about when it would be, counting out the time, and my anxiety has not gone unrewarded. I receive you here after your travels over so many lands and so many seas, harried by so many dangers! How much I feared that Dido in her African kingdom might do you some harm!" Aeneas replied: "The vision of you in your sadness appearing to me again and again compelled me to pursue my way to this realm. My ships are moored on the Italian shore. Give me, give me your right hand, father, do not shrink from my embrace." As he was speaking his face was moist with many tears. Three times he attempted to put his arms around his father's neck, three times he reached in vain as the phantom escaped his hands as light as a breeze, like a fleeting vision of the night.[17]

Meanwhile Aeneas saw in this valley set apart, a secluded grove and the rustling thickets of a wood and the stream of Lethe which

---

[17] Vergil echoes Homer's line about Odysseus trying to embrace the shade of his mother.

flowed by the serene abodes. Around the river countless tribes and peoples were flitting, just as when bees settle on different flowers in a meadow in the calm heat of summer and swarm about the white lilies; the whole plain was filled with a murmuring sound. Aeneas, who did not understand, gave a sudden shudder at the sight, and seeking reasons for it all, asked what the river was in the distance and what crowd of men filled its banks. Then father Anchises replied: "The souls to which bodies are owed by Fate at the stream of the river Lethe drink waters that release them from previous cares and bring everlasting forgetfulness. Indeed I have desired for a long time to tell you about these souls, to show them before your very eyes, and to list the number of my descendants; now all the more may you rejoice with me that you have found Italy." "O father, am I to think that some souls go from here to the upper air and enter sluggish bodies again? What is this dread desire of these poor souls for light?" "To be sure I shall tell you and not hold you in suspense." Thus Anchises replied and proceeded step by step to reveal the details in order.

"In the first place a spirit within sustains the sky, the earth, the waters, the shining globe of the moon, and the Titan sun and stars; this spirit moves the whole mass of the universe, a mind, as it were, infusing its limbs and mingled with its huge body. From this arises all of life, the race of men, animals, and birds, and the monsters that the sea bears under its marble surface. The seeds of this mind and spirit have a fiery power and celestial origin, insofar as the limbs and joints of the body, which is of earth, harmful, and subject to death, do not make them dull and slow them down. Thus the souls, shut up in the gloomy darkness of the prison of their bodies, experience fear, desire, joy, and sorrow, and do not see clearly the essence of their celestial nature. Moreover, when the last glimmer of life has gone, all the evils and all the diseases of the body do not yet completely depart from these poor souls and it is inevitable that many ills, for a long time encrusted, become deeply engrained in an amazing way. Therefore they are plied with punishments and they pay the penalties of their former wickedness. Some spirits are hung suspended to the winds; for others the infection of crime is washed by a vast whirlpool or burned out by fire. Each of us suffers his own shade.[18] Then we are sent to Elysium and we few occupy these happy fields, until a long period of the circle of time has been completed and has removed the ingrown corruption and has left a pure ethereal spirit and the fire of

[18] I.e., each of us has a soul which must bear the consequences of its life on earth.

the original essence. When they have completed the cycle of one thousand years, the god calls all these in a great throng to the river Lethe, where, of course, they are made to forget so that they might begin to wish to return to bodies and see again the vault of heaven."

Anchises then led Aeneas and the Sibyl to a mound from which they could view the souls as they came up, and he pointed out to them with affection and pride a long array of great and illustrious Romans who were to be born. The book ends with Aeneas and his guide leaving by the gate of ivory; why Vergil has it so, no one knows for sure (893–899):

"There are twin gates of Sleep; one is said to be of horn, through which easy exit is given to the true shades. The other is gleamingly wrought in shining ivory, but through it the spirits send false dreams up to the sky." After he had spoken Anchises escorted his son and the Sibyl and sent them out by the gate of ivory. Aeneas made his way to his ships and rejoined his companions.

Vergil is writing in the second half of the first century B.C. and variations and additions are apparent when his depiction is compared to the earlier ones of Homer and Plato. There are, of course, many other sources for the Greek and Roman conception of the afterlife, but none are more complete or more profound than the representative visions of these authors, and a comparison of them gives the best possible insight into the general nature and development of the ancient conception both spiritually and physically.

Vergil's geography is quite precise. Aeneas and the Sibyl go through various regions. First of all a neutral zone contains those who met an untimely death (infants, suicides, and persons condemned unjustly); next the Fields of Mourning are inhabited by victims of unrequited love and warriors who fell in battle. The logic of these allocations is not entirely clear. Is a full term of life necessary for complete admission to the Underworld? Then appear the crossroads to Tartarus and the Fields of Elysium. The criteria for judgment are interesting; like many another religious philosopher and poet Vergil must decide who will merit the tortures of his hell or the rewards of his heaven both on the basis of tradition and of personal conviction. Other writers vary the list.[19] Some have observed that the tortures inflicted are often imaginative and ingenious, involving vain and frustrating effort of mind and body, and therefore characteristically Greek in their sly inventiveness. Perhaps so, but depicted as well is sheer physical agony through scourging and fire. Attempts made to find a logic in the meting out of a punishment to fit the crime are only sometimes successful.[20]

Vergil's paradise is very much the idealization of the life led by Greek and Roman gentlemen and the values illustrated in the assignment of its inhabitants are typical of ancient ethics: devotion to mankind and country, to family, and to the gods. Yet despite the Greek and Roman coloring of the picture, the morality is universal and germane to all humanity and civilization. In Elysium, too, details supplement the religious philosophy of Plato that has been labeled Orphic and Pythagorean in particular, and mystic in general. Man's body is of earth, evil, and mortal; the soul is of the divine upper aether, pure and immortal, and must be cleansed from contamination and sin. Once again we are reminded of the myth of Dionysus, which explains man's dual nature in terms of his birth from the ashes of the wicked Titans (the children of Earth) who had devoured the heavenly god Dionysus.

Presumably in the cycle of rebirth and reincarnation the weary chain is ultimately broken and we are no longer reborn into this world but join the oneness of divinity in the pure spirit of the upper air.

Some identification and clarification of various names and terminology linked with the Underworld are now in order. The realm as a whole may be called Tartarus or Erebus, or these are the names given solely to the region of torment as opposed to Elysium or the Elysian Fields. Sometimes the realm of paradise is located elsewhere in some remote place of the upper world, such as the Islands of the Blessed.

---

[19] The Danaids, the forty-nine daughters of Danaus who killed their husbands on their wedding night, are frequently added to the group in Tartarus; their punishment is that they must attempt in vain to carry water in containers that have no real bottom.

[20] Thus, for example, Tityus has his liver devoured because he attempted to violate Leto, since the liver was believed to be the seat of the passions.

There are usually three judges of the Underworld: Minos, Rhadamanthys (or Rhadamanthus), and Aeacus, whose duties are variously assigned. Aeacus is sometimes relegated to more menial tasks like that of gatekeeper in comedy. The rivers are generally five in number with appropriate names: Styx (the river of hate); Acheron (of woe); Lethe (of forgetfulness); Cocytus (of wailing); Pyriphlegethon or Phlegethon (of fire). It was a custom to bury the dead with a coin in their mouths to provide Charon with his fare. Hermes often plays his role of guide for the souls from this world to the next.

Hades, king of the Underworld, is also called Pluto or (in Latin) Dis, which means the wealthy one, referring to him either as a god of earth and fertility or as a deity rich in the numbers of those who are with him. The Romans called him and his realm Orcus, which probably means "the one or the place that constrains or confines." Sometimes Hades (this word may mean the unseen one) is given no name at all or is addressed by some complimentary epithet, as is the custom for all deities or spirits, such as the devil, whom one dreads. Hades and his realm and its inhabitants are in general called Chthonian, that is, of the earth, as opposed to the bright world of the Olympian gods of the upper air, and he himself may even be addressed as Chthonian Zeus.

The Furies (Erinyes) usually have their home in the realm of Hades; so does Hecate, who sometimes resembles them in appearance and in character. Hesiod, as we have seen, tells how the Furies were born from the blood which fell onto the earth after the castration of Uranus; according to others they are the offspring of Night. Both versions are appropriate in terms of their sphere and their powers. They vary in number but may be reduced to three with specific names: Alecto, Megaera, and Tisiphone. In literature and art they are depicted as formidable, bearing serpents in their hands or hair and carrying torches and scourges. They are the pitiless and just avengers of crime, especially murder; bloodguilt within the family is their particular concern and they may relentlessly pursue anyone who has killed a parent or close relative. It has been conjectured that originally they were thought of as the ghosts of the murdered seeking vengeance on the murderer or as the embodiment of curses called down upon the guilty.

The Furies very definitely represent the old moral order of justice within the framework of primitive society, where the code of an eye for an eye and a tooth for a tooth is meted out by the personal vendetta of the family or the clan. This is Aeschylus's conception of them in his dramatic trilogy, the *Oresteia*. The Furies persecute Orestes after he has murdered his mother but eventually their role is taken over by a new regime of right; the Areopagus, the court of Athens, decides Orestes's case through the due process of law and significantly it is Apollo and Athena (the new generation of progressive deities) who join forces with the justice of advanced civilization. The last play in the trilogy is called *The Eumenides*, which means the Kindly Ones; this is the name for the Furies as they are worshiped in Athens, after having finally been appeased and put to rest once and for all.[21]

The Christian concept of the devil should not be confused with the ancient portrayal of Hades, who is not fighting with his brother Zeus for man's immortal soul. We all end up in his realm where we may or may not find our heaven or our hell. The only exceptions are those who (like Heracles) are specifically made divinities and therefore allowed to join the gods in heaven or on Olympus. Hades, to be sure, is terrible in his severity and inexorable, but he is not in himself evil or our tormentor; we may fear him as we fear death and its possible consequences which we cannot avoid. But he does have assistants, such as the Furies, who persecute with devilish and fiendish torments.[22] Hades's wife, and queen of his realm, Persephone, has been considered in the previous chapter.

The profundity and intensity of the Greek and Roman vision of an afterlife have been all-pervasive in the art and literature of western civilization. Dante was steeped in its radiance which he suffused with Christian imagination and dogma, taking Vergil as his guide.

[21] The Furies also may be called the Eumenides in an attempt to ward off their hostility by a euphemistic appellation, as in the case of Hades.

[22] Zeus and the gods may destroy man and punish evil in this life at times in opposition against one other. And the justice of the moral order of the Olympian gods and the Fates is the same as that of the realm of Hades. It is Prometheus who champions mankind as a whole against the antagonism of Zeus, but this is a quite different story.

It would be misleading to imply that all Greek and Roman literature treats the realm of Hades and the afterlife with such serious profundity. One thinks immediately of Aristophanes's play the *Frogs,* in which the god Dionysus rows across the Styx to the accompaniment of a chorus croaking *brekekekex koax koax;* his tour of the Underworld is different and at times hilarious. From the wealth of material we can only include two dialogues by the satirist Lucian, who wrote in Greek during the second century A.D. A choice among his many brilliant *Dialogues of the Dead* is difficult. Two brief examples of his wit and varying moods must suffice here. The character, Menippus, was a famous Cynic philosopher of the third century B.C. The Cynics were poor and extremely frugal; their dirty and ragged dress usually included a staff and wallet or sack; they were unconventional and outspoken in their indignation at the standard and unthinking attitudes of the individual and society.

22. Charon, Menippus, and Hermes.

Charon: Abominable fellow, pay up the fare.

Menippus: Go ahead and shout, Charon, if this gives you some pleasure.

Charon: Pay up, I say, for ferrying you across.

Menippus: You can't get it from one who doesn't have it.

Charon: Is there anyone who doesn't have an obol for the fare?

Menippus: I don't know whether anyone else has or not, but I don't.

Charon: By Pluto, you rogue, I'll throttle you if you don't pay.

Menippus: And I'll smash your skull open with my stick.

Charon: Then you will have made this crossing to no avail.

Menippus: Let Hermes pay you for me, since he handed me over to you.

Hermes: By Zeus, I'll be damned if I am going to *pay* for the shades, too.

Charon: I won't give in to you.

Menippus: Then haul your boat up and stay here; how can you take what I don't have?

Charon: Didn't you know that you had to bring it?

Menippus: I knew but I didn't have it. What was I to do? Should I not have died on account of it?

Charon: So you will be the only one to boast that you were ferried across free?

Menippus: Not free, my fine fellow. I bailed water and helped row and I was the only one of the passengers who did not weep and wail.

Charon: These things have nothing to do with it. You must pay the obol; no exceptions allowed.

Menippus: Then take me back to life.

Charon: A fine remark, so that I may get a beating from Aeacus if I do.

Menippus: Then don't be so upset.

Charon: Show me what you have in your sack.

Menippus: Legumes, if you want, and one of Hecate's suppers.[23]

Charon: From where did you bring this dog to us?[24] He kept babbling like this during the crossing, laughing and jeering at the other passengers; he alone was singing while they were moaning.

Hermes: Charon, don't you know what man you have ferried across? Scrupulously free, he doesn't care about anyone or anything. This is Menippus.

Charon: Indeed if I ever get hold of you—

Menippus: If you do, my fine fellow. You won't get another chance.

18. Menippus and Hermes

Menippus: Where are the handsome men and the beautiful women, Hermes? Show me the sights, since I am a stranger here.

Hermes: I don't have the time, Menippus. But look over there to the right; there are Hyacinthus, Narcissus, Nireus, Achilles, Tyro, Helen, Leda, and in brief, all the beauties of old.

Menippus: I see only bones and skulls stripped of flesh, many of them alike.

Hermes: These bones that you seem to despise are what all the poets marvel at.

Menippus: But still show me Helen; for I should not recognize her.

Hermes: This is the skull of Helen.

Menippus: Was it for this then that the thousand ships were launched from all of Greece and so many Greeks and non-Greeks fell and so many cities were destroyed?

Hermes: But, Menippus, you did not see the woman when she was alive; you too would have said it worthwhile "to suffer sorrows so much time for such a woman."[25] For if one looks at flowers when

---

[23] Presumably Menippus stole the meal at a crossroads.

[24] Dog was a nickname for the Cynics; "cynic" in Greek means "dog-like."

[25] A quotation from the *Iliad*, 3.157.

they are dry and have lost their hues obviously they will seem ugly, but when they are in bloom and have their color they are most beautiful.

Menippus: And so I wonder at this: whether or not the Achaeans realized that they were toiling for a thing so short-lived and so easily destroyed.

Hermes: I do not have the time to philosophize with you. So pick out a spot wherever you wish and be comfortable there; now I shall go to fetch the other shades.

CHAPTER 14

Orpheus and Orphism

Ovid tells the story of Orpheus and Eurydice as follows (*Metamorphoses*, 10.1–85; 11.1–66):

Hymen, god of marriage wrapped in his saffron-colored cloak, left the wedding of Iphis and Ianthe and made his way through the vast tracts of air to the shores of the Thracian Cicones; he came at the call of Orpheus but in vain, for, although he was to be sure present at the marriage of Orpheus to Eurydice, he did not smile nor bless the pair nor give good omens. Even the torch which he held kept sputtering with smoke that drew tears and would not burn despite vigorous shaking. The outcome was even more serious than this ominous beginning. For while the new bride was wandering through the grass accompanied by a band of Naiads she was bitten on the ankle by a serpent and collapsed in death. After Orpheus, the bard of the Thracian mountains, had wept his fill to the breezes of the upper world he dared to descend to the Styx by the entrance near Taenarus so that he might rouse even the shades.[1] Past the tenuous multitudes of ghosts beyond the grave, he approached Persephone and her lord, who rule this unlovely realm of shadows, and sang his song as he plucked the strings of his lyre: "O deities of the world below the earth, into which all of us who are mortal return, if it is right and you allow me to utter the truth, laying aside evasion and falsehood, I did not come down to see the realms of Tartarus or to bind the triple neck, bristling with serpents, of the monstrous hound descended from Medusa; the cause of my journey is my wife; she stepped on a snake and its venom coursing through her veins stole from her the bloom of her years. I wanted to be able to endure and I admit that I have tried; but Love has conquered. He is a god who is well known in the world above; I suspect

---

[1] One of the many places identified as an entrance to the Underworld was a cave near Taenarus, a town in Laconia.

that he is famous even here as well (although I do not know for sure); if the story of the rape of long ago is not a lie, Love also brought you two together.

"By these places full of fear, by this yawning Chaos, and by the silent vastness of this kingdom, reweave I pray the thread of Eurydice's destiny cut off too soon! We pay everything to you and after tarrying but a little while we hasten more slowly or more quickly to this one abode. All of us direct our course here, this is our very last home, and you hold the longest sway over the human race. Eurydice too, when she in her ripe age has gone through the just allotment of her years, will fall under your power; I ask as a gift her return to me. If the Fates refuse this reprieve for my wife, it is sure that I do not wish to return either. Take joy in the death of us both!" As he made this plea and sang his words to the tune of his lyre, the bloodless spirits wept; Tantalus stopped reaching for the receding waters, the wheel of Ixion stopped in wonder, the vultures ceased tearing at the liver of Tityus, the Danaid descendants of Belus left their urns empty and you, O Sisyphus, sat on your stone. Then for the first time, the story has it, the cheeks of the Eumenides were moist with tears as they were overcome by his song, and the king who rules these lower regions and his regal wife could not endure his pleas or their refusal. They called Eurydice; she was among the more recent shades and she approached, her step slow because of her wound. Thracian Orpheus took her and with her the command that he not turn back his gaze until he had left the groves of Avernus, or the gift would be revoked.

Through the mute silence, they wrest their steep way, arduous, dark, and thick with black vapors. They were not far from the border of the world above; here frightened that she might not be well and yearning to see her with his own eyes, through love he turned and looked, and with his gaze she slipped away and down. He stretched out his arms, struggling to embrace and be embraced, but unlucky and unhappy he grasped nothing but the limp and yielding breezes. Now as Eurydice was dying for a second time she did not reproach her husband; for what complaint should she have except that she was loved? She uttered for the very last time a farewell that barely reached his ears and fell back once more to the same place. At the second death of his wife Orpheus was stunned. . . . The ferryman kept Orpheus back as he begged in vain wishing to cross over once again; yet he remained seated on the bank for seven days, unkempt and without food, the gift of Ceres; anxiety, deep grief, and tears were his nourishment as he bewailed the cruelty of the gods of Erebus. He then withdrew to the mountains of Thrace, Rhodope, and wind-swept Haemus. Three times the Titan sun had rounded out the year with the sign of watery Pisces, and Orpheus the while had fled from love with all women, either because of his previous woe or because he had made a pledge. Many women were seized with passion for union with the bard and many in anguish were repulsed. He was the originator for the Thracian peoples of turning to the love of young boys and of enjoying the brief spring of their youth and plucking its first flowers. . . .

While the Thracian bard was inducing the woods, the rocks, and the hearts of the wild beasts to follow him, Ciconian women, their frenzied breasts clad in animal skins, spied Orpheus from the top of a hill as he was singing to his lyre. One of them, her hair tossing in the light breeze, exclaimed: "Ah look, here is the one who despises us." And she hurled her weapon wreathed with foliage straight at the face of Apollo's son as he sang, and it made its mark but did not wound. The weapon of another was a stone, which as it hurtled was overcome in mid-air by the harmony of voice and lyre and fell prone at his feet like a suppliant apologizing for so furious an assault. But their hostility grew more bold, and restraint was abandoned until the Fury of madness held absolute sway. All weapons would have been softened by his song, but the great clamor, the Phrygian flutes with their curved pipes, the drums, the pounding, and the Bacchic shrieks drowned out the sound of his lyre. Then at the last the stones that could not hear grew red with the blood of the poet. But first the Maenads seized the hordes of birds still spellbound by the singer's voice, the serpents, and the throng of beasts, all testimonies to the triumph of his song. And then they turned with bloody hands on Orpheus himself, like birds that throng together if at any time they see the owl of night abroad by day. They made for the bard, just as the stag about to die is prey for the dogs in the morning sand of the amphitheater, and they flung the verdant leafy thyrsus, not made for such deadly purpose. Some hurled clods of earth, others branches ripped from trees, still others stones. So that weapons might not be wanting for their fury, it happened that oxen were working the earth yoked to the plough-share and nearby sturdy farmers were digging the hard fields with much sweat preparing for the harvest. When they saw the throng they fled, leaving behind the tools with which they worked. Hoes, heavy mattocks, and long rakes lay scattered through the empty fields. The madwomen snatched them up and after they had torn apart the oxen that threatened with their horns, they rushed back again to mete out the poet's fate. In their sacrilege they destroyed him as he stretched out his hands and spoke then for the first time in vain with a voice that touched no one. And through that mouth which was heard, god knows, by stones and understood by bestial senses, his soul breathed forth receding on the winds.

For you, O Orpheus, for you the trees let fall their leaves and shorn of foliage made lament. They say too that rivers swelled with their own tears, and the Naiads and Dryads changed their robes to black and wore their hair dishevelled. His limbs lie scattered in various places; his head and lyre you got, O river Hebrus; and—O wonder—while they floated in midstream, the lyre made some plaintive lamentation, I know not what, the lifeless tongue murmured laments too, and the banks lamented in reply. And then they left his native Thracian river and were carried out to sea, until they reached Methymna on the island of Lesbos. Here they were washed ashore on foreign sands and a savage snake made for the mouth and hair soaked with the dripping foam. At last Phoebus Apollo appeared and stopped the serpent as it prepared to make its bite and froze hard its open mouth and gaping jaws, just as they were, in stone. The shade of Orpheus went down below the earth and recognized all the places he had seen before; he looked amidst the fields of the pious and found Eurydice, and clasped her in his eager arms. Here now they walk together side by side, sometimes he follows her as she precedes, sometimes he goes ahead and safely now looks back at his Eurydice.

As Ovid continues the story we are told that Bacchus was distressed at the loss of the poet who sang his mysteries; he punished the Thracian women by turning them into trees and then abandoned Thrace all together.

The other major classical version of the story of Orpheus and Eurydice is by Vergil.[2] Most, but not all, of the details are similar in both, although the poetic timbre is different. According to Vergil, Eurydice stepped on the snake while running away from the unwelcome advances of Aristaeus.[3]

[2] *Georgics*, 4.452–526.

[3] Aristaeus, the son of Apollo and Cyrene, is the traditional hero or deity of rustic pursuits, especially bee keeping. When Eurydice died, his sister Dryads in their grief and anger caused all the bees of Aristaeus to die. He was perplexed and eventually consulted the wise old man of the sea, Proteus. Aristaeus appeased the nymphs and a new swarm of bees was created. Through the role of Aristaeus, Vergil artfully introduces the touching account of Orpheus and Eurydice in the last book of his didactic poem on farming.

Thus Ovid represents the tradition for the tragic story of music, enchantment, love, and death that has been recreated again and again with imagination, beauty, and profundity whether it be in an opera by Gluck or a movie by Cocteau. But there is another very important side to Orpheus's character of which we can only catch glimpses today because of the inadequacy of our evidence, for Orpheus was considered the founder of a religion, a prophet (*theologos*) who with his priests and disciples committed to writing holy words (*hieroi logoi*) that provided a bible for dogma, ritual, and behavior. Variations and inconsistencies in the tradition make it difficult to know this Orpheus and his religion precisely, but the general nature of their character and development can be discerned, despite the frustrating contradictions and obscurities.[4]

Some of the significant "facts" that can be isolated from the diverse accounts are as follows: Orpheus's home was in Thrace; his mother was one of the Muses, usually Calliope; his father was either Oeagrus, a Thracian river-god, or the great god Apollo, whom he follows. He wooed and won Eurydice, a Dryad, by the charm of his music. When she died, he went to Hades to fetch her but failed. Orpheus was one of the members of Jason's Argonautic expedition.[5] He had a son or a pupil, Musaeus, who assumed many of the characteristics of Orpheus himself. Among the versions of his death, several prove interesting in the quest for the historical religious teacher. He is said to have been struck down by the thunderbolt of Zeus because in his mysteries he taught things unknown before, or he died because of a conspiracy of his countrymen who would not accept his teachings. The common tradition (which both Ovid and Vergil reflect) has the women of Thrace responsible for his death. But the reasons for their hostility vary: they were angry when he neglected them after the

---

[4] An important survey offers the general reader a scholarly examination of the whole question: W. K. C. Guthrie, *Orpheus and Greek Religion, A Study of the Orphic Movement* (New York: W. W. Norton, 1966).

[5] He does not seem really to belong, but the gentle bard was placed among the brawny heroes because of his prestige and the magical powers of his song, which saved them all in more than one crisis; Orpheus appropriately was the leader in religious matters. Also the chronology seems wrong for our historical Orpheus, if we must put him back in the heroic age in the generation before the Trojan War.

death of Eurydice, or refused to initiate them into his mysteries, and enticed their husbands away from them. Sometimes the women are followers of Dionysus, expressly directed by their god against Orpheus, for Dionysus in his attempts to convert Thrace to his religion met the opposition of Orpheus, a devoted follower of Apollo the sun-god, and sent his maenads to tear the bard to pieces. According to some these pieces of his body were buried by his mother and sister Muses in Thrace or in the region of Mt. Olympus. His head and lyre were claimed by Lesbos (as already explained by Ovid) where a shrine was erected in his honor. The head became an oracular source, but its prophecies were suppressed by Apollo. A temple of Bacchus was built over the spot where the head was buried.

The chronological tradition for Orpheus's career is equally muddled. Those who date him in connection with Homer deserve the most credibility. Thus he was the inventor of writing and his works preceded the Homeric epics, or Homer was the first poet and Orpheus followed shortly after.

In these conflicting statements a fundamental and puzzling duality is evident. Orpheus is linked in one way or another to both Apollo and Dionysus. Was there a *real* Orpheus, a missionary in Thrace who met his death violently? Did he champion Apollo against Dionysus, Dionysus against Apollo, or did he compromise and adapt the religion of the oriental Dionysus to that of Hellenic Apollo, taking from both and preaching a message that was new and convincing, at least to some?

However one would like to interpret the evidence, this duality cannot be ignored. The music, magic, and prophecy suggest Apollo, as does the championship of civilization, but Apollo silenced the oracle of Orpheus, whose sermon of gentleness and peace has none of the violence of the archer-god. On the other hand, Orpheus's music is the antithesis of the clashing din of Bacchus; and the tales of the misogyny of Orpheus could imply that at some period his religion was confined to males as opposed to the worship of Dionysus with its appeal to women. Yet Orphic initiation and mysteries are by their very nature Dionysiac. Other elements in the legends of both Orpheus and Dionysus are strikingly parallel: Orpheus is torn to pieces like Dionysus himself (at the hands of the Titans), or like Pentheus, who also opposed the god and was destroyed by his Maenads. Dionysus, like Orpheus, descended to the Underworld, in his case to fetch his mother, Semele; indeed a less common variant has Orpheus successful (just as Dionysus is) in his pursuit of Eurydice.[6]

At any rate, on the side of the historicity of Orpheus is the tradition that he was not a god but a hero who lived, suffered, and died; his tomb was sacred and he had a cult. He was in this view a prophet, a priest, or if you like, a saint, whose god was Apollo or Dionysus or both. Such a belief is ultimately subjective. But the fact is that by the fifth century he *was* accepted as a human religious teacher, whose doctrine was communicated in sacred writings attributed to him and believed to be much earlier in time. Tablets were said to be found in the mountains of Thrace inscribed with his writing, prescribing potent charms, incantations, and spells. Plato in the fourth century quotes hexameter lines of Orpheus and tells of priests who preached his message of salvation. Later, Orpheus is credited with songs about the gods and the origin of all things. The account of the Argonauts and the hymns that have come down to us under Orpheus's name were given their present form in the early centuries of our era. An attractive thesis claims that the religion attributed to the legendary musician was formulated in large part by philosophers in southern Italy and Sicily (although not necessarily confined to this region) in the sixth century. Thus we can explain the elements identified as Orphic in the philosophy of Empedocles and in the religious sect of Pythagoras, and account for the Orphic-Pythagorean thought that is transmitted by Plato. Dominant in the pantheon of Orphism was Dionysus, very often under the name of Zagreus.

Although we hear about initiation into mysteries and a ritual life of purity demanded by the Orphics, we do not know the details.

---

[6] This link with Dionysus might mean that Orpheus is another god (however faded) of the death and rebirth of vegetation; Eurydice, too, has some of the chthonian characteristics of Semele and Persephone. But these parallels could have been added to the legend that grew up about a historical prophet. Some of the themes also look like motifs common to folk tale: conjugal devotion, the journey to Hades's realm, the tabu of looking back.

The shedding of blood and the eating of flesh seem to have been important prohibitions inspired by a fundamental belief in the transmigration of the soul and the sanctity of all life. It is possible to reconstruct the basic themes of the Orphic Theogony with its myth of Dionysus crucial to the doctrine. Parallels to the *Theogony* of Hesiod are apparent, but with meaningful differences and variations. The major stages in the Orphic Theogony run as follows, although divergent statements in the tradition are many.

The first principle was Chronus (Time), sometimes described as a monstrous serpent having the heads of a bull and a lion with a god's face between; Chronus was accompanied by brooding Adrasteia (Necessity), and from Chronus came Aether, Chaos, and Erebus. In Aether Chronus fashioned an egg that split in two and from this appeared the first-born of all the gods, Phanes, the creator of everything, called by many names, among them Eros.[7] He was a bi-sexual deity, with gleaming golden wings and four eyes, described as possessing the appearance of various animals. Phanes bore a daughter, Night, who became his partner in creation and eventually his successor in power. Night then bore Gaea (Earth) and Uranus (Heaven) and they produced the Titans. Next Cronus succeeded to the rule of Night and subsequently (as in the Hesiodic account) Zeus wrested power from his father Cronus.

Then Zeus swallowed Phanes and with him all previous creation (including a special race of men of a Golden Age); Zeus now created everything anew with the help of Night, and Zeus became (as second creator) the beginning and middle and end of all things. Eventually Zeus mated with Kore (Persephone) and Dionysus was born. This myth of the birth of Dionysus is most potent in the dogma it provides but we have related it in connection with the study of Dionysus himself. Its essential features are that the infant god is killed and devoured by the monstrous Titans who are struck down in punishment by the thunderbolt of Zeus. From the ashes of the Titans came mankind; thus man is partly evil and mortal but also partly pure and divine, since the wicked Titans had consumed the god, although not completely. The heart of Dionysus was saved and he was born again.

[7] See Aristophanes' parody translated on p. 19.

In this way the Orphic bible provided the divine authority for belief in man's immortal soul, the necessity for keeping this soul pure as opposed to the contamination and degradation of the body, the concept of a kind of original sin, the transmigration of the soul and an afterlife of reward and punishment, and finally, after various stages of purification, an apotheosis, a union with the divine spirit in the realms of the upper aether. The seeds of everything came from Phanes or Zeus; out of the One all things come to be and into the One are once again resolved.

Plato's myth of Er and Vergil's vision of the afterlife are, as far as we can tell, strongly influenced by Orphic concepts; a reading of both, translated in a previous chapter, will convey most simply and directly a feeling for the basic tenets of Orphism. The ritual purification and catharsis of the great god Apollo are mingled with the Dionysiac belief in the ultimate immortality of the human soul and provide a discipline and control of the ecstatic passion of his Bacchic mysteries.

We cannot distinguish with clear precision among the many different mystery religions and philosophies of the ancient world. It is possible to argue that the mysteries of Demeter with their emphasis on participation in certain dramatic rites lacked the spiritual depth of Orphism with its insistence on the good life as well as mere initiation and ritual. The correspondences between Christianity and other mystery religions of antiquity are perhaps more startling than the differences. Orpheus and Christ share attributes in the early centuries of our era, and of all the ancient deities the god Dionysus has most in common with the figure of Christ. But in any comparison or contrast for the greater glory or detriment of one god and one religion as opposed to another, it must be remembered that we know relatively nothing about the Greek and Roman mysteries as compared with our knowledge, say, of Christianity, particularly in its full development.

Part II

The Greek Sagas: Greek Local Legends

CHAPTER 15

The Theban Saga

The cycles of Greek saga are for the most part connected with cities and areas that were important in the later Bronze Age—that is, from about 1600 to 1100. The richest of these cities, Mycenae, gave its name to the period, and it was the king of Mycenae who led the Greeks on the greatest of their expeditions, against Troy. The great saga cycles concern (1) Mycenae, Tiryns, Argos, Sparta, and Arcadia—all in the Peloponnese; (2) Athens, Thebes, Orchomenus, and Iolcus—cities of Attica, Boeotia, and Thessaly, that is, on the Greek mainland outside the Peloponnese; and (3) Troy, whose connection with the Mycenaean cities was very close. Beyond these Mycenaean sagas there are the stories connected with the Minoan civilization of Crete, the predecessor of Mycenae as the dominant power in the Greek world, whose collapse can be placed at the end of the fifteenth century. Cnossus, its richest city, had close relations with Mycenae. Finally, the story of Odysseus, although basically connected with the Mycenaean world, extends far beyond it, chiefly because it incorporates many folk tales whose origin is quite separate from saga. There is then a definite historical dimension to Greek saga that archaeological discoveries have confirmed, but saga cannot be confused with history, for the former blurs the outlines of the latter and concentrates on a few personages (divine or heroic) and their deeds, ignoring the geographical and economic facts and ordinary men's doings which are the stuff of history. When Schliemann called the great beehive tomb at Mycenae "The Treasury of Atreus" or identified the Scaean Gate at Troy, he was confusing saga and history; there is a relationship between the two, but only a romantic would identify them.

The Founding of Thebes

The most popular cycles of saga among the Greek dramatists were the Theban and Mycenaean, and it is to the Theban cycle that we now turn. The historical Thebes was the leading city of Boeotia, the plain-land area of central Greece ringed by the mountain ranges of Parnes, Cithaeron, Helicon, and Parnassus, and on the east bounded by the Strait of Euboea. Thebes was situated on the low ridge that separates the two chief plains of Boeotia; its citadel was called the Cadmeia, in this preserving the name of Cadmus, legendary founder of the city. Cadmus was son of Agenor, king of Tyre, and brother of Europa; he was sent by Agenor to find his sister; she had been taken to Crete by Zeus who, disguised as a bull, swam across the sea with her on his back. In Crete she became the mother of Minos by Zeus. Cadmus, then, set out with his mother, Telephassa, who died in Thrace, and came to Delphi where he asked the oracle for advice. Apollo told him not to worry about Europa any more but to follow a certain cow until she lay down out of weariness and there to found a city. Cadmus found the cow in Phocis, and she led him to Boeotia, where he founded his city, Cadmeia, later called Thebes. As for the divinely sent cow, it was Cadmus's duty to sacrifice her; to perform the ceremony he needed water, which he sent his companions to draw from the nearby spring sacred to Ares. A serpent, said to be a son of Ares, guarded the spring and it killed most of Cadmus's men, and in return was itself killed by Cadmus. Athena, to whom Cadmus had been sacrificing the cow, now advised Cadmus to take the serpent's teeth and sow them; from the ground sprang up armed men, who fought and killed each other until only five were left. (Cadmus, it was said, threw stones at them and they, thinking that their own fellows were throwing them, started fighting.) From these five survivors, who were called Spartoi (i.e., sown men), descended the noble families of Thebes.

Now Cadmus had to appease Ares for the death of the serpent; he therefore became his slave for a year (which, says Apollodorus, was the equivalent of eight of our years). At the end of this time he was freed, and was given **Harmonia, daughter of Ares and**

Fig. 6. Greece. From Michael Grant, Myths of the Greeks and Romans
(*London: Weidenfeld and Nicholson, 1962*), p. 431.

Aphrodite, as his wife. The marriage was celebrated on the Cadmeia and all the gods came as guests. Among the gifts which the bride received were a robe and a necklace from her husband; the necklace was made by Hephaestus and given by him (or by Europa) to Cadmus; it came to play an important part in the Theban saga. Cadmus and Harmonia had four daughters—Ino, Semele, Autonoe, and Agave—whose stories, with those of their husbands and sons, have been told earlier.

Despite the misfortunes of their daughters, Cadmus and Harmonia reigned a long time, civilizing their people and in particular, introducing knowledge of writing. Eventually they went away to northwest Greece where Cadmus became king of the Illyrians; at the end of their lives they both turned into great harmless serpents (this is the story told by Euripides and Ovid) or were sent by Zeus to Elysium (a detail added by Apollodorus). As serpents or as inhabitants of Elysium they were ancestors worshiped by their descendants, and their departure from Cadmeia was not because of any misdeed or grief, but symbolizes their change from mortal to heroic or divine status.

The House of Labdacus

Cadmus was succeeded as king by his grandson Pentheus, son of Agave, whose misfortunes have been dealt with earlier. A new dynasty was then founded by Labdacus; his origin is obscure, although some authorities make him a grandson of Cadmus.[1] He is said to have perished while pursuing the same policy as Pentheus, leaving as his successor an infant son, Laius. Lycus, a great-great-uncle of Laius, assumed the regency and then made himself king, reigning for twenty years; Lycus was son of Chthonius, one of the five Spartoi, and the story of his family now concerns us, although it is a digression from the story of the House of Labdacus. His brother's daughter, Antiope, was loved by Zeus; while she was pregnant she fled to Sicyon (a city in the northern Peloponnese) to escape from the anger of her father, Nycteus. In despair Nycteus killed himself, and his brother (Lycus) then attacked

---

[1] According to these writers he is the son of Polydorus, son of Cadmus, but generally Cadmus's daughters only appear in the genealogies.

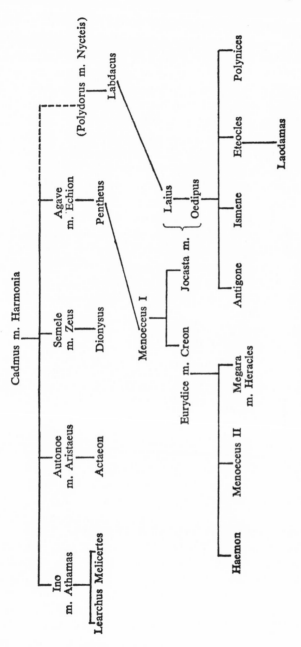

Fig. 7. The dynasties of Thebes.

Sicyon and recovered Antiope. Somewhere in Boeotia, Antiope gave birth to twin sons, who were exposed and found by a shepherd; he named them Amphion and Zethus. Zethus became a skilled herdsman, Amphion a musician, playing on a lyre given him by the god Hermes. Many years later Amphion and Zethus met and recognized their mother, who had escaped from the imprisonment in which she had been kept by Lycus and his wife, Dirce. They avenged Antiope by killing Lycus and tying Dirce to the horns of a bull that dragged her to her death. From her blood sprang the fountain at Thebes that is called by her name.

Amphion and Zethus now became rulers of Cadmeia and built walls for the city, whose stones were moved into place by the music of Amphion's lyre. Laius (who would now have been about twenty-one years old) was banished, while the two rulers married; Amphion's wife was Niobe and Zethus's was the nymph, Thebe, in whose honor the newly walled city was renamed Thebes. After many years Amphion and Zethus died, and Laius returned from exile to resume the kingship of which he had been deprived as an infant.

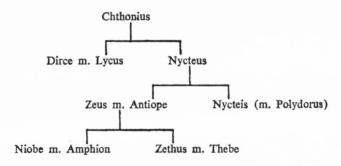

Fig. 8. The descendants of Chthonius.

The story of Lycus and his family is confused, although important; the walling of Cadmeia and its renaming is a doublet of the founding of the city by Cadmus, and just as Cadmus and Harmonia had civilized their people, so Amphion's music demonstrated the power of harmony and beauty over the disunited and inanimate stones.

In exile Laius had been hospitably received by Pelops, king of

Elis. The ties of guest and host were among the most sacred of human relationships, and Laius brought upon himself and his descendants a curse by abducting Chrysippus, the son of Pelops, with whom he had fallen in love. Apollo foretold the working out of the curse in the first generation when Laius consulted the Delphic oracle about the children who should be born to him and his wife Jocasta.[2] "I will give you a son," said the oracle,

1. Cadmus	6. Laius
2. Pentheus	7. Oedipus
3. Labdacus	(regency of Creon)
4. Lycus	8. Eteocles
5. Zethus and Amphion	9. Creon
	10. Laodamas

Fig. 9. The kings of Thebes.

"but you are destined to die at his hands. This is the decision of Zeus, in answer to the bitter curses of Pelops, whose son you abducted; all this did Pelops call down upon you" (*Argument* to Sophocles, *Oedipus Tyrannus*). When, therefore, a son was born, Laius attempted to cheat fate by ordering the infant to be exposed upon Mt. Cithaeron, with a spike driven through his ankles. The servant entrusted with the task pitied the baby, and instead gave him to a Corinthian shepherd (for the Theban and Corinthian summer pastures were adjacent on Cithaeron); the shepherd in turn brought the infant to his master, Polybus, king of Corinth. The child was brought up as the son of Polybus and his queen, Merope, and was called Oedipus (which means Swellfoot) from the injury to his ankles.

Years later Oedipus was jeered at during a feast at Corinth by a drunken companion as not being Polybus's natural son. In alarm and shame at the taunt (which soon spread through the city) he left Corinth and asked the oracle at Delphi who his parents were.

---

[2] She was called Epicasta by some authors, including Homer; the meaning of both names is unknown.

For a reply he received a warning—to avoid his homeland, since he must murder his father and marry his mother. So he determined not to return to Corinth and took the road from Delphi that led to Thebes. What happened then Oedipus himself relates (Sophocles, *Oedipus Tyrannus,* 800–813):

As I came on my journey to this junction of three roads a herald and a man (like him whom you described, Jocasta) riding in a horse-drawn chariot blocked my way; they violently drove me off the road. In anger I struck the driver, who was pushing me aside; and when the old man saw me passing by him, he took aim at the middle of my head and struck me with the two-pronged goad. But he paid for this with interest; struck promptly by the staff in this hand of mine, he quickly tumbled out of the chariot. I killed them all.[3]

The old man, whom Oedipus did not recognize, was Laius. The curse of Pelops was being fulfilled.

So Oedipus came to Thebes where the city was in distress; not only was the king dead, but the city was plagued by a monster sent by Hera, called Sphinx (which means strangler). This creature had the face of a woman, the body of a lion and a bird's wings. It had (says Apollodorus) learned a riddle from the Muses which it asked the Thebans. Those who could not answer, it ate, and it was prophesied that Thebes would only be free of the Sphinx when the riddle had been answered. The riddle was: "What is it that has one name that is four-footed, two-footed, and three-footed?" [4] No Theban had been able to find the answer, and in despair the regent Creon, son of Menoeceus and brother of Jocasta, offered the throne and his sister as wife to anyone who could do so. Oedipus succeeded. "Man," said he, "is the answer: for as an infant he goes upon four feet; in his prime upon two; and in old age he takes a stick as a third foot." And so the Sphinx threw itself off the Theban acropolis; Oedipus became king of Thebes and husband of the widowed queen, his mother.

[3] One of Laius's retainers escaped: in Sophocles's play he is the same servant as the one who originally failed to expose Oedipus, and his story brings about the final discovery of Oedipus's identity.

[4] There are several variants of the riddle and its answer. The shortest (that of Apollodorus, 3.53–54) is given here.

Thus the prophecy of Apollo was fulfilled; what remained was for the truth to be discovered. There are two versions of Oedipus's fate. According to Homer, Epicasta married her own son "and the gods speedily made it known to men. Unhappily he reigned on at Thebes, but she went down to the house of Hades, fastening a noose to the roof of the lofty hall" (*Odyssey,* 11.271). In the *Iliad* Oedipus is spoken of as having fallen in battle. In this version another wife is the mother of the children of Oedipus.

The most widely accepted story, however, is the later version, that of Sophocles. Oedipus and Jocasta lived happily together and she bore him two sons, Polynices and Eteocles, and two daughters, Antigone and Ismene. After many years a pestilence afflicted Thebes, and the oracle of Apollo advised the Thebans that it was the result of a pollution on their state, for the murderer of Laius was in their midst. At this stage Polybus died, and the messenger who brought the news also brought the invitation to Oedipus from the people of Corinth to become their king. Oedipus, thinking that Merope was his mother, refused to return to Corinth, but the messenger—who was the same shepherd to whom the infant exposed on Cithaeron had been given—tried to reassure him by telling him that he was not in fact the son of Merope and Polybus. Oedipus then sent for the servant who had exposed him—who also was the survivor at the death of Laius —and the truth came out. In horror and despair Jocasta hanged herself, and Oedipus, seeing her corpse, blinded himself with the brooches from her robe. Creon became regent again, and Oedipus was banished, in accordance with a curse which he had earlier pronounced on the as yet unknown killer of Laius and in obedience to an oracle of Apollo. He wandered for years accompanied by Antigone, until he finally came to Colonus in Attica. There he was kindly received by the king of Athens, Theseus, who did not allow the Thebans to force him to return (for it had been prophesied that the land in which he was buried would prosper); shortly afterwards he disappeared from the earth.

Sophocles describes the end of Oedipus's life at Colonus and we give the passage in full here, since it clearly tells us how Sophocles viewed the relationship of Oedipus the man to Oedipus the hero. The poet carefully describes the place, for a hero is associated with a particular locality. He connects Oedipus's passing with the powers beneath the earth (Zeus is called by his title "Chthonius," that is, "Zeus of the Earth"); yet Theseus rightly worships the powers of earth and heaven after the miracle, for the hero is part of the array of Greek divinities, those of heaven as well as the chthonic powers. And Oedipus's passing is miraculous and without grief, in this symbolizing his benign influence upon the place where he passed from mortal sight and his power as a hero to perform miracles for those who worship him. Here then is Sophocles's description (*Oedipus Coloneus,* 1587–1665): [5]

You know how he left this place without any of his friends to guide him, himself the leader of us all. When he came to the edge of the ravine which is rooted in the earth by the brazen stairs, he stood in one of the paths which meet there—the place is by the hollow basin where the pact of Theseus and Pirithous was forever made. Around him were the rock of Thoricus, the hollow wild pear tree, and the stone tomb. Here he sat and loosened his dust-stained garments. Then he called his daughters and bade them bring him water from the running stream to wash with and make libations. So they went to the hill of Demeter, bringer of green freshness, which overlooks the place, and soon returned bringing what their father had asked for. Thus they washed and clothed him as custom demands. When he was satisfied with all that they were doing and none of his commands had gone unfulfilled, then Zeus of the Earth thundered, and the girls shuddered as they heard. They clasped their father's knees and wept; continuously they beat their breasts and wailed. But he immediately answered their unhappy cry, clasped his arms around them, and said: "My children, today your father ceases to be. All that is mine has come to an end; no more need you labor to support me. Hard was that task, I know, my daughters; yet one word alone relieves all that toil— for of *Love* you never will have more from any man than me. And now you will pass your lives bereft of me.

In this way they all sobbed and wept, embracing each other. When they came to an end of weeping and were silent, a sudden voice called him and all were afraid and their hair stood on end. It was God who called him repeatedly. "Oedipus, Oedipus," he called, "why wait we to go? Too long have you delayed." Then Oedipus, knowing that God was calling him, called king Theseus to him, and when he drew near said: "Dear friend, give your hand to my children as a solemn pledge,

---

[5] A messenger is the speaker.

and you, my children, give yours to him. And do you, Theseus, swear never knowingly to betray these girls and always to act for their good." And Theseus, without complaint, swore on his oath that he would do as his friend asked, for he was a man of generous nature.

When this was done, Oedipus straightway felt his children with unseeing hands and said: "My daughters, you must resolutely leave this place; you may not ask to see what is not right for you to see, nor hear words that you should not hear. Go then; let only king Theseus stay and behold what will be done."

All of us heard his words, and with groans and tears went with the girls. As we began to leave we turned and saw Oedipus no longer there; the king we saw, shielding his eyes with his hand, as if some dread sight had appeared which he could not bear to look upon. Yet soon after we saw him worship Earth and Olympus, the gods' home above, with the same words.

How Oedipus died no man can tell except Theseus. No fiery thunderbolt from God consumed him, no whirlwind from the sea. Some divine messenger came for him, or the deep foundations of the earth parted to receive him, kindly and without pain. Without grief he passed from us, without the agony of sickness; his going was more than mortal, a miracle.

So Oedipus became a hero, bringing good to the country in which he lay. But, as the ancient commentators pointed out (*Argument* to Sophocles, *Oedipus Coloneus*), Sophocles adopted this version of the story to do honor to Attica and to his own deme (i.e., district) of Colonus. Outside Athens the story was different; Oedipus shut himself up in the palace and lived there while Creon was regent. One day his sons put before him a less honorable portion of meat than was his due; he cursed them, praying that they might fight to divide their kingdom, and after his death the curse was fulfilled.[6]

The story of Oedipus is among the best-known classical legends, largely because of the use made of it by psychologists since Freud's naming of the "Oedipus complex" in 1910. This is a legitimate *use* of a legend, but it must not be taken as an *explanation* of it. Sophocles was aware of the Oedipus complex, in part, at any rate: "Many men," says Jocasta (*Oedipus Tyrannus*, 981) "have in

---

[6] Yet another version is given by Euripides in the *Phoenissae*, where Jocasta kills herself years later during the attack of the Seven against Thebes, and Oedipus is only then driven into exile.

dreams lain with their mothers," and we have already noted how Greek myths of creation are permeated with the concepts of the mother-son relationship and of conflict between father and son. We should be skeptical of attempts to interpret the legend in purely psychological terms; Sophocles and his predecessors were concerned with other aspects—for example, historical and theological —and we must accept the story as the Greeks have transmitted it, whatever use we may make of it.

The Seven Against Thebes

The sons of Oedipus, now of an age to rule, could not decide which of them should be king of Thebes; they agreed that each should rule in alternate years, while the other went into exile. Eteocles ruled for the first year, while Polynices went to Argos, taking with him the necklace and robe of Harmonia. At Argos Polynices and another exile, Tydeus of Arcadia, were given the daughters of the king, Adrastus, in marriage; Adrastus, moreover, promised to restore them to their lands (for it was by now clear that Eteocles would not abdicate at the end of his year as king), and decided to attack Thebes first.

The Argive army had seven leaders: besides Adrastus, Polynices, and Tydeus, there were Capaneus, Hippomedon, Parthenopaeus, and Amphiaraus. Amphiaraus had the gift of prophecy, and he knew that all seven, except for Adrastus, would be killed, and therefore opposed the expedition. But Polynices bribed Amphiaraus's wife, Eriphyle, with the necklace of Harmonia, to persuade her husband to change his mind. As he set out he ordered his sons to avenge his death on their mother, and themselves to make an expedition against Thebes when that of the Seven had failed.

Before the army reached Thebes two episodes intervened. At Nemea (not far from the Isthmus of Corinth) they were led to a spring of water by Hypsipyle, nurse of Opheltes, the infant son of the local king. She left the baby lying on the ground while she showed the way, and he was killed by a serpent. The Seven killed the serpent and celebrated, in honor of the dead child, the athletic contests that became the Nemean Games; his name was changed by Amphiaraus from Opheltes (Snake man) to Archemorus (Beginner of Death), as an omen of what was yet to come.

The second preliminary episode concerned Tydeus. When the army reached the borders of Boeotia, Tydeus was sent to Thebes as an ambassador to demand the abdication of Eteocles in accordance with the agreement with Polynices. While at Thebes, he took part in an athletic contest and beat all comers; the Thebans attempted to avenge their humiliation by setting an ambush for Tydeus as he returned to the army. He killed all fifty of his ambushers, except for one man, who brought the news to Thebes.

Thus the army came to Thebes; each leader attacked one of the city's seven gates, and they all failed. The defenders were in any case assured of success, since the Theban prophet, Tiresias, had prophesied that, if one of the Spartoi sacrificed himself, the city would have atoned fully for the blood-guilt incurred by the killing of Ares's sacred serpent, and so be saved from its attackers. Menoeceus, son of Creon, willingly died for the city; standing on the wall he stabbed himself and fell into the serpent's den. Of the Seven, only Capaneus succeeded in scaling the wall; as he reached the top he boasted that not even Zeus could keep him out and for his blasphemy was struck dead by Zeus's thunderbolt. Eteocles and Polynices killed each other in single combat; Hippomedon, Parthenopaeus, and Tydeus fell in battle. (Tydeus, indeed, could have been made immortal by Athena, whose favorite he was, but she revoked her gift when she saw him eating the brains of the man who had fatally wounded him.) Only Amphiaraus and Adrastus escaped; Adrastus was saved by the speed of his divine horse, Arion, and returned to Argos; Amphiaraus was swallowed up in the earth, with his chariot and driver, as he fled along the banks of the River Ismenus. He became the object of a hero cult at the spot, in this resembling Oedipus who had similarly been "translated" from life.

Creon once more was ruler of Thebes, and he gave orders that the Argive dead were not to be buried, including Polynices. Such treatment of the dead offended Greek religious ideas, and Antigone, daughter of Oedipus, could not allow her brother to be left in this way. She therefore gave him a symbolic burial (by throwing three handfuls of dust over his corpse), and was for this condemned by Creon to be buried alive. Again, such an order defied the law of the gods, and Creon was soon punished; his son, Haemon, attempted to save Antigone (to whom he was engaged to be married) and, finding she had hanged herself in her tomb, ran himself through with his sword; Creon's wife, Eurydice, killed herself when she heard the news. Creon himself, warned by Tiresias, relented too late. According to Euripides, however, Adrastus went to Eleusis (in Attica) as a suppliant and persuaded Theseus to attack Thebes and obtain an honorable burial for the dead Argives; as the corpse of Capaneus was burning on its pyre, his widow, Evadne, threw herself into the flames.

It will be remembered that Amphiaraus had ordered his sons to attack Thebes and to punish their mother. Alcmaeon, one of the sons, carried out these commands ten years later; he and the sons of the other six chieftains (they are known as the Epigoni, i.e., later generation) made an expedition against Thebes and this time were successful. The Thebans abandoned their city on the advice of Tiresias, and it was destroyed. At this point saga touches on history, for the war of the Epigoni took place, it was said, not long before the Trojan War; in the catalogue of ships in the *Iliad,* which is certainly historical, only Hypothebae (Lower Thebes) is mentioned, implying that the ancient town and its citadel had been abandoned.

As for the other part of Amphiaraus's order, Alcmaeon, encouraged by an oracle of Apollo, avenged his father for his mother's treachery by killing Eriphyle. As a matricide he was pursued by the Furies and found temporary shelter in Arcadia where he married the daughter of king Phegeus, giving her the necklace of Harmonia. But the land was afflicted with famine and, since he was responsible as a murderer and therefore a pollution, he had to leave; he was advised by an oracle to go to a land on which the sun had not shone when he killed his mother. He went to western Greece, and found such a land at the mouth of the river Achelous, recently formed by the river's silt. Here he settled and was purified of his guilt by the river-god, whose daughter, Callirhoe, he married. But he did not live on for long; he got the necklace of Harmonia from Phegeus by deceit, so as to give it to Callirhoe, and for this was killed by Phegeus's sons. The necklace eventually was dedicated by the sons of Callirhoe and Alcmaeon at Delphi; it was said to have been stolen from there during the fourth century and, true to its traditional character, to have brought only bad luck to the thief. Alcmaeon's sons became the founders of Acarnania, which is in western Greece.

Tiresias

A recurring figure in the Theban saga is the blind prophet, Tiresias. He was descended from one of the Spartoi and was the son of a nymph, Chariclo, who was a follower of Athena. He lived for seven generations, says Hesiod, and after his death continued to have the gift of prophecy, for in the Underworld, where the souls of the dead are insubstantial and futile, he alone retained his full mental faculties. Accordingly Homer makes him Odysseus's informant when he consults with the dead, and he foretells the end of Odysseus's wanderings and the manner of his death.

There are different stories about his blindness, an affliction shared by many prophets and poets in Greek literature. In one version he once saw two snakes coupling on Mt. Cyllene; he killed the female and was himself turned into a woman. When he later saw another pair coupling and killed the male, he reverted to being a man. Later Zeus and Hera were arguing as to whether men or women enjoyed the act of love more; Tiresias was asked to decide the question and said that whereas the man had one part of the enjoyment, the woman had nine—for which Hera blinded him, but Zeus gave him the gift of prophecy.

In another version, something like the story of Actaeon, he saw Athena naked and was blinded by her. His mother was unable to prevent this punishment, but she made it possible for him, since he had lost his sight, to understand the speech of birds.

At any rate, he was the honored prophet at Thebes. In the story of Oedipus he revealed the truth before Oedipus or the Thebans were ready to understand it; in the story of Antigone he warned Creon of the disastrous mistakes he was making; in the attack by the Seven it was he who advised Menoeceus's self-sacrifice to save the city. Finally, it was on his advice that the Thebans abandoned the city before the attack of the Epigoni and migrated to found the city of Hestiaea. Tiresias never reached the new city; on the way he drank from a spring called Tilphussa and died on the spot.

CHAPTER 16

The Mycenaean Saga

Along with Thebes Mycenae was the most popular source for legends among Greek poets; its sagas are particularly concerned with the House of Atreus and the greatest of its representatives, Agamemnon, leader of the Achaeans against Troy. We shall consider the Trojan War later; in the present chapter we shall discuss the fortunes of the House as they developed in Greece itself.

The family of Atreus was afflicted with a curse which brought evil on its members generation after generation. The father of Atreus was Pelops, son of Tantalus, who came from Asia Minor to Greece as a suitor for the hand of Hippodamia, daughter of Oenomaus, king of Pisa (in Elis). To win Hippodamia, a suitor had first to win a chariot race from Pisa to the Isthmus of Corinth against Oenomaus. He would have a short start and take Hippodamia in his chariot with him; Oenomaus would follow, and if he caught up would kill the suitor. Twelve suitors had failed when Pelops came, and their heads decorated Oenomaus's palace. Pelops, however, bribed Oenomaus's charioteer, Myrtilus (son of the god Hermes), to remove the linchpins from Oenomaus's chariot so that it crashed during the pursuit and Oenomaus was thrown from it and killed. So Pelops won Hippodamia and drove away with her, accompanied by Myrtilus.

Now Myrtilus expected that Pelops would reward him by allowing him to enjoy Hippodamia; at a resting place on the journey he attempted to force her, and when Pelops discovered this he threw Myrtilus from a cliff into the sea; as Myrtilus fell he cursed Pelops and his descendants, and it is this curse and the blood-guilt of the murder of Myrtilus that led to the misfortunes of the House of Atreus.

Pelops returned to Pisa and became king in place of Oenomaus;

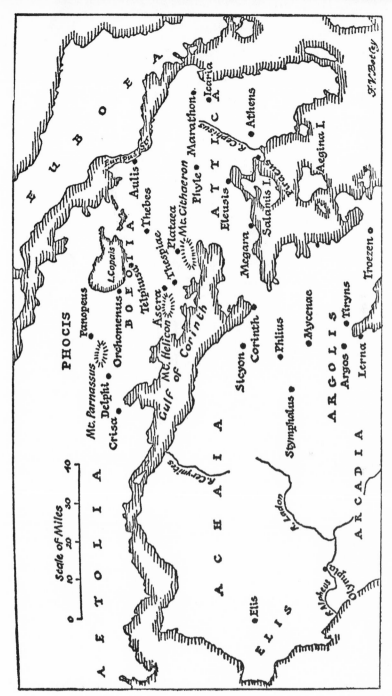

Fig. 10. *Central Greece. From Michael Grant,* Myths of the Greeks and Romans (*London: Weidenfeld and Nicholson, 1962*), *p. 432.*

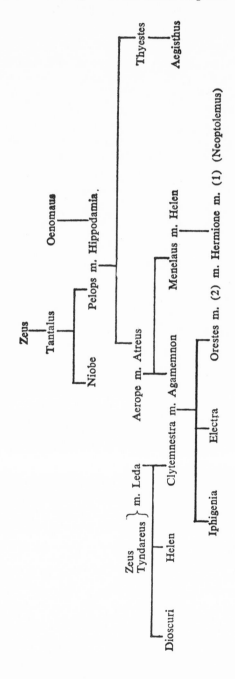

Fig. 11. The House of Atreus.

he extended his power over the nearby areas and the southern part of Greece was called after him "The Island of Pelops" (Peloponnese). His children were Thyestes and Atreus, and they quarreled over the kingdom of Mycenae which had been offered to "a son of Pelops" in obedience to an oracle. It was agreed that the possessor of a golden-fleeced ram should become king; it had been given to Atreus by Artemis, but secretly handed over by Aërope, Atreus's wife, to Thyestes, who had seduced her. So Thyestes was for a time king of Mycenae, but later he was displaced by Atreus and driven into exile, from which Atreus recalled him so as to revenge himself for Aërope's adultery. He invited Thyestes to a banquet and put before him as food Thyestes's own sons; when Thyestes discovered the truth, he went into exile again after cursing Atreus.

Thus the curse of Myrtilus affected the first generation of Pelops's descendants; the quarrel of Thyestes and Atreus was continued by their sons. In his second exile Thyestes lay with his daughter, Pelopia, as he had been advised to do by an oracle, and became the father of Aegisthus; it was he who continued the vendetta against Atreus's son, Agamemnon, who succeeded his father as king of Mycenae. Agamemnon had sacrificed his daughter, Iphigenia, at the start of the Trojan expedition and by doing so had earned the implacable hatred of his wife, Clytemnestra. While he was at Troy she committed adultery with Aegisthus, and the two of them plotted a common vengeance against Agamemnon. He was murdered on his return from Troy: "I struck him twice," boasts Clytemnestra, "and with two cries he let his limbs go slack; a third blow did I add as a thank offering to Hades below the earth, keeper of the dead. . . . And as he fell a rain of blood spattered me with black drops and I rejoiced no less than the fields in Zeus's bright rain at the time of swelling of the buds" (Aeschylus, *Agamemnon,* 1384–1392). Likewise Aegisthus takes full responsibility for the deed which he rejoices in as a just vengeance upon the son of Atreus.

Still the curse continued. Orestes, Agamemnon's son, was not at Mycenae at the time of the murder; while Clytemnestra and Aegisthus usurped the throne, he grew to manhood in exile at the court of Strophius, king of Phocis. It was now his duty to avenge the murder of his father, even though one of the murderers happened to be his own mother, and he was commanded by Apollo to carry out his duty. He returned to Mycenae, and with the encouragement of his sister, Electra, murdered Aegisthus and Clytemnestra. In the *Odyssey* Homer makes Zeus praise Orestes for his piety towards his dead father, but in later authors (most notably Aeschylus) the feeling of revulsion at the matricide predominates. In this tradition, then, Orestes was pursued by the Erinyes, the avenging Furies, who drove him mad. Finally, again on the advice of Apollo, he came to Athens and there pleaded his case before the court of the Areopagus, whose members, citizens of Athens, were the jury. Apollo defended him and Athena presided, while the Erinyes claimed the justice of their punishment. Athena gave her casting vote in favor of Orestes's acquittal, on the grounds that the killing of a mother did not outweigh the murder of a husband and father and that the son's duty towards a father outweighed all other relationships. Thus the curse on the House of Atreus came to an end; the Erinyes were appeased and given a new name, the Eumenides (i.e., Kindly Ones), and worshiped thereafter at Athens.[1]

This version of Orestes's story has attracted poets from Aeschylus to Eugene O'Neill; once again we have a case where an ancient legend has become the vehicle for different interpretations. In its original form the story of the House of Atreus is one of bloodguilt descending from one generation to another; the murder of Agamemnon is an act of vengeance; such things as the pride (hybris) which precedes his fall or the jealousy of Clytemnestra for Cassandra are literary additions. Similarly Orestes acted with piety in avenging his father's death; his "guilt" is a later—if more humane—interpretation; indeed, it is illogical, for it ignores the fact that Apollo had ordered him to murder Clytemnestra. It was the genius of Aeschylus that transformed the primitive legend and in place of the ancient doctrine of bloodguilt and vengeance substituted the rule of Reason and Law.[2]

---

[1] The Areopagus was the court at Athens which heard homicide cases; its members were ex-archons, that is, former state officials. The court had been a center of political controversy shortly before Aeschylus produced his play.

[2] The *locus classicus* for the Orestes legend is Aeschylus's trilogy (*Agamemnon, Choephori, Eumenides*), most especially the *Eumenides,*

It is not surprising that there are other versions of Orestes's story, which allow him to be purified from the bloodguilt either by some ritual or by performing an expiatory deed, without undergoing trial and acquittal. According to one story he was told by the oracle of Apollo to go to the land of the Tauri (the modern Crimea) and fetch a wooden statue of Artemis. It was the custom of the Tauri to sacrifice strangers in their temple, and Orestes was handed over by their king, Thoas, to the priestess of Artemis, who was none other than Orestes's own sister, Iphigenia. She (in this version) had been miraculously saved by Artemis at the moment of sacrifice at Aulis and removed by her to be her priestess among the Tauri. She recognized Orestes; together, under the protection of Athena, they returned to Greece taking the statue with them, which they dedicated at Halae in Attica. Orestes returned to Mycenae, while Iphigenia stayed in Attica as the priestess of Artemis at Brauron, where she died.[3]

Thus Orestes recovered his sanity and reigned at Mycenae; later he is said to have married his cousin, Hermione (daughter of Helen and Menelaus), and by her to have been the father of Tisamenus. He had before his madness been betrothed to her, but she had married Neoptolemus, son of Achilles, and had gone with him to Epirus. Orestes met Neoptolemus at Delphi and there murdered him; in this way he won Hermione. He eventually died from a snake bite. Tisamenus was the Achaean leader against the Heraclidae, at whose hands he perished. As for Electra, she married Orestes's constant friend and companion, Pylades, son of Strophius, and by him had two sons, Strophius and Medon. Thereafter she disappears from the legend.[4]

---

where the profound religious insight of Aeschylus finds it fullest expression. Of the other tragedies on the theme, the *Electra* of Sophocles is closest to the earlier idea of vengeance. Euripides, most especially in his *Electra,* is more melodramatic and more critical of the religious ideas implied by the legend.

[3] This is basically the version of Euripides's *Iphigenia in Tauris;* Euripides combines it with the Aeschylean account by making Orestes travel to the land of the Tauri after his acquittal by the Areopagus; in fact the two versions are mutually exclusive accounts of the purification of Orestes.

[4] A third daughter of Agamemnon, Chrysothemis, has no independent legend attached to her.

CHAPTER 17

The Trojan Saga

The Children of Leda

Leda, wife of Tyndareus, king of Sparta, bore four children to Zeus who visited her in the shape of a swan; the four were born from two eggs—from the one sprang Polydeuces (Pollux) and Helen, from the other Castor and Clytemnestra. Castor and Polydeuces have a mythology of their own quite unconnected with the Trojan War. Known as the Dioscuri (i.e., sons of Zeus), they were heroes on earth and later worshiped as gods. In Homer they are mortal; when Helen in the *Iliad* describes the Greek leaders to king Priam, she says (*Iliad,* 3. 236): "Two only can I not see among the leaders of the people—Castor, tamer of horses, and Polydeuces, skillful in boxing, my own brothers whom one and the same mother bore, my mother. . . ." Homer continues: "Thus she spake; but already the life-giving earth held them there, in Sparta, in their own native land." However, when Odysseus sees Leda in his visit to the Underworld he refers to them as "alive beneath the earth" and passing from death to life and vice versa, and being honored equally with the gods. It was Pindar (in his tenth *Nemean Ode*) who established the most famous version of their death and deification; they quarreled with the two sons of Aphareus, Idas and Lynceus, over the division of some cattle that the four of them had taken in a raid, and in the subsequent fight Lynceus and Castor were killed, while Idas was destroyed by a thunderbolt hurled by Zeus.[1] As Castor lay dying, Polydeuces

---

[1] A popular variant of the story (found, for example, in the twenty-second *Idyll* of Theocritus) makes the quarrel begin when the Dioscuri carry off the daughters of Leucippus from their intended husbands, Idas and Lynceus. The "Rape of the Leucippides" was a common subject in ancient art.

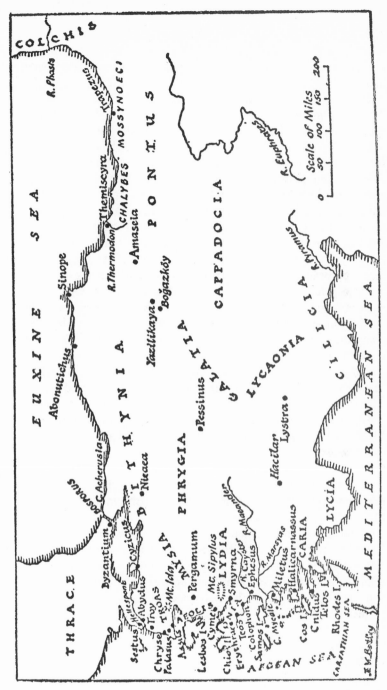

Fig. 12. *Asia Minor.* From Michael Grant, Myths of the Greeks and
Romans (*London: Weidenfeld and Nicholson, 1962*), p. 433.

prayed to Zeus that he might die with him; in reply Zeus gave him the choice either of immortality for himself and death for Castor, or of living together with Castor on Olympus for one day at a time and spending the next together in Hades.[2] Polydeuces chose the latter alternative, and so the Dioscuri shared immortality and death. As gods they were especially connected with seafarers, to whom they appear as St. Elmo's fire. Euripides (writing some sixty years after Pindar) brings them on dramatically at the end of his *Electra,* not only as the protectors of sailors (they have, they say, just calmed a storm at sea), but also as champions of the just and proponents of a better morality and religion than that represented by Apollo. They were especially honored at Sparta, and as early as the fifth century their cult spread to Rome where their appearance (as horsemen on white steeds) at the battle of Lake Regillus in 496 led to a great Roman victory. One of the most prominent buildings in the Forum at Rome was their temple.

Clytemnestra became the wife of Agamemnon, and we have already discussed her part in the Mycenaean saga. Helen grew up to be the most beautiful of women, and many Greek princes (including Theseus and Odysseus) hoped to marry her; she chose Menelaus, who became king of Sparta, and the rejected suitors swore to respect her choice and help Menelaus in time of need.

Helen lived for some years at Sparta and bore Hermione to Menelaus. In time, however, the Trojan prince Paris (who is also called Alexander) visited Sparta while Menelaus was away in Crete, and there seduced Helen and took her back to Troy with him. It was to recover her and vindicate the rights of Menelaus that the Achaean expedition, led by Agamemnon, brother of Menelaus, was raised against Troy.

Another version of Helen's story, however, was invented by the seventh-century poet Stesichorus; although a literary creation rather than truly myth, the story is so famous that it should be related. In his *Palinode,* then, Stesichorus says: "That story is not true; you did not go in the well-benched ships, nor did you go to the towers of Troy." Helen, in this version, only got as far as

---

[2] A variant version has the one in heaven and the other in Hades on alternate days.

Egypt where king Proteus detained her until she was taken back to Sparta by Menelaus after the Trojan War; it was merely an image of Helen, a phantom, that accompanied Paris to Troy, and this was sufficient to give a pretext for the war, which Zeus had determined should occur so as to reduce the population of the earth.

Aphrodite is said (also by Stesichorus) to have made Helen unfaithful as punishment for Helen's father, Tyndareus, who had once omitted to sacrifice to the goddess; this tradition complements the story of the judgment of Paris, in which Aphrodite appears in a gentler (and less superhuman) light. The Olympian gods were once guests at the wedding feast of Peleus and Thetis, and during the feast Eris, goddess of Discord (who was not a guest), threw onto the table an apple inscribed with the words "For the most beautiful." Hera, Athena, and Aphrodite each claimed it, and Zeus decided that the argument should be settled by referring it to Paris. Now Paris had been exposed as an infant because of a dream which his mother Hecuba [3] had had before his birth. She dreamed that she had given birth to a firebrand that consumed the whole of Troy, and the interpretation given by her stepson, the soothsayer Aesacus, was that her baby would be the destruction of the city. The infant was miraculously saved from death; exposed on Mt. Ida, he was suckled by a bear, found by a shepherd, and brought up among the shepherds. It was to him that Hermes led the three goddesses, who appeared before him in their full glory, and each offered the best gift she could give in return for Paris's favorable decision. Hera promised him royal power; Athena promised to make him victorious in war; Aphrodite promised to give him Helen as his wife. He chose Aphrodite, and so the train of events that led to the Trojan War was set in motion, and Hera and Athena were unrelentingly hostile to the Trojans.

It is worth noting, however, that Homer never mentions this story; according to him Paris once insulted Hera and Athena when they visited him, but praised Aphrodite, who gave him the power to attract women irresistibly. This legend is certainly older than

[3] The Greek form of her name is Hecabe; the more familiar Latin form is used here.

the more famous judgment, and closer to genuine myth in that the two insulted goddesses are more imperious in their behavior, while their hostility to Troy is the result of a positive act on the part of Paris; such anger is more in keeping with the ancient gods of mythology than is the more literary anthropomorphism of the judgment story. But it is the latter that has dominated the tradition and fascinated an endless line of poets and artists.

The Preparations for the War

Menelaus and Agamemnon sent heralds throughout Greece and the islands to summon the Greek leaders and contingents to the war; the expedition gathered at Aulis (on the coast of Boeotia, opposite Euboea) numbering nearly twelve hundred ships with their crews and fighting men.[4] Not all the Greek princes came willingly; two of the most important attempted to avoid the war by subterfuge. Odysseus, prince of Ithaca, pretended to be mad; when Agamemnon's envoys came he yoked an ox and an ass and plowed a field, sowing salt in the furrows. One of the envoys, Palamedes, took Odysseus's infant son, Telemachus, from his mother, Penelope, and put him in the path of the plow; Odysseus was sane enough to avoid him; his pretense was uncovered and he joined the expedition. (Palamedes, son of Nauplius, was, along with Odysseus, the cleverest of the Greeks; he was credited with a number of inventions. His unmasking of the "madness" earned him the hostility of Odysseus, who eventually contrived his death.)

The second chieftain who attempted to avoid the war was Achilles, prince of the Myrmidons (a tribe of Phthia, in central Greece) and the greatest of the Greek warriors, as well as the swiftest and most handsome. He was the son of Peleus and Thetis; Thetis was a sea-goddess, daughter of Nereus, and had been loved by both Zeus and Poseidon, who withdrew their attentions when a secret, hitherto known only to Prometheus and Themis, was revealed—that Thetis's son would be greater than his father. Ac-

---

[4] The figure is given in the Catalogue in Book 2 of the *Iliad*. Ancient as this document is and historically of the greatest importance, it is certain that the numbers which it gives are greatly inflated.

cordingly Thetis was married to a mortal, Peleus, king of the Phthians. Peleus is found taking part in a number of famous episodes, including the Argonauts' expedition and the Calydonian boar hunt, but as a mere mortal he was hardly a match for Thetis. It was with difficulty that he married her (for she was able to turn herself into various shapes in attempting to escape from him); and although the gods attended the wedding feast, it was not long after the birth of Achilles that Thetis left her husband for good. She tried to make Achilles immortal, either by roasting him in the fire by night and anointing him with ambrosia by day [5] or by dipping him in the waters of the Styx. (The latter version, which is the more celebrated, is a later story; all parts of Achilles's body that had been dipped were invulnerable. Only his heel, by which Thetis had held him, remained vulnerable, and it was here that he received his fatal arrow wound.) After Thetis had left Peleus, Achilles was sent for his education to the centaur Chiron, from whom he learned the art of music as well as other skills; among his fellow pupils was Jason, the future leader of the Argonauts. It was while Achilles was with Chiron that Thetis learned that Troy could not be taken without Achilles; she further knew that he could live long and die ingloriously or go to Troy and die young and glorious. To circumvent his early death she tried to prevent his going to Troy; she disguised him as a girl and took him to the island of Scyros, where he was brought up with the daughters of Lycomedes, king of the island. One of them was Deidamia, with whom Achilles fell in love; their child, born after Achilles left Scyros, was Neoptolemus (also called Pyrrhus), who took part in the capture of Troy after his father's death. Achilles's disguise at Scyros was discovered by Odysseus and Diomedes; they took with them some armor (as well as less warlike objects) to show Lycomedes's daughters; while the girls were examining it a trumpet sounded and Achilles gave himself away by being the only one not to take fright. So he joined the expedition at Aulis.

Even so there were yet delays before the fleet could sail; for a long time contrary winds blew, and in despair Agamemnon consulted the prophet, Calchas. He knew that Artemis had caused the

[5] Similar magic was practised by Demeter at Eleusis on the child Demophoon.

unfavorable weather because Agamemnon had offended her,[6] and that she could only be appeased by the sacrifice of Agamemnon's daughter, Iphigenia, who therefore was sent for from Mycenae (on the pretext that she was to be married to Achilles) and sacrificed. In another version, however, Artemis saved her at the last moment, substituted a stag as the victim, and took Iphigenia to the land of the Tauri (the modern Crimea) to be her priestess.[7]

We may here consider a famous example of the use to which a mythological legend might be put by the ancients themselves. Lucretius, the Epicurean poet of Rome and contemporary of Cicero, tells the story of Iphigenia with bitterness and pathos in order to show to what lengths men will go in the name of religion (*De Rerum Natura,* 1. 84–101):

Look how the chosen leaders of the Greeks, the foremost of men, foully defiled the altar of virgin Artemis at Aulis with the blood of Iphigenia. As they placed around her maiden's hair the headband which hung down evenly by her cheeks, she suddenly caught sight of her father standing sadly before the altar and at his side his ministers hiding the knife, while the people shed tears at the sight of her. Dumb with fear she fell to the ground on her knees. At such a moment little help to her in her misery was it that she had been his first child, that she had first bestowed upon the king the name of Father. The hands of men brought her trembling to the altar, not that she might perform the customary ritual of marriage to the clear-ringing songs of Hymen, but that at the very time for her wedding she might fall a sad and sinless victim, sinfully butchered by her own father—all for the happy and auspicious departure of the fleet. Such are the monstrous evils to which religion could lead.

Calchas the prophet was an important figure in the Greek expedition, especially in times of doubt or perplexity; at Troy he gave the reason for Apollo's anger and advised the return of Chryseis to her father, and at Aulis he interpreted a famous omen. A snake was seen to climb up a tree and devour eight chicks from a nest high in its branches; it then ate the mother, and was itself turned

---

[6] The commonest version of his offense is that he had killed a stag sacred to the goddess.

[7] This version underlies Euripides's *Iphigenia* tragedies.

into stone by Zeus. Calchas correctly interpreted this as meaning that the Greeks would fight unsuccessfully at Troy for nine years, before capturing the city in the tenth.[8]

The Arrival at Troy

The expedition finally sailed from Aulis, but still did not go straight to Troy. On the way they were guided by Philoctetes, son of Poeas, to the island of Chryse to sacrifice to its goddess. There he was bitten in the foot by a snake and, as the fleet sailed on, the stench from the wound became so noisome that the Greeks abandoned Philoctetes on the island of Lemnos, where he remained alone and in agony for nearly ten years. Now Philoctetes's father, Poeas, had lit the funeral pyre of Heracles, and had in return been given Heracles's bow and arrows, which Philoctetes later inherited. In the last year of the Trojan War Priam's son, Helenus, was captured by the Greeks and prophesied that it was only with the aid of Heracles's bow and arrows that Troy could be captured; accordingly, Odysseus and Diomedes fetched Philoctetes from Lemnos; his wound was healed by the sons of Asclepius, Podalirius and Machaon, who were in the Greek army, and with the arrows he shot Paris and so removed the most formidable of the surviving Trojan champions.[9]

A second diversion on the voyage to Troy concerns Telephus, king of Mysia (a district of Asia Minor) and a son of Heracles. The Greeks landed in Mysia (although it was off their route) and in the battle that followed between them and the Mysians, Telephus was wounded by Achilles. The wound would not heal, and Telephus in despair asked the Delphic oracle for advice and was

[8] The death of Calchas may be mentioned here; after the Trojan War he challenged Mopsus (a prophet who had been on the Argonauts' expedition) to a contest by asking him how many unripe figs there were on a nearby tree. When Mopsus gave the correct answer, Calchas died, for he was fated to do so if he met a cleverer prophet than himself.

[9] The names of minor characters vary in this legend; in some versions it is Calchas who makes the prophecy, and Neoptolemus who accompanies Odysseus to Lemnos. Sophocles and Aeschylus both wrote tragedies on Philoctetes; that of Sophocles is extant.

told that "he that wounded shall heal." He therefore went to the Greek army disguised as a beggar (the action is put variously in Argos or Troy) and asked Achilles to cure his wound. Achilles said he could not, for he was not a doctor, but Odysseus pointed out that it was Achilles's spear that had caused the wound; scrapings from it were applied and Telephus was healed.

Finally, the expedition reached Troy; the first Greek to leap ashore was Protesilaus, and he was killed by Hector. His wife, Laodamia, could not be comforted in her grief. Pitying her, Hermes brought back her husband from Hades for a few hours; when he was taken away again, she killed herself. Another person to die in the first skirmish was a Trojan, Cycnus, son of Poseidon; he was turned into a swan. The Greeks successfully established themselves; they made a permanent camp with their ships drawn up on shore, and settled down to besiege Troy.

The Legends of Troy's Early History

The historical facts about Troy, as established by archaeological discoveries, have already been discussed in the Introduction. In the saga the story is more romantic. Apollo and Poseidon (disguised as mortals) had built the walls of the city for its king, Laomedon, who then cheated them of their pay. In punishment Apollo sent a plague and Poseidon a sea monster to harass the Trojans; the oracles advised that the only way to get rid of the monster was to expose Laomedon's daughter, Hesione, to be devoured by it. At this stage Heracles came to Troy; he agreed to kill the monster and save Hesione in return for Laomedon's immortal horses, which were the gift of Zeus. Once again Laomedon cheated his benefactor; Heracles therefore returned with an army, captured Troy, and gave Hesione as wife to his companion, Telamon, by whom she became the mother of Teucer. Laomedon was killed by Heracles, and his young son, Podarces, was spared by Heracles to become the king of the ruined city; his name was changed to Priam.

Ganymede was an uncle of Laomedon; Zeus loved him for his beauty as a boy, and had sent his eagle to snatch him up to Olympus, where he became the cupbearer of the gods. It was in compensation for this that Zeus gave Tros (father of Ganymede) the divine horses that Laomedon eventually inherited and failed to give to Heracles.

Another early Trojan legend is connected with Athena; she was said to have killed her companion, Pallas, daughter of Triton, during a quarrel; in remorse she made an image of the dead girl which was thrown by Zeus from heaven into Troy, where it was worshiped and looked upon as a talisman for the city's survival. This was the Palladium; when Odysseus and Diomedes stole it, Troy was doomed.

The War

By the time of the Achaean expedition, Troy, under the rule of Priam, had once more become strong and prosperous, with many allies throughout Asia Minor. It is not surprising, then, that the Greeks were unable to take the city easily; nine years were spent in a fruitless siege, varied only by abortive diplomatic exchanges and raids against cities allied with Troy. It was the division of the spoil from these cities that led to the quarrel between Agamemnon and Achilles, the principal theme of the *Iliad*. Agamemnon was given in his share Chryseis, daughter of Chryses, priest of Apollo; to Achilles's lot fell Briseis, whom he came to love greatly. Agamemnon refused to allow Chryses to ransom his daughter, and Chryses therefore prayed to Apollo to punish the Greeks. His prayer was answered and the Greeks were stricken with a plague; Calchas advised that the evil could only be ended by the return, without ransom, of Chryseis. Accordingly she was sent back, but this left Agamemnon without his share of the spoil—a humiliating situation for the greatest of the Greek princes. He therefore took Briseis from Achilles, and Achilles repaid the dishonor done to him by withdrawing his contingent, the Myrmidons, from the war.

This is the opening scene of the *Iliad;* while the events of the first nine years of the war are comparatively obscure (since the epic poems in which they were described survive only in prose summaries), those of the tenth are in part brilliantly illuminated by the *Iliad*. The poem, however, deals only with events from the

outbreak of the quarrel to the death and ransoming of Hector. .
For the subsequent events, including the death of Achilles and
the sack of Troy, we must rely either on the summaries of lost
epics or on the *Aeneid,* whose second book describes the sack
in vivid detail. Homeric epic was composed for aristocratic audiences; the *Iliad* therefore concentrates on the deeds of a comparatively few warriors on either side, whose courage for the most
part is displayed in single combat; we shall best appreciate the
story of the Trojan War if we adopt a similar approach and turn
our attention to the leading individuals on either side, including
some who were not fighting men but were more or less prominent
in the *Iliad.*

The Trojan Leaders

Almost all the chief Trojans belonged to one or other of the two
branches of the royal family. King Priam was father, it was said,
of fifty sons and twelve (or fifty) daughters, of whom nineteen
were children of his second wife, Hecuba (Arisba, his first wife, is
an unimportant figure). In the *Iliad* Hecuba appears as a tragic
figure whose sons and husband are doomed; her most important
legend takes place after the fall of Troy. As she sailed back to
Greece with Odysseus (to whom she had been given as part of the
spoils) she landed in Thrace and there recognized the corpse of
her son Polydorus when it was washed up on the sea shore; he
had been murdered by the local king, Polymestor (to whom he
had been sent for safety during the war), because of the treasure
that had been sent with him. Hecuba, taking advantage of Polymestor's avarice, enticed him and his children into her tent, pre-
tending that she knew the whereabouts in Troy of some hidden
treasure, while she appeared to know nothing of the murder of
Polydorus. Once in the tent, the children were murdered by
Hecuba's women before Polymestor's eyes, and he himself was
blinded by their brooches. After this Hecuba was turned into a
bitch; when she died the place of her burial (in Thrace) was
called Cynossema, which means the dog's tomb.

The most important of the sons of Priam and Hecuba were
Paris and Hector. We have already discussed the circumstances

of the birth of Paris and how he was brought up on Mt. Ida
among the shepherds. It was there that he fell in love with a nymph,
Oenone, who had the gift of healing. He left her for Helen; years
later, when he was wounded by Philoctetes, she refused his request
that she heal him; when he died of the wound Oenone in remorse
killed herself. Paris as a young man had returned to the royal
palace and had been recognized by Priam as his son. As we have
seen, his actions were mainly responsible for the Trojan War; in
it he appears as a brave warrior, if somewhat uxorious. He shot
the arrow that fatally wounded Achilles.

His brother, Hector, was the champion of the Trojans, brave
and honorable and as a warrior excelled only by Achilles, by
whom he was killed in single combat. While Achilles took no part
in the fighting Hector carried all before him; when he was killed,
the Trojans knew they were doomed. His wife was Andromache,
daughter of Eetion (an ally of the Trojans, killed by Achilles). She
became the slave of Neoptolemus after the fall of Troy; she later
married Helenus, one of Hector's brothers, and founded the dynasty
of the Molossian kings. In Book 3 of the *Aeneid* she and Helenus
figure prominently; she is the only one of the Trojan women to
regain some sort of independent status after the fall of Troy. Her
son by Hector was Astyanax, who was still only an infant at the
time of the sack; he was thrown from the walls by the Greeks.

Of Priam's many other sons only Helenus has any importance
in legend, although some—such as Deiphobus (who married Helen
after the death of Paris; his ghost spoke with Aeneas in the Underworld) and Troilus (who was killed by Achilles) [10]—are something more than mere names. Helenus had the gift of prophecy,
for when he was a child serpents had licked his ears. Accordingly
Calchas in the last year of the war advised the Greeks to ambush
and capture him, since he alone could tell what must be done to
end the war successfully. He was caught by Odysseus and honor-
ably treated, so that he alone of Priam's sons survived the war
and, as we have seen, eventually married Andromache and became
a ruler in Epirus. As a prophet he appears for the last time in

---

[10] The story of Troilus's love for Cressida (daughter, in this version,
of Calchas) is entirely medieval; Chaucer and Boccaccio took the story
from the *Roman de Troie* of Benoît de Ste. Maure. Shakespeare's play is
a further variation on the same legend.

the *Aeneid,* where he foretells the course of Aeneas's future wanderings.

Of the daughters of Priam the most important is Cassandra.
She had been loved by Apollo, who gave her the gift of prophecy,
but when she rejected him he added to the gift the fate that she
should never be believed. Thus she foretold the fall of Troy and
warned the Trojans against the Trojan horse all in vain. During
the sack of the city she took refuge in the temple of Athena and was
dragged from this asylum by Ajax the Locrian, son of Oileus. (This
act of sacrilege had a strange and historical consequence; for a thousand years the Locrians sent annually two daughters of noble
families to serve as temple servants of Athena at Troy [11] as a
penance for Ajax's crime. There is concrete evidence for the ending
of this penance not long before 100 A.D.)

Another of Priam's daughters, Polyxena, also has some importance in the Trojan saga. After the fall of Troy, the ghost of
Achilles appeared and claimed her as his share of the spoil; she
was therefore sacrificed at his tomb by the Greeks before they
set sail from Asia. In some versions of the saga (especially popular
in medieval legend) she had been loved by Achilles, and it was
while he was meeting her that he had been ambushed and killed by
Paris.

Of the Trojan leaders outside Priam's immediate family the
most prominent in legend is Aeneas, who belonged to the junior
branch of the royal family; he was the son of Anchises and Aphrodite, but not equal in power or prestige to Priam or Hector. In
the *Iliad* he is a mighty warrior, but a lesser one than Hector or
Achilles; he fights in single combat with Achilles and is saved from
inevitable death by Poseidon, who transports him miraculously
from the fight. Poseidon prophesies that Aeneas and his descendants, now that Zeus has withdrawn his favor from Priam's
family, will be the future rulers of Troy. It is in this respect that
Aeneas is prominent in legend, and we shall consider his story, as
given by Vergil, in a later chapter.

[11] Moreover if any of these girls was caught by the Trojans before she
reached the temple, she was put to death. The "Troy" mentioned here is
a later foundation (Troy VII to the archaeologist) upon the site of the
city sacked by the Greeks. There is a connection between the name Oileus
and the Greek name for Troy, Ilium.

Most of the other Trojans are little more than names, although the brother of Hecuba, Antenor, was conspicuous among those who did not want the war and preferred to avoid it by returning Helen to the Greeks. When the Greeks first landed he saved their ambassadors from being treacherously killed by the Trojans, and in the last year of the war he protested at the breaking of a truce by the Trojans and still proposed the voluntary return of Helen. For this fairness the Greeks spared him at the sack, and he and his wife, Theano, the priestess of Athena, were allowed to sail away; they reached Italy and there founded the city of Patavium (Padua).

Of the allies of Troy the most prominent in the *Iliad* were the Lycians, led by Glaucus and Sarpedon. At one stage Glaucus was about to fight Diomedes, but on discovering that they were hereditary guest friends,[12] they exchanged armor instead and parted amicably. Since Glaucus's armor was made of gold and that of Diomedes of bronze, Diomedes had the better of the exchange. "Zeus," says Homer, "took away Glaucus's wits, for he exchanged golden armor with Diomedes for bronze, armor worth a hundred oxen for that worth nine." Glaucus eventually was killed by Ajax (son of Telamon) in the fight over the corpse of Achilles.

Other allied contingents who appeared at Troy were those of the Thracians, the Amazons, and the Ethiopians. The latter two will be mentioned later; the Thracians were led by Rhesus. Their arrival coincided with a night patrol by Diomedes and Odysseus, during which they caught and killed a Trojan spy, Dolon, who first told them of the Thracians. They went on to kill Rhesus and twelve of his men and to capture his white horses. Rhesus, who was a son of one of the Muses, was worshiped as a hero in Thrace.

The Greek Leaders

The organization of the Greek army was different from that of the Trojans; Troy was a great city led by a powerful king and helped in war by various independent allies. In Greece the Bronze Age system was more like a feudal system; there were a number

---

[12] I.e., that their ancestors had entertained one another and exchanged gifts.

of autonomous princes who were obliged to provide contingents in war if asked to by their suzerain. The overlord–vassal relationship, however, was not as well defined as in the medieval feudal systems, so that a prince such as Achilles might withdraw his services with those of his contingent, however much the suzerain might protest. We have already seen how Helen's suitors swore to help Menelaus if he called for help; in the same way, it appears, the Greek princes were obliged to go to war if the king of Mycenae, greatest of the Bronze Age cities, summoned them.

The Greek leader, then, was Agamemnon, of Mycenae. In the Trojan War he is unquestionably the "lord of men," greatest in prestige among the Greeks, although not the greatest warrior nor the wisest in council. Three other princes from the Peloponnese were prominent; these were Menelaus, king of Sparta, Diomedes, king of Argos, and Nestor, king of Pylos. We have already seen how involved Menelaus was in the origin of the war; he does not play a very distinguished part in the war, his finest hour being the single combat against his arch-enemy, Paris; he had Paris at his mercy, but was thwarted by Aphrodite in his attempts to kill him. Diomedes was a much greater warrior and wiser in council; he was the son of Tydeus and second only to Agamemnon in power and prestige. He was a favorite of Athena and with her help could oppose even the gods in battle—he wounded both Ares and Aphrodite. He was especially associated with Odysseus; with him he had fetched Achilles from Scyros, and later was to fetch Philoctetes from Lemnos. He was his companion in the night patrol, where Dolon and Rhesus were killed, and in the theft of the Palladium from Troy. His meeting with Glaucus has already been described; his adventures after the war will be discussed later.

Nestor, son of Neleus, was the oldest of the Greek leaders; his experience as a child had been similar to that of Priam, for he had become king of Pylos after Heracles had sacked the city and killed Neleus and all his sons except Nestor. At Troy he is among the most respected counselors; his speeches, full of reminiscences, contrast with the impetuosity of the younger princes. He himself survived the war, although his son, Antilochus, was killed by Memnon; strangely enough, for one who was already seventy when the war began, there is no tradition of his death.

The leading princes from central Greece and the islands were

Odysseus, the two Ajaxes, Idomeneus, and Achilles. Although the contingents supplied by Odysseus, prince of Ithaca, and Ajax, prince of Salamis, were among the smallest (only twelve ships each), their personal prowess gave them pre-eminent distinction; Ajax, son of Telamon, was second only to Achilles as a warrior, while Odysseus was the craftiest and wisest of all, as well as a brave fighter. We have seen already that he was involved in a number of missions requiring resourcefulness and courage; his adventures after the fall of Troy are virtually a separate saga.

Ajax the Less (as Homer calls him) and Idomeneus figure prominently in the fighting; each is the leader of a large contingent and therefore important among the leaders. Ajax, prince of the Locrians and son of Oileus, is a less attractive character than his namesake; his sacrilegious violation of Cassandra during the sack led to his death on the voyage back to Greece. Idomeneus, son of Deucalion and leader of the Cretans, stood in a different relationship to Agamemnon from most of the other leaders in that he came as a voluntary ally rather than in any way as owing service. He had long been a friend of Menelaus, and Agamemnon showed him great respect. Good as he was as fighter and counselor at Troy, his legend is chiefly concerned with his return.[13]

Greatest of the champions on either side was Achilles, whose early life we have already discussed. He was the strongest and swiftest of the Greeks, the greatest fighter on either side, and a man of enormous passions, the embodiment of all that was essential in the ethical code of Mycenaean Greece. Thus the slight to his honor justified his withdrawal from the war, even though the whole Greek army suffered terribly by his action. When he killed Hector, his grief at the death of Patroclus (killed by Hector) led him to dishonor Hector's corpse in a way that offended Greek religious conventions, and also to sacrifice twelve Trojan prisoners at the funeral of Patroclus. While Achilles remained in his tent, Hector and the Trojans were victorious and succeeded in entering the Greek camp and almost setting the Greek ships on fire.

[13] The comparative importance in the war (as opposed to the literary legend) of the Greek leaders may be gauged from the size of their contingents as given in the Homeric *Catalogue:* Agamemnon, 100 ships; Nestor, 90; Diomedes and Idomeneus, 80 each; Menelaus, 60; Achilles, 50; Ajax the Less, 40; Ajax, son of Telamon, and Odysseus, 12 each.

Achilles meanwhile had refused the offers of reconciliation made by Agamemnon through an embassy consisting of Ajax (son of Telamon), Odysseus, and Phoenix (a friend of Achilles's father, Peleus). The danger to the ships, however, led him to listen to the pleading of his closest friend, Patroclus, son of Menoeteus, who begged to be allowed to go and fight, clothed in the armor of Achilles. For a while Patroclus was successful and the Trojans were driven back; among those whom Patroclus killed was Sarpedon, leader of the Lycians and a son of Zeus; Zeus could not save him from death and rained down drops of blood on the earth to honor him before the catastrophe. Patroclus himself, however, soon was killed by Hector, who stripped him of Achilles's armor. It was the grief of his death that drove Achilles to end the quarrel with Agamemnon; Briseis was returned to him with costly gifts and Achilles once more took part in the war. Thetis obtained new armor for him from Hephaestus (it is described in detail by Homer), and Achilles in return put such heart into the Greeks that the Trojans were soon driven back to the city. Only Hector remained outside the wall, and it was he whom Achilles sought in his bitterness at the death of Patroclus; the single combat between the two champions (the climax of the *Iliad*) ended with the death of Hector, whose corpse Achilles dragged behind his chariot back to the camp. He celebrated the funeral of Patroclus, and daily for twelve days dragged Hector's body round the city.[14] Finally Priam himself, helped by Hermes, made his way into the camp and ransomed the corpse; Achilles's grief was mitigated, and with the funeral of Hector the *Iliad* comes to an end.

After this Achilles killed the leaders of two contingents that came from the ends of the earth to help the Trojans. From the north came the Amazons—the legendary warrior women—led by Penthesilea; Achilles killed her, yet mourned over her beauty, and killed a Greek, Thersites, who taunted him for this.[15] For this murder Achilles had to withdraw for a time to Lesbos, where he was purified by Odysseus. The second foreign contingent to come to Troy was that of the Ethiopians, from the south; they were led by Memnon, son of Eos (Aurora), goddess of the dawn, and

---

[14] The mutilated corpse was refreshed and restored by Apollo each day.
[15] Thersites appears in the *Iliad* as a troublemaker who speaks out of turn in the assembly of the Greeks and is beaten by Odysseus for it.

of Tithonus (a brother of Priam); after Memnon's death, his followers were turned into birds that fought around his tomb.

Achilles did not long survive these victories. As he pursued the Trojans towards the city he was fatally wounded in the heel by an arrow shot by Paris with the help of Apollo; after a fierce fight his corpse was recovered by Ajax, son of Telamon, and buried at Sigeum, the promontory near Troy. The funeral was a magnificent affair, and among the mourners were Thetis herself and the sea-nymphs; in one version she is said to have removed the corpse to the island of Leuce (in the Black Sea) where she restored it to life and immortality, but Homer sends Achilles to the Underworld, where his ghost later met Odysseus and complained bitterly of his fate.

Achilles's death had two direct consequences; his armor was claimed by both Odysseus and Ajax, son of Telamon, as being the leading warriors surviving on the Greek side. Each made a speech before an assembly of the Greeks, presided over by Athena; Trojan prisoners gave evidence that Odysseus had done them more harm than Ajax, and as a result the arms were awarded to Odysseus. The disgrace of losing sent Ajax mad; he slaughtered a flock of sheep (which he believed were his enemies) and on becoming sane again killed himself for shame by falling on his sword. From his blood sprang a flower (perhaps a type of hyacinth) with the initials of his name (AI-AI) [16] on its petals.

A second legend consequent on the death of Achilles concerns the sacrifice of Polyxena, which has already been mentioned.

The Fall of Troy

After Achilles's death Odysseus took Helenus prisoner; he told the Greeks of a number of conditions that must be fulfilled before they could capture the city. Among these was the summoning of two absent heroes, Neoptolemus and Philoctetes. We have already discussed Philoctetes's part in the war; Neoptolemus killed Priam during the sack of Troy and his share of the spoil included Andromache, Hector's widow, with whom he went after the war to Epirus in northwestern Greece.

[16] Ajax is the Latin form of the Greek Aias.

The Greeks finally took the city by craft; one of them, Epeus, built an enormous hollow wooden horse, in which the leading warriors were concealed.[17] The horse was then left outside the city walls, while the other Greeks sailed off to the island of Tenedos, leaving behind one man, Sinon. The Trojans, thinking that their troubles were over, came out of the city and captured Sinon; he pretended that he was the bitter enemy of Odysseus and the other Greeks and told the Trojans that the horse was an offering to Athena, purposely made too big to pass through the city walls; if it was brought inside, the city would never be captured. Not all the Trojans believed him; Cassandra, the prophetic daughter of Priam, foretold the truth, and Laocoon, son of Antenor and priest of Apollo, hurled his spear into the horse's flank and said that it should be destroyed. Yet the Trojans ignored Cassandra and did not hear the clash of armor as Laocoon's spear struck the horse. Their judgment appeared to be vindicated when two huge serpents swam over the sea from Tenedos, while Laocoon was sacrificing to Apollo, and throttled him and his two sons. The Trojans pulled down part of the city walls and dragged the horse in; Helen walked round it calling to the Greek leaders, imitating the voice of each one's wife, but they were restrained from answering by Odysseus. So the horse achieved its purpose; that night, as the Trojans slept after celebrating the end of the war, Sinon opened the horse and released the Greeks. The other Greeks sailed back from Tenedos and were let into the city; the Trojans were put to the sword and the city burned. Antenor was spared, and of the other Trojan leaders only Aeneas escaped, along with his son, Ascanius, and his father, Anchises. Priam and the others were killed; Hector's infant son, Astyanax, was thrown from the walls, and his widow, Andromache, along with Hecuba and the other Trojan women, were made slaves of the Greek leaders. Cassandra became the slave and concubine of Agamemnon and was taken by him back to Mycenae, where she was murdered with him by Clytemnestra. In Aeschylus's play, *Agamemnon,* she foresees her own death in a moving and famous scene; yet her audience, the Chorus in the play, do not believe her. The curse of Apollo remained with her to the end.

[17] Being descended from one of the heroes shut up in the wooden horse was one of the marks of the *crème de la crème* of the Greek nobility.

CHAPTER 18

The Returns

The Greek leaders met with varied adventures on leaving Troy, which were the subject of a lost epic called *Nostoi* (Returns), as well as of Homer's *Odyssey*. Agamemnon and Menelaus quarreled over the departure and so parted company. Agamemnon sailed for Greece with part of the fleet, including the contingent of the Locrians; off the island of Tenos, Athena, in anger at the sacrilege committed at Troy by the Locrian leader, Ajax, raised a violent storm that wrecked many of the ships, including that of Ajax. He himself escaped drowning and swam to a nearby rock where he boasted that not even the gods could prevent his escape from the dangers of the sea; at this impiety Poseidon struck the rock with his trident, and Ajax was hurled into the sea and drowned. The storm was not the only peril that Agamemnon's fleet encountered; at Cape Caphareus in Euboea Nauplius avenged the death of his son, Palamedes, by decoying many ships onto the rocks with a false beacon. Agamemnon finally reached Mycenae, only to be murdered by Aegisthus and Clytemnestra.

Meanwhile Menelaus, Nestor, and Diomedes set sail together from Troy; Nestor had an easy voyage back to Pylos, but the other two had more to contend with. Menelaus met with a storm and lost all his fleet except for five ships, with which he eventually reached Egypt; he wandered over northern Africa for eight years before returning to Sparta, where he resumed his rule with Helen once more his queen.[1] At the end of his life he was transported to the Elysian Fields (a more suitable destiny for a son-in-law of Zeus than death) where he and Helen live forever.

[1] Helen either rejoined him after the fall of Troy, or (if Stesichorus is followed) it was a phantom like her that did, and he recovered the true Helen in Egypt.

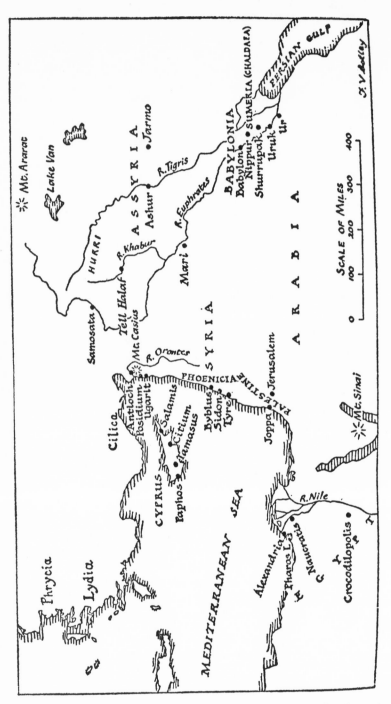

Fig. 13. The East. From Michael Grant, Myths of the Greeks and Romans *(London: Weidenfeld and Nicholson, 1962), p. 434.*

Diomedes, like Nestor, reached his home, Argos, quickly, but there found trouble. Nauplius not only wrecked part of the Greek fleet, as we have seen, but further attempted to satisfy his vengeance by getting the wives of some of the leaders to commit adultery. Among them was Aegialia, wife of Diomedes.[2] As a result of this (or for some other reason) Diomedes left Argos and wandered over the western Mediterranean until he finally came to Italy where he founded several cities. When Aeneas reached Latium, Diomedes refused to send help to the Italians against the Trojans. He was buried in an island off the coast of Apulia (South Italy) and his followers turned into sea birds (said to be shearwaters) that sprinkle the tomb with water and are hostile to everyone except Greeks. He was worshiped as a hero in many places, especially around the Adriatic Sea.

Idomeneus also found trouble at home. His wife, Meda, had committed adultery with a Cretan, Leucus, who had then murdered her and her daughter and made himself king over ten of the one hundred cities of Crete. Idomeneus was unable to reestablish himself on his return and was driven out by Leucus. Quite a different version of the expulsion is given by Servius, the ancient commentator on Vergil, which is similar to the famous story of Jephthah's vow (*Judges,* 11.30 ff.). Idomeneus was caught in a storm during the voyage home and vowed, if he were saved, to sacrifice to Poseidon the first thing that met him; on his safe return it was his son who came out first to meet him. After Idomeneus had fulfilled (or attempted to fulfill) his vow, a pestilence attacked the Cretans; they took it to be a divine punishment for Idomeneus's cruelty, and accordingly drove him into exile. At any rate, Idomeneus left Crete and settled in Calabria (South Italy). The place of his death is variously given as Calabria, Crete, and Colophon (in Asia Minor), and there were cults in his honor in these areas.

Yet another hero to reach Italy was Philoctetes, who was driven from his own city of Meliboea in Thessaly. He came to Campania (the area around Naples) and eventually settled in southern Italy where he founded a number of cities. It was there that he in-

---

[2] Aegialia's unfaithfulness was also Aphrodite's revenge on Diomedes for her wound at Troy.

augurated a cult of Apollo, to whom he dedicated his bow; he died fighting a south Italian tribe, and after his death he was worshiped as a hero.

These three heroes—Diomedes, Idomeneus, and Philoctetes—are clear examples of the workings of saga. Whether or not they were in origin men or gods (both views have been held), they are men in the stories of their lives, who after their death are worshiped as heroes, that is, as men become gods. Moreover their association with Italy has its historical aspect in that southern Italy was one of the major areas of colonization by the Greeks from the eighth century onwards; the legend, in other words, has some connection, however faint, with historical facts.

Achilles's son, Neoptolemus, was warned by Thetis not to return by sea; accordingly he took the land route back to Greece accompanied by Helenus and Andromache. He made his way, not to his father's kingdom of Phthia, but to Molossia (i.e., Epirus) in northwestern Greece, and from there later went to Phthia on the death of Peleus, his grandfather, while Helenus stayed in Epirus and married Andromache. Not long after he married Hermione (daughter of Menelaus and formerly betrothed to Orestes) and as a consequence was killed by Orestes at Delphi; he was buried within the precinct of Apollo's temple there—a unique honor among Greek heroes.[3]

Odysseus

The return of Odysseus forms a saga in itself, to which many folktale elements have accrued. Here is Aristotle's summary of the *Odyssey*: "The story of the *Odyssey* is not long; a man is away from home for many years; Poseidon constantly is on the watch to destroy him, and he is alone; at home his property is being wasted by suitors, and his son is the intended victim of a plot. He reaches home, tempest-tossed; he makes himself known, attacks his enemies and destroys them, and is himself saved. This is the heart of the matter: the rest is episodes" (*Poetics,* 17). The most

---

[3] There are many variants in the legend of Neoptolemus, but of his importance there is no doubt, both in the Trojan saga and as a hero after his death.

interesting part of the legend, however, lies in the "episodes" that comprise Odysseus's adventures on his travels; they have been taken as symbolic (for example, Odysseus conquers death in his visit to the Underworld) or as connected with real places which had become known to the Greeks as their trade and colonization expanded. While it may be probable that the land of the Phaeacians is identified with Corfu, Ithaca with Thiaki, and Charybdis with the currents of the straits of Messina, it is better to accept most of Odysseus's adventures for what they are, romantic legends and folk tales set in imaginary places and grafted on to the saga of a historical prince's return from an ancient war.

It took Odysseus ten years to reach home. When he and his contingent left Troy their first landfall was the Thracian city of Ismarus, home of the Cicones; after sacking it Odysseus and his men were driven off. They had spared Maron, priest of Apollo, in their attack, and he in return gave them among other presents twelve jars of fragrant red wine, which was to prove its value later. As they sailed away they were driven southward by a violent storm and eventually came to the land of the lotus eaters; here their reception was friendly but no less dangerous, for he who ate of the fruit of the lotus forgot everything and wanted only to stay where he was, eating lotus fruit. Odysseus got his men away, even those who had tasted the fruit, and sailed to the land of the Cyclopes.

The Cyclopes were one-eyed giants, herdsmen, living each in his own cave. One of them was Polyphemus, son of Poseidon, and it was his cave that Odysseus and twelve picked companions entered as they explored the area. Polyphemus was out, and in the cave were sheep and lambs, cheeses, and other provisions; the Greeks helped themselves to these and waited for the return of the cave's owner. In the evening Polyphemus returned with his flocks, shut the entrance of the cave with a huge stone, and then caught sight of the visitors, two of whom he ate for his supper; he breakfasted on two more the next day and another two when he returned the second evening. Now Odysseus had with him some of the wine of Maron, and with this he made Polyphemus drunk; he told him his name was Nobody and the giant in return for the excellent wine promised that he would reward Nobody by eating him last. He then fell asleep, and Odysseus took his revenge. He sharpened a wooden stake that was lying in the cave and heated it in the fire; then he and his surviving men drove it into the solitary eye of the sleeping giant. As he cried out in agony the other Cyclopes came running to the cave's entrance, only to hear the cry "Nobody is killing me," so that they assumed that not much was wrong and left Polyphemus alone. Next morning Polyphemus, now blind, removed the stone at the entrance and let his flocks out; he felt each animal as it passed him. But Odysseus had tied his men each to the undersides of three sheep, and himself clung to the belly of the biggest ram; so he and his men escaped. As Odysseus sailed away in his ship he shouted his real name to the Cyclops, who hurled the top of a mountain at him and nearly wrecked the ship. Polyphemus had long before been warned of Odysseus by a prophet, and as he recognized the name he prayed to his father Poseidon (*Odyssey,* 9. 530–535):

Grant that Odysseus may not return home, but if it is fated for him once more to see those he loves and reach his home and country, then let him arrive after many years, in distress, without his companions, upon another's ship—and may he find trouble in his house.

The prayer was heard.

Odysseus, now reunited with the rest of his fleet, next reached the floating island of Aeolus, keeper of the winds, who lived there with his six sons, who were married to his six daughters. After he had entertained Odysseus, Aeolus gave him as a parting gift a leather bag containing all the winds, and showed him which one to release so as to reach home. Thus he sailed back to Ithaca and was within reach of land when he fell asleep; his men, believing that the bag contained gold that Odysseus was keeping for himself, opened it, and all the winds rushed out and blew the ships back to Aeolus's island. Aeolus refused to help them any more, for, he supposed, they must be hated by the gods.

Accordingly they sailed away, this time to the land of the Laestrygonians, who were cannibals; they sank all Odysseus's ships except his own and ate up the crews. So Polyphemus's curse was already working, and Odysseus sailed on with his solitary ship to the island of Aeaea, the home of the witch, Circe. (She was

THE RAPE OF HELEN attributed to a follower of Fra Angelico, London, National Gallery. Reproduced by courtesy of the Trustees, The National Gallery, London.

THE BUILDING OF THE TROJAN HORSE by G. B. Tiepolo (1696–1770), London, National Gallery. Reproduced by courtesy of the Trustees, The National Gallery, London.

AENEAS' FLIGHT FROM TROY by Federico Barocci (ca. 1535–1612), The Cleveland Museum of Art, L. E. Holden Fund. Reproduced by permission of The Cleveland Museum of Art.

*CIRCE AND HER LOVERS IN A LANDSCAPE by Dosso Dossi (ca. 1479–
ca. 1542), Washington, D.C., National Gallery of Art, Samuel H. Kress Collection.
Reproduced by permission of the National Gallery of Art.*

*ODYSSEUS AND
THE SIRENS, from
an Athenian vase (ca.
480 B.C.) London,
British Museum.*

THE RETURN OF ODYSSEUS by Pinturicchio (Bernardo Betti 1454–1513), London, National Gallery. Reproduced by courtesy of the Trustees, National Gallery, London.

ATLAS BRINGS THE APPLES OF THE HESPERIDES TO HERACLES, metope from the Temple of Zeus at Olympia (ca. 460 B.C.), Olympia Museum.

HERACLES SHOWS CERBERUS TO EURYSTHEUS from an Etruscan hydria (ca. 525 B.C.), Paris, Louvre Museum. Photo by Maurice Chuzeville.

THE END OF A MONSTER (1937) by Pablo Picasso (b. 1881). Permission S.P.A.D.E.M. 1970 by French Reproduction Rights, Inc.

PERSEUS AND ANDROMEDA by Annibale Carracci (1560–1609), Rome, Farnese Palace.

THE ROCK OF DOOM (ca. 1885) by
Edward Burne-Jones (1833–1898), London,
The Tate Gallery. Reproduced by permission
of the Trustees of the Tate Gallery.

CLYTIE by Annibale Carracci (1560–1609), Cincinnati Art Museum. Reproduced by permission of
the Cincinnati Art Museum.

Quid Venus in venis possit furor ossibꝰ heres
pyramus hoc thysbes funere mōstrat amās

PYRAMUS AND THISBE, woodcut by Hans Wechtlin (ca. 1480–ca. 1526), Cleveland Museum of Art, John L. Severance Fund. Reproduced by permission of the Cleveland Museum of Art.

Sky-map of the Northern Hemisphere with the twelve signs of the zodiac, by Albrecht Dürer, 1515.

the daughter of the Sun and therefore aunt of the other great enchantress of Greek legend, Medea.) Odysseus divided his men into two groups; he stayed behind with the one while the other, twenty-three men in all, went to visit the ruler of the island. They found Circe with various animals around her, and themselves (except for one, Eurylochus, who brought the news back to Odysseus) were turned, by eating her food, into pigs—swine in appearance and sound, but still with human minds.[4] As Odysseus went to rescue his men he was met by the god, Hermes, who told him how to counter Circe's charms and gave him as an antidote the magic herb *moly,* whose "root is black and flower as white as milk." So he ate Circe's food unharmed; as she tried to transform him into a pig he threatened her with his sword and made her change his men back into their human shape. Odysseus lived with Circe for a year and by her begot a son, Telegonus.[5]

At the end of a year Odysseus, urged on by his men, asked Circe to send him on his way home. She agreed, but told him that he first had to go to the Underworld and there learn from Tiresias, whose prophetic powers were unimpaired even in the world of the dead, the way home. The visit of Odysseus to the Underworld (it is generally referred to as the *Nekuia*) is in some ways the climax of his adventures, for the conquest of death is the most formidable struggle a hero has to face. He who, like Odysseus, Heracles, and Theseus, can return from the house of Hades alive has achieved all that a mortal man can achieve. The *Nekuia* of Odysseus is different in one important respect from its most famous imitation; in the *Aeneid* Aeneas actually descends to the Underworld and himself passes through it. Odysseus goes to the entrance and there performs a ritual sacrifice that enables him to summon up the spirits of the dead; those with whom he wishes to speak are allowed to drink the blood of the sacrificial victim, but the rest are kept away from it by Odysseus, who threatens them with his sword.[6]

[4] Symbolic interpretations are readily devised; the most powerful adaptation of the legend is in the Circe episode in James Joyce's *Ulysses.*

[5] Telegonus is not mentioned in the *Odyssey;* he is the creation of later epic, and by some authorities is said to be the son of Odysseus by Calypso.

[6] We have already dealt with the *Nekuia* in Chapter 13.

Odysseus, then, following Circe's directions, sailed with his men to the River of Ocean at the western limit of the world where, in his words "are the city and the people of the Cimmerians, veiled in fog and mist; never does the bright Sun look upon them with his rays—neither when he climbs toward the starry heavens nor when he returns towards earth from the heavens; a curtain of gloomy darkness envelops those unhappy men" (*Odyssey*, 11. 14–19). Here was the entrance to the world of the dead and Odysseus, alone, performed his ritual. Many ghosts came, most important of whom was the soul of Tiresias, who told Odysseus of the disasters that yet waited for him on his journey; he would reach home, but alone and after many years (in this Tiresias echoes the prayer of Polyphemus). Moreover, at Ithaca things were in a sorry state, with arrogant suitors pressing Penelope hard and wasting Odysseus's substance. But Odysseus would kill them all; yet he would have still more travels ahead of him before death came.

Other ghosts besides that of Tiresias were seen by Odysseus; among them were his mother, Anticlea, Agamemnon, Achilles, and Ajax, son of Telamon; it was Achilles who said that "he would rather be a slave to a poor man on earth than be king over all the souls of the dead." Ajax would not answer Odysseus a word, for he still was grieved by his loss in the contest for Achilles's arms. Eventually Odysseus left the house of Hades for fear that the Gorgon's head (which turns all whom it beholds to stone) might appear; he rejoined his men and sailed back to Aeaea.

Circe sent him on his way after warning him of the dangers that lay ahead. First were the Sirens (said by Homer to be two in number, but to be more by other authors); to Homer these were human in form, but in popular tradition they were bird-like, with women's heads. From their island meadow they would lure passing sailors onto the rocks; all around them were the whitened bones of their victims. Odysseus sailed by them unharmed, stopping his men's ears with wax, while he had himself bound to the ship's mast so that he could not yield to the irresistible beauty of the Sirens' song.[7]

---

[7] There are several late variants of the Sirens' previous history and subsequent fate, which are of little importance. Like the Planctae, they may be interpreted as death symbols; an easier course is to accept them (as Sir

The next danger was the two wandering rocks (*Planctae*) between which one ship only, the Argo, had ever safely passed. Odysseus avoided them by sailing close to two high cliffs; in the lower of these lived Charybdis (she is not described by Homer), who three times a day sucked in the water of the strait and spouted it upwards again; to sail near that cliff was certain destruction, and Odysseus chose as the lesser evil the higher cliff where was the cave of Scylla, daughter of the sea deity Phorcys. Originally a sea-nymph, she had been changed, through the jealousy of Poseidon's wife, Amphitrite, into a monster with a girdle of six dogs' heads and with twelve feet, by means of which she would snatch sailors from passing ships. From Odysseus's ship she snatched six men, whom she ate in her cave; Odysseus and the rest of the crew were unharmed.

Lastly Circe told Odysseus of the island of Thrinacia, where Helius (the Sun) pastured his herds of cattle and sheep; she strictly warned Odysseus not to touch a single one of the animals if he and his men wished ever to return to Ithaca. But Odysseus's men in the event could not show such restraint after weeks of being detained by adverse winds, and while he was sleeping they killed some of the cattle for food. Helius complained to Zeus, and as a punishment (for the sacrilege of killing the god's cattle) Zeus raised a storm when the ship set sail and hurled a thunderbolt at it. The ship sank, and all the men were drowned except for Odysseus, who escaped, floating on the mast and part of the keel.

So much for Circe's prophecy and the subsequent events. After the wreck Odysseus drifted back to Charybdis, where he avoided death by clinging to a tree growing on the cliff until the whirlpool propelled his mast to the surface after sucking it down. From there he drifted over the sea to Ogygia, the island home of Calypso, daughter of Atlas.

He lived with Calypso for seven years; although she loved him and offered to make him immortal, he could not forget Penelope. Finally, after Hermes brought her the express orders of Zeus,

---

J. G. Frazer accepts the Planctae) as "the mere creation of a storyteller's fancy" (ed. of Apollodorus, Cambridge: Harvard University Press, 1921; vol. 2, p. 358).

Calypso helped Odysseus build a raft and sail away. Even now he was not free from disaster; Poseidon saw him as he approached Scheria (the island of the Phaeacians) and shattered the raft with a storm. Odysseus was in the water for two days and two nights, but he survived, helped by the sea-goddess, Leucothea (formerly the mortal Ino, daughter of Cadmus), and by Athena, and he succeeded in reaching land naked, exhausted, and alone.

The king of the Phaeacians was Alcinous, and his daughter was Nausicaa. The very day after Odysseus's landing Nausicaa went to wash clothes near the seashore and came face to face with Odysseus; she gave him her protection and brought him back to the palace. Here he was warmly entertained by Alcinous and his queen, Arete, and related the story of his adventures to them. The Phaeacians gave him rich gifts and a day later brought him back to Ithaca in a deep sleep on one of their ships (they were magnificent seamen). So Odysseus reached Ithaca ten years after the fall of Troy, alone and on another's ship, as Polyphemus had prayed. Yet even now Poseidon did not relax his hostility; as the Phaeacians' ship was entering the harbor of Scheria on its return, he turned it and its crew to stone as a punishment (long foretold) upon the Phaeacians for conveying strangers over the seas, even those who were the objects of Poseidon's hatred.

In Ithaca more than one hundred suitors—young noblemen from Ithaca and the nearby islands—were courting Penelope in the hope of taking Odysseus's place as her husband and as king of Ithaca (for Telemachus, Odysseus's son by Penelope, was considered still too young to succeed). They spent their days feasting at Odysseus's palace, wasting his possessions. Penelope, however, remained faithful to Odysseus, even though he seemed to be dead; she procrastinated with the suitors by promising to choose one of them when she should have finished weaving a magnificent cloak to be a burial garment for Odysseus's father, Laertes. For three years [8] she wove the robe by day and undid her work by night, but in the fourth year her deception was uncovered and a decision was now unavoidable. It was at this stage that Odysseus returned; helped by Athena he gained entrance at the palace disguised as

---

[8] Her weaving begins six years after the fall of Troy.

a beggar, after being recognized by his faithful old swineherd, Eumaeus, and by Telemachus; Telemachus knew, in any case, that Odysseus might be alive, since he had been on a journey to Pylos and Sparta and had learned from Nestor and Menelaus that his father had not perished. (It was outside the palace that Odysseus's old hound, Argus, recognized his master after nineteen years' absence, and died.) At the palace Odysseus was insulted by the suitors and by another beggar, Irus, whom he knocked out in a fight; still in disguise, he had a long talk with Penelope, in which he gave an exact description of Odysseus and of a curious brooch he had worn; as a result she confided in him her plan to give herself next day to whichever suitor should succeed in stringing Odysseus's great bow and shooting an arrow straight through a row of twelve ax heads.[9] Also at this time Odysseus was recognized by his old nurse, Euryclea, who knew him from a scar on his thigh, which he had received in a boar hunt. Thus the scene was set for Odysseus's triumphant return; his son and his faithful retainers knew the truth, and Penelope had fresh encouragement to prepare her for the eventual recognition.

The trial of the bow took place next day; none of the suitors could even so much as string it, and Odysseus asked to be allowed to try. Effortlessly he achieved the task and shot the arrow through the axes; next he shot the leading suitor, Antinous, and in the succeeding fight he and Telemachus and their two faithful servants killed all the other suitors. Next, the twelve maidservants, who had allowed themselves to be seduced by the suitors, were hanged. Even so Penelope could not believe it really was Odysseus who was there, and only when he showed knowledge of the secret construction of their bed did she relent and their twenty years' separation was ended.

Next day Odysseus made himself known to his father, Laertes; the *Odyssey* ends with Athena intervening between Odysseus and the relatives of the dead suitors (who demanded vengeance, blood for blood) and making peace between them.

[9] There is doubt as to what exactly the feat was; probably the arrow had to be shot through twelve double axes placed behind each other. Perhaps their crescent-shaped blades formed a U-shaped alley along which the arrow traveled.

Later authors attempted to "improve" on Homer, and there are many variant stories that concern Penelope, none of which is important. Equally debatable is the subsequent history of Odysseus; here again Homer is our best guide, in the words of Tiresias's prophecy (*Odyssey,* 11. 119–137):

When you have killed the suitors in your palace . . . then you must go, carrying a well-made oar, until you come to men who know not the sea nor eat food flavored with salt; nor know they of red-painted ships nor of shapely oars, which are the wings of ships. This shall be a clear sign that you shall not miss: when another traveler meets you and says that you have a winnowing-fan upon your fine shoulder, then plant the well-turned oar in the ground and sacrifice . . . to Poseidon . . . and to all the immortal gods. . . . And death shall come to you easily, from the sea, such as will end your life when you are weary after a comfortable old age—and around you shall be a prosperous people.

And so it came to pass; after Odysseus's return it still remained for him to appease Poseidon, and this he did in the manner foretold by Tiresias, founding a shrine to Poseidon where he planted the oar. He returned to Ithaca and there, years later, was accidentally killed by Telegonus, who had grown up on his mother's island and sailed across the sea to Ithaca in search of his father.[10]

---

[10] Other details appearing in the last part of Odysseus's legend are: (1) that he spent some time among the Thesprotians (in northwestern Greece) as husband of their queen, Callidice; (2) that he returned to Ithaca (and to Penelope) leaving his son by Callidice, Polypoetes, as king of the Thesprotians; (3) that after his death Telemachus married Circe and Telegonus married Penelope; (4) that Circe made them all immortal.

CHAPTER 19

Heracles

Heracles [1] is the greatest and most popular Greek hero and there-fore has attracted very many legends which range from genuine saga to pure folk tale. His significance—as man, hero, or god—is hotly debated; we shall discuss these matters along with the views held about him in later ages after reviewing his legends.

Birth and Early Life

Heracles is particularly associated with the area around Argos and with Thebes, where his birth is traditionally placed. The two areas are connected in the account of his parents' adventures. Electryon, king of Mycenae, and his sons fought at Mycenae with the sons of Pterelaus, king of the Teleboans (a people of western Greece); all the sons killed one another in single combat; only one son in each family survived and that simply because they had not been present at the battle.[2] The Teleboans then retreated, taking with them Electryon's cattle. Electryon determined to avenge the death of his sons, and made his nephew, Amphitryon, king in his place, so that he could leave Mycenae and make his expedition. More-over, he betrothed his daughter, Alcmena, to him, with the condition that he should leave her a virgin until after his return from the

---

[1] The Greek form of his name, which means glory of Hera, is used in this chapter: Hercules is the Latin form. He is often referred to as Alcides (i.e., descendant of Alcaeus), and this was his name until his visit to Delphi, which immediately preceded the twelve labors. In literature he is also re-ferred to as Amphitryoniades (son of Amphitryon).

[2] Licymnios, surviving son of Electryon, was later murdered by a son of Heracles.

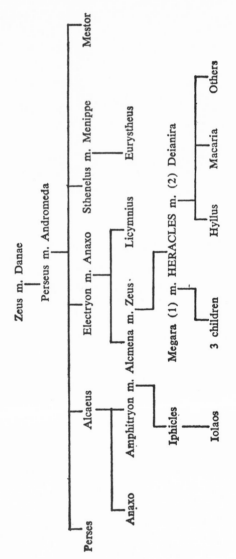

Fig. 14: The family of Heracles.

Teleboans. Now Amphitryon had already recovered the stolen cattle, and while herding them threw his club at one and with the blow accidentally killed Electryon. For this homicide he was exiled from Mycenae, while his uncle, Sthenelus, became king of Mycenae.

Amphitryon, with Alcmena, went to Thebes, where the king, Creon, purified him of his blood-guilt. The death of Alcmena's brothers, however, still remained unavenged, and Alcmena refused to give herself to Amphitryon until he should have completed the expedition that Electryon had planned. To do this he needed the help of Creon and his forces, and Creon would only support him if he first got rid of a fox that was ravaging the Theban territory. The Thebans offered it one of their youths each month, and their distress was increased by the knowledge that the fox was fated never to be caught. Among Amphitryon's helpers in performing the task was Cephalus, who brought with him the hound of his wife, Procris, which was fated to catch whatever it pursued. Zeus resolved the impasse by turning both the fox and the hound into stone, and Amphitryon was now free to make war on the Teleboans. His expedition was partially successful, but Pterelaus was immortal and so long as he lived his territory could not be taken; his immortality depended on a golden hair on his head. Now his daughter, Comaetho, fell in love with Amphitryon, and to help him pulled out her father's golden hair so that he died and Amphitryon was completely victorious. Amphitryon returned to Thebes with the spoils, having first put Comaetho to death.[3]

Amphitryon expected on his return to lie with Alcmena and was surprised to find her less than welcoming. Zeus, in the likeness of Amphitryon, had visited her the previous night, which he made three times its proper length, and had told her the full story of the Teleboan expedition; the truth was revealed to Amphitryon by Tiresias, and he then lay with Alcmena. Thus she conceived twins (it was said); the elder by one night was Heracles, son of Zeus, and the younger, the son of Amphitryon, was Iphicles.

The birth of Heracles had its complications, and introduces an unaltering feature of his story until after his death, the hostility of Hera. Zeus had boasted on Olympus, on the day on which

---

[3] The story of Comaetho is similar to that of Minos and Scylla.

Heracles was to be born, saying: "Today Eileithyia, helper in childbirth, will bring to the light a man who shall rule over all that dwell around him; he shall be of the race that is of my blood" (Homer, *Iliad,* 19. 102–105). Hera deceived Zeus by hastening on the birth of the child of Sthenelus, whose wife was seven months pregnant, and sending Eileithyia to delay the birth of Alcmena's sons.[4] Sthenelus, king of Mycenae, was the grandson of Zeus, and so his son, rather than Alcmena's, fulfilled the terms of Zeus's boast; he was Eurystheus, for whom Heracles performed the Labors.

Hera, unable to prevent the birth of Heracles, attempted to destroy him in infancy by sending a pair of snakes into the twins' cradle; while Iphicles was terrified, Heracles strangled them both with his bare hands. Thus he survived and grew to manhood; in his education he was taught chariot driving by Amphitryon, wrestling by Autolycus, archery by Eurytus, and music by Linus. Eurytus, prince of Oechalia (a city of Euboea), was the grandson of Apollo and in some versions of his legend was killed by Apollo for challenging him in archery. Others, however, make Heracles responsible for his death when, many years later, he stormed Oechalia. Heracles also caused the death of Linus, who was a son of Apollo, by striking him with his lyre. As a result of this homicide Heracles was sent away to the Theban pastures on Mt. Cithaeron.

Here he performed a number of exploits; he killed a lion which was preying on the cattle of Amphitryon and of Thespius, king of the Boeotian town of Thespiae. During the hunt for the lion Heracles was entertained for fifty days by Thespius, who gave him a different one of his fifty daughters to lie with each night; one version, indeed, improves on this and makes Heracles lie with all fifty in the same night. Another exploit of this part of his career was to free the Thebans from the necessity of paying tribute to the Minyans of Orchomenus, leading the Theban army himself into

[4] Eileithyia achieved this by sitting outside Alcmena's door with her hands clasped around her knees (a common piece of sympathetic magic); the spell was broken by Alcmena's maid, Galanthis, rushing from the house crying "My mistress has borne a son"—which so astonished Eileithyia that she leapt up and unclasped her hands. Thus the birth took place: but Galanthis was turned by Eileithyia into a weasel.

battle. In gratitude for this Creon gave him his daughter, Megara, as wife, and by her he had three children.

Some time later Hera again attacked Heracles; in a fit of madness caused by her he killed Megara and her children. When he recovered his sanity he left Thebes and went first to Thespiae, where Thespius purified him, and then to Delphi for further advice. Here the priestess of Apollo called him Heracles for the first time —before he had been known as Alcides—and told him to go to Tiryns and there for twelve years serve Eurystheus, performing the Labors that he would impose; if he did them, she said, he would become immortal.

This is the simplest story of the origin of the Labors; there is, however, great confusion over the chronology of Heracles's legends. Thus Euripides, in his *Heracles,* puts the murder of Megara and her children after the Labors; Sophocles, in his *Trachiniae,* has Heracles marry his second wife, Deianira, before the Labors, whereas Apollodorus places the marriage after them. All are agreed, at any rate, that for a number of years Heracles served Eurystheus. As Heracles's ghost says to Odysseus (Homer, *Odyssey,* 11. 620–623): "I was a son of Zeus, but infinite was my suffering; for I was slave to a far inferior mortal, and heavy were the labors he laid upon me."

The Twelve Labors

The Greek word for labors is *athloi,* which really means contests undertaken for a prize. In Heracles's case, as the Delphic oracle's advice made clear, the prize was immortality, so that we should not be surprised to find that at least three of the Labors (and possibly more) are variations on the "conquest of death" theme.[5] Heracles did not necessarily perform the Labors unaided; sometimes Athena helped him, sometimes his nephew, Iolaus.[6] The first six Labors all take place in the Peloponnese; such localization is to be expected, since the servitude to Eurystheus brought Heracles

---

[5] Cattle of Geryon; apples of the Hesperides; Cerberus.
[6] Iolaus was the son of Iphicles and Creon's younger daughter.

back to the area of Argos, the home of his parents.[7] The second group takes place in different parts of the world; in them Heracles has passed from being a local hero into being the benefactor of all mankind. The list of the Labors varies, but the twelve given here represent a widely accepted tradition.

1. *The Nemean Lion.* Heracles was required to bring the skin of this beast to Eurystheus; at Nemea he cut himself a club with which he killed the monster. This is the early tradition of the story; later authors (of whom Theocritus gives the fullest account in his twenty-fifth *Idyll*) made the lion invulnerable, so that Heracles was obliged to strangle it with his hands after clubbing it, and then to flay it by using its claws to cut the invulnerable hide, At any rate, the club and lion's skin henceforth were Heracles's weapon and clothing *par excellence;* in art, as in literature, they are invariably associated with him.

2. *The Lernaean Hydra.* This serpent (*hydra* is the Greek word for a water snake) lived in the swamps of Lerna, near Argos; it was said to have had nine heads, of which eight were mortal and the ninth immortal. Moreover, each time Heracles clubbed a head off, two grew in its place. The Labor was made the harder by a huge crab, which Hera sent to aid the Hydra. Heracles killed this monster, and then, with the assistance of Iolaus dealt with the hydra; each time he removed one of the heads Iolaus cauterized the stump with a burning brand so that another could not grow. Heracles chopped off the immortal head and buried it under a huge rock. He then dipped his arrows in the hydra's poison—an act which led indirectly to his own death. As for the crab, Hera took it and made it the constellation, Cancer.

3. *The Cerynean Stag.* This miraculous animal, with golden horns, was sacred to Artemis; it took its name from Mt. Cerynea in Arcadia.[8] It was harmless nor might it be harmed without incurring Artemis's wrath.[9] So Heracles pursued it for a whole year and eventually only caught it by lightly wounding it with an arrow as it crossed the river Ladon. He then carried it back on his

---

[7] The three cities of the Argolid—Argos, Tiryns, and Mycenae—are often confused in accounts of the Labors.

[8] It is also called the Cerynitian stag, from the river Cerynites in Achaea.

[9] Only Euripides makes it a destructive beast that Heracles kills.

shoulders to Eurystheus; on the way, however, Artemis met him and claimed her sacred animal, but she was appeased (both for the theft and the wounding) when Heracles laid the blame on Eurystheus.

This version of the story is entirely set in the Peloponnese. A different account, however, is given by Pindar in his beautiful third *Olympian Ode*. In this Heracles went to the land of the Hyperboreans—on the northern confines of the world—in search of the stag, on whose golden horns the nymph Taygete, a daughter of Atlas, had stamped the name of Artemis. In this version we have a certain clue that allows us to connect this Labor with that of the apples of the Hesperides; in the latter story Heracles goes to the limits of the world in search of a miraculous golden object, and again Ladon (in the form of a dragon) and Atlas [10] appear. We shall see that the Hesperides Labor is in fact a conquest of death, and at this point we can say that the story of the Cerynean stag is another version of the same theme.[11]

4. *The Erymanthian Boar.* This boar was ravaging the land around Mt. Erymanthus and had to be brought back alive; Heracles chased the animal out of its hiding place into some deep snow and there trapped it with nets. He brought it back to Eurystheus, who cowered in terror in a large jar. This rather unexciting Labor resulted in a side adventure (or *parergon*)[12] of some interest; on his way to the chase Heracles was entertained by the centaur Pholus, who set before him a jar of wine that belonged to all the centaurs in common. When it was opened the other centaurs, attracted by its fragrance, came and attacked Heracles, who repelled and pursued them. Most of them were scattered all over Greece, but one who was wounded by one of Heracles's poisoned arrows was Chiron. Since he was immortal, he could not die, but had to suffer incurable agonies until Prometheus interceded with Zeus and took upon himself the immortality of Chiron. Heracles's

[10] Atlas was the name of a mountain in Arcadia, as well as of the more famous range in North Africa, into which the Titan Atlas had been turned.
[11] The stag appears beside the tree of Hesperides in several Greek vase paintings.
[12] In the traditional classification of Heracles's legends the *parerga* are the adventures incidental to the Labors.

host, Pholus, also met his death from a poisoned arrow that he accidentally dropped on his foot as he was examining it out of curiosity.

5. *The Augean Stables.* Augeas, son of Helius (the Sun) and king of Elis, was the owner of vast herds of cattle, whose stables had never been cleaned out. Heracles was commanded by Eurystheus to perform the task, and successfully achieved it within one day by diverting the rivers Alpheus and Peneus so that they flowed through the stables. Augeas had agreed to give Heracles one tenth of his herds as a reward, but refused to keep his promise after the performance of the task and expelled Heracles and his own son, Phyleus (who had taken Heracles's part in the quarrel), from Elis. Heracles was received by a nearby prince, Dexamenus (whose name, indeed, means the receiver or the hospitable), and was able to save his host's daughter from an unwanted marriage to the centaur Eurytion by killing Eurytion. Years later, when the Labors had been completed, Heracles returned to Elis at the head of an army, and after an initial setback took the city and killed Augeas, making Phyleus king in his place.

It was after this expedition that Heracles was said to have instituted the Olympic Games, the greatest of Greek festivals, held every four years in honor of Zeus.[13] He marked out the stadium by pacing it out himself; he was even said to have fetched from the land of the Hyperboreans an olive tree to be, as Pindar described it (*Olympian Odes* 3. 16–18), "a shade for the sacred precinct and a crown of glory for men"—for at that time there were no trees at Olympia, and at the Games the victors were awarded a garland of olive leaves.[14]

6. *The Stymphalian Birds.* Heracles was required to shoot these creatures, which flocked together in a wood by the lake of Stymphalus (a town in Arcadia); he frightened them out of the wood by clashing a pair of brazen castanets given him by Athena and

---

[13] Olympia was in the territory of Elis, beside the river Alpheus.

[14] A strange version recorded by the Greek traveler, Pausanias, attributes the institution of the Olympic Games to "Heracles the Dactyl," a Cretan dwarf, attendant on the great Cretan goddess, and having nothing to do with the Heracles of Greek legend. (The story is almost certainly a late fabrication, designed to detract from the glory of the Argive hero.)

then shot them. Apparently these birds were not harmful; they were said, however, to have had feathers that they shot like arrows, together with other attributes varying with the imagination of individual authors.[15]

This ends the Peloponnesian Labors; the remaining Labors take Heracles all over the world; as is to be expected when so wide a geographical range is involved, this group is far richer in *parerga*.

7. *The Cretan Bull.* This bull was either the one that had brought Europa to Crete [16] or the one that Minos had refused to sacrifice to Poseidon; Heracles caught it and brought it back alive to Eurystheus. It was then turned loose and eventually came to Marathon, where in time Theseus caught and sacrificed it.

8. *The Mares of Diomedes.* Diomedes, son of Ares, was a Thracian king who owned a herd of mares that were fed on human flesh. Heracles, alone or with an army (the accounts vary), got possession of them and tamed them by feeding them Diomedes himself; he then sailed back to Argos with the horses, where Eurystheus set them free and dedicated them to Hera.

It was on his way to Thrace that one of Heracles's most famous victories over death was won. He was entertained by Admetus, king of Pherae, who disguised his grief at the recent death of his wife Alcestis; Heracles discovered the truth and himself wrestled with Thanatos (i.e., Death) and made him give up Alcestis, whom he restored to her husband.

9. *The Girdle of Hippolyta.* Hippolyta was queen of the Amazons, the warlike women from the northern limits of the world, whom we have already mentioned in connection with the Trojan War. Heracles was sent to fetch her girdle (which evidently was thought to bestow some magical properties on its possessor), and in the fight against the Amazons killed Hippolyta and took her girdle. It was displayed at Argos in historical times.

It was while returning from this Labor that Heracles came to Troy and there rescued Hesione from the sea monster. On this occasion he was cheated by king Laomedon of the agreed reward;

[15] Pausanias has a minute description of the birds; it and many other sources are gathered in D'Arcy W. Thompson's *Glossary of Greek Birds,* 2nd ed. (New York: Oxford University Press, 1936), p. 273.

[16] In which case it would not have been Zeus in disguise.

he therefore returned later (after his time as the servant of Omphale) with an armed force and sacked the city, giving Hesione to his ally, Telamon, and leaving Podarces (Priam) on the throne of the ruined city.

10. *The Cattle of Geryon.* The last three Labors are most clearly conquests of death, with the "harrowing of hell" in the abduction of Cerberus as their climax. Geryon lived in the island of Erythia, far away to the west; to place Erythia in Spain (or anywhere else for that matter) is mistaken, for in Greek legend the kingdom of death is generally symbolized by a mysterious land to be found somewhere far away toward the sunset. Geryon was a three-bodied monster, offspring of the Oceanid, Callirhoe, and Chrysaor; he tended a herd of cattle that Heracles was to bring back to Eurystheus, helped by a giant herdsman, Eurytion, and a two-headed hound, Orthus (or Orthrus). To reach Erythia Heracles was helped by Helius (the Sun), who gave him a golden cup in which to sail upon the River of Ocean (which girdles the world).[17] On the island he killed Orthus, Eurytion, and finally Geryon, and then sailed back to Tartessus (i.e., Spain) in the cup with the cattle. He gave back the cup to Helius and then began to drive the cattle back to Greece. As a monument of his journey to the western edge of the world he set up the Pillars of Heracles at the Atlantic entrance to the Mediterranean; some authorities identified them with the rocks of Calpe (Gibraltar) and Abyla (Ceuta), which flank the Straits of Gibraltar, but there were many other opinions about them.

Heracles's journey back to Greece has many *parerga;* while crossing the south of France he was attacked by the tribe of the Ligurians and exhausted his supply of arrows defending himself. He prayed for help from Zeus, who sent a rain of stones which gave Heracles the ammunition he needed to drive off the at-

---

[17] To get the cup Heracles threatened Helius with his bow and arrows. There were several ancient accounts of the cup and explanations of how Helius traveled from West to East at his setting, of which a number are quoted by the second-century A.D. author, Athenaeus, in Book 11 of his *Deipnosophistae,* ch. 38–39. There are also vase paintings showing Heracles sailing in the cup.

tackers.[18] He then crossed the Alps and traversed Italy; since he was very widely worshiped both at Rome and throughout Italy, it is not surprising that Heracles was credited by the Romans with a number of conquests during his journey there and with the foundation of several cities. One legend in this group, however, is particularly famous, that of Cacus, which Vergil relates in the eighth book of the *Aeneid*. Cacus, son of Vulcan, was a fire-breathing monster living in a cave on the Aventine Hill (part of the future city of Rome) beside the Tiber; he lived by brigandage and stole some of the cattle of Geryon, dragging them backwards to his cave, so that their hoof marks appeared to lead away from the cave. As Heracles, who had been unable to find the stolen cattle, was leaving with the remaining cattle, one of the stolen animals in the cave answered the lowing of its former companions. Thus the hiding place was discovered and Heracles broke into the cave, throttled Cacus, and recovered his cattle. The legend touches closely on Roman religion, for Heracles, it was said, left instructions for his cult at Rome, where he was in fact worshiped at the Ara Maxima (near the reputed site of his fight with Cacus) as well as in the several temples dedicated to him. Cacus, like his sister Caca, was probably an old Italian fire-god; his name is remembered by the rock staircase on the Palatine Hill called *Scalae Caci* (the steps of Cacus).

Heracles's wanderings in Italy also took him across the strait to Sicily. Here he wrestled with Eryx (king of the mountain of the same name at the western end of the island), whom he killed. Eventually he returned to Greece, passing around the head of the Adriatic and through Dalmatia; his last adventure before reaching Argos was at the Isthmus of Corinth, where he killed the giant and brigand, Alcyoneus.[19] As for the cattle, Eurystheus sacrificed them to Hera.

Quite a different version of the Geryon legend is implied by

[18] An area called the Stony Plain near the confluence of the Rhone and Durance was identified with the scene of this adventure.

[19] He is generally confused with the giant of the same name whom Heracles killed in the battle between the gods and giants, in those versions which include him in the Gigantomachy.

Herodotus. In this, Heracles's journey brought him to the cold lands beyond the Danube; there Heracles met and lay with Echidna (Snake woman), a monster who was half woman and half serpent; she bore him three sons, Agathyrsus, Gelonus, and Scythes. When the three grew up, only Scythes was able to draw a bow and put on a belt that Heracles had left behind; the other two were driven away by Echidna, and Scythes became king and ancestor of the Scythians.[20]

11. *The Apples of the Hesperides.* The Hesperides were the three daughters of Night, living far away to the west; they passed their time in singing and guarding a tree in their garden, upon which grew golden apples, and in this were helped by the dragon (or serpent) Ladon, who was coiled around the tree. The apples had originally been given by Ge to Hera when she married Zeus and put by her in the garden of the Hesperides. To get them Heracles first had to find the sea-god Nereus and learn from him the whereabouts of the garden; Nereus would only tell him after he had turned himself into many different shapes, being held all the while by Heracles. At the garden, in Euripides's version, he killed Ladon and plucked the apples himself, but in the more well-known tradition he got the help of the Titan, Atlas, who held up the heavens. Heracles took the heavens on his own shoulders while Atlas fetched the apples for him; he then returned the load to Atlas's shoulders (outwitting Atlas in doing so, since Atlas had no desire to resume it) and brought the apples back to Eurystheus. In the original version of the legend Heracles probably kept the apples, for they are symbols of immortality, and the tree in the garden of the Hesperides is the Tree of Life; we have already seen how the journey to a mysterious place in the farthest West is really a journey to the realm of death. But the original story acquired new details, for example that Athena took the apples back from Argos to the garden of the Hesperides, since they were too holy to be put down anywhere in the mortal world.

On his journey across northern Africa to the garden of the

[20] The Agathyrsi and Geloni were tribes to the northwest and northeast, respectively, of Scythia, whose area, strictly speaking, is immediately north of the Danube. But Scythia generally was taken to refer to the whole area between the Danube and the Don.

Hesperides, Heracles conquered two dangerous enemies. The giant Antaeus, son of Ge and Poseidon, ruled over Libya and would wrestle with those who came to his kingdom. He was invincible, since every time he came in contact with his mother (Earth) he rose again with renewed strength. Thus he had beaten and killed all comers and had used their skulls in building a temple to his father, Poseidon. Heracles destroyed his invincibility by holding him aloft and crushing him to death. In Egypt he killed king Busiris,[21] who used to sacrifice all strangers to Zeus.

As in the third and tenth Labors, some versions of this story take Heracles to the North, where he came to the Caucasus mountains. Here Prometheus was chained to a rock; Heracles released him after killing the eagle that tormented him, and in return Prometheus advised him to use Atlas in getting the apples and foretold the battle against the Ligurians. On this occasion, too, Prometheus took over the immortality of Chiron and satisfied Zeus by letting Chiron die in his place.

12. *Cerberus.* The final Labor was to fetch Cerberus, the three-headed Hound of Hell. In this legend Heracles's conquest of death is found in its most open form; Heracles himself (in the *Odyssey*) says that it was the hardest of the Labors, and that he could not have achieved it without the aid of Hermes and Athena. In the Underworld he wrestled with Cerberus, brought him back to Eurystheus, and then returned him to Hades.

In Hades Heracles saw Theseus and Pirithous, chained fast there because of their attempt to carry off Persephone. He was able to release Theseus, and Theseus out of gratitude sheltered him after his madness and the murder of Megara. Another person whose ghost Heracles saw in Hades was Meleager; when he told Heracles of his death, Heracles offered to marry his sister, if he still had one living. Meleager named Deianira, "upon whose neck was still the green of youth, nor did she know yet of the ways of Aphrodite, charmer of men" (Bacchylides, 5. 56); thus the train of events that led eventually to the death of Heracles was set in motion.

---

[21] His name is really the name of a place, "the house of Osiris." Herodotus, pointing out that the Egyptians did not indulge in human sacrifice, discredits the story of Busiris.

Other Deeds of Heracles

We can only select a few of the very many legends that became
attached to the name of Heracles. He fought and killed a number
of monstrous beings; one of these was Cycnus, son of Ares, who
used to rob men passing on their way through Thessaly to Delphi
of the victims that they were taking to sacrifice to Apollo. In one
version of the story the fight ended when Zeus threw a thunderbolt
between Cycnus and Heracles, but in the commoner variant Heracles, helped by Athena and with Iolaus as charioteer, killed
Cycnus (for whom Ares also fought) in single combat. Another
robber was Syleus, who lived by the straits of Euboea; Heracles
destroyed his vineyard (in which Syleus compelled passers-by to
work) and then killed Syleus himself.

Quite a different legend, with much more of the folk-tale element, is Heracles's encounter with the Cercopes, whose home is
placed by different authors in various parts of Greece or Asia
Minor. They were a pair of dwarfs who spent their time playing
tricks on people; they had been warned by their mother "to beware of the black-bottomed man." Now as Heracles was asleep
under a tree they attempted to steal his weapons, but he awoke,
and when he had caught them he slung them from a pole across
his shoulders upside down. They thus had an uninterrupted view
of his rump which, since the lion skin did not cover it, had been
burned black by the sun. They roared with laughter and joked
about the sight so much that Heracles, himself amused, let them
go. Later they tried to trick Zeus and were punished by being
turned into apes, or into stones.

While Heracles was alive the expedition of the Argonauts took
place, and he was among the heroes who sailed on the *Argo*. But
he is too important to be subordinate to other heroes in the saga,
and so generally he soon drops out of the expedition. The most
well-known account concerns his love for the boy Hylas (son of
Theodamas). When the *Argo* put in at Cios (in Asia Minor),
Hylas went to a nearby spring to draw water for himself, Heracles,
and Telamon; the water-nymphs were so entranced by his beauty
that they pulled him into the water, to remain with them forever.

Heracles spent so long searching for him that the rest of the Argonauts sailed away without him and he returned on his own to Argos. A cult of Hylas was established at Cios by Heracles, it was said; in late antiquity the people still searched for him annually, calling out his name.[22]

Heracles was also credited with a number of campaigns; sometimes he takes part in Zeus's battle against the Giants, during which he slew the terrible Alcyoneus. We have already mentioned the expeditions against Laomedon, king of Troy, and Augeas, king of Elis. Other Peloponnesian expeditions were made against Neleus, king of Pylos, who perished with all his sons excepting Nestor, and against Hippocoon, king of Sparta, and his sons, who had given assistance to Neleus; although Heracles was again successful, his brother, Iphicles, was killed in this campaign. It was while returning home from Sparta that Heracles lay at Tegea with Auge, whose father, fearing an oracle that Auge's son would kill her brothers, had made her priestess of Athena. The son she conceived was Telephus; either he was exposed on Mt. Parthenion and miraculously saved from death, or else he was born while his mother was being taken down to the sea (on the orders of her father) to be drowned. At any rate, he and his mother crossed the sea, floating in a chest or by some other means, to Asia Minor, where Telephus eventually became king of the Mysians.

In Thessaly Heracles appeared as an ally of Aegimius, king of the Dorians, against the attacks of his neighbors, the Lapiths and the Dryopes. Whether or not this legend is a fabrication of the Dorian peoples in an attempt to claim Heracles for themselves, it brings Heracles back to central Greece (Thessaly and the area immediately south of it), where the legends of the last part of his life are placed.

Deianira and Iole

Sometime after the completion of the Labors, Heracles fulfilled the promise he had made to the soul of Meleager, to marry his

[22] Vergil has the custom in mind when he writes of the seashore re-echoing "Hylas" (*Eclogue*, 6. 44—*ut litus Hyla, Hyla, omne sonaret*).

sister, Deianira. She was the daughter of Oeneus, king of Calydon (in western Greece), and to win her Heracles had to wrestle with a rival suitor, the river-god Achelous, who was horned like a bull and had the power of changing himself into different shapes. "They came together," says Sophocles (*Trachiniae,* 513–525), "desiring marriage; alone between them as umpire was Aphrodite, maker of marriages. Then was there confusion of sounds—the beating of fists, the twang of bow, the clash of bull's horns; there were the wrestling holds, the painful collision of heads, and the groans of both. But she, the prize, fair and delicate, sat afar upon a hill, waiting for him who was to be her husband." In the struggle Heracles broke off one of Achelous's horns and after his victory gave it back to Achelous, receiving in return the miraculous horn of Amalthea, which could supply its owner with as much food and drink as he wished.[23]

Having thus won Deianira, Heracles returned with her to Tiryns; on the way they came to the river Evenus, across which the centaur Nessus carried Deianira. On the far bank he attempted to rape her, but Heracles shot him with his bow; as he was on the point of death he advised Deianira to gather some of the blood that flowed from his wound (the arrow that caused it had been dipped in the Hydra's poison); it would be efficacious in preventing Heracles from loving any other woman more than Deianira. She therefore kept the blood, and for a number of years she and Heracles lived at Tiryns, where she bore him children, including a son, Hyllus, and a daughter, Macaria.

At some time (whether before or after the marriage with Deianira is unclear) Heracles fell in love with Iole, daughter of Eurytus, king of Oechalia, a city generally placed in Euboea. Eurytus refused to let him have Iole, even though he won in the archery contest that was to decide whose wife (or concubine) Iole should be. Heracles for the time being returned to Tiryns, bitter at the insult; later the brother of Iole, Iphitus, came to Tiryns

---

[23] This is the *cornu copiae* (horn of plenty). Amalthea is either a goddess of Plenty or else the goat which suckled the infant Zeus. According to Ovid it was Achelous's horn that became the cornucopia when the Naiads picked it up and filled it with fruit and flowers. It has remained one of the most popular symbols and ornaments in art.

in search of some lost mares (or cattle), and Heracles threw him
to his death from the citadel. For this murder he had to leave
Tiryns, and went first to Pylos, where Neleus refused to purify
him; it was because of this that Heracles later made his expedition
against Neleus. Having eventually obtained purification (from the
king of Amyclae), he went to Delphi to find out what more he
should do to be cured of the disease of madness that had caused
him to kill Iphitus; at first the priestess would not give him any
reply, and he attempted to carry off the sacred tripod, intending
to establish an oracle of his own. Apollo himself wrestled with
him to prevent this, and their fight ended when Zeus threw a
thunderbolt between them. Finally Heracles obtained the advice
he had asked for, which was that he must be sold as a slave and
serve for one year.

Accordingly Hermes auctioned Heracles, and he was bought
by Omphale, queen of the Lydians; he served her for the stipulated
year and performed various tasks for her in keeping with his
heroic character. Later versions, however, make Heracles perform
women's work for the queen and picture him dressed as a woman
and spinning wool.[24] At the end of his year he mounted the expedition against Troy and then returned to Greece, determined to revenge himself upon Eurytus, whom he blamed for his misfortunes,
and to get Iole.

Deianira meanwhile was in Trachis, where king Ceyx had received her and Heracles after they had left the Peloponnese. According to Sophocles, whose *Trachiniae* is the most important
source for the last part of Heracles's life, she knew nothing of
Oechalia and Iole until the herald, Lichas, brought news of the
sack of the city; she had not seen Heracles for fifteen months,
since before his servitude to Omphale. In this account, then,
Heracles kills Eurytus and destroys Oechalia on his way back
from Asia, sending Iole and the other captive women back to
Trachis with Lichas. In her despair at Heracles's love for Iole,
Deianira made use of Nessus's charm; she dipped a robe in the
poisoned blood and sent it to Heracles by Lichas's hand for him

---

[24] Thus Ovid says (*Heroides*. 9. 55): "The Meander saw a necklace upon
Hercules's neck . . . and Hercules did not shrink from putting his hand,
victor in a thousand labors, to the smooth baskets of wool."

to wear at his thanksgiving sacrifice to Zeus. As the flames of the sacrificial fire warmed the poison, the robe clung to Heracles and he was burned by it with unendurable torment. In his agony he hurled Lichas to his death in the sea and had himself carried back to Trachis, where a huge funeral pyre was made for him upon Mt. Oeta. Deianira stabbed herself when she realized what she had done, while Hyllus went with his father to Oeta; there Heracles instructed Hyllus to marry Iole after his death and gave his bow to the shepherd, Poeas (father of Philoctetes), as a reward, since he alone of those present dared to light the pyre. So the mortal part of Heracles was burned away and he gained immortality, ascending to Olympus, there to be reconciled with Hera and to marry her daughter, Hebe. "To Olympus went Alcmena's son," says Pindar (*Isthmian Ode,* 4. 61–67), "when he had explored every land and the cliff-girt levels of the foaming sea, to tame the straits for seafarers. Now beside Zeus he enjoys perfect happiness; he is loved and honored by the immortals; Hebe is his wife, and he is lord of a golden palace, the husband of Hera's daughter."

Heracles: Man, Hero, and God

The extent of the problems that confront the student of Heracles becomes clear as soon as we read of Odysseus's meeting with his ghost (Homer, *Odyssey,* 11. 601–603): "Then saw I mighty Heracles—his ghost, but he himself delights in feasting among the immortal gods, with fair-ankled Hebe for his wife." Here, in this very early passage, the ambiguity of Heracles's status as man and god is evident. That he was a man before he became a god is shown by his name (which means glory of Hera), since Greek gods do not form their names from compounds of other gods' names. Since his legend is particularly associated with the area of Argos, that part of it which is truly saga may very probably have its origin in a real man, the lord of Tiryns, who, although himself a great warrior, was vassal to the lord of Mycenae; this certainly fits with the theme of subservience to Eurystheus. But other areas with which he is especially associated are Boeotia (the traditional setting of his birth and of a group of his exploits) and Trachis, scene of his final exploits and death. This leads to one of two conclusions: either legends of the hero of Tiryns spread to Boeotia and other parts of Greece (possibly as a result of military conquest), where his fame attracted local legends to himself; or else he was brought into Greece by very early settlers from the North and his fame spread all over Greece. The latter explanation seems the more acceptable, but it has led many people to believe that Heracles was a Dorian hero, brought in by waves of Dorian invaders who swept over Greece around 1100 and put an end to Mycenaean civilization. Some of the legends, however—in particular that of Aegimius—are probably no more than fabrications designed to claim Heracles for the Dorians, and it has been decisively shown that the "Dorian" theory cannot stand. Instead it is better to suppose that Heracles is older than the Dorian invasions and that he is a hero common to all the Greek peoples, but associated more with certain areas (Argos, Thebes, Trachis) than others. Thus we find his exploits covering the whole of the Greek world and his legends and cult flourishing in areas of Greek colonization, such as Asia Minor and Italy (where, as Hercules, he passed into the Roman state religion).

Many people, however, have thought of him primarily as a god. The ancient historian Herodotus believed that Heracles the god was quite distinct from Heracles the man and that the god was one of the twelve ancient gods of Egypt. Herodotus himself even traveled to the Phoenician city of Tyre, whose chief god, Melkart, was identified with Heracles, to find support for his theory. Since, however, the mythology of Melkart is virtually unknown we cannot be certain what exactly were the similarities between him and Heracles. Nor can we establish the exact relationship between Heracles and other Oriental figures with whom he shares many similarities—the Jewish hero, Samson, the Mesopotamian Gilgamesh, and the Cilician god, Sandas.[25] All that can be said is that these figures may have contributed elements toward the Greek hero's legend; the reverse process can also be shown to have taken place in some cases—for example, the Lydian Omphale—where

[25] A definitely non-Greek element in Heracles's legend is his self-immolation, which is a conspicuous feature of the myth of Sandas.

the Greek legend spread and became attached to already existing Oriental legends. In general, however, it is safe to reject Herodotus's theory and to accept the nearly unanimous view of the ancients that Heracles the man became a god.

It was inevitable that so diverse a character should have attracted a variety of interpretations and that different uses should have been made of Heracles and his legend. Indeed, as Aristotle pointed out in the *Poetics* (Chapter 8), his very diversity made it impossible for a unified epic or tragedy to be written about him; only three extant Greek tragedies deal with his legend—Sophocles's *Trachiniae,* Euripides's *Heracles* and *Alcestis* (the latter almost incidentally). To the comic poets, such as Aristophanes, he is good material for slapstick; in the *Frogs,* for example, he is largely motivated by gluttony and lust. More significant was the use made of his virtues by the moralists and philosophers, to whom he became a model of unselfish fortitude, laboring for the good of mankind and achieving immortality (or at any rate conquest over the most formidable of human difficulties) by his virtue. This process began early and is best typified by the famous parable told by Prodicus of Ceos.[26] In this, Heracles as a young man was faced with the choice between two women, representing Vice (with ease) and Virtue (with hardship), and chose the latter.

Perhaps we would do better to leave Heracles by returning to the ancient invocation to him in the *Homeric Hymn* (number 15); here we may forget the perversions of his legend and the theories of scholars, ancient and modern, concentrating instead on the man who, after a lifetime of toil, became a hero and a god: "Of Heracles will I sing, son of Zeus, whom Alcmena bore in Thebes, city of delightful dances, when she had lain with the son of Cronus, lord of the dark clouds, to be by far the greatest of men on earth. He traversed long ago vast distances of land and sea at the order of king Eurystheus; many were the bold deeds he did, many

---

[26] Recounted at length by Xenophon, *Memorabilia,* 2. 21–34; more briefly by Cicero, *De Officiis,* 1.118. The parable has been very important in western art; see E. Panofsky, *Hercules am Scheideweg* (Leipzig, 1930). The copious illustrations in this book make it valuable even to those who know no German.

were the things he endured. Now he dwells in joy in the beautiful palace of snowy Olympus and has for wife slender-ankled Hebe." [27]

The Heraclidae

After the death of Heracles his mother, Alcmena, and children were persecuted by Eurystheus; unable to find safety in Trachis, they came to Attica and were given protection by the king of Athens, Demophon (son of Theseus). This led to war between Eurystheus and the Athenians, in which Eurystheus and his five sons perished; to secure the victory, according to Euripides, Heracles's daughter by Deianira, Macaria, offered herself as a sacrifice to Persephone, in obedience to an oracle. During the battle Heracles's nephew, Iolaus, was miraculously rejuvenated and killed Eurystheus. The head of Eurystheus was brought to Alcmena, who gouged out the eyes with brooches; his body was buried separately from the head and, like the dead Oedipus, became a guarantee of protection for the Athenians against invading enemies.

As for Alcmena, she had, after the death of Amphitryon and long before these events, married Rhadamanthys, brother of Minos. When Rhadamanthys died he became a judge in the Underworld, and Alcmena at her death was taken by Hermes to rejoin him. Her body was not buried; as it was being carried to burial in its coffin Hermes, at the command of Zeus, substituted for it a large stone, which the sons of Heracles discovered (for the coffin had suddenly become very heavy) and set up in a shrine sacred to Alcmena.

The descendants of Heracles (the Heraclidae) have a saga of their own, which is clearly connected with the historical

[27] The curious may wish to consult the following for further information and discussion of the question of Heracles: L. R. Farnell, *Greek Hero-cults and Ideas of Immortality* (New York: Oxford University Press, 1921), chs. 5–7; Herodotus, Book 2. 43–44. For those who read German, there is a full discussion and a persuasive presentation of the "Dorian" theory by U. von Wilamowitz-Moellendorff in his edition of Euripides's *Heracles,* vol. 2, 2nd ed. (Darmstadt, 1959), pp. 1–107.

Dorian invasions. Hyllus married Iole, as his father had commanded, and consulted Delphi about his return to the Peloponnese. He was advised to wait "until the third fruit" and that victory would come "from the Narrows." Accordingly, after waiting two more years, he attacked by way of the Isthmus of Corinth. He himself was killed in single combat by Echemus, king of Tegea; his army withdrew, and a truce of one hundred years was agreed upon. At the end of that time the Heraclid Temenus again consulted the oracle, who told him that the "third fruit" meant not the third harvest but the third generation, and that "the Narrows" meant the entrance to the Gulf of Corinth. Temenus therefore invaded the northwest Peloponnese, crossing over near Patrae and taking as a guide a "three-eyed man" in accordance with the advice of the oracle; this was an Aetolian exile named Oxylus, whom he found riding a one-eyed horse. Helped by him the Heraclids defeated the Peloponnesian defenders, who were led by Tisamenus, son of Orestes.

Thus the "Return of the Heraclidae" took place; the leaders now divided up the three principal areas which they had conquered. Lacedaemon (Sparta) was given to Procles and Eurysthenes, sons of the lately dead leader, Aristodemus, and they became founders of the two royal houses of Sparta. Argos fell to the lot of Temenus, and Messene to Cresphontes. Temenus was killed by his sons, whom he had passed over in the succession to his throne; Cresphontes was also murdered, along with two of his sons, by a rival Heraclid, Polyphontes. His widow, Merope, was forced to become Polyphontes's queen, but she succeeded in getting her surviving son, Aepytus, out of the kingdom to Aetolia, where he grew up. Later he secretly returned to Messene and was recognized by Merope, with whose connivance he killed Polyphontes and recovered his father's throne. The saga of the Heraclidae ends at this point, for the history of the Dorian states can be more or less accurately recovered from this stage; of the three Dorian kingdoms whose establishment we have described, Sparta and Argos flourished for many centuries, but Messene within a comparatively short time was subjugated by the Spartans.

CHAPTER 20

The Argonauts

The saga of the Argonauts covers almost the whole of the Greek world in its geographical scope and includes many of the leading Greek heroes of the age before the Trojan War; just as the finest of the Greek leaders were shut up in the Trojan horse, so the crew of the Argo was made up of the flower of Greece, ancestors of Greek nobles and themselves descended from gods. They are often referred to as Minyae; the Minyae as a people were particularly associated with the Boeotian city of Orchomenus (which appears in this saga only incidentally); among cities that claimed Minyan descent were Iolcus in Thessaly and Miletus in Ionia. Jason belonged to the ruling family of Iolcus, and the Black Sea, where the main part of the saga takes place, was an area particularly colonized by the Milesians. The name Minyae therefore tells us something about the origin of the saga; it is certainly an old story, for Homer refers to it and calls the Argo "all men's concern," reflecting the adventures of the seamen of Mycenaean Greece; to it have been added later accretions—part saga, in particular reflecting the expansion of the Greeks into the Black Sea area from the eighth century onwards, and part folk tale. This latter element can be seen in the name which Homer uses for the country to which the Argo sailed—Aea—which means no more than land, and its king, Aeetes (man of the land); it is a mysterious land on the edge of the world, a suitable setting for a story in which magic and miracle play a big part. The folk tale element can further be distinguished in the formal outline of the legend, where a hero is set a number of impossible tasks that he performs unscathed and is helped by the local princess, whom he

337

then marries. However the legend developed, it has always been among the most important, and in antiquity Greek cities and individuals were eager to claim a part in the saga for their ancestors.

The Golden Fleece

The saga concerns the adventures of Jason and the crew of the *Argo* in their quest for the golden fleece, and some knowledge of the previous story of the fleece is necessary. The Boeotian king, Athamas, married as his first wife, Nephele, whose name means cloud; after bearing Athamas two children, Phrixus and Helle, she returned to the sky. Athamas then married Ino, one of the daughters of Cadmus, who attempted to destroy her stepchildren. She persuaded the Boeotian women to parch the seed grain so that when it was sown nothing grew. In the ensuing famine Athamas sent to Delphi for advice, but Ino suborned the envoys to say that the god's advice was for Athamas to sacrifice Phrixus if he wanted the famine to end. As he was about to perform the sacrifice, Nephele caught up Phrixus and Helle to the sky and set them on a golden-fleeced ram that Hermes had given her. The ram carried them eastward through the heavens; over the straits between Europe and Asia (the Dardanelles) Helle fell off and was drowned; the straits were called the Hellespont after her. Phrixus continued his flight safely, and was brought by the ram to Colchis, at the eastern end of the Black Sea, where King Aeetes (son of Helius and brother of Circe and Pasiphae) received him kindly, and gave him his elder daughter, Chalciope, as wife. Phrixus sacrificed the ram to Zeus Phyxius (i.e., Zeus as god of Escape) and gave the golden fleece to Aeetes, who hung it up on an oak tree in a grove sacred to Ares, where it was guarded by a never sleeping serpent. Phrixus himself lived on at Colchis, where he finally died; his four sons by Chalciope—Argus, Melas, Phrontis, and Cytisorus—play a minor part in the Argonauts' saga.

In itself the story of Phrixus and the golden fleece has no necessary connection with the story of Jason. But the golden treasure guarded by a dragon—reminiscent of the apples of the Hesperides —is a suitable goal for heroes to search for; and as we have already seen, the saga of the Argonauts is in this respect more folk tale than saga. We now turn to see how Jason came to undertake the mission.

Jason and Pelias

Cretheus, brother of Athamas, was king of Iolcus; at his death the throne was usurped by his stepson, Pelias (son of Poseidon and Tyro, wife of Cretheus), who deposed the rightful heir, Aeson, son of Cretheus and Tyro, and father of Jason. Out of fear of Pelias, Jason's mother [1] sent the boy away to the hills to be educated by the centaur Chiron and to be cared for by the centaur's mother, Philyra; there he remained until he was twenty years old. Now Pelias knew that he was fated to be killed by a descendant of Aeolus and more recently had received an oracle from Delphi telling him to "beware of the man with one sandal"; he therefore realized that his fate was approaching him when Jason, now a handsome young man of twenty, returned to Iolcus to claim the throne that rightly belonged to his family. On the way down from the hills he had come to the river Anaurus in full spate; beside it stood an old woman, whom he carried across, losing one sandal as he tried to get a foothold in the mud. The old woman was in fact the goddess Hera, who thereafter favored Jason, just as she was hostile to Pelias, who had neglected to sacrifice to her. [2]

Pelias did not refuse Jason's request outright; instead he promised to yield the throne if Jason would bring him first the golden fleece, which the soul of Phrixus, appearing to him in a dream, had ordered him to obtain. Whether for this reason or for some other [3] Jason readily undertook the task.

[1] Her name is variously given as Polymede, Alcimede, or Amphinome.

[2] There are many variations in this story; in some versions Jason claims the throne for himself, Aeson being already either too old or dead. In some he is summoned to Iolcus by Pelias to attend a sacrifice, or he meets Hera while out hunting. Again different explanations are given for his being shod on one foot only.

[3] For example, one version has it that Pelias tricked Jason by asking him what he would do if an oracle had warned him that he would be killed by a citizen: "I would order the citizen to fetch the golden fleece," Jason replied—and this was the order Pelias gave him.

The Argonauts

In preparation for the expedition the *Argo* was built, said by some
to have been the first ship—"the wondred *Argo*" as Spenser called
it, "which . . . first through the Euxine seas bore all the flower
of Greece" (*Faerie Queen,* 2.12.44). Its name means swift, and
it was built by Argus, son of Arestor,[4] with the help of Athena;
in its bows she put a piece of wood, made from an oak of Dodona
(the oracle of Zeus), which had the power of speech. The crew
came from all over Greece, the finest of its noble heroes. "Hera,"
says Pindar, "kindled all-persuading sweet desire in the sons of
gods for the ship *Argo,* so that none should be left behind to nurse
a life without danger at his mother's side, but rather that he should
find even against death the fairest antidote in his own courage along
with others of his age" (*Pythian Odes,* 4. 185–188). Lists of the
names of the Argonauts vary from author to author, since the
Greeks of later ages were eager to claim an Argonaut for an ancestor; thus, for reasons of family pride or local patriotism, authors
inserted names of their own ancestors in the catalogue. Two heroes
who figure prominently in all the lists also have no place in the
original story, Orpheus and Heracles. The former is a post-Homeric
figure (and we have already seen that Homer knew of the Argonauts); while Heracles, the most important of the Greek heroes,
could hardly be left out of a saga that occurred in his own lifetime.
But his eminence could only obscure the parts played by the leaders
of the Argonauts; he therefore refuses at Iolcus to accept the
leadership, in favor of Jason, and disappears from the expedition
before the *Argo* has even reached the Black Sea.

Of the fifty or so names included among the Argonauts (fifty
was the standard number of rowers in an ancient Greek warship)
certain groups stand out. These are the heroes from Thessaly, such
as Jason himself, and those from the Peloponnese, such as Augeas,
king of Elis; a third group consists of Meleager and other heroes
who took part in the Calydonian boar hunt; a fourth includes the
parents of Trojan War heroes, such as Peleus (father of Achilles),

---

[4] This Argus is sometimes confused (as for example by Apollodorus)
with Argus, son of Phrixus.

Telamon (father of Ajax Telamonius), Oileus (father of Ajax the less), and Nauplius (father of Palamedes). An important group (some of whom may be already included in the other groups) are the heroes with special gifts—the seers Idmon and Mopsus; Castor and Polydeuces, excellent, respectively, as horseman and boxer, with their later enemies, Idas and Lynceus, the latter of whom had such keen sight that he could see even beneath the earth; Periclymenus, son of Neleus, who could take whatever shape he liked in battle (this was Poseidon's gift); Euphemus, son of Poseidon, who could run so fast over the waves of the sea that his feet stayed dry; Zetes and Calais, the winged sons of Boreas (the North Wind); Argus, the skilled shipwright; and, finally, the helmsman, Tiphys. Of these only Polydeuces, the sons of Boreas, Argus, and Tiphys have any significant part in the legend as we now have it; in an earlier form, before the witch Medea took over so much of the superhuman element, the individual Argonauts must have had a more independent part in helping Jason perform his otherwise impossible tasks.

The Voyage to Colchis

After leaving Iolcus the *Argo* sailed across the Aegean to the island of Lemnos, where the sailors found only women, under their queen, Hypsipyle. Aphrodite had punished them for neglecting her worship and had made them unattractive to their husbands (either through a noisome smell or in some other way). The men therefore turned their attentions to Thracian concubines whom they had captured in war. In revenge the Lemnian women murdered every male on the island, with the single exception of Thoas, father of Hypsipyle and king of Lemnos; he was saved by his daughter and escaped over the sea, either through the help of his father, Dionysus, or floating in a chest. In these circumstances the women were glad to receive the Argonauts, who stayed on the island for a year. Among the many children born as a result of these unions were the twin sons of Jason and Hypsipyle, Euneus and Thoas (or Nebrophonus). Some time after the departure of the Argonauts Hypsipyle was captured by pirates and sold into slavery under king Lycurgus of Nemea;[5] many years later she was rescued by her sons and brought back to Lemnos.

After touching at Samothrace, where they were initiated into the local mysteries, they sailed on to the Propontis and put in at Cyzicus, where the Doliones lived under king Cyzicus. They were well received by Cyzicus, and in return Heracles killed the earth-born giants who lived around Cyzicus and menaced the Doliones. When the Argonauts had sailed from Cyzicus, contrary winds drove them back to land; the Doliones took them for night raiders, and the Argonauts, not knowing where they were, failed to recognize their former friends. A fierce battle followed, in which Cyzicus himself was killed; next day, when they realized what they had done, the Argonauts helped bury Cyzicus and mourned for him before sailing off again.

Their next call was at Cios, farther eastward along the Asiatic shore of the Propontis, where they landed so that Heracles could replace his broken oar. It was here that the loss of Hylas occurred, and as a result the withdrawal of Heracles with his companion, Polyphemus, from the expedition, as we have already seen.[6] Sailing on without these three, the Argonauts passed into the Euxine (the Black Sea) and came to the land of the Bebryces, a Bithynian tribe, whose custom was to compel strangers to box with their king, Amycus, a son of Poseidon and hitherto an invincible boxer. On this occasion Polydeuces fought Amycus and killed him. In their dismay the Bebryces attacked the Argonauts but were defeated with great loss.

The next landfall was at Salmydessus on the Euxine shore of Thrace; here the Argonauts were received by king Phineus, who was blind and a prophet. Different versions are given of his story; he is variously said to have been the son of Agenor or of Poseidon and by some to have been the husband of Cleopatra, daughter of Boreas (the North Wind). Again, there are different versions of the reasons for his blindness—either it was a punishment of Zeus for revealing the secrets of the gods, or a punishment inflicted by

[5] The story varies; in some versions she is driven out of Lemnos by the other women for having saved Thoas. Pindar puts the visit to Lemnos during the Argonauts' return from Colchis.

[6] There are many different versions of Heracles's part in the expedition; a number are listed by Apollodorus, 1. 9, 19.

Boreas (with the help of the Argonauts, according to Apollodorus) because he had blinded his sons by Cleopatra, or one inflicted by Helius because he preferred long life to sight. At any rate, in most versions he is old, blind, and a prophet; in addition he was tormented by the Harpies, two winged monsters (their name means the snatchers) who, every time a meal was set before Phineus, would swoop down upon it, snatch away most of the food, and render what was left untouchable. Here the winged sons of Boreas, Zetes and Calais, proved their especial value; when the Harpies next appeared they rose into the air and pursued them with drawn swords to the Strophades Islands (i.e., the islands of turning), where Iris put an end to the chase by making the sons of Boreas return and the Harpies swear never to go near Phineus again.[7]

Phineus was able to repay the Argonauts for their services by telling them of the rest of their voyage and forewarning them of its dangers. In particular he told them of the most formidable danger, the Symplegades (clashing rocks), two huge rocks near the western end of the Black Sea that clashed together driven by the force of the winds; nothing had ever yet passed between them, and it was fated that they should remain fixed once a ship had made the passage. Phineus advised the Argonauts to release a dove and, if it succeeded in flying between the rocks, then themselves to row hard between them as they recoiled; if the dove failed, they were to turn back. In the event, the dove was successful and the Argonauts, with the help of Athena (or Hera), got through before the rocks clashed for the last time—only part of the ship's stern ornament was trapped. So the greatest danger was passed; the Black Sea lay before the Argonauts, clear and open, and the Symplegades remained fixed, never to threaten seafarers again.[8]

[7] Again there are variant versions of the fate of the Harpies—for example, that both died or that they returned unharmed to their den.

[8] The "clashing rocks" appear elsewhere in Greek legend as the Planctae (wandering rocks), in the return voyage of the Argonauts and in the *Odyssey*, where Odysseus chooses to avoid them and face the dangers of Scylla and Charybdis. They are identified with the Cyaneae (i.e., the dark rocks) by Herodotus and many other authors. Whether the Symplegades are a memory of the straits of the Bosporus or not is a matter of mere conjecture; that Phineus's kingdom lay on the shores of the Euxine, as most authors maintain, militates against such a supposition.

The remaining incidents before the Argonauts reached Colchis were comparatively innocuous; not far along the Asiatic coast of the Euxine lived the Mariandyni, whose king, Lycus, received them hospitably. Here one of their seers, Idmon, was killed by a boar, and their helmsman, Tiphys, died after a short illness. Nevertheless, with the Arcadian hero Ancaeus, son of Lycurgus, as the new helmsman, they sailed on past the land of the Amazons and that of the iron-working Chalybes and came to the Island of Ares, where the Stymphalian birds that had been frightened away from Greece by Heracles in his sixth Labor now lived; these they kept at bay by clashing their shields together. It was here that they also found Phrixus's four sons, who had been shipwrecked during an attempted voyage from Colchis to Boeotia; they took them on board the *Argo* and were to find them of no little help when they reached Colchis.

Thus they sailed up the river Phasis, on which stands Colchis, and came to their journey's end.

Jason at Colchis

Aeetes did not give a friendly welcome to the Argonauts and was prepared to let Jason take the fleece only if he first performed a series of impossible tasks. These were to yoke a pair of brazen-footed and fire-breathing bulls, the gift of Hephaestus to Aeetes, and with them to plough a large field and sow in it dragon's teeth from which armed men would spring up; he would then have to kill these.[9] At this point the legend leaves the realm of saga and with the introduction of Aeetes's younger daughter, Medea, takes on an aura of magic more typical of folk tale. Through the agency of Hera and Aphrodite, Medea was made to fall in love with Jason; when therefore Chalciope, at the request of her son, Argus (who, as we have seen, had returned to Colchis with the Argonauts), approached Medea on Jason's behalf, she was more than willing to help him perform the tasks. She was herself priestess of Hecate

[9] These teeth came from the dragon of Thebes and had been given to Aeetes by Athena.

and a witch, as skilled in magic as her aunt Circe; she therefore was able to give Jason (whom she met at the shrine of Hecate) a magic ointment that would protect him from harm by fire or iron for the space of a day. So he performed the allotted tasks; like Cadmus, he threw a stone among the armed men who sprang from the dragon's teeth to set them fighting one another, and so easily disposed of them.

Even now Aeetes did not intend to hand over the fleece but rather was planning to destroy the Argonauts. Medea therefore advised Jason to take the fleece himself and escape immediately; with her help he found the fleece, drugged its guardian serpent, and took possession of it. Then he and the Argonauts set sail, taking Medea with them; according to Apollodorus she brought her younger brother, Apsyrtus, with her and used him to delay the pursuit of Aeetes by cutting him up and throwing his limbs into the sea for Aeetes to collect piecemeal. But in other versions Apsyrtus is a grown man and leads the pursuers, being treacherously murdered by Jason in an ambush near the mouth of the Danube.

The Return of the Argonauts

We have seen that up to this point the legend of the Argonauts falls into two clearly distinguished parts—the saga of their journey to Colchis and the events at Colchis where the magic of Medea is predominant. A third division of the legend concerns the return voyage; the variety of accounts, and the very confused geographical notions that they embody, have led many people to dismiss them as merely fanciful. But it has been shown that the northern routes do correspond to some extent with the great early trade routes between northern Europe and the Mediterranean (in particular the amber routes), while the places at which the Argonauts touched in the Mediterranean reflect the actual trade and colonization from the eighth century onwards. It is impossible to arrive at a synthesis of the different versions, but it is reasonable to say that these versions do reflect ancient commercial voyages (if not a single voyage) and that therefore they have some claim to be saga rather than folk tale.[10]

In the simplest account the Argonauts return by the way they came; the three other versions take them much farther afield. In the oldest surviving literary account (that of Pindar) they sailed eastward up the Phasis until they came to the River of Ocean, along which they sailed southward and westward to Africa; they then carried the *Argo* across north Africa for twelve days until they came to the Mediterranean, and so sailed home.

The third version takes them up the Phasis and northward through Russia to the northern seas (either in the far north or the Gulf of Finland), then round the British Isles and back into the Mediterranean through the Pillars of Heracles. Finally there is the commonest version (that of Apollonius Rhodius), in which they sailed up the Ister (Danube) and crossed overland to the head of the Adriatic; here their way southward was blocked by the Colchians, and instead they sailed up the Eridanus (apparently this is the Po) and into the Rhone, down which they sailed to the Mediterranean. Here the speaking oak of the *Argo* told them of the wrath of Zeus at the murder of Apsyrtus; if they did not wish to wander interminably they must go to Circe in Aeaea and be purified by her. Aeaea here is located on the coast of Italy; after the purification by Circe, they sailed past the dangers that were later to menace Odysseus—the Planctae, Scylla and Charybdis, the Sirens—and came to Corcyra, the land of the Phaeacians, where Jason and Medea were married. Here they were driven southward to Libya and stranded on the shoals of the Syrtes; they carried the *Argo* on their shoulders to Lake Tritonis (again, a twelve-day journey), past the garden of the Hesperides (where lay the dragon, Ladon, lately killed by Heracles). On the way they lost Mopsus, killed by a snake bite. From the lake they made their way back to the Mediterranean guided by the sea-god Triton.[11]

[10] The subject is discussed by Miss J. R. Bacon in Chapter 9 of her book *The Voyage of the Argo* (London: Methuen, 1925).

[11] On this occasion Triton gave a clod of earth to the Argonaut Euphemus as a token that his descendants would rule in Libya; the clod, dropped into the sea, eventually became the island of Thera from which, generations later, the Libyan colony of Cyrene was founded by the descendants of Euphemus.

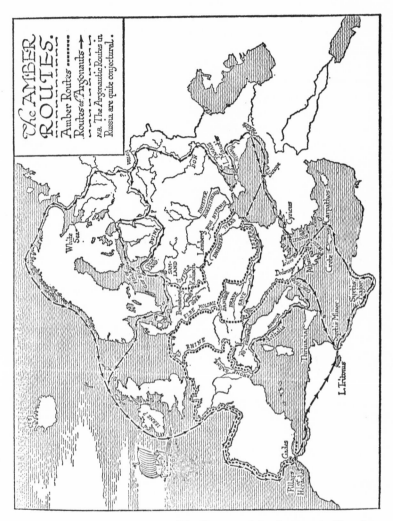

Fig. 15. From Janet R. Bacon, The Voyage of the Argonauts (*London: Methuen, 1925*), *p. 122.*

One adventure remained on the voyage back to Thessaly; the island of Crete was guarded by the bronze giant, Talus, who walked round it three times a day and kept strangers from landing by throwing rocks at them. His life depended on a membrane (or bronze nail) that closed the entrance to a vein above one ankle; if this was opened, the ichor (the divine equivalent of human blood) would flow out and he would die. And this came to pass —either because Medea drugged him and removed the nail, or because he was shot in the ankle by Poeas, or because he grazed his ankle on a rock and broke the membrane.[12]

Finally the Argonauts sailed home, stopping only to get water at Aegina. With their arrival at Iolcus their legend, strictly speaking, comes to an end (as does the epic of Apollonius Rhodius); there is no tradition of the later history of the fleece itself, except that Jason did hand it over to Pelias. As for the *Argo,* Jason dedicated it to Poseidon at the Isthmus; years later, while he was resting under the ship (which was propped up on dry land), he was struck on the head and killed by a piece of timber that fell from its stern.

Jason and Medea in Greece

We may here relate something of the sequel to the Argonauts' expedition. At Iolcus Pelias showed no intention of standing by his part of the agreement with Jason and (in one version) had already driven Jason's parents to suicide. In the best-known story, however, Medea used her magic arts first to rejuvenate Aeson by cutting him up and boiling him in a cauldron, along with certain herbs; she further demonstrated the efficacy of her method by turning an old ram into a lamb. Persuaded by these examples the daughters of Pelias attempted to rejuvenate their father in the same way; since Medea failed to give them the magic herbs, the experiment led only to his death.

---

[12] Talus was said by some to be the creation of Hephaestus and the gift of Zeus to Minos or Europa. Others say that he killed his victims by becoming extremely hot and burning them in his embrace. Modern speculation on his origin is as varied as the ancient stories.

Thus Jason was revenged on Pelias, but he did not gain the throne of Iolcus, for, being defiled by the murder of Pelias, he and Medea were driven out of the city by Acastus, son of Pelias. They came to Corinth, and here, some years later, Jason divorced Medea and married Glauce,[13] the daughter of Creon, king of Corinth. In revenge, Medea sent by the hand of her two children a robe and a crown as wedding gifts to Glauce; the magic ointment with which Medea had smeared them burned Glauce and Creon to death. After this Medea killed her two children [14] as a final act of vengeance against Jason, and escaped to Athens in a chariot drawn by winged dragons, which her grandfather, Helius, provided. Jason lived on in misery at Corinth; Medea was given asylum at Athens by king Aegeus, by whom she became the mother of Medus. Later she nearly caused Aegeus to poison his son, Theseus; failing in her plot, she fled from Athens to Persia, where Medus established the kingdom of Media. Medea herself eventually returned to Colchis and the rest of her legend is lost in the ingenious fancies of individual authors.

[13] Also called Creusa.
[14] In another version the Corinthians killed Medea's children after her flight; they performed expiatory rites for this murder in historical times.

CHAPTER 21

Local Legends

In the previous six chapters we have been concerned with the cycles of saga that had become the concern of the whole of Greece, either through their variety and geographical range or because of their literary importance. Every district of Greece, however, had its local heroes and legends; some are famous because the city had a persuasive literary tradition (for example, Athens and its local hero, Theseus), but many more are comparatively obscure, although none the less interesting, because there were no local authors to carry the fame of their heroes beyond the borders of the district, or because the city never emerged into the first rank. In this chapter we shall discuss some of these local legends.

Central Greece

We have already seen something of Ixion as a sinner being punished in the Underworld; the earlier version of his story, however, puts his punishment in the sky. He was the first to shed kindred blood; he invited his father-in-law, Eioneus, to come and collect the price that Ixion was to pay for his bride, Dia. Eioneus came, but Ixion had dug and camouflaged a pit full of burning coals into which Eioneus fell. Since this was a new crime no mortal was able to purify Ixion, and it was Zeus himself who purified him, receiving him as a guest at his own hearth. Yet Ixion repaid him with a second crime, an attempt to rape Hera. Zeus, to whom Hera complained, made a cloud upon which was a likeness of Hera; Ixion took it for the real Hera, lay with it and made his guilt clear to

Zeus. He was punished by being bound to a wheel of fire that ever revolves through the heavens: [1] "They say that Ixion, through the gods' commands revolving upon the winged wheel, cries out to men that they should always hasten to pay back their benefactor with kind deeds" (Pindar, *Pythian Odes,* 2. 21–24).

The cloud that Ixion had impregnated gave birth to a monster, Centaurus, human in form; he mated with the mares that grazed the slopes of Mt. Pelion, and thus became the father of the Centaurs, creatures with the upper half of a man and the legs and body of a horse. Some of these we have already met in the stories of Achilles, Heracles, and Jason; the most famous centaur was Chiron, who differs from the other centaurs in that by nature he was wise and gentle, skilled in medicine and music. His parentage, too, is different from the other centaurs; Pindar calls him the son of Cronus and the nymph Philyra.[2] The other centaurs, however, are generally portrayed as violent beings, and their best-known legend is their fight with the Thessalian tribe of the Lapiths; since the Lapith chieftain, Pirithous, was the son of Ixion, the Lapiths and centaurs were related, and therefore the centaurs were invited to the wedding of Pirithous to Hippodamia. At the feast they got drunk and attempted to rape the bride and the other Lapith women; the ensuing fight, in which the centaurs were routed, was especially celebrated in Greek art; it was represented in the sculptures of important Greek temples—upon the west pediment of the temple of Zeus at Olympia and in the metopes of the Parthenon at Athens.

Another Lapith with a legend of his own was Caeneus; he had been born a girl, Caenis, but after being raped by Poseidon and being granted anything she wanted by him, she asked to be turned into a man and to become invulnerable. As a man Caeneus set up his spear and ordered people to worship it as a god; this impiety drove Zeus to bring about his death, despite his invulnerability. He was attacked by the centaurs and buried under an enormous pile of tree trunks that they hurled at him; either his body was driven down into the Underworld by their weight or else a yellow-

---

[1] Many scholars have therefore identified Ixion with the sun god.

[2] Among his pupils were Achilles, Jason, and Asclepius.

winged bird was seen to emerge from the pile; the seer Mopsus announced the bird to be Caeneus transformed.

On the southern border of Thessaly lies the district of Phthia; we have already discussed some of the adventures of its prince, Peleus, the father of Achilles. He was the son of Aeacus, king of Aegina, and brother of Telamon; he (or Telamon) killed his half brother Phocus, and therefore had to leave Aegina. He came to king Eurytion of Phthia, who purified him and gave him part of his kingdom. Peleus accompanied Eurytion on the Calydonian boar hunt (discussed later in this chapter) and accidentally killed him with a javelin intended for the boar; for this homicide he once again went into exile, this time being purified by Acastus (son of Pelias), king of Iolcus. Now the wife of Acastus, Astydamia, fell in love with Peleus, and when he refused her advances accused him before her husband of trying to seduce her.[3] Acastus, rather than kill his guest, took Peleus out hunting on Mt. Pelion and after the hunt left him there asleep, but not before hiding his invincible sword (a gift from Hephaestus) in a pile of dung.[4] Peleus awoke to find himself surrounded by wild animals and centaurs, who would have killed him had not Chiron protected him and given him back his sword. Later, as we have seen, Peleus married Thetis upon Mt. Pelion and returned to Phthia; in one version he first revenges himself on Acastus by sacking Iolcus and leading his army between the severed portions of the body of Astydamia.

Boeotia

A number of stories are associated with the families of northern Boeotia and Thessaly; one group concerns the children of Aeolus. Salmoneus, as king of Salmone (in the Peloponnesian district of Elis where he had gone from Thessaly), dressed himself as Zeus

[3] In Pindar's fourth *Nemean Ode* her name is given as Hippolyta. Similar stories of the unchaste wife and chaste hero appear later in this chapter in the legends of Theseus and Phaedra, and Bellerophon and Stheneboea. The legend appears in the Bible (*Genesis,* ch. 39) with Joseph and Potiphar's wife.

[4] The magic sword is an evident folk tale element, as is the detail, related by Apollodorus, that Peleus cut out the tongues of the animals that he killed in the hunt and used them as proof of his skill as a hunter.

and imitated the god's thunder and lightning by driving in a chariot with brazen vessels attached to it and by hurling lighted torches; for this impiety he was killed by Zeus's thunderbolt. A similar crime was committed by Ceyx, king of Trachis and son of Eosphoros (Lucifer, the Morning Star), and his wife Alcyone, daughter of Aeolus. They called themselves Zeus and Hera, and for this were turned into sea birds (alcyone and ceyx) of doubtful identification. In Ovid, however, they are romantic lovers; Ceyx left Trachis on a sea voyage to visit the oracle at Claros, and on the way was drowned during a storm. Alcyone, who had been left in Trachis, learned of her husband's death in a dream; going down to the sea shore she found his corpse washed up by the waves and in her grief was turned into a sea bird. As she flew by the corpse and touched it, it came to life and was also turned into a bird. For seven days each winter Aeolus forbids the winds to blow while the halcyon (*alcyone*) sits on the eggs in her nest as it floats upon the waves.

Tyro, daughter of Salmoneus, was loved by Poseidon, who disguised himself as the Thessalian river Enipeus: "In the form of Enipeus did the Earthshaker lie by her at the mouth of the eddying river. About them rose a crested wave, mountainous in size, which hid both god and mortal woman" (Homer, *Odyssey,* 11. 245). The children born of this union were twins, Neleus and Pelias; Pelias's story has already been told; Neleus settled in the Peloponnese where he founded the Messenian city of Pylos, which was sacked, as we have seen, by Heracles; Neleus and all his sons, save only Nestor, were killed.

Tyro later married her uncle, Cretheus, the founder and king of Iolcus, and by him became the mother of Aeson, Pheres, and Amythaon; the story of Aeson and his son, Jason, has already been discussed. Pheres, founder of the Thessalian city of Pherae, was the father of Admetus. The famous legend of Admetus and Alcestis has already been mentioned in connection with Heracles; here we may add that Admetus in order to marry Alcestis had to perform the apparently impossible task of harnessing a lion and a boar together to a chariot. Of greater interest are the children of Amythaon, Bias and Melampus; [5] Melampus was a seer who had the power of understanding the speech of animals. This gift

---

[5] Amythaon and his children, like Neleus, are associated with Pylos.

was a return for the kindness he showed to a pair of snakes killed by his servants; he burned their bodies (a mark of honorable burial) and reared their young, who later licked his ears and so enabled him to understand the tongues of animals and birds and from them be able to foretell events. Now his brother, Bias, was a suitor for the hand of Pero, daughter of Neleus, for whom the bride price required by Neleus was the cattle of Phylacus, the king of Phylace (a city in Phthia, on the borders of Thessaly). Bias appealed to Melampus for help, and Melampus agreed to get the cattle even though he knew that he would have to spend a year in prison at Phylace. The cattle were guarded by a monstrous dog, and Melampus, as he had foreseen, was caught in the act of stealing them and imprisoned. After nearly a year he heard two woodworms saying to each other that they had very nearly finished gnawing through the roofbeams of the cell; he insisted on being moved to another cell, and shortly afterwards the first cell collapsed. This clairvoyance so impressed Phylacus that he set Melampus free and asked him how the impotence of his son, Iphiclus, might be cured; Melampus agreed to tell him, on condition· that he would be given the cattle. He then sacrificed a pair of bulls and left some of their flesh for vultures to feed on; from one vulture he learned that Iphiclus's debility was due to his having as a child been frightened while watching his father gelding rams; on that occasion Phylacus had stuck the knife, still bloody, in an oak tree, and the tree's bark had by now covered it over. If it could be found and the rust from its blade scraped off and put in Iphiclus's drink for ten days, he would recover his power.[6] All this came to pass; Iphiclus became the father of two sons (Podarces and Protesilaus), and Melampus was given the cattle, which he drove back to Pylos and handed over to Neleus; in return he got Pero and gave her to Bias.

Melampus himself later left Pylos and settled at Argos, where he gained a share in the kingdom by healing the madness of the daughters of Proetus; from him descended Amphiaraus, the seer of the Seven against Thebes.

---

[6] The details of this story, although lengthy, are given since they display recurring features of folk tale—the task to be performed by the bridegroom, the magician who can understand the talk of animals, the cure of a disease by sympathetic magic. For this last detail compare the story of Telephus.

Another family from northern Boeotia to have some importance in mythology is that of Minyas. We have seen that the Argonauts' legend is connected with the Minyae, and earlier have mentioned the legend of his daughters and their resistance to Dionysus. Minyas himself has no legend, although he is connected with a particular place, Orchomenus. His daughter, Clymene, however, appears as the wife of five different husbands and thus is made the grandmother of Jason (through her marriage to Pheres) and the mother (by Iasus) of Atalanta (whose legend is discussed later). As wife of Helius (the Sun) she became the mother of Phaethon, whose story has already been related.

At this point we may digress to consider other women who were loved by Helius; one was the eastern princess, Leucothoe, to whom Helius gained entrance by disguising himself as her mother. A former mistress, the Oceanid Clytie, in jealousy at Helius's preferring Leucothoe to herself, told Leucothoe's father of the seduction of his daughter, and he in anger had Leucothoe buried alive. Helius attempted to save her, but was too late in uncovering her corpse; upon it he shed drops of nectar so that it grew into a frankincense tree. Meanwhile Clytie could not persuade Helius to forgive her; he ignored her love and all she could do was sit, without food or drink, following the Sun's progress with her eyes until she too turned into a flower—the sunflower which forever turns its face towards the sun.[7]

The famous oracle of the hero, Trophonius, lived at Lebadeia, in northern Boeotia; as his name (he who fosters growth) implies, he is a chthonic deity and he was therefore consulted in a subterranean setting with an awesome ritual. A considerable legend was attracted to him, quite separate from his role as an earth deity, which is similar to a number of eastern stories; of these the best known is that of the Egyptian Pharaoh Rhampsinitus (Rameses) and his treasury, which Herodotus tells (2. 121). Trophonius, then, and his brother, Agamedes, were skilled builders, sons of Erginus of Orchomenus. They built for king Augeas of Elis (or, as some say, the Boeotian king Hyrieus) a treasury with a movable stone, which they made use of to steal the king's treasure. In time the

---

[7] Two other consorts of Helius are named—Perse, the mother of Aeetes and Circe, and Rhodos (or Rhode), nymph of the islands of Rhodes.

king set a trap for the unknown thief and Agamedes was caught; at his own suggestion his head was cut off by Trophonius (who then escaped), so that both avoided recognition. Trophonius fled to Lebadeia, where he was swallowed up by the earth and thereafter worshiped as a god.

Pindar, however, has a different story of the brothers' death, one that is very similar to Herodotus's story of the Argives, Cleobis and Biton; in this version Trophonius and Agamedes built the temple of Apollo at Delphi and on asking the god for their wages were told that he would pay them on the seventh day. At the time appointed they fell asleep, never to wake.

Aetolia

Among the descendants of Aeolus was Oeneus, king of Calydon, whom we have already mentioned as the father of Heracles's wife, Deianira; his son was Meleager. Shortly after the birth of Meleager the Fates (Moirae) appeared before his mother, Althaea, and told her that Meleager would die when a log, which was burning on the hearth, had burned out; Althaea snatched up the log, extinguished it and kept it in a chest. Years later, when Meleager was a young man, Oeneus offended Artemis by failing to sacrifice to her her share of the first fruits, and she sent a huge boar to ravage Calydon. Meleager gathered many of the noblest Greek heroes to hunt the boar, among whom came Atalanta, daughter of the Boeotian king Schoeneus. In the hunt Atalanta was the first to wound the boar after several heroes had been killed. Meleager gave the *coup de grâce* and therefore received the boar's skin, which he presented to Atalanta, whom he loved. Such an act was an insult to his uncles, the brothers of Althaea, who were slighted at being given less honor than a girl; a quarrel ensued in which Meleager killed his uncles. When this news reached Althaea, in her grief she took the unburned log from its chest and cast it on the fire; as it was consumed so Meleager's life waned and he died. Althaea and Meleager's wife, Cleopatra, hanged themselves, while the women who mourned for him at his funeral were turned into guinea fowl, which the Greeks called *meleagrides*.

This is the most famous version of the Calydonian boar hunt as it is found in Ovid: in Homer, however, Artemis sent the boar to ravage the land while war was going on round the city of Calydon between the Aetolians (i.e., Calydonians) and the Curetes (an Acarnanian tribe); Meleager killed it and then withdrew from the war in anger at his mother, who had cursed him for killing her brothers (how or why he killed them is not stated). In his absence the Calydonians were routed, and it was only in reply to Cleopatra's urgent entreaties that Meleager consented to go back and fight and defeat the Curetes. Homer does not record his death; but his soul talked with Heracles in the Underworld.

Atalanta, daughter of the Boeotian Schoeneus cannot be distinguished from Atalanta, daughter of the Arcadian Iasus. In both cases she is a virgin huntress, brave enough to join the Greek heroes in the Calydonian boar hunt and on the Argonauts' expedition. As a baby she had been exposed by her father (whether Iasus or Schoeneus—both names are given) and kept alive by a she-bear that suckled her until some hunters found her and brought her up. Grown up, she was recognized by her father, but she refused to let him give her in marriage unless her suitor could win a footrace against her. Those who lost were executed. When many young men had died in this way, Milanion (also called Hippomenes) raced with her; with him he had three golden apples (said by some to be the apples of the Hesperides) given him by Aphrodite, and these he dropped one by one during the race to delay Atalanta. So he won the race and his wife, but in their impatience to lie together they mated in a sacred place (a precinct of either Zeus or Cybele) and for their sacrilege were turned into a lion and lioness.[8]

Attica

It was the Athenians' boast that they were autochthonous, that is, that they were not descended from any invaders of Attica. Cecrops,

---

[8] The ancient belief was that lions never mated with lionesses, but with leopards; the lovers were therefore never able again to fulfill their desires. Others, however, ignore this picturesque story and make Atalanta the mother of Parthenopaeus, one of the Seven against Thebes.

their earliest king, therefore, was sprung from the earth, and was serpent-shaped in the lower half of his body; he has little importance in legend except as the founder of Attica, which he called Cecropia after himself. It was in his time that the contest between Poseidon and Athena for the possession of Attica took place. Another early figure in Attic mythology is Erichthonius, who again was partly serpent-shaped and, in a manner of speaking, sprung from the earth. The story of his birth is as follows: Hephaestus attempted to violate Athena, and as she repelled him his seed fell on the ground; from it sprang Erichthonius. Athena took him up and put him in a chest, which she gave to the daughters of Cecrops to look after; two of them could not resist the temptation to look inside and were driven mad by what they saw,[9] so that they hurled themselves off the Acropolis. After this Athena took back Erichthonius and brought him up herself. As king of Athens he was credited with instituting the great annual festival of the Panathenaea.

The daughters of Cecrops were called Aglauros, Herse, and Pandrosos, whose names, meaning bright, dew, and all-dew, show that they are truly mythological beings, in origin fertility-goddesses. Herse was loved by Hermes, and by him was the mother of Cephalus, who has already been mentioned as beloved by Eos (the dawn) and in connection with Amphitryon. In later legend he is the husband of Procris, daughter of Erechtheus.[10] In Ovid's story he was tempted by Aurora (the Latin form of Eos), who also loved him, to make trial of Procris's faithfulness; in disguise he attempted to seduce her and when he was on the point of succeeding revealed himself. In shame Procris fled and joined Artemis as a huntress; Artemis gave her a hound, Laelaps, that always caught its quarry, and a javelin that never missed its mark. Later she was reconciled to Cephalus and returned home bringing with her the magic gifts. Cephalus used to go out hunting alone with them; when hot he would call for the wind (*aura* in Latin) to cool him, and the gossip came to the ears of Procris that Cephalus was making love in the forest with a girl named Aura. So

[9] According to some, a pair of snakes, or Erichthonius with his snake-like lower half.

[10] The parentage of Cephalus and Procris varies.

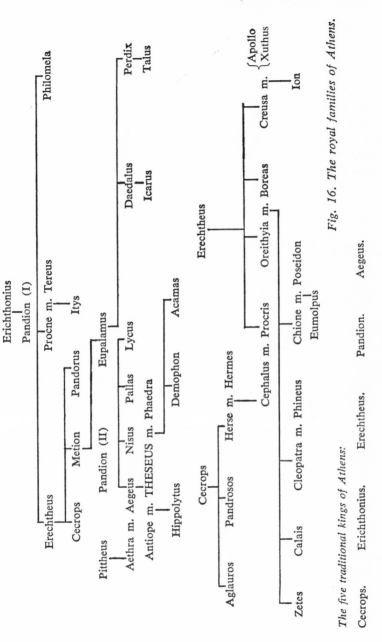

Fig. 16. The royal families of Athens.

The five traditional kings of Athens:

Cecrops.   Erichthonius.   Erechtheus.   Pandion.   Aegeus.

she hid in the undergrowth to watch for herself; as Cephalus called on the wind—"Come, Aura, and cool my heat"—Procris moved and made the undergrowth rustle. Cephalus, thinking it was an animal, threw the javelin and, too late, realized that he had killed his wife.

This is the most famous version of the story; in another, however, Procris was less chaste and, being discovered by Cephalus with a lover, fled to Minos, king of Crete, who himself fell in love with her. Now he had been bewitched by his wife, Pasiphae, so that whenever he lay with a woman he discharged snakes and other creatures; Procris was able to cure him and then lay with him, being rewarded with the gift of the hound and the javelin. Later she returned to Athens and was reconciled with Cephalus.

To return to the line of Athenian kings, the successor of Erichthonius was Pandion (Apollodorus distinguishes between two kings of this name), who is famous in legend chiefly for his daughters, Philomela and Procne. The Thracian king Tereus came to help Pandion in a war against Thebes and was rewarded with the hand of Procne; he took her back to Thrace and by her became the father of Itys. Later Philomela came to visit her sister; Tereus seduced her and then cut out her tongue to prevent her telling Procne what had happened. She embroidered the story, however, on a robe which she sent Procne, and Procne, in revenge, killed Itys and served him to Tereus at dinner. When Tereus realized what he had eaten he attempted to kill Philomela and Procne; as they fled they were turned into birds—Philomela into a swallow, Procne into a nightingale—while Tereus himself became a hoopoe. This is the Greek version where the nightingale (Procne) mourns for her dead son, and the tongueless swallow (Philomela) tries to tell her story by her incoherent chatter. The Latin authors, however, changed the names, making Philomela the nightingale and Procne the swallow; it is this version that has survived in later European literature.

Pandion is said to have been succeeded by Erechtheus, who again claimed to be earth-born. He made war on the people of Eleusis, who were helped by Eumolpus, a Thracian son of Poseidon, and in obedience to an oracle sacrificed one of his daughters (the name varies with different authors) to secure the death of Eumolpus and his own victory. Poseidon, in anger at the death of his son, persuaded Zeus to kill Erechtheus and his family with a thunderbolt.

Another daughter of Erechtheus was Orithyia; she was loved by the North Wind, Boreas, who carried her off to Thrace as she was playing by the river Ilissus.[11] In Thrace she became the mother of the winged heroes Zetes and Calais, and of two daughters, Cleopatra and Chione. Zetes and Calais were prominent in the Argonauts' expedition, in which they saved Phineus from the Harpies; Phineus himself was married to Cleopatra. Chione became the mother, by Poseidon, of Eumolpus, whose death we have just discussed.

A third daughter of Erechtheus was Creusa, who was loved by Apollo and bore to him a son, Ion, whom she exposed out of fear of her father. Ion was saved by Hermes at Apollo's request and taken by him to Delphi, where he was brought up as a temple servant and became treasurer of the sanctuary. Creusa, meanwhile, was given as wife to Xuthus as a reward for his aiding Erechtheus in defeating the Chalcodontids of Euboea. After years of childlessness, Xuthus and Creusa consulted the Delphic oracle as to how they might have children; Xuthus was told to greet as his son the first person he met on going out of the temple.[12] This person was Ion, but Creusa, who did not know that he was her own son, took him for a bastard son of Xuthus, and attempted to kill him. The attempt miscarried and in the end, with the intervention of Athena, mother and son recognized each other; Xuthus, Creusa, and Ion returned together to Athens, where Ion became the ancestor of the four Ionic tribes (which were the main units of the early Athenian political struc-

---

[11] The chief source for this story is Plato, *Phaedrus,* 229B; the passage provides an interesting rationalization of the legend. "If I were skeptical, like clever men," says Socrates, when asked if he thinks the story true, "I would not be extraordinary; then I would rationalize and say that the North Wind pushed her, as she was playing, down from the nearby rocks. She died in this way; but her death was described as her being ravished by Boreas."

[12] There is a pun here on Ion's name, which is also the Greek word meaning "going."

ture). His descendants colonized part of the coast of Asia Minor and the islands, thereafter called Ionia.

The legend of Ion is not mentioned in most of the ancient sources —it stems almost entirely from Euripides's play, *Ion*. Nor does Ion have any genuine mythological significance. The story is in fact largely an artificial myth composed to explain a historical fact, that is, the colonization of Ionia by mainland Greeks (principally from Athens, but including also Achaeans) moving out because of the pressure of the Dorian invasions.

The lists of the Athenian kings are incredibly confused, as a glance at the genealogical tables will show. According to our most explicit ancient source, Apollodorus, Erechtheus was succeeded by his son Cecrops, and Cecrops by his son Pandion; Cecrops and Pandion thus repeat the names of earlier kings. Pandion was driven out of Attica by his uncle, Metion, and fled to Megara, where he became the father of four sons, Aegeus, Pallas, Nisus, and Lycus. The four brothers, after Pandion's death, recovered the throne at Athens and shared the power; Aegeus, however, as the oldest, was in effect the sovereign, while Nisus returned to Megara as its king.

Aegeus, like Erechtheus, is in fact an Athenian form of the god Poseidon; this is indicated by his connection with the Aegean sea, by the Troezenian version of the legend, in which Poseidon was Theseus's father rather than Aegeus, and by his connection with the cult of Apollo Delphinius, that is, Apollo as a god of spring, when the sea once more is navigable and the dolphins appear as portents of good sailing weather. As king of Athens he was threatened by the opposition of his brother, Pallas; childless, he traveled to Delphi for advice and was told by the oracle "not to undo the wineskin's mouth" until he had returned home. Perplexed by this riddle, he asked the advice of Pittheus, king of Troezen, his host on his journey. Pittheus, who understood the oracle, made Aegeus drunk and gave him his daughter, Aethra, to lie with.[13] When Aegeus (now sober) left Troezen, he told Aethra that if their child were a boy she must bring him up without saying who his

---

[13] The oracle is difficult to reconcile with this story if the "home" referred to should be Athens. It is more readily comprehensible in the version given by Euripides, which has Medea cure Aegeus of his sterility after she has joined him in Athens.

father was; she was to send him to Athens when he was old enough to lift a rock by himself, under which Aegeus would leave a sword and a pair of sandals as tokens by which he could recognize his son.

In due time Aethra bore a son, Theseus, who grew up and set out for Athens after securing the tokens. Theseus is the great national hero of Attica, and his sagas are a good example of national propaganda at work on mythological material. Athens came to be the focal point of his legends, and so his earlier association with Marathon (in Attica) and Troezen (in the northeast Peloponnese) has become vague. He is associated with Heracles in some of his adventures and his deeds are consciously modeled after those of Heracles, for example his ridding the land of brigands and monsters or his expedition against the Amazons. Some of the characters in his sagas were themselves heroes with a cult of their own, whom he absorbed; examples are Sciron and Hippolytus. As a mythological character Theseus is less interesting than many lesser, but more genuine, figures; his legends owe their fame as much to the fact that he was the hero of a city whose writers dominated the classical Greek literary tradition as to their intrinsic interest. The idealization of Theseus was especially developed in the latter part of the sixth century, when the tyrant Pisistratus encouraged the development of an Athenian historical tradition. There was another period of interest in Theseus immediately after the Persian Wars (around 475), during a time of patriotic fervor at Athens.

The adventures of Theseus fall into fairly well-defined groups, of which the first contains the six deeds that he performed while traveling to Athens from Troezen; the easiest way to make this journey is by sea, but Theseus chose the land route so as to expose himself to the challenge of more dangerous adventures. At Epidaurus he killed the brigand Periphetes, a son of Hephaestus, who was armed with a club and so generally called Corynetes (club man); Theseus took the club for himself in imitation of Heracles. Since the story of Periphetes is a century later than the other adventures of Theseus, it is not surprising that the club plays no further part in these stories (except in artistic representations). At the Isthmus of Corinth he killed the robber Sinis; Sinis also had earned a surname—Pityocamptes (pine bender)—from the way in which he killed his victims. The commonest version is that he would bend two pine tree saplings to the ground, tie each end of his victim to one of the two trees, and then release the trees; Theseus killed him by this method.

On the border of the Isthmus and the Megarid lies the village of Crommyon; in the nearby ravines lived a huge gray man-eating sow, which Theseus killed. After this adventure he found the brigand Sciron blocking his way at the so-called Cliffs of Sciron. Sciron was originally an independent hero, with a considerable legend and cult of his own at Megara, on the island of Salamis, and at certain places in Attica where there were limestone outcrops; his name means limestone. The legends of Megara and Salamis that make him a local leader related to many of the heroes prominent in saga have been obscured by the Athenian version; in this he blocked the path along which travelers through the Megarid must go to pass the cliffs and compelled all comers to stoop and wash his feet. He would then kick his victims into the sea where a gigantic turtle ate them up. As with the other brigands, Theseus killed him by his own methods.

Drawing closer to Athens Theseus met Cercyon at Eleusis. Like Sciron, Cercyon was originally a local hero, with connections in Arcadia; he too becomes in the Athenian tradition a mere brigand, who compels passers-by to wrestle with him to the death. (A similar, and more original, mythical wrestler was Antaeus, who undoubtedly contributed to the Athenian version of Cercyon.) Theseus defeated him in wrestling, held him high in the air, and then dashed him to his death upon the ground.

Finally, between Eleusis and Athens, Theseus met the brigand Procrustes,[14] who possessed a hammer, a saw and a bed; he compelled passers-by to lie on the bed, and those who were too long for it he would cut down to size; those who were shorter than the bed he would hammer out until they fitted it exactly. He too perished at Theseus's hands in the way in which he had killed his victims.

So Theseus came to Athens; his arrival is dramatically described by the lyric poet, Bacchylides of Ceos, writing about 475 (which, as we shall see, was a significant time at Athens for Theseus's

---

[14] The name means the stretcher; he is also called Damastes (Subduer), Procoptes (Slicer) and Polypemon (Troubler).

legend); in reply to the citizens' questions Aegeus speaks (Bac-chylides, *Dithyramb,* 18. 16–60):

"A messenger has come, traversing the long road from the Isthmus; incredible are the deeds of a mighty man that he relates. This man killed violent Sinis, strongest of mortals . . . he killed the man-slaying sow in the glens of Cremmyon and killed the cruel Sciron. The wrestling ring of Cercyon has he suppressed; Procoptes has dropped the mighty hammer of Polypemon, for he has met a more valiant man. I fear what this news portends." "Who is this man?" [ask the citizens, and Aegeus continues]: "Two companions only come with him, says the messenger; upon his shoulders he wears an ivory-hilted sword and in his hand he carries two polished spears; upon his red-haired head is set a Spartan cap, well-made; around his body he has cast a purple tunic and over it a woolen cloak from Thessaly. From his eyes darts blood-red flame, as from Lemnos's volcano. Yet he is but a youth in his first prime, whose skill is in the delight of war and the brazen blows of battle. In quest of shining Athens does he come."

Theseus's recognition by his father was hedged with further dangers. Aegeus was married to Medea, who expected their son Medus to succeed as king of Athens. Medea immediately recognized Theseus as Aegeus's son and a rival to Medus; she therefore attempted to have Theseus poisoned before Aegeus could recognize him. She advised Aegeus that the newcomer would be a threat to his power; he should entertain Theseus at a banquet where he would drink poisoned wine, for which Medea would provide the poison. Theseus at the banquet carved his meat with the sword that he had recovered from under the rock at Troezen; Aegeus recognized the sword, dashed the cup of poison out of Theseus's hand, and publicly recognized Theseus as his son and successor.

Medus had not been the only contender for the succession. Pallas, brother of Aegeus, and his sons had hoped and plotted to take over Aegeus's power and resorted to violence upon Theseus's recognition. Theseus killed all the members of one of the two groups into which they had divided; Pallas himself and his sur-viving sons ceased to be a threat.[15]

[15] Other versions make Theseus kill Pallas and all his sons.

Theseus's next exploit was to catch the bull of Marathon, which was troubling the northeastern part of Attica; the bull was said to have been that which Heracles had brought from Crete. He mastered the bull and drove it back to Athens, where he sacrificed it to Apollo Delphinius. Among the many ancient variants on this legend is the story of an old woman, Hecale, who entertained Theseus on his way to Marathon. She promised she would sacrifice to Zeus if Theseus returned successful, but on his return he found her already dead and he ordered that she share the honors henceforth paid to Zeus Hecalus at an annual festival by the people of that locality.

The greatest and best-known of Theseus's exploits as heir apparent is his adventure with the Minotaur. Androgeos, son of the Cretan king Minos, had been killed in Attica because of the jealousy he had aroused by winning all the contests at the Panathenaic games; either he had been ambushed or sent by Aegeus against the bull of Marathon, which killed him. In revenge Minos mounted an expedition against Athens and her ally Megara, where Nisus, brother of Aegeus, was king. Megara was attacked first and some time after its fall Athens made a treaty with Minos. Part of the terms were that at intervals (variously stated as being of one or nine years) seven Athenian youths and seven girls, children of noble families, should be sent to Crete as tribute, there to be shut up in the Labyrinth and devoured by the Minotaur. The details of the story vary considerably; according to the fifth-century historian, Hellanicus, Minos himself chose the victims and took them with him on his ship back to Crete; as might be expected, Theseus, the son of the king of Athens, was among them.[16] On the voyage to Crete, Minos attempted to seduce one of the maidens, Eriboea, who called on Theseus for help. In reply to Theseus's remonstrations, Minos prayed to Zeus for a sign that he was indeed Minos's father (and therefore that his son need be under no restraint in dealing with other men); Zeus sent lightning and Minos then challenged Theseus's claim to be the son of Poseidon by throwing a ring overboard which Theseus was to recover. The sequel forms the subject of a famous and beautiful poem by

[16] The more common version is that the victims were chosen by lot and that Theseus volunteered to go.

Bacchylides; Theseus jumped into the sea and the boat sailed on. (Bacchylides, *Dithyramb,* 17. 92–116):

The Athenian youths trembled as the hero leaped into the sea, and tears poured from their lily-like eyes as they awaited the sorrow of what had to be. Yet the dolphins, dwellers in the sea, swiftly brought great Theseus to the palace of his father, the ruler of horses. There with awe he saw the noble daughters of rich Nereus . . . and in the lovely palace he saw his father's own wife, the beauteous Amphitrite, in all her majesty. Round him she cast a purple robe, and upon his thick hair the unwithered wreath, dark with roses, which subtle Aphrodite had given her at her own marriage.

With these gifts (the poet does not mention the ring) Theseus returned miraculously to the ship and so came to Crete. Here the daughter of Minos, Ariadne, fell in love with him and, in the best-known version of the story, gave him a thread with which he could trace his way back out of the Labyrinth. With this aid, he entered the Labyrinth, killed the Minotaur, and emerged unharmed; he then sailed from Crete with his thirteen Athenian companions, taking Ariadne with him.

An equally ancient tradition, however, makes Ariadne give Theseus a wreath that lights up the darkness of the Labyrinth and so helps him escape. In the poem of Bacchylides this wreath is made the gift not of Ariadne, but of Amphitrite—in other words it is Theseus himself who brings it to Crete. Ariadne wore the wreath on her flight with Theseus until he deserted her on Naxos and she was found by Dionysus; the god took the wreath and set it in the heavens, where it became the constellation Corona.

Ariadne is originally a divine person, perhaps another form of Aphrodite; Hesiod (*Theogony,* 947–949) describes her as the "wife of Dionysus, whom Zeus made immortal." Later and more romantic versions of the Theseus legend make her a forlorn heroine, deserted by her lover Theseus upon the island of Dia (the early name for Naxos) during the voyage back to Athens. In the original form of the legend, however, Theseus forgot Ariadne [17] and sailed away, leaving her to be claimed as wife by Dionysus.

---

[17] Such forgetfulness is a common feature of *märchen.*

Yet another version, that of Homer, says that Ariadne was killed by Artemis upon Naxos as a punishment for eloping with Theseus when she was already betrothed to Dionysus. Finally, there is another legend of her death set in Cyprus; in this version, Theseus and Ariadne came to Cyprus; here they were separated during a storm, and Ariadne died in giving birth to Theseus's child. When Theseus returned he instituted a ritual in her honor; in historical times she was honored under the title of Ariadne Aphrodite, part of the ritual being for a young man to lie down and imitate a woman in childbirth. In all these conflicting stories it is clear that Ariadne is no ordinary mortal and that her partner was not a man, Theseus, but a god.

After touching at Delos, Theseus returned to Athens. Now he had arranged with Aegeus that he should change the black sail of his ship for white if he had been successful. This he forgot to do, and Aegeus, as he saw the black-sailed ship approaching, threw himself from a cliff into the sea, which thereafter was called the Aegean sea. So Theseus became king of Athens. At this point saga and history join, for Theseus was credited with reforms and institutions that are historical facts; the most famous are the "synoecism" of Attica (that is, the union of the different villages into one political unit with Athens as its center) and the refounding of the Isthmian games,[18] in this emulating Heracles's founding of the Olympian games. He was also said to have organized the Athenian people into three classes (nobles, farmers, and craftsmen)—again a feature of the early stages of historical Athens.

The chronology of Theseus's career is incredibly confused. If he is a historical king of Athens who was responsible for the synoecism, we should expect him to belong after the Dorian invasion, in the period 1000–700. But his exploits in Crete surely must be dated earlier, in the Late Bronze Age (1600–1100). Such are the historical problems created by the cumulative growth of saga.

As king, Theseus was involved in several legendary campaigns, two of which were the subjects of some of the most famous works of art in antiquity. He joined with Heracles in his expedition against the Amazons, and as his share of the spoil received the

---

[18] They had previously been founded in honor of Melicertes (Palaemon).

Amazon Antiope, by whom he became the father of Hippolytus. The Amazons in revenge invaded Attica and were defeated by Theseus. There are several variant versions of the Amazon saga; it partly owes its origin to the existence in Attica and other parts of Greece of prehistoric burial mounds, which were described as tombs of Amazons. It was during the Amazon attack that Antiope died (there are, however, conflicting accounts of her death). The battle between Theseus and the Amazons was depicted in the Hephaestaeum at Athens and in the Stoa Poecile (the Painted Colonnade); these paintings dated from the period immediately after the Persian Wars (i.e., after 479), when Athenian national pride and interest in the national hero, Theseus, was at its height. The Amazons were then seen as legendary symbols of the barbarian world, who, like the contemporary barbarians (the Persians) had been defeated by the Greeks. For this reason also, the battle with the Amazons formed one of the subjects of the metopes of the Parthenon (about 445) and was again depicted on the shield of Pheidias's great statue of Athena Parthenos upon the Acropolis, as well as on the pedestal of the statue of Zeus at Olympia.

A second campaign was the result of Theseus's friendship with Pirithous, king of the Thessalian tribe of the Lapiths, and son of Ixion. Theseus was among the guests at the marriage of Pirithous, and took part in the fight against the Centaurs; as we have already seen this episode was also important in Greek art.

The friendship between Theseus and Pirithous led (in the earliest form of the saga at any rate) to their destruction. They vowed to help each other in securing a wife; Theseus attempted to secure Helen, and Pirithous, Persephone. Helen, who at the time was only a child, was kidnapped from Sparta and brought back to Attica, where she was put in the care of Theseus's mother, Aethra, in the Attic village of Aphidnae.[19] While Theseus and Pirithous were away on their attempt against Persephone, the Dioscuri invaded Attica and recovered their sister. Despite their violence, the Dioscuri were favorably received in Athens itself, where the regent Menestheus instituted a cult in their honor; they were called by the title of *Anakes* or *Anaktes* (Kings) and

---

[19] Aethra had left Troezen to rejoin her son.

their temple in historical times was called the *Anakeion*. A further sequel to the legend is that Aethra was taken back to Sparta as Helen's slave and went with her to Troy.

Theseus, then, failed to keep Helen; Pirithous failed even more finally in attempting to abduct Persephone. Theseus and Pirithous descended to the Underworld and there were held fast in magic chairs, never to return to earth again. This is the earliest version of the saga, but the Athenian literary tradition altered it and made Heracles intercede for Theseus's release, while Pirithous stayed forever in Hades: [20]

> And Theseus leaves Pirithous in the chain
> The love of comrades cannot take away.

Thus the Athenian hero was again associated with Heracles, in this case in his last and greatest Labor, the conquest of death.

At some stage in his saga Theseus was married to Phaedra, another daughter of Minos, and by her was the father of two sons, Demophon and Acamas. The origin of Phaedra (whose name means bright) cannot be established, although she may originally have been a Cretan goddess, like Ariadne; the outlines of the legend associated with her are clear enough. She fell passionately in love with Hippolytus, Theseus's son by Antiope, but did not tell him of her desire. During an absence of Theseus her old nurse found out the secret and told Hippolytus; Phaedra, in shame at the discovery of her secret, hanged herself and left behind a letter falsely accusing Hippolytus of attempting to seduce her. When Theseus returned, saw Phaedra's corpse, and read the letter, he banished Hippolytus and called on Poseidon to destroy him.[21] As Hippolytus left on his way into exile and was driving his chariot along the seashore, Poseidon sent a bull from the sea, which so frightened Hippolytus's horses that they bolted; Hippolytus was

---

[20] The rationalizing account of the descent to the Underworld given by Plutarch, *Theseus,* Chapter 31, is worthless as mythology. The quotation is from A. E. Housman's translation of Horace, *Odes,* 4. 7.

[21] Poseidon was said to have granted Theseus three wishes, of which this was the third. (The others were to escape from the Labyrinth and to return from Hades.)

thrown from the chariot and dragged almost to his death. He was carried back to Theseus and died after being reconciled with his father and assured by Artemis of his future honor as a hero with a cult.

The legend of Hippolytus owes its fame largely to Euripides, who wrote two tragedies on the subject (one of which is extant), and to Seneca, whose *Phaedra* was the model for Racine's *Phèdre.* There are several variants of the saga, and some apparently insoluble problems. In Euripides's extant *Hippolytus,* the drama is set at Troezen, but most other authors make Athens the scene. Hippolytus himself was honored with a cult at Troezen and was closely connected with Artemis, in whose honor he avoided all women. At Athens he was connected with Aphrodite, whose temple on the south side of the Acropolis was called "Aphrodite by Hippolytus." He himself was said to have been brought to life by Asclepius, and in his resurrected form he was absorbed by the Italians with the name of Virbius. Whether he is in origin a god or man cannot be established; all that can be said is that his legend is of the greatest literary importance and that historically it connects Attica and Troezen and links Theseus to the great goddesses worshiped in Crete, Troezen, and Athens.

Theseus originally was not a member of the great expeditions of saga, but so important a national hero naturally came to be included in the roster of heroic adventurers, so that he was said to have been an Argonaut and present on the Calydonian boar hunt. Indeed, "not without Theseus" became an Athenian proverb, and he was called "a second Heracles." These exploits and many others credited to him need not be detailed here.

Theseus's life ended in failure, and here again the legend appears to reflect historical events, that is, political dissension in early Athens. He was said to have been driven out of Athens and his power to have been usurped by Menestheus, who is mentioned in the *Iliad*'s Catalogue of Ships as the Athenian leader at Troy. Theseus went to the island of Scyros, where he possessed lands, and was there killed by Lycomedes, the local king. Menestheus continued to reign at Athens, but died at Troy; the sons of Theseus then recovered their father's throne, and we have already seen how Demophon helped the children of Heracles. At this stage the legend passes over into history, and it was in historical times that Theseus finally returned to Athens. After the Persian Wars the Greek allies, led by the Athenian Cimon, captured Scyros in the year 476–475.[22] There Cimon, obedient to a command of the Delphic oracle, searched for the bones of Theseus; after near failure he found the bones of a very large man with a bronze spearhead and sword, and brought them back to Athens. So Theseus returned, a symbol of Athens' connection with the Heroic Age and of her claim to lead the Ionian Greeks; in the same way the Spartans a century before had claimed the leadership of the Peloponnese by recovering the bones of Orestes from Tegea.

There are a number of minor legends attached to Demophon, son of Theseus. He was said to have succeeded Menestheus as Athenian leader at Troy and to have brought his grandmother Aethra back to Athens. His best-known legend concerns his love for the Thracian princess, Phyllis. Leaving her in Thrace he swore to return soon; when he never came back, she hanged herself and was turned into an almond tree. Too late he returned and embraced the tree, which burst into leaf.[23]

The last king of Athens was said to have been Codrus, who sacrificed himself for his city. The Peloponnesians invaded Attica, being assured by the Delphic oracle that the side would win whose king was killed. When Codrus learned of the oracle he disguised himself as a peasant and provoked a quarrel with some enemy soldiers, who killed him; the Peloponnesians were defeated.

Mention has been made above of Daedalus, son or grandson of Metion (younger brother of Cecrops), and therefore a member of the cadet branch of the Athenian royal house. Daedalus, as well as being a royal prince, was a skilled craftsman and inventor; his assistant was his nephew Perdix.[24] Perdix one day invented the saw, getting the idea from a fish's backbone; Daedalus in a fit of jealousy hurled him from a rock, and as he fell he was turned

[22] Athenian years were dated by archons (magistrates) whose year of office began in mid-summer.

[23] The Greek word for leaves is *phylla*. The version given above is one of several variants.

[24] In other versions the boy is called Talus and his mother, Daedalus's sister, Perdix.

into a partridge, which still bears the name *perdix*. Being now guilty of homicide Daedalus had to leave Athens and went to Crete; here his skill was employed by Minos and Pasiphae. Now Minos had prayed to Poseidon to send him a bull from the sea for sacrifice; when Poseidon answered his prayer Minos was so covetous that he sacrificed another and less beautiful bull, keeping Poseidon's animal for himself. As a punishment, Poseidon caused the wife of Minos, Pasiphae, to fall in love with the bull, and it was to satisfy her passion that Daedalus was called in to help. He constructed a lifelike hollow cow, in which Pasiphae was shut up, and so mated with the bull. Her offspring was a monster, with a man's body and the head of a bull, called the Minotaur; it was kept shut up in a maze, called the Labyrinth, of Daedalus's devising, and we have already seen how Theseus destroyed it.

The famous discoveries at Cnossus in Crete have shown that the strange legend of the Minotaur has a basis in fact, for the bull played a significant part in Cretan ritual, and a common sacred object was the *labrys* or double-headed axe, which is certainly to be connected with the word *labyrinth*. The idea of the maze has plausibly been thought to have its origin in the huge and complex palace of Cnossus, with its many passageways and endless series of rooms. Moreover, Minos and Pasiphae, like their daughters Ariadne and Phaedra, are probably divine figures; Minos was son and friend of Zeus,[25] while Pasiphae (the All-Shining) was the daughter of Helius.

Daedalus eventually tired of his life in Crete, and Minos would not let him go. He therefore contrived feathered wings, held together by wax, by means of which he and his son Icarus could escape. As they flew high above the sea, the wax on Icarus's wings was melted by the heat of the sun and he fell into the sea, which thereafter was called *Mare Icarium;* Daedalus himself successfully reached Sicily,[26] where Cocalus, king of the city of Camicus, received him. Here he was pursued by Minos, who discovered him by

[25] Homer (*Odyssey,* 19. 178–179) describes him as the intimate friend of Zeus, and Hesiod (fragment 103) calls him "the most kingly of mortal kings, who ruled over most subjects and held his scepter from Zeus."

[26] A well-known variant, which appears in the opening lines of the sixth book of Vergil's *Aeneid,* brings him to Cumae in Italy.

the ruse of carrying round a spiral shell, which he asked Cocalus to have threaded; Cocalus gave the shell to Daedalus, who alone of men was ingenious enough to succeed, and Minos knew that Daedalus was there when Cocalus gave him back the threaded shell. However, Daedalus still stayed out of Minos's reach; as Minos was being entertained by Cocalus, the daughters of Cocalus drowned him in the bath in boiling water. There is no reliable legend about the further history or death of Daedalus.

The Family of Minos

Several of the children of Minos and Pasiphae have their own legends; there were four sons, Catreus, Deucalion, Glaucus, and Androgeos, and four daughters, of whom only Ariadne and Phaedra have important legends, and these we have already discussed.

Catreus, who became the Cretan king, had a son, Althaemenes, of whom an oracle foretold that he would kill his father. Althaemenes, therefore, like Oedipus, tried to avoid this fate by leaving Crete and going to Rhodes with his sister Apemosyne.[27] She was seduced by Hermes and killed by Althaemenes, who did not believe her story, as a punishment for her unchastity. Years later Catreus himself came to Rhodes in search of his son; he and his party were taken for pirates and in the ensuing skirmish he was killed by his son. When Althaemenes learned how the oracle had been fulfilled, he avoided the company of other men and was eventually swallowed up by the earth; the Rhodians honored him as a hero.

Of the other sons of Minos, Deucalion (who should not be confused with Deucalion of the flood legend) became the father of Idomeneus, but is otherwise unimportant in saga. Glaucus figures in a legend that is more folk tale than saga. As a boy he fell into a vat of honey and was drowned; Minos could not find him and

---

[27] Two other sisters are mentioned: Aerope, who became the wife of a Mycenaean prince, either Pleisthenes or Atreus, and Clymene, who became the wife of Nauplius and the mother of Palamedes.

was told by the oracle that that person who could find an exact simile for a magic calf in Minos's herds would be able both to find Glaucus and restore him to life. This calf changed color every four hours, from white to red to black, and it was the seer Polyidus who most fittingly likened it to a mulberry, which changes from white to red and finally black as it ripens. With the help of various birds Polyidus found Glaucus's corpse in the vat; it was duly placed in a tomb and Polyidus was then shut up in the tomb and ordered to bring Glaucus back to life. While he was wondering what to do a snake came; Polyidus killed it with his sword, whereupon another snake came, looked at the dead snake and went away, returning with a herb, which it put on the dead snake's body. The dead snake then came to life again, and Polyidus took the herb and used it on Glaucus, who likewise came to life. Even now Minos was not satisfied and compelled Polyidus to teach Glaucus the seer's art before he would let him return to his home in Argos. Polyidus obeyed, but before he left he told Glaucus to spit into his mouth, whereupon Glaucus forgot all that he had learned.[28]

Androgeos, as we have already seen, had been killed in Attica; his death led to Minos's expedition and the attack on Megara. The king of Megara, Nisus, had a purple lock of hair, which was the city's talisman; the city would fall if the lock were cut off. Now Scylla, daughter of Nisus, fell in love with Minos (whom she could see from the city walls), and to please him cut off her father's purple lock and brought it to Minos. When the city fell Minos rejected Scylla and sailed away; she clung to the stern of his ship and was turned into a sea bird called *ciris*,[29] while Nisus turned into a sea eagle, forever pursuing her.

We may now continue with the legends of the Greek mainland; Megara has no significant legends beyond that of Scylla, but its neighbor Corinth has a number of figures with important sagas.

---

[28] Forgetfulness induced by spitting is a folk tale *motif,* as is also the seer who can understand the ways of birds and snakes.

[29] Its identification is unknown. According to Aeschylus, who does not mention the metamorphosis, Scylla was bribed by Minos with a golden necklace to betray Nisus.

Corinth

Homer calls Corinth by its ancient name, Ephyra, and says that it was part of the territory of Argos. Its founder and earliest king was Sisyphus, whose punishment in Hades we have already discussed. As son of Aeolus he was connected with Athamas's family; we have described already how Athamas's wife, Ino, leaped into the sea with her child, Melicertes, and how she became the sea-goddess Leucothea, and her child, the god Palaemon. Melicertes's body is said to have been brought ashore on the Isthmus by a dolphin; it was found and buried by Sisyphus, who instituted the Isthmian games in the child's honor.[30] At first the games were mainly religious and ritualistic; Theseus is said to have founded them a second time and to have given them the character which they had in historical times.

The legends of Sisyphus are less concerned with him as king than as the craftiest of men. One story makes him the father of Odysseus, whose mother, Anticlea, was said to have consorted with Sisyphus before marrying Laertes. Anticlea's father was the master thief Autolycus, son of Hermes, who gave him the power of stealing undetected whatever he wished. For a long time he was in the habit of stealing Sisyphus's cattle until Sisyphus (unknown to Autolycus) branded the animals on their hoofs and so easily recognized and recovered those that Autolycus had stolen. The two heroes became friends, and Autolycus gave Sisyphus his daughter.

Sisyphus's greatest exploit was the outwitting of Death (Thanatos) himself. He had aroused the anger of Zeus by telling the river-god, Asopus, of Zeus's rape of Asopus's daughter Aegina, and Zeus sent Death to carry Sisyphus off. Sisyphus successfully resisted Death and chained him; so long as he was bound, no mortals could die. Eventually Ares freed Death and handed Sisyphus over to him, but before he went down to the Underworld Sisyphus left instructions with his wife Merope, not to make the customary

[30] The legend of Melicertes is of great interest; for a discussion see L. R. Farnell, *Greek Hero-Cults and Ideas of Immortality* (New York: Oxford University Press, 1921), pp. 39–47.

sacrifices after his death; when Hades found that no sacrifices were being made he sent Sisyphus back to remonstrate with Merope. So he returned to Corinth and stayed there until he died in advanced old age. It was for his treatment of Death and Hades that he was punished in the Underworld.

The greatest of Corinthian heroes was Bellerophon, grandson of Sisyphus. His legend was told in Homer by the Lycian leader Glaucus, when he met Diomedes in battle; it is set both in the Argolid and in Asia Minor. Whether Bellerophon himself was always a Greek or whether he was rather introduced into Greek legend from the East cannot be established.

Born in Corinth, he left home, perhaps because of bloodguilt after unintentionally killing a brother, and went to the court of Proetus, king of Argos, who purified him. There the wife of Proetus, Stheneboea (or Antea, as Homer calls her), fell in love with him and on being rejected accused him before Proetus of having tried to seduce her. Proetus therefore sent him to his wife's father, Iobates, king of Lycia, with a sealed letter in which Proetus told of Stheneboea's accusation and asked Iobates to destroy Bellerophon. Accordingly he sent him on a number of dangerous expeditions (Homer, *Iliad,* 6. 179–193):

First he bid him kill the fearsome Chimaera, which was of divine, not mortal, breed—a lion in its forepart with a serpent's tail and in the middle a goat, and it breathed fire. He killed it, trusting in the gods' signs. Next he fought the mighty Solymi, and this was his most violent battle with men. Third, he slew the warrior Amazons. And as he returned the king devised another plot against him; he chose the most valiant men in all Lycia and set them in ambush. Not one of them returned home, for gallant Bellerophon killed them all. So when the king realized that he was truly of divine descent, he kept him there in Lycia and gave him his daughter and the half of his kingdom.

Bellerophon became the father of Hippolochus (Glaucus's father) and of Isandrus, who was killed fighting the Solymi, and of a daughter, Laodamia; she was loved by Zeus and by him was the mother of Sarpedon, whom Patroclus killed at Troy. Laodamia was "killed by Artemis in anger," and Bellerophon ended his days in sorrow; "hated by the gods he wandered over the Alean plain alone, eating out his heart and avoiding the paths of men" (Homer, *Iliad,* 6. 200–202).[31]

Homer's story is filled out by later authors, notably Pindar. Poseidon gave Bellerophon the winged horse Pegasus to ride. It stood by the Corinthian spring, Pirene, and Bellerophon could not master it until Athena appeared to him in a dream and gave him a magic bridle with golden trappings (Pindar, *Olympian Odes,* 13. 63–92):

> Much did he labor beside the spring in his desire to harness the off-spring of the snake-girdled Gorgon, until the maiden Pallas brought him the gold-accoutred bridle and quickly his dream became reality. "Are you sleeping," said she, "King, descendant of Aeolus? Come, take this charm to soothe the horse and sacrifice a white bull to your forefather, Poseidon, the Tamer of Horses." These were the words which the maiden with the dark aegis seemed to speak as he slept; he leaped to his feet and took the divine object that lay beside him. . . . And strong Bellerophon, after all his efforts, caught the winged horse by putting the gentle charm around its mouth. Mounting it straightway he brandished his arms, himself in armor of bronze; with it he slew the archer army of women, the Amazons, shooting them from the unpeopled bosom of the cold upper air, and he slew the fire-breathing Chimaera and the Solymi. His fate I shall not mention; the ancient stalls of Zeus's stable in Olympus shelter the horse.

Bellerophon, then, met his end in attempting to rise too high: "If any man sets his eye on a distant target, he is too short to reach the brass-paved home of the gods. For winged Pegasus hurled his rider Bellerophon, who wished to enter the palaces of Heaven and join Zeus's company" (Pindar, *Isthmian Odes,* 7. 60–68). This is as far as Bellerophon's legend can be taken; no reliable details about his fate and that of Stheneboea can be added. Bellerophon joins other heroes, such as Ixion, Tantalus, and Sisyphus, as someone who abused the friendship of the gods and ended his career in disaster.

In Chapter 20 we have seen how Medea was brought to Greece

---

[31] Two etymologies have been suggested for Alean plain—either "the plain of wandering" or "the plain of avoiding."

from Colchis and how she came to Corinth. The version given there follows Euripides's play, *Medea,* in making Medea herself responsible for the death of her children. At Corinth itself, however, it was believed that Medea was much more than a foreign witch. The Corinthian legend is that originally the sons of Helius, Aeetes and Aloeus, divided the kingdom of Corinth; Aeetes received the city itself (Ephyra), but went to Colchis leaving a certain Bounos (and his descendants) to rule Corinth. After some generations the Corinthians called on Medea to be their queen, and it was through her that Jason became king of Corinth.

Whatever the value of this legend, the sequel, especially insofar as it concerns Medea's children, is extremely interesting. Medea rejected the advances of Zeus, who had fallen in love with her, out of respect for Hera; in return Hera promised to make her children immortal. But the process of making them immortal was interrupted perhaps by Jason, and the children died; in one version they were killed accidentally by Medea herself; in another they were killed by the Corinthians after Medea had left them for asylum in the precinct of Hera Acraea, when she herself fled from Corinth on the death of Creon. It was because of this crime that expiatory rites were performed by the Corinthians in historical times. The story of Medea as the murderess of her children was, in this version, originally a rumor spread by the Corinthians who actually killed them, and it is the persuasive advocacy of Euripides that has led to the universal acceptance of her guilt. Whether, as some supposed, the legend has its origin in a ritual child sacrifice or whether Medea was herself originally a Corinthian goddess who gave way to the more powerful Argive goddess, Hera, cannot be established. It is enough to observe the variations in her legend and to see how the genius of Euripides stabilized the tradition.

Argos

The reader will now be aware how far the history of Greece in the Bronze Age was bound up with the three great fortresses of the Argolid—Argos, Tiryns, and Mycenae. We have seen, too, that Argos was connected, in history and in legend, with Corinth and Thebes; the Argive sagas will demonstrate the many contacts of Argos with the eastern Mediterranean, notably the Levant and Egypt. While some of the legendary heroes are associated with a particular city—for example Heracles with Tiryns, Diomedes with Argos, and Perseus with Mycenae—it is often hard to distinguish between the separate cities; as in earlier chapters we shall generally use "Argos" to cover the whole Argolid and its cities. Argos was the greatest center for the worship of Hera, and the Heraeum, the hill where Hera's sanctuary stood, was the religious center of the whole area. In the Argive saga the first of men was Phoroneus, who established the kingdom of Argos and decided the contest for the land between Poseidon and Hera in favor of Hera. In anger Poseidon dried up the Argive rivers, one of which, Inachus, was the father of Phoroneus, and ever after the Argive rivers have been short of water. The richness of Argive saga can be seen from the opening lines of Pindar's tenth *Nemean Ode:*

> Sing, O Graces, of the city of Danaus and his fifty daughters on their shining thrones, of Argos, dwelling of Hera, a home fit for the gods; bright is the flame of her brave deeds unnumbered in their excellence. Long is the tale of Perseus and the Gorgon, Medusa; many are the cities of Egypt founded by the wisdom of Epaphus; Hypermestra kept to the path of virtue and alone did not draw the dagger from its sheath. Fair Athena once made Diomedes divine; in Thebes the earth struck by Zeus's thunderbolts received the seer, Amphiaraus, the storm cloud of war. Ancient is Argos's excellence in beautiful women; Zeus revealed this truth when he came to Alcmena and to Danae. . . .[32]

First in importance, though not in time, of the heroes of Argos is Perseus. His great-grandfather, Abas, had twin sons, Proetus and Acrisius (we have met Proetus in the saga of Bellerophon); the twins were enemies and quarreled even before their birth. Acrisius, who became king of Argos itself while Proetus ruled Tiryns, had no sons and one daughter, Danae; an oracle foretold that her son would kill Acrisius. To prevent her having children

---

[32] Pindar goes on to refer to Amphitryon and Heracles, whom we have discussed in Chapter 19.

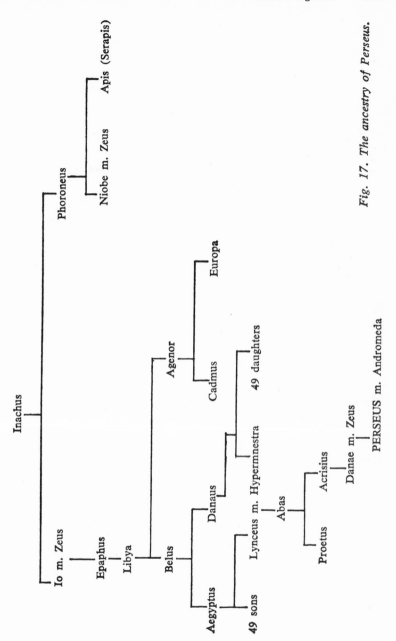

Fig. 17. The ancestry of Perseus.

Acrisius shut Danae up in a brazen underground chamber in his palace,[33] but Zeus loved her and entered the chamber in the form of a shower of gold and lay with her. Their child was Perseus, and Danae kept him in the chamber for four years, unknown to Acrisius, until he was discovered from the noise he made while playing. Then Acrisius, refusing to believe Danae's claim that Zeus was the child's father, put her and the child in a chest and set them afloat on the sea. The chest floated to the island of Seriphos where the fisherman, Dictys (whose name means net), found it; he rescued Danae and Perseus and gave them shelter in his own home.

Now Polydectes, brother of Dictys, was king of Seriphos, and as Perseus grew to manhood Polydectes fell in love with Danae; protected by Perseus she refused Polydectes. He therefore summoned the leading men of the island to a banquet at which each man had to present him with the gift of a horse; Perseus boasted that he could just as easily give Polydectes the Gorgon's head, and Polydectes, eager to get Perseus out of the way, took him literally and ordered him to perform the task. In despair Perseus wandered to a lonely part of Seriphos, and there Hermes and Athena came to his help with advice. That two gods should assist him is remarkable; Hermes belongs more than Athena to the Peloponnese, and he very likely was originally the hero's only supernatural helper. Since the Gorgon's head was an attribute of Athena's aegis, she may very early have been associated with the saga, especially since much of the literary tradition was in the hands of Athenians (an early fifth-century Athenian historian, Pherecydes, is one of the earliest and best authorities for the legend). At any rate, Pindar, writing in the first half of the fifth century, makes Athena the sole helper: "Breathing courage Danae's son joined the company of blessed men, and Athena was his guide" (*Pythian Odes,* 10. 44–46)—and Athena generally in the literary tradition has obscured Hermes's part.

Perseus, then, advised by these gods, made his way to the three daughters of Phorcys, who were sisters of the Gorgons and old women from their birth (hence they were called in Greek the

---

[33] The Roman poet Horace (*Odes,* 3. 16) changed Danae's prison to a brazen tower and his version has become the accepted tradition.

Graeae). They alone could tell Perseus the way to some nymphs, who possessed certain magic objects which he would need for his task, but the Graeae could only be compelled to part with their information. Now between them they had one eye and one tooth, which they passed to each other in turn; Perseus got hold of these objects, and only gave them back when the Graeae had told him the way to the nymphs.

From the nymphs he received three objects—a Cap of Darkness, which made its wearer invisible, a pair of winged sandals, which enabled him to fly, and a wallet or *kibisis*.[34] Finally from Hermes he received a scimitar; it is worth noting that while this object alone comes from Hermes, the cap and sandals are elsewhere associated with Hermes, for he wore the Cap of Darkness in the Gigantomachy, and winged sandals are a regular feature of his iconography. (Athena, however, is also said by Homer to have worn the Cap of Darkness at Troy when she joined in the battle.)

Perseus now flew to the Gorgons; their home was somewhere on the edge of the world (i.e., beyond the limits of reality) and was variously said in antiquity to be in the far North among the Hyperboreans, in the far West by Ocean, or the far South among the Ethiopians; it was most generally placed in north Africa. As we have seen, they were three in number and Medusa alone of the three was mortal. They were of terrifying aspect, and those who looked upon their faces were turned to stone. They were asleep when Perseus came; guided by Athena and looking at the Gorgon's reflection in his burnished shield he beheaded Medusa and put the head in the *kibisis*. As she was beheaded, Chrysaor (He of the Golden Sword) and Pegasus, the winged horse, sprang from her body. Their father was Poseidon; Chrysaor became father of the monster Geryon, and Pegasus we have met in the legend of Bellerophon.

Perseus was able to fly away from Medusa's sisters unharmed, since he was invisible wearing the Cap of Darkness. In the original version of the saga he would have returned directly to Seriphos and have dealt with Polydectes. At a very early stage, however,

[34] The word *kibisis* is non-Greek and in antiquity was believed to be Cypriote; here is one concrete connection between the Argive saga and the Levant.

a second saga, the legend of Andromeda, was added to the story of Perseus's return. Andromeda was daughter of king Cepheus and his queen, Cassiepea; the exact location of his kingdom is a matter of doubt, but he is referred to as "King of the Ethiopians," [35] while as late as the first century A.D. the marks of Andromeda's fetters were shown on the rocks near the Palestinian city of Joppa. Although the names of the characters in the story are Greek, it seems almost certain that the setting of the story was always in the Levant.

At any rate, Cassiepea boasted that she was more beautiful than the Nereids; as a punishment Poseidon flooded Cepheus's kingdom and sent a sea monster to ravage the land. Cepheus consulted the African oracle of Jupiter Ammon and was told that the monster could only be appeased if Andromeda were offered to it, chained to a rock. Cepheus obeyed, and it was at this point that Perseus flew by; he fell in love with Andromeda and agreed with Cepheus to kill the monster if he could marry Andromeda— an offer that was willingly accepted by Cepheus and Andromeda. So Perseus, making use of his sandals and cap, killed the beast with Hermes's scimitar and released Andromeda; he soon married her (after using the Gorgon's head to deal with the opposition of Cepheus's brother, Phineus, to whom Andromeda had previously been betrothed) and stayed long enough with Cepheus for a son to be born. Leaving the child, Perses, behind as heir to Cepheus's kingdom, Perseus then completed his flight back to Seriphos, taking Andromeda with him.[36]

Although the legend of Andromeda, as we have seen, was not part of the original saga, it was an early and important enough addition to be accepted as a genuine part of the tradition. The same cannot be said of a number of late details added to the original account of Perseus's flight with the Gorgon's head. The Gorgon's blood is said to have dripped through the *kibisis* as

[35] The "Ethiopians" in antiquity were vaguely thought of as the peoples living to the south and east of Egypt.

[36] The principal characters in this legend became constellations, even the monster (*Cetus* is the Greek word for a sea monster). Perses became ancestor of the kings of Persia; Aeschylus in his *Persians* refers to Xerxes as a godlike mortal, descended from the shower of gold.

Perseus flew over Libya, and from the drops sprang the infinite number of poisonous snakes that, according to the belief of the ancients, infested the Libyan desert. The giant Atlas, supporter of the heavens, refused to show Perseus any hospitality, and Perseus turned him into stone with the Gorgon's head; his head and body became a mountain range, his hair the forests upon the mountains. Finally, after Perseus had rescued Andromeda, he put the *kibisis* down on the seashore, resting on some leaves and seaweed; they were petrified and became coral.

When Perseus and Andromeda reached Seriphos they found that Danae and Dictys had taken refuge at an altar from the violence of Polydectes; Perseus displayed the Gorgon's head before Polydectes and his assembled followers, who were all turned to stone. Thus Danae was released and, with Perseus and Andromeda, returned to Argos; before leaving Seriphos Perseus made Dictys king of the island and gave back the magic objects to the gods— the sandals, *kibisis,* and cap to Hermes [37] (who returned them to the nymphs) and the Gorgon's head to Athena, who set it in the middle of her shield.

This completes the saga of Perseus and the Gorgon's head. There have been very many interpretations and rationalizations, which can for the most part be safely ignored. One interesting feature of the saga is the predominance of folk tale motifs, more so than in any other Greek saga. These include the magic conceiving of the hero by the princess, his mother; the discovery of the hero as a child by the noise of his playing; the villainous king and his good and humble brother; the rash promise of the hero, which he performs with the aid of supernatural helpers and magic objects; the three old women ("Old, Older, and Oldest") from whom advice must be sought; the Gorgons, imaginary monsters of ferocious ugliness; and finally the vindication of the hero and the punishment of the villain.

With the return of Perseus to Argos his saga comes closer to history, and the story of Acrisius is brought to its end. When he heard that Danae's son was indeed alive and returning to Argos, Acrisius left the city and went to the city of Larisa, in Thessaly,[38]

[37] The scimitar is not mentioned again in the sources.
[38] The acropolis of Argos was also called Larisa.

where Perseus followed him. And here Acrisius met his long-foretold death; Perseus competed in the athletic games that the king of Larisa was celebrating in honor of his dead father, and threw a discus that accidentally wounded Acrisius fatally in the foot. Acrisius was buried outside Larisa and honored there as a hero; Perseus, having shed kindred blood, returned not to Argos but to Tiryns, whose king, Megapenthes, son of Proetus, exchanged kingdoms with him. As king of Tiryns, Perseus founded a nearby city, Mycenae, where in historical times he was honored as a hero. The children of Perseus and Andromeda became kings of Mycenae and from them descended Heracles and Eurystheus.[39]

From Perseus we may return now to the earliest legends of Argos and to the family of Inachus. The daughter of Inachus was Io, who was loved by Zeus; she was priestess of Hera, and could not avoid detection by Hera. Zeus attempted to deceive Hera by turning Io into a white cow which Hera asked to have for herself.[40] To guard her new possession she set Argus over her. Argus, whose parentage is variously given (most probably he was Earth-born), had many eyes (the number varies from four in Aeschylus to one hundred in Ovid) and was called Argus Panoptes (the all-seeing); his eyes never all slept at once so that he could have Io under constant surveillance. Zeus therefore sent Hermes to rescue Io; Hermes lulled Argus to sleep by telling him stories and then cut off his head; hence his title Argeiphontes or slayer of Argus; Hera set Argus's eyes in the tail of the peacock, the bird with which she is especially associated. Io still could not escape Hera's jealousy; Hera sent a gadfly which so maddened her that she wandered miserably over the whole world, until finally she came to Egypt. There, by the Nile, Zeus restored her human form, and she gave birth to a son, Epaphus, whom the Egyptians identified with Apis, the sacred bull. Even now Io's wanderings were not over; Hera had the child Epaphus kidnapped, and Io set out in search of him, eventually finding him in Syria.[41]

---

[39] A daughter, Gorgophone (*phone* = slayer), is sometimes added, who becomes ancestress of Clytemnestra and Helen.

[40] According to Aeschylus, Hera herself transformed Io.

[41] This part of the legend appears to reflect the Egyptian myth of Isis's search for Osiris.

She now returned to Egypt and eventually was worshiped there as Isis.

The story of Io has many confusing elements. An Apis was said to have been a son of Phoroneus and to have given the Peloponnese its ancient name of Apia; after his death he was identified with Serapis, who is the same as the Egyptian bull-god Apis. Io was originally a goddess; she may have been a form of Hera herself. Herodotus, who himself visited Egypt, said that Isis was identified there with Demeter, whose image Io had first brought there, and also said that Isis was always represented as a woman with cow's horns (in this being similar to the great Phoenician moon-goddess, Astarte). The versions of Io's legend vary considerably; Aeschylus, for example, gives different reasons for her leaving home and her transformation in his two plays, the *Supplices* and the *Prometheus Bound,* and is inconsistent in his accounts of her wanderings. All we can say is that in this Argive legend we are dealing with a divine rather than a human heroine, and that, through Greek contacts with the East and especially with Egypt, Io has been assimilated into Egyptian mythology.

Through Epaphus Io was the founder of the royal families of Egypt and Argos, as well as of Phoenicia, Thebes, and Crete. Epaphus himself was said to have founded many cities in Egypt, including the royal city of Memphis. His daughter was Libya, who gave her name to part of north Africa; he had twin sons, Agenor and Belus, the former of whom became the Phoenician king, father of Cadmus (founder of Thebes) and Europa (mother of the Cretan king Minos). Belus stayed in Egypt and was also the father of twin sons, Aegyptus and Danaus, who, like their descendants, Proetus and Acrisius, were bitter enemies. They quarreled over the kingdom so that Danaus was compelled to leave Egypt; sailing with his fifty daughters via Rhodes he came to Argos and there peaceably established himself as king. (His subjects were called after him *Danai,* and this is the term by which Homer generally refers to the Greeks.) Now Aegyptus had fifty sons who claimed, as next of kin, to marry their cousins, and they pursued them to Argos. Danaus allowed their request and gave his daughters in marriage, but to each he gave a dagger with orders to kill her husband that night. All obeyed, save one only, Hypermnestra,[42] who spared and hid her husband Lynceus. As to the sequel, accounts vary; the most popular version, which is not recorded in the earlier authors, is that the forty-nine Danaids who obeyed their father were punished in the Underworld by eternally having to fill water jars, through which the water leaked away. According to Pindar, however, Danaus gave them as wives to the winners of an athletic contest. Hypermnestra, after a period of imprisonment by Danaus, was reunited with Lynceus and became the mother of Abas, father of Proetus and Acrisius. Thus the line of descent of the Argive kings from Inachus to Heracles remained unbroken.

One other of the Danaids has an independent legend; Amymone was once sent by her father to search for water and came upon a Satyr who attempted to seduce her. She was saved by Poseidon, who then himself lay with her and as a reward caused a spring to burst from a rock with a stroke of his trident. In historical times the spring Amymone was still shown near Argos.

The remaining Argive legends have been dealt with earlier in this book; the most important figures in the local sagas were the prophet Melampus, who became king of Argos, and the heroes who took part in the expedition of the Seven against Thebes. Among these was Tydeus, whose son Diomedes was prominent in the Trojan War and is the last great mythical prince of Argos. As we have seen, he was widely worshiped as a hero after his death; Pindar says that Athena gave him the immortality that she denied Tydeus. Finally, an important group of Argive heroes is found in the family of Heracles.

Other Peloponnesian Legends

The most significant legends of Sparta, Pylos, Arcadia, and Elis have already been dealt with. Two legends concerning the Alpheus, the river at Olympia, may be told here. The river-god loved the nymph Arethusa, a follower of Artemis.[43] As he pursued her

---

[42] Her name is also spelled *Hypermestra*.

[43] According to Telesilla, an Argive poetess of the sixth century, Alpheus loved Artemis herself.

along the riverbank, she prayed for help to Artemis, who covered her with a cloud; as the god watched the cloud, it and the nymph melted into a stream, for which Artemis cleft the earth; flowing underground, where it was united with the waters of Alpheus, and under the sea, it emerged at Syracuse in Sicily and is still called by the same name, the fountain Arethusa.

It was also by the banks of the Alpheus that a daughter of Poseidon, Evadne, secretly bore her son Iamus, whose father was Apollo, and left him there. Her foster father Aepytus, aware of Evadne's condition, inquired at Delphi about the child and learned that he would be the greatest of human seers; he returned and found the child, who had been miraculously fed on honey by two serpents, and brought him up. When he grew up, Iamus was brought by Poseidon and Apollo to Olympia, where he received the gift of prophecy. His oracle, says Pindar, was established by Heracles upon the altar of Zeus at Olympia.[44]

The Islands

Every Greek community had its own local legend and cult, and this is just as true of the Aegean islands. The islands with the most important religious cults were Delos and Samothrace; at Delos Apollo was honored, and in Samothrace the Cabiri were worshiped with mystery rituals. Delos was the home of Anius, son of Apollo, as well as his father's priest, and king of the island at the time of the Trojan War. He had three daughters, Elais (Olive girl), Spermo (Seed girl), and Oeno (Wine girl), who received from Dionysus (from whom they were also descended) the power of producing, respectively, oil, grain, and wine, at will. Agamemnon attempted to compel them to go to Troy with the Greeks and there supply the army with these essential provisions. As they resisted and tried to escape, they were turned by Dionysus into white doves; ever after doves at Delos were sacrosanct.

Ceos was the home of Cyparissus, a boy loved by Apollo. On the island was a beautiful stag, a favorite of Cyparissus; as it was resting in the woods one day, he accidentally killed it with his

---

[44] That is, divination was practiced by inspecting the entrails of sacrifices at the altar, and requests for omens were made to Iamus.

javelin. In grief at the deed he turned into a tree, the cypress, ever after called by his name and associated with mourning. Ceos is the setting, too, of the romance of Cydippe, who was loved by Acontius, a youth who was not her social equal. He put in her way an apple on which were inscribed the words, "I swear before Artemis to marry only Acontius"; she picked it up and read the words out loud, thus binding herself by the vow. Each time her parents found a suitable husband for her, she fell so ill that she could not be married; eventually the truth was revealed and she and Acontius were united.

The island of Rhodes was sacred to Helius, the Sun. When Zeus was dividing up the lands of the world among the gods, Rhodes had not yet appeared above the surface of the sea. Helius was accidentally not given a share, but refused Zeus's offer of a re-division, for he could see the future island below the sea; he took it as his possession when it appeared. There he loved the island's nymph, Rhode, and one of her seven sons became the father of the heroes of the three principal cities of Rhodes, Camirus, Ialysus, and Lindus. Even late in historical times the people of Rhodes would throw a chariot and four horses into the sea every October, as a replacement for the old chariot and horses of the Sun that would be worn out after the labors of the summer.

Rhodes was associated with several figures from sagas that we have already discussed. From Crete came Catreus and Althaemenes; from Egypt came Danaus, who visited the island on his journey to Argos and there founded the great temple of Athena at Lindus. A son of Heracles, Tlepolemus, murdered his uncle Licymnius at Tiryns and on the advice of Apollo fled to Rhodes. Rhodes was also the home of the Telchines, who were skilled craftsmen and metalworkers; they were also credited with having the evil eye and for this reason (says Ovid) were drowned by Zeus in the sea.

On the island of Lesbos lived Macareus, a son of Aeolus, ruler of the winds, whose story was told by Euripides in his lost play *Aeolus*. He fell in love with his sister Canace and by her became father of a child. When Aeolus discovered the truth he sent Canace a sword with which she killed herself; later Macareus himself committed suicide.

Asia Minor

Electra, daughter of Atlas, had two sons by Zeus, Iasion and Dardanus. On the death of Iasion (which was said by some authorities to have taken place in Samothrace), Dardanus sailed to the Troad where Teucer, son of the river-god Scamander, was king. There Dardanus married the king's daughter and built a city called by his name. On the death of Teucer, the land was called Dardania and its inhabitants (as in Homer), Dardani. From Dardanus was descended the Trojan royal house.

A late but famous story comes from the Hellespont. Leander, a young man from the city of Abydos on the Asiatic shore, loved Hero, priestess of Aphrodite in Sestos, the city on the European shore. He would swim the Hellespont each night to visit her, being guided by a light placed by her in a tower on the shore. One stormy night the lamp was extinguished, and Leander, bereft of its guidance, was drowned; his body next day was washed up on the shore near the tower, and Hero in grief threw herself from the tower and joined her lover in death.

This chapter ends with two stories (both related by Ovid) that are almost certainly not Greek in origin, although the names of the principal characters are Greek. From Phrygia comes the legend of Baucis and Philemon, a poor and pious old couple who unwittingly entertained Zeus and Hermes in their cottage. The gods, who had not been received kindly by anyone else on their visit to the earth, saved Baucis and Philemon from the flood with which they punished the rest of Phrygia; they saw their cottage become the gods' temple and, being granted each a wish, prayed that they might together be priest and priestess of the shrine and die together. And so it happened; full of years, they at the same time turned into trees, an oak and a linden.

Finally, Ovid's setting for the story of Pyramus and Thisbe is Babylon; perhaps Cilicia (a district of southern Asia Minor) is the home of the legend, for the river Pyramus was there, and the name Thisbe was variously associated with springs in Cilicia or Cyprus. Pyramus and Thisbe were next-door neighbors in Babylon, forbidden by their parents to marry or even to meet each other. They conversed through a crack in the common wall of their houses and arranged to meet at the tomb of Ninus outside the city. Thisbe arrived first and was frightened by a lioness that had come to drink in a nearby fountain. As she fled, she dropped her veil, which the lioness mangled with her jaws, bloodstained from a recent kill. Pyramus came, found the footprints of the lioness and the bloodstained veil, and concluded that the lioness had eaten Thisbe. He therefore fell on his sword; as he lay dying Thisbe returned and in grief killed herself with the same sword. They lay together in death beneath a mulberry tree, whose fruit, which before had been white, henceforward was black, in answer to Thisbe's dying prayer that it be a memorial of the tragedy.

Part III

The Survival of
Classical Mythology

CHAPTER 22

Roman Mythology

The gods and legends of Rome would require a separate book; in this chapter we can only outline some of the differences between Greek and Roman mythology and show how the native Italian myths have in very many cases succumbed to the Greek legends. The two basic differences, which account in large measure for the comparative dearth of Roman mythological material, lie in the nature of the Italian gods and in the way in which their characters and legends were perpetuated. In the first place, the Italian gods were not originally thought of in anthropomorphic terms, which is typical of Greek religion. The Greeks therefore more readily developed legends of their gods, and their mythology is far richer in legends than Italian mythology. The Roman gods were associated more with cult than with mythology. It requires more imagination than the Romans possessed to create a legend, for example, about Robigo, the goddess who prevents blight.

In the second place, it was not until a comparatively late stage in Roman history that historians and poets began to record the earliest historical events; Greece could boast a Homer and a Hesiod early in her literary history, but Rome could not. In the third century, when the first historians and epic poets began to write in the Latin language, the influence of Greek literature was already too strong for purely Italian legends to maintain an independent existence. Many of the early authors were themselves Greeks, whether writing in Greek or Latin, and this fact served to emphasize the predominance of Greek mythology. The Roman legends, then, are often adaptations of a Greek legend; often they are literary creations owing their present form to the genius of sophisticated authors (most especially of the Augustan Age), such as Vergil and Ovid, and therefore far removed from genuine myth, saga, or folk tale.

Yet we should not dismiss Roman mythology as being a mere extension of Greek mythology. Roman religion has its roots in the ancient religions of the pre-Roman Italic tribes, such as the Sabines, and in the religion of the Etruscans. Unfortunately it was a tendency in classical antiquity to equate the gods of one religion with those of another: Herodotus identifies Isis with Demeter; Caesar identifies the Celtic Sul with Minerva. As a result the great native Italian gods tended to lose their independent identities and to be equated with Greek gods—Saturnus with Cronus, Jupiter with Zeus, and so on. The poet Ennius (a south Italian, Greek by birth, but the greatest of early Latin literary geniuses), writing in the early years of the second century, named the twelve principal Roman gods and equated them with the twelve Olympians: the order in which he names them is due to the exigencies of the Latin hexameter, and does not represent their order of importance. His list, with the Greek equivalents, was:

Iuno (Hera), Vesta (Hestia), Minerva (Athena), Ceres (Demeter), Diana (Artemis), Venus (Aphrodite), Mars (Ares), Mercurius (Hermes),[1] Iovis (Zeus),[1] Neptunus (Poseidon), Vulcanus (Hephaestus), Apollo.

Of these only Apollo is truly identical with his Greek counterpart. Some of the others have gained from their Hellenization—Venus advances from a mere fertility spirit to become the great goddess underlying all growth and love; others lose by the identification— the great Italian agricultural and war deity, Mars, becomes identified with Ares, the least attractive and almost the least important of the twelve Olympians.

We cannot attempt here to cover the complex subject of Roman religion. We will give some idea of the Roman gods, however, and such legends as they have, and then we will consider the Roman equivalent of saga, that is, the legends attached to the foundation and early history of Rome.

[1] Ennius's forms of the names are given here. We shall refer to Mercury and Jupiter.

The Italian Gods

Among the gods of the Roman state, Janus takes first place; in formal prayers to the gods he was named first. He is a very ancient god, and there is no equivalent for him in other mythologies. He is principally thought of as a god who presides over beginnings, and it is in this connection that we preserve his name in the month that begins our year. It is more than likely, however, that in his earliest form he was connected with water and especially with crossing places and bridges. Thus in the city of Rome there were five shrines to Janus, all placed near crossings over the river or water courses, and he was intimately connected with the boundaries of the earliest settlements at Rome, the approaches to which involved crossing the Tiber or one of its tributary brooks. As the city expanded these early crossing places lost their importance and Janus's original functions were obscured. Yet they can be detected in later times; the gates of his shrine near the Argiletum entrance to the Forum were open in time of war and closed in time of peace. They were closed with great ceremony, for example, by Augustus, as a sign of the ending of the civil wars that had brought him to power. In the early days of Rome the bridges would have been broken when the city was threatened by an enemy; an analogy for the opening of the gates of Janus in time of war would be the raising of a drawbridge over a moat. In later times "Janus" was used not only as the name of a deity but also as a common noun (a janus), which Cicero (*De Natura Deorum*, 2. 67) defined as "a crossing place with a roadway" (*transitiones perviae iani nominantur*), in this recalling the god's early functions. While his significance as a god of bridges waned, he attracted to himself other functions; he was the god of going in and coming out, and therefore of doors, entrances, and archways, as well as of beginnings. In another form, as the youthful god Portunus, he was god of harbors (which are the entrances to lands from overseas) and ferries; in the boat race in the *Aeneid* it was with his help that the winners were successful.

There are few legends of Janus; it was said that after the Sabines under Titus Tatius had captured the Capitol they were kept from entering the Forum by jets of boiling water that Janus caused to gush forth. The only ancient statues of Janus surviving are two four-faced marble "herms" upon the parapet of the Pons Fabricius in Rome; on coins he is portrayed with two faces, for as a god of entrances and exits he could look both before and behind.

Mars (or Mavors) was much more important as an Italian deity than his equivalent in Greece, Ares. In origin he was an agricultural deity, worshiped by many Italian tribes. His association with spring, the time of regeneration and growth, is shown by naming after him the month of March, which began the Roman year under the pre-Julian calendar. As an agricultural god he is associated with a number of rural deities, such as Silvanus and Flora; the latter deity was said to have provided Juno with a magical flower, the touch of which enabled her to conceive Mars without any father. Mars sometimes has as his consort the Sabine fertility goddess Nerio, who is often identified with Minerva; in this connection Ovid tells a story of his wooing her. He asked Anna Perenna (i.e., the goddess of the year) to act as his go-between; when he came to lie with Nerio, he found on unveiling her that his bride was none other than Anna, who was old and wrinkled and thoroughly enjoyed her deception. This, says Ovid, was the origin of jokes and obscenities at marriage parties.

Just as the Roman people turned from farming to war, so Mars became a war god, until this aspect of him predominated over his agricultural character. Sacrifices were offered to him before and after a battle, and a portion of the spoils was dedicated to him; the most famous of his temples at Rome was that of Mars Ultor (Mars the Avenger) vowed by Augustus at the Battle of Philippi (42 B.C.) and dedicated forty years later. The Campus Martius (Field of Mars) was the open space outside the gates of the ancient city, where the people could assemble under arms and where they could practice their military skills. As the god of war Mars often had the title Gradivus (perhaps meaning the marcher); he was also closely associated with the Sabine war deity Quirinus, with whom Romulus was later identified. In battle Mars was generally accompanied by a number of lesser deities and personifications, of whom the war goddess Bellona is the best known.

Mars is particularly associated with two animals, the wolf and the woodpecker; it was a she-wolf that suckled the infants Romulus and Remus. The woodpecker, *picus,* was said in one legend to have been a Latin king, Picus, whose wife was the nymph Canens (Singer). One day in the woods the witch Circe tried to seduce Picus; when he rejected her she turned him into a woodpecker, and Canens, after searching in vain for him for six days and six nights, wasted away into nothing more than a voice.[2]

The great Italian sky god was Jupiter, the forms of whose name are etymologically connected with other Indo-European sky gods, such as Zeus. Very early in the history of the Roman Republic the great temple of Jupiter was built on the Capitoline Hill and the great sky god became, so to speak, localized in a temple with a statue like a Greek city god. A further Hellenization of Jupiter was his association in the Capitoline temple with Juno, the chief Italian goddess of women, and Minerva, who was an Italian fertility and war goddess but at Rome was worshiped principally as the patroness of handicrafts and wisdom. These three deities formed the "Capitoline Triad," and their triple temple was the most conspicuous religious edifice of Republican Rome. Jupiter was called by many titles; on the Capitol he was worshiped as Jupiter Optimus Maximus (The Best and Greatest), and it was to worship him that the triumphal procession celebrating a successful campaign would wind its way up from the Forum to the Capitoline temple. This was the most visible way in which Jupiter was seen as the source of Roman greatness and military might. As sky-god Jupiter was constantly concerned with Roman public life in which the weather omens of thunder and lightning, his special weapons, played an important role. After lightning had struck, a ritual purification or expiatory rite was required, and Jupiter himself was said to have given king Numa the original instructions for the sacrifice. Advised by the nymph Egeria, Numa captured the two forest divinities, Picus and Faunus, upon the Aventine Hill, and compelled them to tell him how to summon Jupiter. When Jupiter himself came, Numa asked what objects were necessary

[2] There are many variants of Picus's legend that marry him to Circe or to Pomona, or make him the father of Faunus. It is better merely to think of him as originally a woodland divinity.

for the expiatory rite; "a head," the god replied and was interrupted by Numa with "of an onion." "Of a man," Jupiter went on, and Numa added "hair"; finally Jupiter demanded "a life"—"of a fish," said Numa—and Jupiter good-naturedly agreed to have these objects (a head of an onion, human hair, and a fish) as part of the expiatory ritual.

At this same interview Jupiter promised to give Numa a sign of Rome's claim to exercise power over other communities; next day, in full view of the people of Rome, he caused a shield to fall miraculously from heaven. This was the *ancile,* and was of the archaic figure 8 shape; since it was a talisman of Roman power, Numa had eleven others made exactly like it, so that it would be all the harder for the genuine *ancile* to be stolen. The twelve *ancilia* were kept in the Regia, the official headquarters of the Pontifex Maximus, and were used by the priests of Mars, the Salii, in their sacred war dance which was performed each spring. As they danced they sang an ancient hymn, in which were the words *mamuri veturi,* whose meaning had been very early forgotten. The tradition was that the name of the craftsman who made the eleven pseudo-*ancilia* was Mamurius, and that as a reward he asked for his name to be included in the hymn.

The many titles of Jupiter, which are more the concern of the student of cult rather than mythology, indicate his supreme importance in all matters of the state's life in war and peace. As Jupiter Latiaris he was the chief god of the Latins and was worshiped by the Romans in an annual ceremony upon the Mons Albanus (the modern Monte Cavo) twenty miles from Rome. As the god before whom the most solemn oaths were sworn, he was closely associated with the goddess Fides (Good Faith), and identified with the old Sabine god Dius Fidius; the identification is shown by the fact that oaths sworn by Dius Fidius had to be sworn under the open sky (i.e., Jupiter). An obscure Latin deity, Semo Sancus (the name is from the same root as *sancire,* the Latin word for ratifying an oath), is also identified with Dius Fidius and Jupiter.

Another title of Jupiter is Indiges, by which he was worshiped near the river Numicus. The word *Indiges* has never been explained. It evidently refers to a state god, and the Di Indigetes were a well-known group of state gods, the exact role of whom remains unknown. At any rate Jupiter Indiges was believed to have been none other than the deified Aeneas, who disappeared (i.e., was transported) after a battle by the Numicus.

The second member of the Capitoline triad, Juno, originally was quite distinct from Jupiter; through the influence of Greek mythology she became the consort of Jupiter. She was in fact an independent and ancient Italian deity, who presided over every aspect of the life of women. She was especially associated with childbirth (with the title of Lucina) and marriage, and her importance for married women is indicated by the name of her chief festival, the Matronalia, which was celebrated in March (and not, as might be expected, in the goddess's own month of June). Besides her part in the Capitoline temple of Jupiter Optimus Maximus, Juno was also worshiped on the Arx (Citadel), which was a second peak of the Capitoline hill. There her title was Juno Moneta, that is Juno the Adviser (from the same root as the Latin word *monere*); the origin of this title was soon forgotten; it survived in later times and even in our language in connection with a secondary function of Juno's temple on the Arx, for it was also the *mint* at Rome.

Minerva, the third member of the Capitoline triad, is again an Italian deity, but was not worshiped at Rome as early as the other gods whom we have discussed. Her first appearance is in the Capitoline temple, which indicates that the Etruscans introduced her to Rome. Very soon she attracted Greek legends of Athena to herself, so that it is hard to distinguish her original functions, which may have been as a war goddess. Like Athena she was represented in later art as armed and she shared her great festival, the Quinquatrus, with Mars, whose consort, the Sabine goddess Nerio, is often identified with Minerva. Her chief importance for the Romans, however, was as the goddess of all activities involving mental skill; [3] she was the patroness of craftsmen and skilled workers, among whom Ovid (in his invocation to Minerva in the *Fasti*) includes authors and painters. She was also the goddess of school children, and the Quinquatrus was the time of the chief

[3] Her name is evidently connected with the Latin words for mind and remembering, *mens* and *memini*.

Roman school holidays, as well as the time for the payment of school fees.

The most important of the other Roman state gods who were of Italian origin were the two concerned with fire, Vesta and Volcanus. Vesta (whose name is etymologically identical with the Greek Hestia) was the goddess of the hearth as the center of family life. Since the State was a community of families, it too would have as the symbolic center of its life a hearth with an ever-burning fire; this fire was kept alight in the round temple of Vesta in the Roman Forum and tended by the six Vestal Virgins. These were daughters of noble families, who entered the service of Vesta as small girls (before their tenth year) and remained until their fortieth year or even longer. Their life was hedged with many tabus and rituals, and their vow of chastity was strictly observed; burial alive was the penalty for breaking it. On the other hand, the Vestals were treated with the highest honor and were among the most important personages in the whole apparatus of the state religion. Their elaborate quarters are still among the most evocative remains of the Forum; together with the Regia they formed a complex that bears vivid witness to the importance of the cult of Vesta throughout the history of pagan Rome.[4]

The cult went back almost to the beginning of Rome's history and its foundation was ascribed to Numa. Yet the myths of Vesta are few and uninteresting. Closely attached to her, however, were the household spirits of the Romans, the Penates, whose name derives from the *penus* or store cupboard, source of food and therefore symbol of the continuing life of the family. Originally the spirits on whom the life and food of the individual family depended, they became equally closely associated with the life of the state. Even the Romans were vague about their number or identity; one ancient definition of them was "all the gods who are worshiped in the home" (*omnes dii qui domi coluntur:* given by Servius on *Aeneid,* 2. 514). In origin they are undoubtedly Italian, being especially associated with the Latin town of Lavinium; in one legend, when an attempt was made to remove the Penates from

[4] The official residence of the Pontifex Maximus was also in this complex until 12 B.C., when Augustus, on becoming Pontifex Maximus, continued to live on the Palatine hill.

Lavinium to Alba Longa, they miraculously returned to their original home, where they were thenceforth left undisturbed. Roman tradition came to identify the Penates with the Trojan gods entrusted by Hector to Aeneas on the night of Troy's destruction and brought by him to Italy. From this legend it is not a long step to identify the sacred objects kept in the *penus Vestae* (i.e., the sacred repository in the temple of Vesta) with the Palladium of Troy, said to have been given by Diomedes to one of Aeneas's followers. When the temple of Vesta was burned in 241 the consul L. Caecilius Metellus earned great glory by saving the Palladium with his own hands, yet he was blinded for the act because he had looked upon a sacred object that it was not lawful for a man to see.

Vulcan (Volcanus) was the chief Italian fire deity, of greater importance than his Greek equivalent, Hephaestus. The Greek god was the god of industrial, creative fire; Vulcan was the god of destructive fire, and therefore a potent force to be worshiped in a city frequently ravaged by conflagrations.[5] With his Hellenization Vulcan acquired the more creative aspect, as his alternative name, Mulciber (he who tempers), shows. With him were associated some minor fire deities of whom one, Cacus, is the subject of a legend that we have related in connection with Heracles.

Saturn was an ancient god at Rome, perhaps of Etruscan origin. His temple dated from the early days of the Republic; beneath it was the state treasury, and no great skill in etiology is required to connect the god of the Golden Age (*Saturnia regna*) with the treasury. The origins of Saturn are extremely obscure; he was evidently an agricultural deity and his festival, the Saturnalia, celebrated on December 17th, was possibly a celebration of the winter grain sowing originally. Like many country festivals it was accompanied by a relaxation of the normal social inhibitions, and this was a prominent feature of the Saturnalia in historical times, when slaves had almost complete freedom of speech. The Saturnalia came to be linked with the festival of Ops, which was celebrated two days later, and eventually the festival period lasted for a week. Saturn was very soon identified with the Greek Cronus, and his

[5] Some years after the great fire of 64 A.D., for example, the emperor Domitian had an altar to Vulcan set up in each of the fourteen districts of the city.

myths and symbols are indistinguishable from those of his Greek counterpart. Rhea, the Greek consort of Cronus, was identified with the Italian goddess of plenty, Ops, who was the partner of Saturn in popular mythology; his partner in cult, however, was another and more obscure Italian deity, Lua. In the cult of Ops her partner was Consus, an Italian harvest deity; he was honored with a festival, in August and December, the Consualia, and Livy tells us that the rape of the Sabine women took place at the games held during the Consualia.

It will by now have become clear that agricultural deities were very prominent in early Roman religion; we have so far considered Mars and Saturnus and their associates, and we may now mention a number of other Italian deities connected with the fertility of the land. One such deity was the grain goddess Ceres; her cult at Rome went back at least to the earliest days of the Roman Republic, when in 493 a temple was dedicated on the Aventine to her, with Liber and Libera. Liber likewise was an old Italian god and became associated with the vine; it was natural for him to be identified with Dionysus, and Ceres with Demeter, while his Italian cult partner, Libera, became identified with Kore (i.e., Persephone, Demeter's daughter). Thus the Eleusinian triad of Demeter, Kore, and Iacchus/Bacchus had its exact counterpart at Rome. The mythology of Ceres and Liber is entirely Hellenized; it is worth noting, however, that the wine-god Liber did not share in the ecstatic aspects of Dionysus. For example, in the notorious suppression of the Bacchanalia in 186, we find no mention of Liber either in the senate's decree or in Livy's account of the episode. The Aventine temple of Ceres, Liber, and Libera was also important as a political and commercial center; it was a center of plebeian activity, being especially concerned with the plebeian aediles and tribunes, and in front of it was the headquarters of the state-subsidized grain supply (*statio annonae*).

Also associated with Ceres was the Italian earth goddess, Tellus Mater, with whom she shared the festival of the sowing of the seed (*feriae sementivae*) in January. Thus the grain was watched over from seed to granary by three divinities—Ceres before it is sown; Tellus Mater when it is put in the earth; Consus when it is harvested and stored.

Not far removed from these deities are Flora and Pomona. The former of these is the goddess of flowering—not only of flowers in general, but especially of the flowering of grain and of the vine. We have already related her part in the birth of Mars; in Ovid she is the consort of the West Wind, Zephyrus. Pomona is also an ancient but obscure goddess, whose realm was fruit that could be picked from trees. Ovid has a romantic and late story linking her with Vertumnus, an obscure Etruscan deity whose functions are unknown; his name, however, is linked with the Latin word *vertere* (to change). In the story he loved Pomona and, changing himself into an old woman, advised her to marry Vertumnus with such eloquence that when he resumed his normal form she accepted him.

The deities who presided over the livestock of the farm were called Pales; originally a pair, their name was later used for one deity, either male or female. The festival of Pales, the Parilia (or Palilia) was celebrated in April and for an unknown reason was also considered to be the anniversary of the foundation of Rome.

Moving away from the farm we find two Italian gods of the woods and forests, Silvanus (the forester) and Faunus (the favorer). The former was popular at Rome and was sometimes associated with Mars, but had no official cult or temple. He was the god who especially would need propitiating when a forest was being cleared or trees felled. Faunus has more mythological significance, although he is sometimes confused with Silvanus. In Vergil, Faunus is made the son of Picus and grandson of Saturn, and the father of Latinus by the obscure Italian birth goddess, Marica. This is a later development, for originally Faunus is a woodland spirit, occasionally mischievous but generally favorable (as his name implies) to the farmer who worshiped him. His consort (or daughter) was Fauna, who was identified with the Bona Dea (the good goddess), a divinity worshiped only by women and in reality the feminine form of the male deity, Faunus. Not surprisingly, both Faunus and Silvanus were identified with the Arcadian pastoral god, Pan; Faunus and Fauna were further identified with minor gods of woodland sounds because they were considered responsible for strange and sudden forest noises. Thus, in Livy, the night after a closely fought battle against the Etruscans, the Romans heard Silvanus (whom Livy here confuses with Faunus) cry out from a nearby forest that they had won the victory, with the result that the Etruscans acknowledged defeat and returned home. Faunus was credited also with oracular powers; Latinus consulted him about the prodigies that accompanied the arrival of Aeneas in Italy, and Numa received advice from him in a time of famine.

Faunus was officially worshiped at Rome, where there was a temple to him on the Tiber island. His own festival was in December, but he was closely connected with the more famous festival of the Lupercalia, which took place in February. The Arcadian king, Evander, was said to have come to Rome and there to have founded the first settlement upon the Palatine hill. On the side of the hill is a cave, the Lupercal, where the she-wolf (*lupa*) was said later to have suckled Romulus and Remus, and here in former times Evander worshiped his Arcadian god, Pan, who (as we have seen) was the equivalent of Faunus. Faunus was therefore connected with the Lupercalia, the central feature of which was a sacrifice in the Lupercal, at which two young noblemen were smeared with the victims' blood. They were called the *luperci,* and after the sacrifice they ran nearly naked around the boundary of the Palatine, striking those women whom they met with leather straps; barren women, it was believed, became fertile by this act.

Ovid relates a Greek folk tale explaining the nudity of the Luperci. Hercules (to give him his Latin name) and the Lydian queen, Omphale, came once to a cave and there exchanged clothes while supper was being prepared. After the meal they went to sleep, still each in the other's clothes. Meanwhile Faunus (in Greek he would have been Pan) had seen Omphale and determined to seduce her. He entered the cave and proceeded to lie with the person dressed as a girl; his reception was far from warm, and ever after he ordered his followers (i.e., the Luperci) to be naked at his cult, to prevent the repetition of so painful a mistake.

A minor Italian fertility god, who became a great Roman goddess through Hellenization, was Venus. Her original functions are obscure, and she was worshiped in a number of places under titles that indicate that she had as much to do with luck and the favor of the gods as with beauty and fertility. She seems, however, to have been particularly the protector of gardens, and her name has been taken to indicate the neat appearance of a well-kept garden. Her official worship at Rome began in 215 during the Punic Wars on the advice of the Sibylline books; no one has yet satisfactorily explained how she came to be identified with the great Greek goddess of love, Aphrodite. Aphrodite herself had a famous shrine at Eryx in Sicily; her influence may have spread from there and have led to the transformation of Venus. At any rate, by the end of the Republic Lucretius (writing around 55) could begin his poem, *On the Nature of Things,* with an eloquent invocation to Venus as the creative principle of life, and at about the same time Pompey could dedicate a temple to her as the bringer of victory (*Venus Victrix*). With the success of Julius Caesar and the establishment of the principate by Augustus, Venus became one of the greatest of the state gods because the family of the Julii traced its ancestry back to her. Julius Caesar dedicated a temple to her in his forum; Vergil gave her a prominent part in the *Aeneid;* finally, more than a century later, Hadrian dedicated Rome's most magnificent temple to the two goddesses, Venus and Rome.

Another group of ancient Italian divinities of importance to the early Italian farmer are the water gods. Each river and spring had its deity who would need to be propitiated by offerings—Horace's *fons Bandusiae* was propitiated by the sacrifice of a kid; the Tiber by the annual offering of twenty-seven straw dummies called *Argei.*[5] The Italians did not, however, have a sea god of their own. Neptunus (Neptune), who was identified with the Greek sea god Poseidon, was originally a fresh-water divinity whose festival occurred in July, when the hot Italian summer was at its driest. Of the river gods the most important for the Romans was Tiberinus, god of the Tiber; we have seen already in our discussion of Janus how important a religious matter the bridging of a river was at Rome, and it may be (as most ancient and modern scholars have believed) that the Latin word for a priest, *pontifex,* really means bridge builder. At any rate, the chief

[5] The ceremony of the Argei is the cause of unlimited controversy; the explanation given here is but one of many theories.

public ceremony concerned with the Tiber, that of the Argei, was attended by the great dignitaries of the state religion, the *pontifices* and the Vestal Virgins.

Springs of running water were each under the protection of a minor deity, identical with the Greek nymphs. In the Forum at Rome was the spring of Juturna, who in Vergil appears as the sister of Turnus and the object of Jupiter's love; as a reward Jupiter had made her more important than other Latin water nymphs. In Rome she was worshiped at shrines in the Forum and in the Campus Martius, and in Imperial times the headquarters of the city's water administration was in her precinct. She was important enough, at any rate, to have a feast of her own (the Juturnalia) and to be associated in myth with a number of deities —Jupiter, Juno, and the Dioscuri (Castor and Pollux) whose temple was next to her precinct.

Outside the Porta Capena at Rome was a spring and a small park dedicated to the Camenae, water nymphs of great antiquity but vague origin. Later they were identified with the Greek Muses who, it will be recalled, were associated with various springs. It was from the fountain of the Camenae that the Vestals drew water for the purification of the temple of Vesta. Closely associated with the spring of the Camenae was the nymph Egeria, said to have been the counselor and consort of Numa to whom so much of Roman religious custom was ascribed. Egeria is also found in the precinct of Diana at Aricia, and her spring was one of those that fed Lake Nemi; she was believed to be able to help pregnant women and may indeed have been a birth goddess. Another nymph associated with the Camenae is Carmentis (or Carmenta), who also has the double association with water and with birth. As water nymph she shared the festival of Juturna; some authors make her the mother of the first settler at the site of Rome, Evander. Like the Parcae (the Roman birth goddesses identified with the three Fates, the Greek Moirae) she had prophetic powers, and this is indicated by her name, for *carmen* means a song or prophetic utterance.

The Italian goddess Diana was worshiped at Aricia near Lake Nemi; the ancient cult had considerable political importance in the days of the Latin league, before Rome came to dominate the area. It is famous in modern times because it is the starting point for Sir James Frazer's *The Golden Bough;* the priest of Diana was a fugitive slave, who had the title of "King of the Grove" (*Rex nemorensis*). He became priest by killing his predecessor in single combat, having challenged him by plucking a bough from a sacred tree; as priest he always went armed, watching for his challenger and would-be murderer. In fact, as Frazer's critics have pointed out, the cult of Diana and the *rex nemorensis* were probably not originally connected at all; the sacred grove was, in this interpretation, an asylum for runaway slaves and the sacred bough no more than the branch usually carried by suppliants at an altar. The nature of Diana, then, is not explained by the cult at Aricia; it is true, however, that Lake Nemi was known as "Diana's mirror," and this has been used as evidence for Diana's being originally a moon goddess (the moon reflected in the waters of the lake). She was, too, a goddess intimately concerned with the affairs of women (especially childbirth), as a number of dedications at Aricia show. She was also worshiped with an important cult in Campania, at Mt. Tifata near Capua; since this was an area where Greek influence was strong, it is possible that the Greek Artemis began to be identified here with Diana and to bring to her not only the attributes that they already shared but also her powers as goddess of the hunt and (as Hecate) her association with the Underworld. At Rome she was worshiped from early days upon the Aventine Hill, that is, outside the early city's walls, and was especially honored by women and slaves. With the increase in Apollo's prestige under Augustus, Diana (as the equivalent of Artemis and sister of Apollo) also gained; the importance of the pair in state cult is dramatically expressed in Horace's *Carmen Saeculare.*

We have already mentioned that the resurrected Hippolytus was identified at Aricia with a minor Italian divinity, Virbius, and associated with Diana. Who Virbius originally was is unknown; nor can we tell how he came to be associated with Diana. Vergil explains the tabu on horses at Aricia by the death of Hippolytus (dragged by his horses), but this is etiology rather than genuine mythology.

The god Mercurius (Mercury) was early worshiped at Rome as a god of trading and profit (the Latin word *merces* means merchandise), and his temple was therefore by the Circus Maximus in the busiest commercial center of Rome. He appears as a character in Plautus's play *Amphitryon* and in the prologue describes himself still as the god of commerce and gain; as he came to be identified with the Greek Hermes, however, he acquired Hermes's other functions—musician, messenger of Jupiter, and escorter of the dead.

We have already seen something of the Roman idea of the Underworld and its system of rewards and punishments. This conception, which is found principally in Vergil, is largely a literary one, a sophisticated creation put together from different philosophical, religious, and literary sources, most of them Greek. The native Italian ideas of the Underworld and its spirits are more primitive and have their origin, once again, in the simple religion of the early agricultural communities. Here the propitiation of the spirits of the dead ancestors of the family was commemorated by the ancient festival of the Parentalia that took place from February 13th to 21st (which in the old Roman calendar was the last month of the year). During this period no one would get married, the temples were closed, and offerings would be made to the spirits by the head of the family as a guarantee of their friendliness to the family in the ensuing year. The whole festival was a private, family affair; there were no named gods (and therefore no mythology attached to the cult). A related, yet very different, festival was the Lemuria, celebrated on May 9th, 11th, and 13th, when the head of the family would propitiate the Lemures, spirits who could do great harm to the household if not propitiated. The ceremony was conducted by night with a certain amount of magic ritual—the *paterfamilias* was barefoot, his fingers and thumb forming an "O," his hands ritually washed before he threw behind him black beans for the Lemures to pick up, while uttering nine times a formula to drive the spirits from the house.

Ovid identifies (or confuses) the Lemures with the Manes, who in Imperial times are synonymous with the dead. They again have no individual identity, but each man has his Manes; from the first century B.C. onwards, epitaphs would begin with *Dis Manibus Sacrum* (sacred to the divine Manes of . . .) followed by the person's name.

The Manes and the apparatus of the Parentalia and the Lemuria involve no mythology or legend and are far removed from the elaborate structure of the Underworld that we find in Vergil and other authors. Roman religion owed this to Greek and Etruscan sources, and it is not possible always to distinguish between the two. Certainly from the Etruscans came the custom of propitiating the dead by an offering of human blood spilled on the earth, and this is the origin of the gladiatorial games, which were first celebrated at Rome in 264 at the funeral games for Decimus Junius Brutus. The Etruscans shared with the Greeks many Underworld divinities, such as Charon and Persephone, while adding some of their own, such as the demon Tuculcha. The Underworld itself in Roman literature is commonly called Orcus (sometimes personalized as a god) and its ruler was Dis Pater, whose name (Dis = *dives*) is but a literal translation of the Greek Pluto (wealth). The worship of Dis Pater was established at Rome in 249, although he was certainly known there long before. He and Proserpine shared a cult at an underground altar in the Campus Martius; the precinct was called Tarentum (the etymology of the name is still unexplained), and the cult was associated with the great festival of the Secular Games. The altar was said to have been miraculously discovered by a certain Valesius (or Valerius) at a depth of twenty feet below the ground; since our chief source for the legend is called Valerius, and since the foundation of the Secular Games is attributed to a consul Valerius, we must suspect the legend of Valesius as being invented to glorify the family of the Valerii rather than being a genuine saga. Finally, the burial goddess Libitina, whose name, origin, and associations have never been satisfactorily explained, was used by the later poets as synonymous with Death.

We have mentioned the *Penates* in our discussion of Vesta and have seen how intimately they were connected with the life of the Roman family. Another group of divinities with whom the Penates are often linked was the Lares. The origin of those gods and the etymology of their names are subjects of endless controversy; they have been identified with spirits of the dead, particularly of ancestors, but this theory is almost certainly wrong. Rather the Lares should be thought of as household spirits in origin who, in the agricultural community, could bring prosperity and happiness to the farmer and his farm. This agricultural origin remained visible for centuries in the festival of the Compitalia (crossroads festival), a winter feast celebrated when the labor on the farm had been completed; a crossroads, in the primitive communities, was regularly the meeting point of the boundaries of four farms, and the Lares honored at the Compitalia were the protecting spirits of the farms. At each crossroads was a shrine, with one opening corresponding to each property whose boundary was there; at the festival the farmer would hang in the shrine a doll for each free member of his household and a ball of wool for each slave. Although it is easy to explain this ritual as an offering of substitutes for the lives of members of the household, it has been much more plausibly suggested that this is a purification ritual at the end of the farmer's labor, where the substitutes for the human beings are hung up to be purified by the air.

The Lares, then, are basically kindly spirits, protecting the household. Transferred from farm to city, they kept this function; each house had its *Lar familiaris* to whom offerings of incense and wine and garlands would be made. In Plautus's play *Aulularia* the *Lar familiaris* speaks the prologue and describes how he can bring happiness and prosperity, if he is duly worshiped; if he is neglected, the household will not prosper. Just as each household had its Lar, so the city had its Lares (called the *Lares praestites* or guardian Lares), who were worshiped on May 1st; their cult, however, was not as important as that of the Penates. Finally, Lares, with appropriate titles, were worshiped as protectors of different activities—for example, marching or making a sea voyage.

One other household spirit should be mentioned before we leave the native Italian divinities; this is the Genius, which represented the creative power of a man. The creative aspect is seen most especially in the *lectus genialis* or marriage bed, symbol of the continuing life of the family. The Genius, however, came to be associated more generally with the continued well-being of the family, and in this respect the Genius of the head of the family was pre-eminent; slaves swore oaths by his Genius and offerings were made to it on his birthday. The woman's counterpart to a man's Genius was her Juno, but its exact meaning and development is hard to ascertain, and the matter lies outside the scope of this chapter.

We may complete this discussion of the gods of Rome by reviewing the foreign deities who had an important place in Roman religion. In most cases they come from Greece or the East, and in many cases we can actually date their arrival.

The earliest newcomer was the Greek Heracles, called Hercules at Rome; Livy says that when Romulus founded the city the cult of Hercules was the only foreign one that he accepted. We have seen how Hercules visited Rome with the cattle of Geryon and there killed the monster Cacus. To commemorate the event his cult was established, either by Hercules himself or by Evander, in the Forum Boarium (the cattle market between the Circus Maximus and the Tiber). His precinct there was the Ara Maxima (the Great Altar), and the cult was in the hands of two noble families until 312, when it was taken over by the State. The Forum Boarium area was a natural landing place from the Tiber; it and the Circus Maximus area were the earliest commercial quarters at Rome, and Hercules was especially worshiped as the patron of traders. He also, like Mercury, was a bringer of luck (responsible for chance finds) and of profit, so that successful traders would on occasion dedicate a tithe of their profits to him. Various stories are told of him at Rome, which we omit here; his popularity is attested to by the fact that besides the Ara Maxima there were at least twelve shrines or temples dedicated to him in the city.

Very early in the Republic the worship of the Dioscuri, Castor and Pollux, was introduced at Rome; their appearance at the battle of Lake Regillus (probably in 496) led to the dedication of a temple in the Forum to them twelve years later (its official name was the Temple of Castor). In the battle against the Latins the Romans were being hard pressed, when the Dioscuri appeared before them on horseback and led them to victory. They then appeared in the Roman Forum and announced the victory; hot from the battle they watered their horses at the Fountain of Juturna and then vanished. The appearance of the Dioscuri in battle is fairly common in ancient legend—they had been seen, for example at the sixth century battle of the Sagra, in south Italy, between the Locrians and men of Croton; they appeared at other battles, it was said, in later Roman history. Their connection with Juturna, however, is obscure, as is that with the Penates in the

Temple of Vesta, with whom they were sometimes identified in antiquity. It has been clearly established that they came to Rome from the Greek cities of southern Italy (perhaps from Tarentum) after a period as important deities at Tusculum, a Latin city near Lake Regillus. At Rome they were especially the patrons of horsemen and of the knights (that is, the next highest class in Roman society after the senators); as a final note we may add that only women swore by them (the oath was *ecastor*).

An even older arrival in Rome than the Dioscuri were the Sibylline oracles, which were traditionally associated with the Greek colony of Cumae. Collections of oracles written in Greek hexameters were common throughout the Greek world and were especially associated with the Sibyls, prophetesses said to be inspired by Apollo. One such Sibyl was at Cumae and was said to have been granted a life of one thousand years by Apollo, but without the compensation of eternal youth. She appears as Aeneas's guide in the Underworld and in the following legend of the arrival of the Sibylline Books at Rome. She mysteriously appeared at Rome before the last king, Tarquinius Superbus, and offered to sell him nine books of oracles for a high price; when he refused she burned three of the books and offered the remaining six at the same price. Again he refused, and again she burned three books and offered the last three at the same price. This time Tarquin, on the advice of the augurs (an important group of priests), bought the books, and the Sibyl disappeared after handing them over. The books were stored in the Capitoline temple of Jupiter and were consulted only on the orders of the senate for guidance in times of calamity and perplexity or during a pestilence or after the appearance of disturbing prodigies. The priests who had charge of them—two at first then ten, then, in the last century B.C., fifteen—were men of distinction. The books were considered so important that after the great Capitoline fire of 83 had destroyed them, a new collection was made, which Augustus later deposited in the base of the statue of Apollo in his new temple upon the Palatine hill. The political importance of the Sibylline books lies outside the scope of this chapter; in religion they are significant, firstly, as an example of an early Greek influence at Rome (coming, it is true, by way of the Etruscans, for Tarquinius was an Etruscan); secondly, for the introduction of new cults that they advised —for example, those of Ceres, Liber, and Libera in 496 and of Apollo in 433.

Apollo—the only one of the great Greek gods not to change his name at Rome—arrived as the result of a pestilence, and his temple was dedicated two years after the Sibylline books had been consulted, in 431. Until the time of Augustus this remained his only temple at Rome, and except for his cult under Augustus and to a lesser extent under Nero, he never achieved such prominence at Rome as his importance in the Greek world might have suggested. He was worshiped originally as Apollo Medicus (corresponding to his Greek title of Paean, the Healer), and it was only much later that his other attributes and interests were introduced; it was in 212 that the Ludi Apollinares, an annual festival, were instituted, and these for the first time broadened the popularity of the god. Augustus had a special regard for Apollo and in 28 dedicated to him a magnificent new temple on the Palatine hill, but this effort to make him a rival to the great Capitoline deities did not outlast the reign of Augustus, who died in 14 A.D. Apollo was too uncompromisingly Greek to become a permanent favorite of the Roman people.

With Apollo we complete our discussion of Ennius's twelve Olympians; a formal indication of the pre-eminence of these twelve Greek gods was the *lectisternium* of 217, when for the first time the twelve were so honored. A *lectisternium* was a public ceremony at which images of gods were laid on couches (two to a couch) and a feast set before them. Such ceremonies had been held from early times—Livy records the first in 399—but the ceremony of 217 was the first in which the supremacy of the Greek myths was so openly acknowledged. From then on, with the development of Roman literature based on Greek models, we can see the increasing domination of Roman mythology by Greek legends.

Two other newcomers to Rome should be mentioned. In 293, again during an epidemic, the Sibylline books counseled the bringing to Rome from Epidaurus of the Greek god of healing, Asclepius. He came in the form of a sacred serpent; when the ship bringing him came up the Tiber to Rome, the serpent slipped onto the island that is in the middle of the present-day city, and there made its home. A temple to Aesculapius (his Latin name) was built on the island and his cult established.

In another period of distress and doubt, the second Punic War, the Sibylline books in 205 again counseled the bringing of a foreign deity if Hannibal were to be driven out of Italy. This was the Phrygian mother goddess, Cybele, known also at Rome as the Magna Mater (Great Mother). A solemn embassy, after a visit to Delphi, went to the city of Pessinus in Phrygia and there was given a black stone, which was said to be the goddess. It was brought to Rome with much ceremony; a temple was built and games (the festival of the Megalensia) were instituted in honor of Cybele. The ferocity and ecstatic nature of her worship was hardly abated at Rome; Roman citizens for many years were forbidden to become her votaries (her priests were "Galli" who practiced, among other things, self-castration), but the annual festival and its processions remained a colorful and popular feature of the Roman calendar.

With Cybele we may suitably end our discussion of the Roman gods. Other eastern gods continued to make their way to Rome —Isis from Egypt, Ma from Asia Minor, Baal from Syria, Mithras from Persia—and helped destroy what remained of Roman religion. But an account of their coming, and of the spread of Christianity, lies outside the bounds of classical mythology, to which we now return with a survey of the legends of the founding and early history of Rome.

The native gods of Rome, as we have seen, can be traced in cult rather than in literature. It is different with the legends of early Rome, which are recorded for us in the writings of sophisticated authors, who were deeply influenced by Greek literature. The most important of these for our purpose are Livy, Vergil, and Ovid, all of whom lived under Augustus (his reign was from 27 B.C. to 14 A.D.); when we remember that Augustus, the second founder of Rome, encouraged an interest in the "founding fathers" of Rome and in her early customs and virtues, we realize that the legends that we have are very different from the genuine sagas of the Greeks. All the same, these legends are famous, however artificial they may be, and therefore deserve to be related.

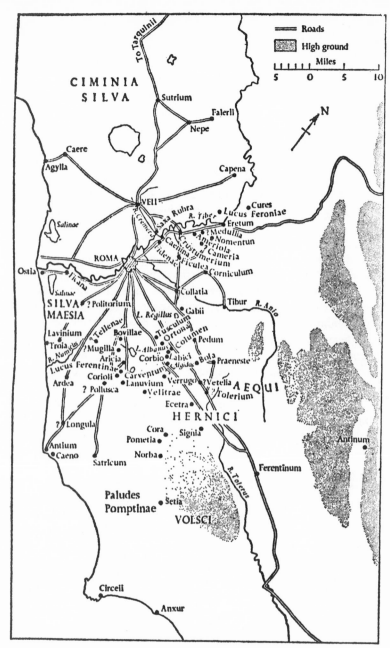

Fig. 18. *The Campagna. From R. M. Ogilvie,* A Commentary on Livy, Books 1–5 *(Oxford: Clarendon Press, 1965).*

The origins of Rome perplexed ancient scholars as much as they perplex modern researchers. Traditionally her roots went back to Aeneas, whose son Iulus was ancestor of the *gens Iulia,* the family of Augustus. But Aeneas left Troy some 475 years before the traditional date for the founding of Rome in 753; in the tradition, then, Aeneas reached Italy and established his men in Latium but soon died; his son founded the city of Alba Longa and it was from there that Romulus came to found Rome itself. Roman legend fills in the gap with a line of kings at Alba Longa. In fact, the earliest settlement at Rome may plausibly date from not long before the traditional date of 753, and it is known that early Rome was not one city, but an alliance of villages on the different hills by the Tiber, which in time were unified. The city, as it became, was sometimes under the control of surrounding peoples (the Tarquins, the fifth and seventh kings of Rome, were Etruscans), but by the early part of the fifth century it was strong enough to be independent and to extend its authority over surrounding Etruscan, Sabine, and Latin tribes, whose customs and gods it often absorbed. The legendary connection between Rome and Alba Longa is historically tenable; that between Rome and Troy is more obscure, despite the persistence of legends that connected Italy and the peoples of Asia Minor.

Aeneas, prince of the junior branch of the Trojan royal house and son of Aphrodite and Anchises, left Troy on the night of its fall and fled to Mt. Ida, taking with him his young son Ascanius (also called Iulus) and his father; his wife Creusa perished in the sack. On Mt. Ida he gathered enough men to build some ships and set sail, looking for a land in which to found a new Troy. The story of his journey is full of variations that cannot now be reconciled. His arrival in Italy is an old tradition; it was recorded by the fifth-century Greek historian, Hellanicus, and seems to have been generally accepted by Greek writers. Various traditions connected him with shrines of Aphrodite in the Aegean and Mediterranean islands. More significant are the Roman literary traditions as exemplified by the historians Cato the Elder and Livy, and in the early epics of Naevius and Ennius. In Vergil's *Aeneid* the legend of Aeneas finds its most developed form.

According to Vergil, Aeneas sailed by way of Thrace and Delos

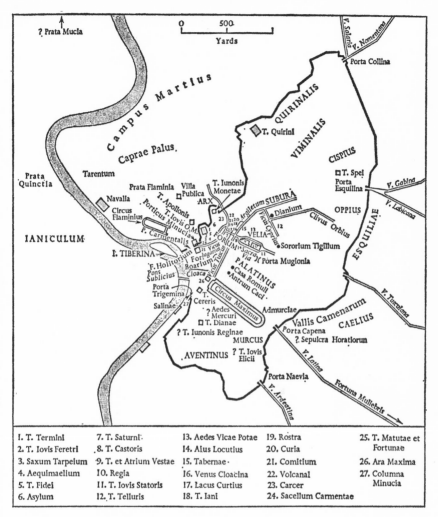

I. T. Termini	7. T. Saturni·	13. Aedes Vicae Potae	19. Rostra	25. T. Matutae et
2. T. Iovis Feretri	8. T. Castoris	14. Aius Locutius	20. Curia	Fortunae
3. Saxum Tarpeium	9. T. et Atrium Vestae	15. Tabernae·	21. Comitium	26. Ara Maxima
4. Aequimaelium	10. Regia	16. Venus Cloacina	22. Volcanal	27. Columna
5. T. Fidei	11. T. Iovis Statoris	17. Lacus Curtius	23. Carcer	Minucia
6. Asylum	12. T. Telluris	18. T. Iani	24. Sacellum Carmentae	

Fig. 19. Rome. From R. M. Ogilvie, A Commentary on Livy, Books 1–5 *(Oxford: Clarendon Press, 1965).*

to Crete, where he stayed a year, believing that this was the place from which Dardanus came and that therefore it was the future home foretold him by the oracle at Delos. But a pestilence and a vision of the Penates led him to sail on again in search of Italy, which proved to be Dardanus's original home. He sailed to Epirus, where Helenus and Andromache had settled; here Helenus foretold some of his future wanderings, and in particular told of their ending, which Aeneas would know had come when he saw on a river bank in Italy a white sow with thirty piglets. This prophecy complemented one that Aeneas had received from the Harpy, Celaeno, who had foretold that he would reach Italy and would only found his new city when hunger had compelled the Trojans to eat the tables upon which their food lay.

Leaving Helenus Aeneas reached Sicily, sailing past the shore of southern Italy and avoiding the perils of Charybdis. A direct link with Odysseus was provided by the appearance of one of his men, Achaemenides, a survivor of the adventure with the Cyclopes, who warned Aeneas of Polyphemus and other dangers. It was in Sicily, too, that Anchises died and was buried.

After setting sail from Sicily, Aeneas's fleet was scattered by a storm; the survivors were reunited in northern Africa, where Dido, queen of Carthage, hospitably received them. She fell deeply in love with Aeneas, who would himself have been content to stay with her, had not Mercury appeared to him and bidden him sail away to fulfil his destiny in Italy. At his departure Dido laid a curse on Aeneas and his descendants that they should always be the enemies of Carthage, and then stabbed herself with the sword that Aeneas had given her.

Meanwhile Aeneas sailed back to Sicily and was welcomed by the king of Egesta, the Trojan Acestes. Here he celebrated funeral games in honor of Anchises, during which the Trojan women set fire to some of the ships, the rest being saved by Jupiter in a miraculous rainstorm.[6] Aeneas left some of his followers behind in Sicily and now sailed on to Italy where he reached Cumae; here the Sibyl foretold the wars he must fight in the new land and escorted him to the Underworld, where he talked with many of the dead and most especially with Anchises, who foretold the greatness of Rome and showed Aeneas a pageant of future Romans. The visit to the Underworld is the turning point in Aeneas's saga;

[6] The ships are later turned into sea nymphs, after the landing in Italy, by Cybele.

after it he is sure of his destiny and determined to settle in Italy, whatever obstacles must be surmounted.

From Cumae Aeneas sailed to the mouth of the Tiber, where the prophecy of Celaeno was fulfilled; as the Trojans ate the flat cakes upon which their food was placed, Iulus said, "Why, we are even eating our tables." In Latium, king Latinus had betrothed his daughter, Lavinia, to the prince of the tribe of the Rutuli, Turnus. Worried by prodigies, Latinus consulted the oracle of Faunus, who advised him to give Lavinia to a foreigner instead. Latinus attempted to obey this advice by giving Lavinia to Aeneas, but Juno intervened and urged Lavinia's mother, Amata, and Turnus to oppose Aeneas. War became inevitable, and Latinus was left unhappily in the middle. Turnus and the Latins, with other Italian leaders (notably the Etruscan exile, Mezentius), opposed the Trojans, who had for allies the Etruscans under Tarchon and the men of Pallanteum, Evander's city on the future site of Rome. (Aeneas's visit to Evander had been preceded by a vision of the river god Tiberinus, which led to the finding of the white sow and her thirty piglets. Evander himself showed Aeneas the city that was to become Rome and sent back with him his own son, Pallas, who later was killed by Turnus.) The fighting was hard and bloody; in the end Aeneas and Turnus met in single combat and Turnus was killed. At this point the *Aeneid* ends.

Peace was now made; Aeneas married Lavinia and with her settled in Lavinium, a historical town that appears to be identical with the mythical Laurentum (Cato calls the town Laurolavinium), while the Latins gave their name to the combined peoples. Three years later Aeneas died (or rather was transported) while fighting against the Etruscans near the river Numicus, where he was worshiped as Jupiter Indiges.

The legend as given here is chiefly that of the Roman poets. The early historian Cato has Latinus grant Aeneas some territory and the hand of Lavinia, but a quarrel broke out between the Latins (who are also called the Aborigines) and the Trojans, and in the following year both Latinus and Turnus (who came to help the Aborigines) were killed, and Aeneas disappeared from sight. Mezentius, in this version, continued the war against Iulus, by whom he was eventually killed. Iulus then ruled over Laurolavinium; thirty years after the arrival of the Trojans in Italy he left Laurolavinium and founded Alba Longa. Livy also attributes the foundation of Alba Longa to Iulus; as we have already seen, the basis for this legend is the need to reconcile two mutually exclusive legends, those of Aeneas and of Romulus.

Ovid tells a legend of how Anna, Dido's sister, came to Italy after various vicissitudes and was there welcomed by Aeneas. But Lavinia was jealous of her, and Anna, warned by a vision of Dido's ghost, left Lavinium and disappeared in the river Numicus, becoming a goddess, Anna Perenna. The story may be genuine, but the identification of Anna of Carthage with the Roman year goddess is totally false.

The Romans filled in the gap between Iulus and Romulus with a line of kings of Alba Longa. The last of these was Amulius, who had usurped the throne from his brother Numitor. Numitor's daughter was Rhea Silvia, also called Ilia, whom Amulius attempted to keep from marriage by making her a Vestal Virgin. Mars loved her, however, and she bore him twin sons; Amulius made away with Rhea, but the boys were put in an ark and exposed in the Tiber. Miraculously they were brought to land near the Palatine hill and there found by a she-wolf, who suckled them. Thus they were saved. Later one of Amulius's shepherds, Faustulus, found them and brought them to his home, where he and his wife, Acca Larentia, brought them up.[7] When they were grown up and already distinguished for their strength and skill, Remus was captured by Numitor's shepherds in a quarrel; he was brought before Numitor, but his punishment was prevented by the appearance of Romulus, to whom Faustulus had told the story of the twins' rescue. So father and sons recognized each other, and together they brought about the death of Amulius and the restoration of Numitor to the throne of Alba. Romulus and Remus preferred to leave Alba and found their own city by the site of their miraculous rescue from the Tiber.

We have frequently met with the theme of fraternal rivalry—Amulius and Numitor here, Atreus and Thyestes in Greece, to

[7] Faustulus and Acca are originally divine figures; the former is identified with Faunus. Acca presents many problems; the late story that makes her the wife of the shepherd conveniently solves a number of difficulites.

name but two examples. The same motif now appears in the story of Romulus and Remus; rivalry over the founding of the city led to the death of one brother. To decide which should give his name to the city, Romulus and Remus resorted to augury, that is, the taking of omens from the flight of birds. Romulus watched for his omen from the Palatine hill, Remus from the Aventine, and it was to Remus that the first omen, six vultures, appeared, only to be followed by twelve appearing to Romulus. In the ensuring quarrel as to whether the winner was he who saw more birds or he who saw the omen first, Remus was killed; Romulus gave his name to the new city of Rome and became its king.

A more famous version, however, of Remus's death is also given by Livy. Romulus was the winner in the augury and began to build his city on the Palatine. When the walls had risen a little way Remus scornfully leaped over them and was killed by his brother for what was in essence the act of an enemy—for a friend enters a city by the gate.[8]

Romulus now set about establishing his kingdom and laying the foundations of Rome's political structure. He was especially concerned with increasing the population, which he did in the first place by declaring the area between the two parts of the Capitoline hill an *asylum* (that is, a sanctuary where any man could be assured of freedom from violence or prosecution). To this place men came from many directions to become Rome's future citizens. There was a shortage of women, however, and attempts to remedy this situation led to a long series of incidents involving the Romans and the Sabines.

In the first place, the surrounding tribes refused requests from Roman embassies for young women as wives for Roman men. Romulus decided therefore to use deceit and force; men and women from the Sabine tribes were invited to attend the festival games of the Consualia, and at a given signal the Roman men seized the young Sabine women, whose relatives fled. Such an act could not go unavenged, and the Sabines under the leadership of Titus Tatius organized themselves for war on the Romans. In the

[8] Ovid relieves Romulus of part of the guilt by making one of his followers the murderer.

first encounter Romulus killed the king of the Sabine town of Caenina and dedicated his armor to Jupiter Feretrius (perhaps Jupiter "to whom one brings"). This was the first of only three occasions in the history of the Roman Republic that a Roman commander dedicated the armor of an enemy commander whom he had personally slain; such dedications were known as the *spolia opima* (the finest trophy). In the second battle, when Romulus was again victorious, Hersilia, the wife of Romulus, acted as conciliator and persuaded her husband to accept the defeated Sabines as Roman citizens.

Finally the Sabines attacked Rome itself and through the treachery of Tarpeia captured the Capitoline hill. In the legend Tarpeia was the daughter of the Roman commander upon the Capitol; greedy for gold, she agreed to let the Sabines in if they would give her "what they had upon their left arms"—meaning their gold bracelets. After the capture they crushed her to death under their shields, for the left arm is the shield arm.[9] Yet the Sabines, although masters of the citadel, could not capture the Forum, immediate entrance to which was barred by the miraculous jets of boiling water emitted by Janus. In the low ground where the Forum lay, fierce fighting took place in which the Sabines were successful until Romulus turned the tide of battle by vowing a temple to Jupiter Stator (Jupiter the Stayer).

The next stage of the battle is associated with a cavity in the Roman Forum called in ancient times the Lacus Curtius. The fiercest of the Sabine soldiers was a knight, Mettus Curtius; pursued by the Romans he rode on his horse into the marshy ground and miraculously escaped, to continue the fight; the low-lying depression was named after him. Livy elsewhere gives another account of the Lacus Curtius which, because of its patriotic character, has proved the more popular. In 362 a chasm mysteriously opened up in the Forum, and the Roman soothsayers announced that it could only be closed by putting into it that which was most valuable to Rome; if it were so filled, the Roman state would endure forever. A young Roman, Marcus Curtius, saw that military courage was Rome's greatest treasure; in full panoply and

---

[9] In another version, which recalls the story of Scylla and Minos, Tarpeia's treachery was motivated by love for Tatius.

before the assembled people he prayed to the gods and rode into the chasm. Thus it was closed, and the traces of it that remained took their name from the hero who had been swallowed up by the earth.

To return to Romulus and the Sabines; the fighting was brought to an end by the Sabine women themselves, wives (and now mothers) of Romans and daughters of Sabines. They ran into the middle of the battle and by their direct appeals brought about a truce. Peace was made and the Sabines and Romans agreed to live together at Rome, with Titus Tatius becoming Romulus's colleague in the kingship, while the Sabines provided the word by which the Roman citizens were known, *Quirites*.[10]

Thus the unification of the two peoples was achieved. Titus Tatius was killed some years later by the people of Lavinium in the course of a personal quarrel. Romulus himself, after a long and successful reign, disappeared, while reviewing his army in the Campus Martius, to the accompaniment of thunder and lightning. His disappearance was rather a transportation, for he became a god, Quirinus, and appeared to an Alban farmer, Proculus Julius. His final words to Proculus eloquently summarize the ideals that later Romans attributed to the founder of their state (Livy, 1. 16): "Go," said he, "and tell the Romans that it is the gods' will that my city of Rome should be the capital of the world. Let them exercise their military skill and let them know—and let them tell their descendants—that no mortal power can resist the Romans."

The saga of Romulus is the most important group of Roman historical legends. While much of it is rooted in fact, as has been proved by recent archaelogical discoveries, much of it also owes its origin to more artificial sources so that the legend as a whole is not so much a saga as a collection of literary stories—historical, romantic, and etiological—many of them composed by late authors on Greek models. Romulus himself is but the eponym [11]

[10] The etymology of *Quirites* is unknown; the Romans themselves erroneously connected the name with the Sabine town of Cures. It has the same root as the god Quirinus and the Quirinal hill.

[11] That is, a person who takes his name from a place—for example, Corinthus at Corinth. In many cases the eponymous hero is the city's founder.

of Rome, to whom many features of the Roman constitution are ascribed. His deification is problematic; Quirinus, as we have seen, was a Sabine god with whom Mars was associated. Sometimes his name stands by itself; sometimes it is attached to Mars (Mars Quirinus) or Janus, Jupiter, or even Hercules. One ancient Roman scholar (Servius on *Aeneid,* 1. 292) described Quirinus as "Mars when he presides in peace time," and the idea of a god of a military state when it is not at war is particularly suitable for Romulus, organizer of the peaceful state and its successful leader in the first wars. Quirinus, moreover, being Sabine, is suitably fused with the Roman Romulus; there were separate communities upon the Palatine, Oppian, and Quirinal hills in the eighth century, with different cultures, and the legend of a fusion, symbolized by the god Romulus-Quirinus, has good archaeological evidence to support it.

Several other characters in the Romulus legend are themselves minor deities—Faustulus and Acca Larentia; Hersilia, who becomes the goddess Hora, the consort (or perhaps merely a personification of the power) of the deified Romulus; Tarpeia, at whose supposed tomb libations were offered. Some of the elements in the legend are clearly intended to explain features of the Roman constitution; the most obvious case is the dual kingship of Romulus and the colorless Titus Tatius, which foreshadows the collegiate principle of Republican magistracies and in particular the dual consulship.

With Aeneas and Romulus, Roman saga is virtually complete. The period of the kings (which traditionally ended in 509) and of the early Republic is full of stories, however, that are more justly called legends than history—"more suited," as Livy remarked, "to poetical writing than to sober history." Some of these legends we have already touched on; we give a few of the more famous remaining ones here.

In the reign of the third king Tullus Hostilius there was war between Rome and Alba Longa, which ended in the destruction of Alba. At an earlier stage the two sides had agreed to decide the issue by a battle between champions, three brothers on each side; the Alban champions were the Curiatii, the Romans were the Horatii. Two Romans were quickly killed, but the third, who was unwounded, separated and despatched singly his wounded opponents. Now his sister had been betrothed to one of the Curiatii, and as her brother was triumphantly entering Rome, bearing the spoils of the dead Curiatii, she cried out in grief. Horatius killed her immediately for her inopportune and un-patriotic gesture. As a murderer he was accused and condemned to death by the two judges appointed to try such cases, but on appeal to the people he gained a reversal of the verdict ("more because of his popularity as a courageous soldier than because he had a good case," says Livy) and underwent a ritual purification by offering a sacrifice and then passing with veiled head beneath a kind of yoke or crossbar (i.e., a horizontal beam supported by two upright poles). The crossbar, often renewed, was still visible in the fourth century A.D.; it was called the *tigillum sororium* and was flanked by two altars, one to Janus Curiatius, the other to Juno Sororia.

The association of Horatius with the *tigillum sororium* is based on false etymology, a confusion of the archaic title of Juno Sororia with the Latin word *soror,* a sister. Passing under the yoke was indeed a ceremony of purification, but, as the titles of the two divinities prove, the purification in this case was of boys and girls reaching the age of puberty. The boys, initiated at the altar of Janus Curiatius, went out to their first battle and on their return were purified from bloodguilt by passing beneath the *tigillum*. Juno Sororia likewise presided over the initiation of girls into adult life. As for other details of the legend, some are merely etiological—for example, the right of appeal to the people was a prominent feature of Roman Republican law. While a battle between champions is common enough in national legends, the legend of the Horatii and Curiatii was given a firmer basis by the existence of five ancient tombs, in two groups of two and three, respectively, outside Rome in the direction of Alba. Another ancient stone tomb stood near the place where Horatia was said to have been killed by her brother.

The last three kings of Rome were Tarquinius Priscus, Servius Tullius, and Tarquinius Superbus. The two Tarquins (if indeed they are not two versions of the same person) were Etruscans, while Servius was a Latin—an indication of the unsettled conditions that faced the early Romans. Servius, in Roman tradition, was as good a king as Tarquin was a bad tyrant. As a founder of Roman institutions he was considered second only to Romulus, and therefore a number of legends gathered round him. His mother, Ocrisia, was a slave who had been captured in war and assigned to the household of Tarquinius Priscus. She was of the royal house at Corniculum. Who Servius's father was is a matter for conjecture; legend made him the son of Vulcan, who miraculously appeared in phallic form to Ocrisia as she was sitting by the fire in the palace. When she had thus conceived and borne Servius, Vulcan showed his favor by causing a miraculous flame to play around the child's head without harming him. Favored by such portents Servius was assured of special treatment in the palace; he was brought up in the king's family and married to his daughter. When Tarquin was murdered by two men in the pay of the sons of Ancus Martius (the fourth king of Rome), his widow, Tanaquil, skilfully arranged for the transfer of power to Servius.

The reforms and institutions of Servius are matters more for the historian than the mythographer. He is credited with introducing the cult of Diana to Rome, and like king Numa he is said to have had a divine counselor and consort, in this case the goddess Fortuna. The legend of his death deserves more than a passing mention. His two daughters (both called Tullia) were married to two Etruscan brothers, Tarquin and Arruns, sons of Tarquinius Priscus. Arruns's wife had her husband and her sister murdered and then married Tarquin, whom she urged to usurp the throne and to murder Servius. The corpse of Servius lay in the street called the Clivus Urbius; Tullia drove her coach over her father's body, and the name of the street, because of the crime, was changed to the Vicus Sceleratus (Crime Street).

Thus Tarquinius Superbus became king; in the historical tradition he is a tyrant and his expulsion is the achievement of Rome's liberty. Whatever the historical facts may be—and they are much disputed—Tarquin's expulsion was the occasion of one of the most famous of Roman legends. In the Roman army besieging the Rutulian capital of Ardea were a number of young nobles, including Tarquinius Collatinus and Tarquinius Sextus, the son of the Roman king. Full of wine one evening, they rode off to pay surprise visits to their wives in order to see who was the most virtuous and faithful. Alone of all whom they visited the wife of Collatinus, Lucretia, was acting in a chaste and matronly way; they all judged her to be the best and returned to camp. Now Sextus Tarquinius had been so taken by Lucretia's beauty that he returned alone to Collatia some nights later and surprised and raped her. Next day she sent for her father and husband, who came together with Lucius Junius Brutus; she told them of the violation of her chastity and made them promise to avenge themselves on her defiler. Then she plunged a dagger into her heart and died.

Lucretia's martyrdom led to the end of the monarchy; the gates of Rome were closed against Tarquinius Superbus, and he was driven into exile with two of his sons, while Sextus Tarquinius went to the Latin town of Gabii, where he was murdered. Rome became a Republic, the chief power being exercised by two annual praetors (the title was changed to "consuls" some sixty years later), one of whom was Brutus.

With the establishment of the Republic we are on the threshold of passing from legend to history. The subsequent wars between the Etruscans and Rome, and especially the capture of Rome by the Etruscan prince Porsenna, have their own crop of legends and heroic deeds. These have passed so far from the realm of mythology that we may suitably leave them to the historians of Rome and conclude our survey with Lucretia and the expulsion of the Tarquins.

CHAPTER 23

The Survival of Classical Mythology

The Myths in Later Antiquity and the Dark Ages

Religion and the state were intimately connected in classical Greece. The highest expression of Greek religion is to be found in the plays of Aeschylus or the pediment sculptures of the temple of Zeus at Olympia or the Parthenon sculptures at Athens; Aeschylus and Pheidias speak for the Greek city-state at its zenith in the mid-fifth century. As the independence of the city-state declined and the public initiative of its citizens weakened, so anthropomorphic Homeric religion began to lose its force, and in the fourth century men sought from religion not the civic self-confidence of Homeric cult, but comfort for their individual doubts and problems. Ever since the seventh century the potentiality for undermining Homeric religion had existed. The early Greek philosophers of Ionia had explained man's relationship to the macrocosm in nontheological terms. A whole world separates Hesiod's cosmogony and theogony from the Ionians' theories of the elements of the universe. Anaximenes of Miletus (ca. 545) said that air was the elemental substance of the universe (including the gods) and did not hesitate to refer to it as *theos* (God). Heracleitus of Ephesus (ca. 500) taught that fire was the prime element and further criticized the ritual of Homeric religion, in particular its central feature, the animal sacrifice; purifying oneself with blood, said he, was like washing in mud. The most outspoken of these early critics was Xenophanes of Colophon (ca. 525) who attacked Homeric anthropomorphism: "Homer and Hesiod," he said, "have attributed to the gods everything that is shameful and a reproach among men: theft, adultery and deceit."

The potential weakness of Homeric religion was obvious to thinking men long before it was fatally exploited. Towards the end of the fifth century the criticisms of the philosophers became common currency among educated men, whose confidence in the old order and established religion was shaken by the political, moral, and intellectual upheavals that surrounded them. The greatest of these upheavals, the Peloponnesian War (431–404), coincided with the flourishing of the Sophists at Athens. These practical philosophers, who professed to teach virtue, so threatened the traditional religion that they called forth a violent conservative reaction; in literature this finds its expression in Aristophanes's play the *Clouds* (423), and in history its climax is the condemnation and execution of Socrates in 399 for atheism. Nevertheless, Homeric religion had been undermined, and the following century saw Plato banish Homeric legends from his ideal educational curriculum. Thinking men turned more and more to philosophy for assurance, and the great philosophical schools—the Academy of Plato, the Lyceum of Aristotle, the Porch of the Stoics, and the Garden of Epicurus—were founded during the fourth century.

The weakening of traditional religion was further compounded by the phenomenon of Alexander the Great, who died in 323. His conquests brought the Greeks into contact with Oriental ideas and religions, whose effect on Greek mythology will be discussed later. He and his father, Philip II of Macedon, put an end to the autonomous city-state as a living institution in Greece, further weakening the hold of traditional religion. His death ushered in the so-called Hellenistic Age, which is taken to cover the period from 323 until the final absorption of Greece into the Roman Empire in 146 B.C. The intellectual center of the Greek world in the Hellenistic Age was the Egyptian city of Alexandria, and its library was the greatest of the Greek centers of scholarship.

The deadening effect upon mythology of the processes just outlined are not surprising. The legends of the gods ceased to be a vehicle for a living religion and became material for scholars and pedants. Thus the third century saw a great flourishing of interest in traditional mythology, but it took the form of explanation, classification, and standardization. Callimachus of Alexandria (ca. 265) is the most distinguished of the Alexandrian scholar-poets. His interest in mythology found literary expression in a vast poetic output, including a four-thousand line poem called *Aetia* (Causes), a storehouse of legend, and a series of six hymns modeled on the *Homeric Hymns*. In his work, as in that of his contemporaries like Apollonius (author of an epic on the Argonauts), learned allusion and romantic coloring are prominent features, and traditional mythology is already far on its course toward becoming material for literary ornamentation or learned pedantry. This tendency was amplified in Roman literature; the *Lock of Berenice* of Catullus (poem number 66) is a translation of one of Callimachus's *Aetia,* and Ovid's *Metamorphoses* owes much of its romantic detail to Alexandrianism. A parallel development may be seen in Greek art; the sentimental and sensuous creations of Praxiteles express an individualism that is utterly alien to the creator of the Apollo at Olympia.

Callimachus and other scholars were also interested in explaining myths, and in so doing succeeded in explaining away the gods. We need not go into these vagaries of ancient scholarship, which are as multifarious and as desiccating as the equally fanciful theories of nineteenth century classical researchers. The work of Euhemerus of Messene (ca. 300), however, requires special notice since it achieved an influence out of all proportion to its merits and led to the coining of the term *Euhemerism,* that is, the theory that the gods were originally men who had been kings or otherwise distinguished men.[1] Euhemerus claimed in his book *The Sacred Scripture* to have journeyed to the Indian Ocean and on an island there to have seen a golden column in the temple of Zeus, upon which were inscribed the deeds of Uranus, Cronus, and Zeus; from this, he claimed, he discovered that the gods were men deified for their great deeds. Euhemerus's book was translated into Latin by Ennius (ca. 180) and summarized in Greek by the historian Diodorus Siculus (ca. 30); Ennius's version was summarized by the Christian writer Lactantius (ca. 300 A.D.). Euhemerism owed its importance in the Christian era to the fact

---

[1] A tendency toward deification of living men was a feature of the Hellenistic Age.

that it provided pagan material with which to attack the pagan gods. St. Augustine, writing around 415 A.D., can explain the errors of pagan religion "most reasonably," he says, "by the belief that the pagan gods were once men" (*De Civitate Dei*, 7. 18). The seventh-century bishop of Seville, Isidore, begins his chapters on the pagan gods with the Euhemeristic statement: "Those whom the pagans call gods are said to have once been men" (*Etymologiae*, 8. 11). Isidore elsewhere exhibits an interesting side effect of Euhemerism, namely a concern for dating the men who became gods. In his summary of world history (*Etymologiae*, 5. 39) myth and fact are inextricably combined, and among the "historical facts" dated are, for example, the invention of the lyre by Hermes and Heracles's self-immolation. Euhemerism survived throughout the Middle Ages and, while Christian polemicists used it to attack pagan religion, it also proved to be an important element in the survival of the pagan, anthropomorphic gods.

To return to the Hellenistic Age; another aspect of scholarly interest in mythology was the work of the mythographers, who summarized and classified Greek mythology. Handbooks on mythology, now lost, are known to have been written by the Alexandrian polymath Eratosthenes (ca. 225) and by the Athenian scholar Apollodorus (ca. 145), and their names are attached to two surviving mythological compendia. That of "Apollodorus" (perhaps ca. 120 A.D.) is the most complete and provides the most accessible versions of many of the legends, especially in saga. The shorter work of pseudo-Eratosthenes, called *Catasterisms*, deals exclusively with metamorphoses of people into stars. The development of astral legends was a feature of Alexandrianism; genuinely early Greek astral myths are rare (the myth of Orion is one example), but the *Catasterisms* contains no less than forty-four such legends, including such famous (but new) ones as the origins of the Great Bear (Callisto), the signs of the Zodiac, and the Milky Way. This manufacturing of astral myths reflects the advances being made in astronomy at Alexandria, as well as the growth of the pseudoscience of astrology. The legends are not genuine myth; they are nevertheless important because the names of classical mythology often owe their survival to their use in astronomy and astrology. We give two examples of these catasterisms. The constellation Gemini (the Twins) was formerly the Dioscuri (Castor and Pollux) who, says the author, "exceeded all men in brotherly love, for they never quarreled about power or about anything else. So Zeus, wishing to make a memorial of their unanimity, called them 'the Twins' and placed them together among the stars" (number 10).[2] Catasterism number 44, the origin of the Milky Way, is given thus: "The sons of Zeus might only share in divine honors if Hera had suckled them. Hermes, therefore (so they say), brought Heracles at his birth to Hera and held him to Hera's breast and she suckled him. But when she realized it was Heracles, she shook him off and the excess milk spurted out to form the Galaxy." [3]

Other mythological handbooks survive and still have some value. The first-century B.C. Greek slave, Parthenius, compiled a collection of love stories for the use of his friend, the Roman poet Gallus; they show clearly the romanticizing tendency of Hellenistic mythographers. A Latin compendium dating from around 160 A.D. is attached to the name of Hyginus (who in reality was the librarian of the Emperor Augustus, around 10 B.C.); it contains in bald summary more than two hundred and fifty legends. More attractive is the *Mitologiae* of the African bishop Fulgentius (late fifth century A.D.), in which the pagan myths are summarized and explained, very often by means of shaky etymologies. While we may deplore the low literary level to which the gods of Homer and Aeschylus have fallen, we must acknowledge that works like that of Fulgentius at least helped keep the pagan myths alive through the early Middle Ages.

It was through astronomy and astrology that the names of mythology often survived. The interest of the Alexandrians is proved by literary works other than the handbooks of astral legends already mentioned. The astronomical poem of Aratus (ca. 275) called the *Phaenomena* was one of the most popular of all Hellenistic works; it was frequently translated into Latin (Cicero being among the translators) and more than two dozen ancient commentaries are known. Astrology, however, had greater in-

---

[2] The author then proceeds to describe the position of the stars in the constellation.

[3] *Gala* is the Greek word for milk, hence *Galaxy* for the Milky Way.

fluence on the survival of the pagan gods. It had been of importance in the East since the time of the Sumerians, but in Greece it was the conquest of Alexander that laid the Greeks open to Oriental influences and led to the popularity of astrology and its related superstitions. Homer, to be sure, had explained the friendship of Hector and Polydamas by their having been born in the same night, and for this he was criticized by Heracleitus for being an "astrologer." The common sense of Heracleitus was the prevailing Greek attitude toward astrology until the third century B.C. From then on the influence of the stars on the life of man was widely studied and feared. Astrology was not confined to the uneducated or the superstitious; it was encouraged by the Stoic philosophers and among the Romans even so rational a man as Cicero admitted that there was "divinity in the stars." Indeed, astrology was in many ways closer to religion than science; its fundamental belief lay in the "sympathy" of the heavenly bodies and mankind on earth. Human life, therefore, was bound up with the movements of the heavenly bodies, so that the stars came to have the power formerly held by the gods. It was an easy step then to give them the names of gods and to link these names with existing legends, as was done in the *Catasterisms*. At the same time, a host of foreign gods joined the classical pantheon, and they led to a profound transformation in men's ideas of the classical gods. In literature the greatest classical work on astrology is the *Astronomica* of Manilius (ca. 15 A.D.), and it has its place in the continuation of the mythological tradition despite Manilius's own scorn for saga and epic (expressed in the opening lines of Book 3 of the poem). Far more influential was the work of the Greek-Egyptian astronomer and mathematician Ptolemy (Claudius Ptolemaeus, ca. 140 A.D.), especially his astrological treatise, the *Tetrabiblos,* which explained scientifically the heavenly bodies and the nature of their influence upon human character and action.

Christianity was unable to resist the popularity of astrology. St. Augustine vigorously attacked astrology in his *City of God* (especially Book 5), yet even he believed that the stars did have an influence, to which God and human free will were nevertheless superior. In any case astrology was too much a part of late-classical and early-medieval culture to be extirpated. It therefore survived the coming of Christianity and with it the classical gods prolonged their existence, often, it is true, in scarcely recognizable forms.

In the previous chapter we discussed the transfer of Greek mythology to Rome and saw that the standardization of literature meant virtually the end of classical mythology as a living force. It was the literary, scholarly, and astrological traditions that accounted for the continued survival of classical mythology in the pagan Roman world. Even the critics of mythology acknowledged its uses. The poet Lucretius (ca. 55) found the names of the gods useful as symbols: "let us allow a man to use 'Neptune' and 'Ceres' for 'sea' and 'grain,' 'Bacchus' for the proper word 'wine,' 'mother of the gods' for 'earth,' provided that he does not in fact allow his mind to be touched by base superstition" (*De Rerum Natura,* 2. 655–660). Elsewhere (3. 978–1023) Lucretius uses myths as allegory, explaining the sinners in the Underworld (Tantalus, Tityus, Sisyphus) as allegories of human passions: "Tityus is in us here, whom the birds tear as he lies in the throes of love and as painful anxiety eats him up or as the cares of some other desire consume him" (3. 992–994). In the same way, the classical myths survived the attacks of the Christian fathers. The greatest of these, St. Augustine's monumental *City of God,* was written explicitly "to defend the City of God against those who prefer their gods to its founder" (quotation from Augustine's *Preface*)—that is, as a reasoned attack on the pagan gods and classical mythology. Yet St. Augustine himself was too good a classical scholar to be able to throw out pagan mythology, and the same is true of other Christian Fathers, such as St. Jerome. The critics of classical mythology, then, actually assisted in the process of keeping it alive; the myths survived not only in classical literary texts (most especially the works of Vergil), but also in the religious tradition, where they were used by the Christians and can claim even to have enriched the religion that sought to destroy them. This process of absorption and mingling throughout the Middle Ages finds its ultimate medieval synthesis in the work of Dante, where the classical myths are used and criticized, and in the process, vindicated.

The mythological figures, then, did indeed survive despite the passing of the religion that created them. In western literature they were used as symbols or as allegories; they became vehicles for romantic storytelling, or identified with constellations. They traveled to the East, often to be depicted in Arab manuscripts in forms unrecognizable to their Greek originators. But however "mutilated, botched, crippled" (to quote the words of a French historian) they were, the important fact is that they survived and at the end of the Middle Ages returned to a new lease on life that still endures.

Literary Uses of the Myths

The age in European literature that began toward the end of the eleventh century has rightly been called the *aetas Ovidiana;* "a history of mythology and the Renaissance tradition," wrote Douglas Bush, "must be largely an account of the metamorphoses of Ovid." Although Ovid's other works had their influence in this period, it is his *Metamorphoses* that were supremely important in bringing about the revival of classical mythology in Renaissance literature and art. The Middle Ages had, in Gilbert Highet's phrase, a "unitary view of history," in which classical and Biblical history and mythology were all mingled together. This lack of historical perspective and failure to distinguish between history and legend in part accounts for the transformation of Ovid during the eleventh to the thirteenth centuries. His legends are retold not merely for their own sake, but still more as vehicles for moralizing allegory. The goddesses and heroines of the *Metamorphoses* even appear as nuns in one work and a whole series of poems and prose works explain the *Metamorphoses* in Christian terms. The climax of this process is in the enormous *Ovide Moralisé* of the early fourteenth century, a French reworking of the *Metamorphoses* in which the legends are interpreted as moral allegories. As an example we give here a translation (from a fifteenth century French prose summary of the poem) of one of the several interpretations of the legend of Apollo and Daphne: "Here we may suppose that by the maiden Daphne is meant the glorious Virgin Mary, who was so lowly, pure, and beautiful that God the Father chose her to conceive his only Son by the work of the Holy Spirit. She carried him for nine months and then bore him, virgin before the birth and at the birth; virgin after the birth she remained without ever losing her virginity. This sovereign Virgin is the laurel, always green in virtue, which God planted in the garden of his paradise."

A similar approach is to be found in the translation (from the French of Raoul le Fèvre) of the *Metamorphoses* by William Caxton (*Ovyde Hys Booke of Methamorphose*, 1480).

> Another sentence may be had for the storye of Daphne which was a ryght fayre damoysel. . . . On a tyme he [*sc.* Apollo] fonde her alone and anone beganne to renne after her. And she for to kepe her maydenhode and for to eschewe the voice of Phebus fledde so faste and asprely [i.e., roughly] that al a swoun she fel down dede under a laurel tree. In which place she was entered [i.e., interred] and buryed without deflourynge or towchynge of her vyrgynyte. And therefore fayneth the fable that she was chaunged and transformed into a laurel tree, whiche is contynuelly grene. Which sygnefyeth the vertu of chastete.[4]

Quaint as the medieval uses of Ovid may seem, they indicate a lively interest in classical mythology, far removed from the stark summaries of the late classical mythographers. Ovid's legends were to return in their full glory in the poetry of the English Renaissance and in Renaissance art, and his poem still remains the single most fruitful ancient source of classical legend.

Medieval use of classical mythology was not limited to allegory. The romantic side of Ovid's legends was often preserved: the "most lamentable comedy and most cruel death of Pyramus and Thisby" presented by the "rude mechanicals" in *A Midsummer Night's Dream* has as its predecessors a number of versions of the legend in French, Italian, and English. They appear in the works of Chaucer and Boccaccio, in the songs of the medieval troubadours, and in a nine-hundred line twelfth century *Piramus et Tisbé*. All go back finally to Ovid.

A different romantic tradition is embraced by the medieval versions of the Trojan legend. The twelfth and thirteenth centuries

---

[4] Chapter 18 in the Phillips manuscript of Caxton's translation, now in the possession of Magdalene College, Cambridge. Transcribed from the facsimile edition published by George Braziller (New York, 1968).

saw the production in France of a number of epic *Romances,* including a group whose themes were classical. The most influential of these was the *Roman de Troie* by Benoît de Ste. Maure, a 30,000-line romance written around 1160. In scope it extends from the Argonautic expedition through the founding and destruction of Troy to the death of Odysseus. As his source Benoît was using not Homer but two Latin prose versions of the Trojan legend. The first, by "Dictys of Crete," describes the war and the returns from the Greek point of view; it is a forgery of uncertain date (second to fourth century A.D.), purporting to be a translantion from the Greek version of a diary written "on bark in Phoenician script" by Dictys of Crete during the Trojan War. The second of Benoît's sources, the *De Excidio Troiae* of "Dares Phrygius" is likewise a late Latin forgery (perhaps of the sixth century A.D.), purporting also to be a translation from the Greek, this time of the eyewitness diary of the war kept by the Phrygian Dares, and therefore pro-Trojan in attitude. These works, forgeries as they were, were preferable to Homer and Latin accounts based on Homer, because they were by eyewitnesses, says Benoît. More significantly, they have many more realistic details about the war and its participants and more touches of romantic interest. They therefore appealed to the medieval taste and they are, through Benoît, the ancestors of a great quantity of literature on the Trojan legend. Joseph of Exeter wrote a Latin verse paraphrase of Dares, and it and Benoît were used by Chaucer for his *Troilus and Criseyde* (ca. 1380). The legend of Troilus and Cressida, first elaborated by Benoît, shows how classical mythology was transformed in the Middle Ages and the Renaissance. Benoît was paraphrased in Latin by an Italian, Guido delle Colonne (ca. 1275); Guido was put into French by Raoul le Fèvre (1464). Chaucer and Caxton were the principal sources for Shakespeare's *Troilus and Cressida.* "Shakespeare's bitter play is therefore a dramatization of part of a translation into English of the French translation of a Latin imitation of an old French expansion of a Latin epitome of a Greek romance." [5] As an example of what Shakespeare had to work with we give a few

---

[5] G. Highet, *The Classical Tradition* (New York: Oxford University Press [Galaxy ed.], 1959), p. 55.

lines from Caxton's *Recuyell of the Historyes of Troye* in which
the medieval romantic interest is evident.[6]

> Whan Troylus knewe certaynly that Breseyda [i.e., Cressida] shold
> be sente to her fader he made grete sorowe. For she was his soverain
> lady of love, and in semblable wyse Breseyda lovyd strongly Troylus.
> And she made also the grettest sorowe of the world for to leve her
> soverayn lord in love. There was never seen so much sorowe made
> betwene two lovers at their departyng. Who that lyste to here of alle
> theyr love, late [let] hym rede the booke of Troyllus that Chawcer
> made wherein he shall fynde the storye hooll [whole] whiche were
> to longe to wryte here.

The gradual transformation of medieval literature into the full
flowering of the Renaissance is best exemplified in Dante (1365–
1421), the last of the great medieval writers and the forerunner
of the Italian Renaissance. He took Vergil as his guide, and singles
out Homer, Horace, Ovid, and Lucan as the "great shades"
(*quattro grand' ombre*) of classical literature. It was in Italy that
the figures of classical mythology first returned to their classical
forms, after the centuries of metamorphosis.

Both Petrarch (1304–1374) and Boccaccio (1313–1375) made
use of classical mythology in their Latin and Italian poems—
Petrarch, for example, in his Latin epic *Africa,* Boccaccio in his
Italian epic of the *Theseid.* A particular aspect of Italian Renaissance literature was pastoral Latin poetry, modeled on the
Eclogues of Vergil. In these poems the form and language are
Vergilian; the characters have classical names with figures from
classical mythology used for ornament and allusion. Only the
setting is Renaissance Italian; in the *Eclogues* of Sannazaro (1458–
1530), the Vergilian shepherds have become Neapolitan fishermen. In one eclogue, for example, two fishermen sailing back from
Capri meet with Proteus and a band of Tritons.

In the English Renaissance the uses of classical mythology
were varied and extensive. Ovid was the most popular source and
the *Metamorphoses* at least was known to educated men, whether
in Latin or in medieval versions or contemporary translations. At

---

[6] Taken from *Recuyell,* edited by H. Oskar Sommer (London: David
Nutt, 1894), p. 604.

the same time, there were important contemporary collections of classical myths, mostly Italian. Boccaccio's *De Genealogia Deorum* is the earliest; equally influential and more modern were the *De Deis Gentium* by Giraldi (1548); *Mythologiae* by Conti (1551), and Cartari's *Le Imagini degli Dei Antichi* (1556). These handbooks not only provided sources for writers, but also described the figures of classical mythology as they should appear in art. Relying on them and on collections of legends in English, English authors could and did make extensive use of classical mythology even when, like Shakespeare, they had "small Latin and less Greek." Mythological figures appeared in many guises; they might be ornamental, as is often the case in Elizabethan lyric; Ben Jonson will address the moon (i.e., Diana-Artemis) as "Queen and huntress, chaste and fair." Sometimes the mythological allusion has a universal application, as in Thomas Nashe's famous lines where pagan imagery and Christian prayer go together in perfect harmony:

> Beauty is but a flower
> Which wrinkles will devour:
> Brightness falls from the air,
> Queens have died young and fair,
> Dust hath closed Helen's eye.
> I am sick, I must die.
> Lord, have mercy on us!

The classical myths need not, of course, be explicitly alluded to. In Shakespeare's *Twelfth Night,* the Duke describes his first sight of Olivia (act 1, scene 1, 19–23):

> O! When mine eyes did see Olivia first,
> Methought she purg'd the air of pestilence.
> That instant was I turn'd into a hart,
> And my desires, like fell and cruel hounds,
> E'er since pursue me.

Ovid's Actaeon has become at the same time an allegory of desire and a poetic symbol.

In the Ovidian tradition, classical mythology provided legends for development into narrative poems, the great examples being Marlowe's *Hero and Leander* (1598, completed by Chapman) and Shakespeare's *Venus and Adonis* (1593), which show the strengths and weaknesses of Elizabethan treatment of the classics. In drama, history rather than mythology provided Renaissance authors with material, but one peculiar dramatic use of mythology was in masques, that is, short dramatic productions usually with an allegorical purpose, in which the characters are drawn from classical mythology. The most distinguished example of the genre is Milton's *Comus* (1634), which combines a pastoral setting with classical allegory. More representative is the masque in Shakespeare's *The Tempest* (act 4, scene 1). The custom of having aristocrats dress up as classical gods and goddesses survived in France and England well into the eighteenth century.

The most important uses of mythology in the English Renaissance are for didactic purposes, as allegory, and as symbolic of universal truths. Its greatest exponents are Spenser and Milton. In the second book of Spenser's *Faerie Queen* Guyon journeys with the good Palmer and destroys the evil Bower of Bliss. On the way the Sirens try to lure him:

> O turne thy rudder hither-ward a while:
> Here may thy storme-bet vessell safely ride;
> This is the Port of rest from Troublous toyle,
> The worlds sweet In, from paine and wearisome turmoyle.

Guyon finds his:

> Senses softly tickeled
> That he the boateman bad row easily
> And let him heare some part of their rare melody.

But "him the Palmer from that vanity,/With temperate advice discounselled," and Guyon is saved. Classical mythology here is symbolic of evil, even while we (with Guyon) feel its attraction in the poet's beautiful words. Yet more explicit is Spenser's use of the tale of Ares and Aphrodite at the end of the same canto (Book 2, canto 12): the enchantress lies voluptuously with her lover "arayd, or rather disarayd,/All in a vele of silke and silver thin . . . More subtile web Arachne cannot spin"; and over them Guyon and the Palmer throw "a subtile net" and "tooke them both." The Bower of Bliss is destroyed and its bewitched animals restored to human shape. Circe and Aphrodite have combined to assist Spenser's allegory of Temperance.

Spenser was capable of feeling the sensuous attraction of Ovid's fables—"her snowy brest was bare to readie spoyle/Of hungry eies," he says, for example, of the enchantress. More severe is Milton, who of all English writers displays the deepest knowledge and most controlled use of classical mythology. In an allusion to the Adonis legend he describes the Garden of Eden as a "spot more delicious than those gardens *feigned* or of revived Adonis;" ornamental simile and adverse judgment are combined. In *Paradise Lost* his classical allusions are especially associated with Satan and his followers, and Milton's Hell is peopled with the full complement of the classical Underworld. The violence of the fallen angels is described in a simile drawn from Heracles's death (*Paradise Lost,* 2. 542–546):

> As when Alcides, from Oechalia crowned
> With conquest, felt th'envenomed robe, and tore
> Through pain up by the roots Thessalian pines,
> And Lichas from the top of Oeta threw
> Into th' Euboic sea.

And this passage is followed by one describing the more peaceful fallen angels in terms of the Elysian fields. Throughout all of Milton's poetry classical mythology is intertwined with Biblical and contemporary learning. Milton knows and loves it, yet his opinion of its value appears in the invocation to his Muse, Urania (*Paradise Lost,* 7. 1–39); after describing the fate of Orpheus, whose mother (a Muse) could not save him, Milton concludes:

> So fail not thou, who thee implores
> For thou art heav'nlie, shee an empty dreame.

The tension between classical paganism and puritan Christianity is yet more explicitly put by Milton's contemporary, Abraham Cowley:

> Still the old heathen gods in numbers dwell.[7]
> The heav'nliest thing on earth still keeps up hell.

Milton represents the climax of the Renaissance use of classical mythology. Already in his own time the French writer, Paul Scarron, had perfected the *burlesque,* the comic and trivial (if tasteful) treatment of noble themes from classical mythology; his most famous such work was the unfinished parody of the *Aeneid, Virgile Travesti.* The appearance of a host of tasteless and less skillful travesties in England imitating Scarron heralded a long period of aridity in the literary uses of classical mythology. In France and Germany things were better; the classicism of Corneille (d. 1684) and Racine (d. 1699) showed how drama could still be inspired by mythology. In French prose, Fénelon (d. 1715) used the *Odyssey* as the model for his *Télémaque* (1699), and Telemachus as a vehicle for his moral and political teaching.

While in England classical mythology became for nearly a century a quarry for correct (but too often soulless) allusion, German writers of the eighteenth century launched a full-scale classical renaissance. Its basis is expressed in Schiller's *Gods of Greece* (1788), unfavorably contrasting Christianity with the Greek deities, and in the theories of Winckelmann (d. 1768) and Lessing, whose *Laocoon* (1766) proclaimed the ideal of classical art. Above all stands Goethe (1749–1832), whose work constantly uses the classical myths. In drama he wrote an *Iphigenia,* and in poetry countless works evoking the Greek legends—*Ganymede* and *Prometheus* are but two of the most famous ones. In *Faust,* Helen symbolizes all that is beautiful in classical antiquity, most specifically the beauty of Greece. More than two centuries earlier she had been the symbol of surpassing sensual beauty in Marlowe's *Faustus* (scene 13):

> Sweet Helen, make me immortal with a kiss!
> Her lips suck forth my soul. See where it flies!
> Come, Helen, come, give me my soul again.
> Here will I dwell, for heaven be in these lips,
> And all is dross that is not Helena.

Goethe went far beyond this in his symbolism.

[7] By "numbers" is meant "poetry."

Classical legends continued to inspire the Romantic poets of the late eighteenth and nineteenth century in England. Greece inspired Keats (who knew no Greek) and Shelley (who was an excellent Greek scholar). Nineteenth century authors found in the classical myths opportunities for escapism (as in Poe's *To Helen*), or as allegories of their own aspirations (e.g., Tennyson's *Ulysses*); occasionally even they could become vehicles for narrative for its own sake, as in William Morris's *Life and Death of Jason* (1867). Whatever purposes they served, the classical myths survived; with the expansion of classical scholarship they gained new force and have found fresh expression in the twentieth century.

The most conspicuous modern use of the myths has been in prose by James Joyce (1882–1941); by T. S. Eliot (1888–1965) in poetry; and in drama by the French authors, Gide (1869–1957), Cocteau (1889–1963), and Anouilh (b. 1910); by Eliot; and in America by Eugene O'Neill (1888–1953). The most extended modern treatment of an ancient myth is Joyce's *Ulysses;* yet in the Circe episode (Bloom at Bella's house) the allegory is hardly different from that of Spenser. But there the parallel stops, for Joyce's work is unheroic in its characterization. So Eliot for Sweeney and J. Alfred Prufrock uses classical mythology, but in an antiheroic framework. Perhaps the tragic figures of classical mythology have fared best in our century; Cocteau and Anouilh have both turned to Orpheus and to the Theban sagas for modern dramas on classical themes, while the Mycenaean saga has provided the material for Eliot's *Family Reunion* (1939) and the trilogy by Eugene O'Neill, *Mourning Becomes Electra* (1931), where the saga of the House of Atreus is played out in post-Civil War New England.

For all their viscissitudes the classical myths have not died, even in an age where classical learning has declined. Their literary tradition is too strong and their beauty too great for them to be dispensable. Even where they are not found to be beautiful or noble they remain an inexhaustible mine of image and symbol.

Classical Myths in Medieval and Renaissance Art

The decline of the pagan gods in literature and religion was paralleled in artistic representations. By the time of the triumph of

Christianity in the Roman Empire (fourth century A.D.) classical mythology had virtually ceased to be a source of artistic inspiration. The popularity of astronomy and astrology, however, proved to be the chief means by which the pagan mythological figures survived, with surprising transformations. It is mainly in the illustrations of astronomical and astrological manuscripts that classical mythological characters find pictorial representation during the Dark Ages. The ninth century manuscripts of Aratus (in Cicero's Latin translation) show Perseus still in recognizable classical form, with cap, sword, winged sandals, and Gorgon's head, and this tradition of fidelity to the antique classical model is maintained in a few manuscripts even into the eleventh century.

Two other traditions, however, combined to change the classical gods beyond recognition, the one western and the other Oriental. In the former case the artist would plot the position of a constellation and then link up the individual stars in the form of the mythological figure whose name the constellation bore. The artists were generally more interested in the pictorial qualities of the subject, so that the illustrations were usually astronomically inaccurate. In the Oriental tradition, however, as handed down by the Arabs, the approach was scientifically more accurate; they had the advantage of having Ptolemy's astronomical work, which (by a corruption of the word *megiste* in the Greek title) they called *Almagest*. The Arab artists therefore plotted the constellations accurately, and the pictorial aspects of the mythological figures were of subsidiary importance. Hercules appears as an Arab, with scimitar, turban, and Oriental trousers; Perseus carries, in place of the Gorgon's head, a bearded demon's head, which gave its name *Algol* (the Arab for demon) to one of the stars in the constellation of Perseus.

Another strange Oriental metamorphosis has been shown to go back to Babylonian religion. In the Arab manuscripts Mercury is a scribe, Jupiter a judge; in Babylonian mythology the god Nebo had been a scribe, Marduk a judge, and the ancient tradition had survived to merge with the classical figures. It continued to yet a further stage in the West, where, in thirteenth century Italian sculpture, Mercury appears as a scribe or teacher, Jupiter as a monk or bishop, and other classical gods in similar guises.

In a few cases the classical gods survived outside the domain of astrology and astronomy. Christian sarcophagi show Dionysus as a symbol of immortality; Apollo could be mingled with Christ. In the Byzantine empire the classical forms continued to appear in non-astronomical manuscripts; as late as the fourteenth century, Pan appears still with his goat-like attributes. The same is true also of figures carved on Byzantine ivory caskets.

As the Middle Ages progressed, handbooks appeared giving detailed instructions for the appearance of the gods; it was important in astrology and magic to have an accurate image of the divinity whose favor was needed. One Arab handbook of magic appeared in a Latin translation in the West after the tenth century, with the title *Picatrix,* and contained, besides ritual and prayers, fifty minute descriptions of gods. Some, like Saturn with "a crow's head and the feet of a camel" were changed into Oriental monsters, but in some, for example, Jupiter, who "sits on a throne and he is made of gold and ivory," the classical form remains.

Other handbooks of iconography circulated in the West at the end of the Middle Ages. Influential was the *Liber Ymaginum Deorum* of "Albricus" (perhaps Alexander Neckham, who died in 1217), which was certainly used by Petrarch in his description of the Olympian gods (*Africa,* 3. 140–262), from which we give a short extract (140–146): "First is Jupiter, sitting in state upon his throne, holding scepter and thunderbolt. Before him his armor bearer [i.e., the eagle] lifts the Trojan boy [i.e., Ganymede] above the stars. Next with more stately gait, weighed down with gloomy age, is Saturn; with veiled head and a gray cloak, holding a rake and sickle, a farmer in aspect, he devours his sons. . . ."

A third type of handbook is represented by the *Emblemata* of Alciati (1531), which is based on the *Hieroglyphica* of Horapollo, an Alexandrian work of the fourth century A.D. In this type the gods are given allegorical symbols; Venus is represented, for example, with her foot on a tortoise (the symbolism goes back into classical antiquity), indicating that women should remain silently at home.

These handbooks are the forerunners of the Renaissance mythological encyclopedias mentioned earlier, which were of such importance in Renaissance literature and art. The classical gods had survived, but in many disguises; just as Renaissance humanism had led in literature to a rediscovery of the classical forms, so the Renaissance artists returned to the classical images. In Florence, Botticelli (1444–1510) combined medieval allegory with classical mythology in his allegorical masterpieces, *The Birth of Venus, Primavera, Venus and Mars,* and *Pallas and the Centaur,* and in Venice, Giovanni Bellini (1430–1516), Giorgione (1478–1510), and his pupil Titian (1487–1576), all displayed the same mingling of traditions. Two Renaissance works perhaps best illustrate the return of the classical gods to their antique forms; the one is the map of the sky published in 1515 by the German, Albrecht Dürer. In this the classical forms of the western astronomical tradition combine with the scientific accuracy of the Arabs. Dürer gives the mythological figures their ancient forms; Hercules is a Greek once more and recovers his club and lion skin. In the Vatican Stanza della Segnatura, decorated by Raphael after 1508, the classical, allegorical, and Christian traditions combine to exalt the glory of the Church and its doctrine. And in the place of honor (though not supreme) is Apollo, surrounded by the Muses, the poets of antiquity, and Renaissance humanists. Classical mythology and Renaissance humanism have achieved the perfect synthesis.

The uses of the figures of classical mythology in art from the Renaissance to our own day are too many to be discussed in this brief survey. In Italy, Michelangelo in Florence and Rome, Correggio at Ferrara, and Titian, Paolo Veronese, and Tintoretto at Venice, are sixteenth century masters who found inspiration in classical mythology. The great series of paintings by the Carracci brothers in the Gallery of the Farnese Palace at Rome (1597–1604) depicts the triumph of Love by means of one classical legend after another. In the seventeenth century it is in Flanders and France that the classical myths found their most eloquent interpreters, Rubens (1577–1640) and Poussin (1594–1665). Rubens reflects the energy and self-confidence of classical culture at its height, as can be seen in such paintings as his *Judgment of Paris* and *Venus and Adonis.* For Poussin the world of classical mythology is an age of perfection, gone never to return. Among painters he is the most perfect interpreter of the classical myths, and those who wish to understand best what "classicism" means in Renaissance art should study the long series of drawings and paintings done by Poussin on mythological themes.

From the time of Poussin to our own day artists have returned again and again to the classical myths, and the ancient gods and heroes have survived in art as in literature. To select but one modern example, Picasso has found in the Minotaur legend the source of inspiration for protest against horror and violence in modern life. There is no sign that future artists will be any less ready to turn to the ancient legends. To use an often quoted passage of Coleridge (*Wallenstein*, I. 2, 4. 130–131), "The intelligible forms of ancient poets" may have vanished:

> but still the heart doth need a language, still
> Doth the old instinct bring back the old names.

APPENDIX TO CHAPTER 23

The subject of the post-classical uses of mythology is so vast that there is virtually no end to the books written on it. The two most useful works available in English are:

J. SEZNEC. *The Survival of the Pagan Gods* (New York: Pantheon Books, 1953). First published in French as *La Survivance des dieux antiques, Studies of the Warburg Institute,* vol. XI, London, 1940.

DOUGLAS BUSH. *Mythology and the Renaissance Tradition in English poetry* (Minneapolis: The University of Minnesota Press, 1932; New York: W. W. Norton, 1963). Includes a chronological list of poems on mythological subjects.

Among other works the following are helpful and readily available:

GILBERT HIGHET. *The Classical Tradition* (New York: Oxford University Press, 1939; Harper and Row, 1962).

J. E. SANDYS. *A History of Classical Scholarship,* 3 vols. (New York: Cambridge University Press, 1903–08).

E. K. RAND. *Ovid and his Influence* (Boston: Marshall Jones Company, 1925).

L. P. WILKINSON. *Ovid Recalled* (New York: Cambridge University Press, 1955); published in paperback as *Ovid Surveyed*.

F. CUMONT. *Oriental Religions in Roman Paganism* (Paris: P. Geuthner, 1929; New York: Dover Publications, n.d.). Chapter 7 is an excellent introduction to ancient astrology. For the history of astrology there is a good short article by M. Graubard, "Under the Spell of the Zodiac," *Natural History* 78 (1969), 10–18.

STUART GILBERT. *James Joyce's Ulysses* (London: Faber and and Faber, 1930).

DOUGLAS BUSH. *Mythology and the Romantic Tradition in English Poetry* (Cambridge, Mass.: Harvard University Press, 1937; New York: W. W. Norton, 1963). This is more summary than Professor Bush's earlier work; it also contains a chronological list of poems on mythological subjects.

See the bibliographies of Seznec, Bush, and Highet for further suggestions.

CHAPTER 24

Classical Mythology in Music

It is impossible in a brief compass to survey with any kind of justice the use of mythology in the field of music. The topic is too vast, rich, and important. We attempt here merely to suggest the significance and vitality of Greek and Roman inspiration in this area as well as to introduce (to those for whom an introduction may be necessary) a whole fascinating world to be explored with joy and profit. The genre of opera provides the most obvious and significant focal point for the most cursory discussion. Emphasis is placed upon works that may be seen or heard in contemporary performances; fortunately the ever expanding repertoires of the recording companies are making the more esoteric works available for entertainment and study. One should have by one's side the latest issue of the *Schwann Long Playing Record Catalog*.

Music was an art inherent in the culture of ancient Greece and Rome. Drama, for example, was rooted in music and the dance and its origins were religious. Music is again linked with drama, and again the impetus is religious, in the liturgical mystery and miracle plays of the Middle Ages. During the Renaissance, with its veneration of antiquity, tragedy and comedy were often inspired by Greek and Roman originals and quite elaborate musical choruses and interludes were sometimes added. But the years ushering in the Baroque period (ca. 1600–1750) must provide the real beginning for our survey. In 1581 Vincenzo Galilei (father of the renowned astronomer) as the spokesman for the Camerata, a literary and artistic society of Florence, published his *Dialogo della Musica Antica e della Moderna,* which was an attack on the composition of vocal counterpoint then in vogue and advocated a doctrine for the correct method of setting words to music. The new style was labeled monodic; the goal was to revive the principles of ancient Greek drama, which was believed to have been sung in its entirety. Members of the Camerata produced in 1594 or 1597 what may be called the first opera; its title *Dafne* and its theme reflect the spell cast by the ancient world. Ottavio Rinuccini wrote the text (which is still extant); Jacopo Peri composed the music, with the help of Jacopo Corsi (some of his music alone survives), and Giulio Caccini too may have contributed as well. A second opera, *Euridice,* followed, which has survived and on occasion receives scholarly revivals. Peri again wrote most of the score, but apparently Caccini added some music and then composed another *Euridice* of his own.

The first great genius in the history of this new form was Claudio Monteverdi; his first opera *Orfeo* (1607) lifts the musical and dramatic potential initiated by his predecessors to the level of great art that can be appreciated to this day. The subjects of some of his subsequent works reveal the power and impetus provided by Greece and Rome. *Arianna* (her "lament" is all that survives; it was a hit in its day); *Tirse e Clori; Il Matrimonio d'Alceste con Admeto; Adone; Le Nozze d'Enea con Lavinia; Il Ritorno d'Ulisse in Patria.* His opera perhaps best-known to modern audiences,, *L'Incoronazione di Poppea,* is based upon Roman history.

Monteverdi's pupil, Cavalli, wrote over forty operas. His best-known, *Giasone* (1649), concerns the legend of Jason. His contemporary, Marc Antonio Cesti, is said to have composed over one hundred operas; of the eleven surviving (all from the years 1649–1669), *Il Pomo d'Oro,* which deals with the contest for the Apple of Discord, was the most famous—a superspectacle in five acts and sixty-six scenes, including several ballets in each act and requiring twenty-four separate stage sets. And thus opera developed in Italy. The list of composers is long and the bibliography of their many works inspired by classical antiquity impressive; particularly startling is the number of repetitions of favorite subjects.

Alessandro Scarlatti (1660–1725) in the years following emerges as one of the more vital and influential forces in music; his son, Domenico who became famous for his composition of keyboard music, also wrote operas on Greek and Roman themes.

Many of the operatic composers of the early period wrote

cantatas as well. But as examples of this musical form, we shall mention two works by Johann Sebastian Bach (1685–1750) in the catalogue of his secular cantatas. Some of these he himself entitled *dramma per musica,* and modern critics have gone so far as to label them "operettas." In cantata 201 (*Der Streit zwischen Phoebus und Pan*) Bach presents the contest between Phoebus and Pan as a musical satire against a hostile critic of his works, Johann Adolph Scheibe. The text is derived from Ovid's version. Mt. Tmolus and Momus, god of mirth, award the victory to Pan, while Midas is punished with a pair of ass's ears. Cantata 213 (*Hercules auf dem Scheidewege*) depicts Hercules at the crossroads; he rejects the blandishments of Pleasure in favor of the hardship, virtue, and renown promised to him by Virtue. The more familiar *Christmas Oratorio* presents a reworking of the musical themes of this cantata.

In England during the Baroque Period, plays with incidental music and ballet became very much the fashion; such productions, inevitably influenced by foreign developments, led eventually to the evolution of opera in a more traditional sense. John Blow wrote (ca. 1684) a musical-dramatic composition, *Venus and Adonis.* Although the work bears the subtitle "A masque for the entertainment of the king," it is in reality a pastoral opera constructed along the most simple lines. But it was Blow's pupil, Henry Purcell, who created a masterpiece that has become one of the landmarks in the history of opera, *Dido and Aeneas* (ca. 1689). The work was composed for Josias Priest's Boarding School for Girls in Chelsea; the libretto by Nahum Tate comes from Book 4 of Vergil's *Aeneid.*[1] The artful economy and tasteful blending of the various elements have often been admired in Purcell's score. Dido's lament as she breathes her last surely must be one of the most noble and touching arias ever written:

---

[1] A fascinating series of brief articles by James S. Constantine ["Vergil in Opera," *Classical Outlook* 46 (1969), 49; 63–65; 77–78; 87–89] traces the history of the musical treatment of Vergilian themes and characters from the *Aeneid;* some twenty-four titles are listed in operatic annals. Cavalli wrote *La Didone* in 1641. A libretto by Metastasio, *Didone Abbandonata,* was set to music first by D. A. Sarro (1724); subsequently twenty other composers wrote music for this same poem, among them Luigi Cherubini (1786).

> When I am laid in earth, may my wrongs create
>   No trouble in thy breast.
> Remember me, but ah! forget my fate.

In France operatic development was very much influenced by spectacle and ballet as well as by the works of dramatists like Corneille and Racine. Jean-Baptiste Lully (1632–1687), a giant in the development of opera in general and of French opera in particular, worked with Molière in the composition of opera-ballets. In 1673 Lully produced *Cadmus et Hermione* in collaboration with the poet Philippe Quinault; this was the first of a series of fifteen such tragic operas (twelve of them to texts by Quinault). Some of the other titles confirm the extent of the debt to Greece and Rome: *Alceste, Thésée, Atys, Proserpine, Persée, Phaéton, Acis et Galatée*. Jean-Philippe Rameau (1683–1764) was the most significant heir to the mantle of Lully. He too created many operas and opera-ballets on Greek and Roman themes, for example, *Hippolyte et Aricie, Castor et Pollux, Dardanus, Les Fêtes d'Hébé*.

George Frederic Handel (1685–1759) was one of the greatest composers of the first half of the eighteenth century with a musical idiom that was international and universal. He was a prolific musician and although the general public knows him primarily for his oratorios, he was very much concerned during much of his career with the composition of operas. In fact many of his oratorios are operatic in nature, and his operas often strike the modern listener as oratorio-like in their structure and movement. Certainly several of his oratorios are on secular themes, intended for the concert hall and in spirit much closer to the theater than to the church, and some deal with mythology, for example, *Semele* and *Hercules*. Handel wrote forty operas, but they are little known today because they are not in fashion. Standard criticism complains about the stylization, the lack of drama, and the complexity and absurdity of the plots. Fortunately, however, they are sometimes revived and reveal the abundant beauties and subtleties that they contain. Many of Handel's operas are historically orientated, for example, *Attone, Agrippina, Giulio Cesare, Serse;* some are more strictly mythological—*Acis and Galatea* (a pastorale)*, Admeto,* and *Deidamia*.

Christoph Willibald Gluck is the composer of the earliest opera
to maintain any kind of regularity in the standard repertoire, *Orfeo
ed Euridice* (first version 1762). This beautiful work, restrained in
its passion and exquisite in its melody, remains one of the most
artistically rewarding settings of this eternal myth. The libretto, by
Raniero Calzabigi, proved a great help to Gluck, whose avowed
purpose was to compose music that would best serve the poetry
and the plot. Orpheus's arias expressing his anguish at the loss of
his wife, *Che puro ciel* and *Che farò senza Euridice* well illustrate
the highest embodiment of these ideals. Gluck again worked with
Calzabigi for *Alceste,* derived from Euripides's play (first version
1767), another impressive achievement more monumental in character than *Orfeo,* but nevertheless equally touching in its nobility
and sentiment. Their third collaboration, *Paride ed Elena* (1770),
was a failure. Subsequent operas by Gluck were *Iphigénie en
Aulide, Iphigénie en Tauride,* and *Echo et Narcisse.* Niccolò (or
Nicola) Piccinni, a rival of Gluck (they were both commissioned
by the French Opéra to write an *Orfeo*), composed over a hundred
operas, many of them on classical subjects. Gluck's new style
greatly influenced Maria Luigi Cherubini, who also turned to ancient mythology. His *Médée* (1797) is sometimes revived for a
prima donna of the caliber of Maria Callas or Magda Olivero, who
can meet the technical and histrionic demands of the title role.
Another of Gluck's many and far reaching influences was on Antonio Sacchini, who wrote *Dardanus* (1784) and a popular master-
work, *Oedipe à Colone* (1786).

The two musical giants of the second half of the eighteenth century, Franz Joseph Haydn and Wolfgang Amadeus Mozart, were
not generally drawn to Greek and Roman subjects. But Haydn's
Orfeo ed Euridice (1791) is considered by many to be the finest
of his many operas, and Mozart's *Idomeneo, Rè di Creta* (1781)
is a fascinating, although imperfect, masterpiece, well worth in-
vestigation. Ludwig von Beethoven, another of the very great composers, found little direct influence from Greece and Rome. His
Coriolanus overture (1807), inspired by the legendary Roman
hero, might be mentioned; more to the point is his ballet music
The Creatures of Prometheus (1801). The thematic material of
this work seems in a special way to epitomize the indomitable

spirit of the composer. He arranged it as a set of variations for piano and it appears again in the final movement of his great third symphony (the *Eroica*). The whole aura of defiance conjured up by the romantic image of the life and music of Beethoven is strikingly parallel to that evoked by the Titan Prometheus. At any rate, Beethoven's career (1770–1827) provides the chronological and spiritual link between eighteenth-century Classicism and nineteenth-century Romanticism.

The German *lied* of the nineteenth century embodies much of the passion and longing that are the exquisite torture and delight of the Romantic soul. The musical mood runs parallel to that of the *Sturm und Drang* movement in literature as typified by the works of Goethe. Several of the songs of Franz Schubert (1797–1828), for example, are set to poems on ancient themes: *Der Atlas, Fahrt zum Hades, Orest auf Tauris, Der zürnenden Diana, Fragment aus dem Aeschylus* (a chorus from the *Eumenides*), *Memnon, Philoctete,* and *Orpheus.* Two songs by a later Romantic composer, Hugo Wolf (1860–1903), *Prometheus* and *Ganymede,* are staples of the lieder repertoire. On the other hand, his one symphonic work, a tone poem entitled *Penthesilea,* is an interesting piece of program music that is not so well-known.

The operatic achievements of the nineteenth century are among its most conspicuous glories, but Greek and Roman themes no longer generally held the vogue that they once had. Many of the illustrious composers of the period (the list is impressive) remained virtually untouched by traditional classical motifs, for example, Giacomo Meyerbeer, Giachino Rossini, Gaetano Donizetti, Vincenzo Bellini, Giuseppe Verdi, Carl-Maria von Weber, Richard Wagner.[2] Operas like Bellini's *Norma* (the tragic story of a Druid priestess) are, it is true, built upon Roman historical legendary themes, but such an exception only brings home to us more forcefully the changes being wrought in subject matter and style. But as always it is rash to generalize too broadly. Charles Gounod wrote an opera *Philémon et Baucis* (1860), and Hector Berlioz with his *Les Troyens* (1856–1858) has achieved one of the most monumental and important

---

[2] Of historical interest is a mammoth work inspired by Wagner's *Ring,* a cycle of operas entitled *Homerische Welt* by August Bungert (1845–1915), which failed to win favor.

masterpieces ever created on an ancient mythological subject. The work, which draws heavily upon Vergil, comprises two full-length operas: *La Prise de Troie* (based upon Book 2 of the *Aeneid*) and *Troyens à Carthage* (the Dido and Aeneas episode from Book 4). Of a very different tone and spirit are the boisterous works of Jacques Offenbach. His opera bouffe, *Orphée aux Enfers* (*Orpheus in the Underworld,* 1858) is a delight; and so is his later *La Belle Hélène* (1865).[3]

Some of the later works of Jules Massenet are on classical subjects; his opera *Bacchus* (1909), for example, might be of some interest if only a revival were possible. Similarly, two operas by Gabriel Fauré, *Prométhée* (1900) and *Pénélope* (1913), should be rewarding experiences. Verismo opera, which became the rage at the turn of the century because of the genius of composers such as Giacomo Puccini, Pietro Mascagni, and Ruggiero Leoncavallo, turned away from classical themes in favor of the realistic and shocking or the Oriental and exotic. Yet it may be a surprise to some that Leoncavallo has written an *Edipo Rè* (posthumously produced in 1920), which on occasion is revived. This is in keeping with the trend in the twentieth century of returning to classical subjects. Gian Francesco Malipiero, for example, has used the Orpheus theme for a trilogy, *L'Orfeide* (1925), and his *Ecuba* (1941) is modeled on Euripides.

The works of Richard Strauss are towering achievements of the twentieth century. His reworkings of Greek myth in terms of modern psychology and philosophy are among the most rewarding artistic products of this or any age. Strauss was fortunate in having as his librettist the brilliant dramatist Hugo von Hofmannsthal. Their collaboration for *Elektra* (1909), a work based upon Sophocles but startling in the originality of its conception, is a brilliant and profound *tour de force.* Strauss and Hofmannsthal again worked together to create the charming and sublime *Ariadne auf Naxos* (the original version of 1912 was redone in 1916); this opera within an opera focuses upon the desolate and abandoned

[3] Twentieth century musical comedy has sometimes drawn upon mythology. Those interested in this popular genre will find Cole Porter's *Out of This World* a particularly witty and frothy satire on the amatory pursuits of Jupiter.

Ariadne, who longs for death but finds instead an apotheosis through the love of Bacchus. The Holy Marriage has never found more ecstatic expression. The last three mythological operas of Strauss are not worthy of the relative neglect that they have received. *Die Aegyptische Helena* (1929, again Hofmannsthal is the librettist) plays upon the ancient version of the myth that distinguishes between the phantom Helen who went with Paris to Troy and the real Helen who remained faithful to Menelaus in Egypt. *Daphne* (1938, the text this time is by Joseph Gregor) is a most touching treatment of the same subject as that of the very first opera; its final scene (for soprano and orchestra) depicts a magical and evocative transformation that soars with typical Straussian majesty and power. Gregor is also the librettist for *Die Liebe der Danae* (1940), although he drew upon a sketch left by Hofmannsthal. The plot is evolved from an ingenious amalgamation of two originally separate tales concerning Midas and his golden touch and the wooing of Danae by Zeus in the form of a shower of gold.

The works of other twentieth-century composers are by no means negligible. Among the operas of Darius Milhaud are *Oreste* [a trilogy comprising *Agamemnon, Les Choéphores, Les Euménides,* (1913–1924)], composed to a translation of Aeschylus by Paul Claudel; *Les Malheurs d'Orphée* (1924); and *Médée* (1938). In 1927 he wrote three short operas (each only about ten minutes long): *L'Enlèvement d'Europe, L'Abandon d'Ariane,* and *La Délivrance de Thésée.* One of Arthur Honegger's most impressive operas, *Antigone* (1927), is set to a libretto by Jean Cocteau based upon Sophocles. Benjamin Britten deserves special mention for his chamber opera, *The Rape of Lucretia* (1946), a beautifully taut and concise rendition of the Roman legend; the libretto by Ronald Duncan is derived from the play by André Obey, *Le Viol de Lucrèce.* The text of a scene from Euripides's *The Trojan Women* (in a special translation by the poet John Patrick Creagh) has been scored for soprano and orchestra by Samuel Barber (1963) under the title *Andromache's Farewell;* a messenger has come to tell Andromache that she must relinquish her son Astyanax to the Greeks, who have decided to hurl the boy to his death from the walls of Troy. Andromache's scena begins with the words, "So you must die, my son."

Igor Stravinsky has also been drawn to classical subjects. He has written for string orchestra the score of a ballet, *Apollon Musagète* (1928), taking for its subject Apollo and his association with three of the Muses, Calliope, Polyhymnia, and Terpsichore (i.e., Poetry, Mime, and Dance).[4] Stravinsky too has composed a melodrama entitled *Perséphone* (1934), a work utilizing orchestra, narrator, tenor soloist, mixed chorus, and children's chorus. But his *Oedipus Rex* is his most significant achievement on a classical theme—a highly stylized opera-oratorio, liturgical, ritualistic, and statuesque, composed to a Latin text provided by Jean Cocteau, who telescoped Sophocles' play into six episodes (Cocteau's French version was given to Jean Danielou who translated it into Church Latin). This ecclesiastical work, in spirit more akin to a Christian morality play than ancient Greek drama, is scored for six solo voices, a narrator, a male chorus, and orchestra.

The twelve-tone (or "atonal") school of musical composition founded by Arnold Schönberg has produced some works on classical themes, for example, Egon Wellesz has an *Alkestis* (1924, libretto by Hofmannsthal) and *Die Bakchantinnen,* both from Euripides. Ernest Křenek, who has adopted various styles in his career (jazz idiom, romanticism, and atonality), has treated the Orestes myth in his *Leben des Orest* (1930). His other operas include *Orpheus und Eurydike* (1923) and *Pallas Athena Weint* (1952).

Carl Orff has won considerable renown with his operatic treatment of mythological subjects. In 1925 he adapted Monteverdi's *Orfeo;* he has written an *Antigone* (1949) and subsequently *Oedipus der Tyrann,* both of which follow Sophocles closely. His recent opera, *Prometheus,* is set to the classical Greek text of Aeschylus.

---

[4] The wealth of mythological repertoire in ballet must be ignored in this brief survey. But it is worthwhile to single out the dynamic and imaginative works for dance theater of this century by Martha Graham on Greek themes, for example, *Clytemnestra, Phaedra, Night Journey* (the Oedipus legend), *Cave of the Heart* (concerning Medea and Jason), *Alcestis, Errand into the Maze* (the story of the Minotaur). Many of her works are or will be on film.

APPENDIX TO CHAPTER 24

The following books are suggested for further reading:

WALLACE BROCKWAY, and HERBERT WEINSTOCK. *The World of Opera* (New York: Random House, 1941).

JAMES S. CONSTANTINE. "Vergil in Opera," *The Classical Outlook* 46 (1969), 49, 63–65, 77–78, 87–89.

DAVID EWEN. *Encyclopedia of the Opera* (New York: Hill and Wang, 1955).

DONALD JAY GROUT. *A Short History of Opera.* 2 vols. (New York: Columbia University Press, 1947).

Grove's Dictionary of Music and Musicians. 5th ed. Edited by Eric Blom. 9 vols. (New York: St. Martin's Press, 1954. Supplementary vol., 1961).

PAUL HENRY LANG. *Music in Western Civilization* (New York: W. W. Norton, 1941).

Select Bibliography

Only a few of the basic works in English (many of which are available in paperback) have been listed with a view to the interests of the general reader. Subsidiary references will be found in the text and in the notes; see in particular the bibliographies at the end of Chapters 23 and 24. Translations of ancient sources and, for the most part, highly specialized works of scholarship are not included.

E. R. Dodds. *The Greeks and the Irrational* (Berkeley: University of California Press, 1964 [1951]).

Mircea Eliade. *Myth and Reality,* translated from the French by Willard R. Trask (New York: Harper & Row, 1963).

L. R. Farnell, *Greek Hero-Cults and Ideas of Immortality* (New York: Oxford University Press, 1921).

James G. Frazer. *The New Golden Bough, a New Abridgement of the Classic Work,* ed. Theodor H. Gaster (New York: Criterion Books, 1959; Mentor Books, 1964).

Charles Mills Gayley. *The Classic Myths in English Literature and in Art,* new edition (New York: Ginn and Co., 1939 [1911]).

Michael Grant. *Myths of the Greeks and Romans* (New York: Mentor Books, 1964).

Robert Graves. *The Greek Myths,* 2 vols. (Baltimore: Penguin Books, 1955).

W. K. C. Guthrie. *The Greeks and Their Gods* (Boston: Beacon Press, 1955).

Edith Hamilton. *Mythology* (New York: Mentor Books, 1953 [1942]).

E. O. James. *Seasonal Feasts and Festivals* (New York: Barnes and Noble, 1961).

C. Kerenyi. *The Heroes of the Greeks,* translated by H. J. Rose (New York: Grove Press, 1960).

C. Kerenyi. *The Gods of the Greeks,* translated from the German by Norman Cameron (New York: Grove Press, 1960).

G. M. Kirkwood. *A Short Guide to Classical Mythology* (New York: Holt, Rinehart and Winston, 1959).

Larousse Encyclopedia of Mythology (New York: Prometheus Press, 1960).

MARTIN P. NILSSON. *The Mycenaean Origin of Greek Mythology* [New York: W. W. Norton, 1963 (1932)].

MARTIN P. NILSSON. *A History of Greek Religion,* translated from the Swedish by F. J. Fielden, 2nd ed. revised 1952 (New York: W. W. Norton, 1964).

H. J. ROSE. *A Handbook of Greek Mythology,* 6th ed. (London: Methuen, 1958; New York: Dutton, 1959).

H. J. ROSE. *Religion in Greece and Rome* (New York: Harper & Row, 1959). Originally published as *Ancient Greek Religion* (1946) and *Ancient Roman Religion* (1948).

INDEXES

A. Passages Translated from Ancient Authors

B. Mythological and Legendary Persons and Subjects; Mythical and Non-Mythical Place-Names

C. Persons, Subjects, Titles